METHODOLOGY IN THE ACADEMIC TEACHING OF JUDAISM

Studies in Judaism

METHODOLOGY IN THE ACADEMIC TEACHING OF JUDAISM

Edited by

Zev Garber

UNIVERSITY PRESS OF AMERICA

LANHAM • NEW YORK • LONDON

University Press of America,® Inc.

4720 Boston Way
Lanham, MD 20706

3 Henrietta Street
London WC2E 8LU England

Printed in the United States of America

ISBN (Perfect): 0-8191-5724-4
ISBN (Cloth): 0-8191-5723-6

All University Press of America books are produced on acid-free paper which exceeds the minimum standards set by the National Historical Publications and Records Commission.

For Asher and Dorit Garber

Children of the Fourth Generation

Contents

Contributors

Introduction: Thoughts on the Text, Teachers, and *Talmidim*

ZEV GARBER, is Professor of Jewish Studies, Los Angeles Valley College, and Visiting Professor of Religious Studies, University of California at Riverside. He also serves as Vice President, National Association of Professors of Hebrew.

The Contemporary Study of Religion and the Academic Teaching of Judaism

CHARLES ELLIOT VERNOFF, is Associate Professor of Religion, Cornell College, Mount Vernon, Iowa.

During the past generation, the academic study of religion in America has moved rapidly toward autonomy as a field. This has forced an unprecendented engagement with the theoretical and methodological questions of what religion is, why it should be studied and how it should be investigated and taught. Jacob Neusner's book *Take Judaism, For Example: Studies Toward the Comparison of Religions* underscores the need for contemporary scholars and teachers of Judaic religion to inform their own work with recent developments in the study of religion generally. This paper examines one prominent line of development and considers its possible influence upon the study and teaching of Judaism.

Ninian Smart, a noted theoretician of religious studies, has proposed "worldview" as a characterization of the focal subject area for this new academic realm. Smart's proposal reflects a broader consensus emerging within the field, which includes scholars studying Judaism such as Jonathan Z. Smith and Neusner himself. An exchange between the latter two suggests that a study whose proper object is "worldview" can be neither history nor philosophy, although it is tangent with both, as well as with the social sciences. A worldview manifests itself in history, seeks like philosophy to interpret the world as coherent system, and contributes functionally to the constitution of social reality. Yet the study of worldview can in principle be reduced to no other study insofar as adequate understanding of its "object" methodologically requires the investigator's full acknowledgement of his or her own "subjective" worldview: and that entails an eventual theoretical definition of worldview to which the conventional dichotomy of subject and object itself proves inadequate.

An interest in studying religion in its own terms, i.e., religiologically, may thus require approaches capable of probing worldview as ground of *both* the outward coherence of the world as "objectively" apprehended *and* the necessarily related inward coherence of consciousness as "subjectively" maintained. Such approaches to scholarly research and reflection, although distinctively inspired by thinkers like Mircea Eliade and Martin Buber, may be adapted from the classical Aristotelian method of hypothesis which is applicable to all empirical realities.

Since religiological insight into a body of data ultimately aims at larger patterns of coherence which must be humanistically construed, however technically assembled, a strong continuity exists between research scholarship and classroom instruction in the study of religion. This is apparent in examples of pedagogical strategy for the four typical sorts of offerings in a basic Judaica curriculum: general and particular courses in Hebrew Bible, and general and particular courses in post-biblical Judaism. Novel modes of pedagogy which seek to convey distinct forms of *religious* reality may encourage some teachers of Judaism who already are moving toward them, and salutarily challenge others who have been for the most part content with established instructional practices. At any event, the concern of religion to view "the world" in its wholeness could eventually, albeit indirectly, aid in restoring an often absent wholeness to contemporary education as such.

Jewish Literary Themes in the Teaching of Judaica

S. DANIEL BRESLAUER, is Associate Professor of Religious Studies, University of Kansas.

The chapter proposed would argue that using Jewish literary themes is an effective way to convey basic concepts, historical data, and theological ideas when teaching Judaica. It would fall into four different sections. The first would suggest the place of narrative and literature in Judaism in general, drawing heavily upon the works of Joseph Dan. This section would explain why a student of Jewish religion may want to take the narrative tradition seriously.

Not only should Jewish literature be taken seriously, but it also provides an introduction to an often overlooked aspect of Jewish religiousness — imagination. The second section would argue that the imaginative element in Judaism is often neglected, but is central to an understanding of Jewish religion in all its aspects — writings by David Roskies, Barry Holtz, Arthur Green and Elie Wiesel among others will be used in making that argument. This section will show how the study of literary themes corrects the imbalance which a focus on either history alone or theology alone or both in combination produces.

If the study of Jewish literary themes is important, the next problem is defining how it should proceed. The third section will look at three approaches to Jewish narratives: that of Richard Rubenstein in *The Religious Imagination*, that of Robert Alter, focusing on both *After the Tradition* and *Defenses of the*

Imagination, and that of Yoav Elstein, looking at his analysis of Hasidic stories and of Agnon. None of these approaches is finally satisfying, although each has a particular use. An eclectic method, in view of the goal which is not literary criticism for its own sake but the study of literature for the illumination of Jewish religion, may prove the most satisfying.

The study of literature may help place Jewish studies within the broader context of the humanities in general. The humanities ask questions about how human beings respond to themselves, their world, and other people. They investigate ideas, psychology, and social institutions to find clues about the nature of being human. The final section will examine one particular theme: Torah and Creation in order to show how such a study illuminates the basic concerns of the humanities. The chosen theme can be used to illuminate the varied ways human beings have grappled with a world which presents itself as a given, as independent of human creativity. The theme also enables an exploration of the psychology of creaturehood as it interacts with the human quest for meaning and personal significance. Finally the discovery that stories of creation often reflect the social realities experienced by the author will help put the claims of various cosmologies into sociological perspective. The conclusion, then, will be that using literary themes is a means of transmitting the vital and varied nature of Jewish religion.

The Methodology of Hebrew Language and Literature: Some Basic Needs

ALBERT T. BILGRAY, is Professor Emeritus, University of Arizona and currently President, National Association of Professors of Hebrew.

After discussing the present academic climate in the instruction of foreign languages and literature, the chapter describes the current teaching of classical (Biblical and Rabbinics) and modern Hebrew language, and proceeds to analyze some methodological problems confronting the professor in the classroom.

Attention is then directed to some basic needs in the current teaching of Hebrew language and literature, and the following topics are addressed:

A. A Bibliography of Methodological Materials
   1. Possible sources for such a bibliography
   2. The use of unpublished as well as published materials

B. An Updated Survey of Hebrew Instruction
   1. Exploration of changes since the most recent survey (1973)
   2. Analysis of current textbooks
   3. Analyses of current aids and techniques

C. Fostering Workshops in Methodology
   1. Sharing disparate individual experiences
   2. Analyzing collective efforts

D. Current Research Needs
 1. A study of motivations for Hebrew study
 2. Exploring innovative aids and techniques
 3. Coping with individual student differences and other specialized problems.

The article concludes with brief summaries of the roles of the campus, the professional associations, and the foundations in meeting the challenge of effective teaching of Hebrew language and literature in American institutions of higher learning.

Choosing Among the Strands: Teaching Old Testament Survey to Undergraduates at a Secular University

BRUCE ZUCKERMAN, is Assistant Professor of Religion, University of Southern California.

The intent of this study is to consider issues and problems involved in teaching what is generally called "Old Testament" at an undergraduate university not associated with any religion and/or religious institution. The type of course targeted for particular consideration is the standard, one semester, survey course in OT; i.e., a course that endeavors to cover the Bible — from Genesis to Daniel — in a limited period of time. Such an "Introduction to the Old Testament" is inevitably a most visible part of any curriculum in a college level department of religion and, more importantly, is the most likely means by which an undergraduate will ever have a chance to consider the Hebrew Bible in an academic context. The issue then is: how does one teach such a course as part of a "liberal arts" education?

The following issues and problems are considered:

The problem of time: This is always a major difficulty in any survey course — the choice of what materials to cover and what to exclude in consideration of the limited time frame. It is argued that all aspects of biblical thought should be touched upon and that care must be taken to avoid "cramming in" huge sections of biblical writings at the end of a course (e.g., wisdom literature) because too much time was devoted to other sections (e.g., Genesis) at the beginning of the course. A doctrine of "educated ruthlessness" is proposed — that is, a recognition that one must sacrifice a serious consideration of much vital material in order to leave time to consider absolutely essential material. Strategies for teaching sections in OT in line with the "ruthlessness" doctrine are considered.

The issue of overall emphasis: This is related to the time problem. Once again, hard choices must be made regarding what to stress within areas of OT study — especially considering that one is teaching to undergraduate students (as opposed to a graduate or seminary audience). It is suggested that issues of particular concern to graduate OT study should not be at the forefront of the undergraduate curriculum, e.g., source and form criticism. Rather, stress should be placed upon overreaching ideas, how they developed in biblical times and how they affect western civilization. In this regard, even the extra-biblical historical record as well as the burgeoning archaeological data must be handled judiciously. These sources should not be presented as an end in themselves but instead as a means of more clearly setting the Hebrew Bible within its Ancient Near Eastern cultural context.

Biblical and secondary texts: The choice of biblical text edition or editions are considered and the advantages of allowing students to use a wide variety of texts in class. The problems of finding the right supporting literature is also discussed.

Issues of faith: What stance should a teacher of OT take in regard to his students' faith commitments or lack thereof? It is argued that the teacher should not make clear precisely what his own system of belief is, since this has too prejudicial an effect on students. Strategies for handling "fundamentalist" students or others with well-defined belief systems are brought forward. An argument is made that the religious aspects of the Bible should not be deemphasized as a means of side-stepping issues of faith. Thus, the popular approach of teaching the "Bible as Literature" or even the "Bible as History" is criticized. Instead, an approach that emphasizes modern scholarly issues and basic rational problems (e.g., theodicy), but also leaves room for and respect for individual faith positions is proposed. The teacher should make clear the difference between his role and that of a minister or rabbi — how he, as a representative of the secular world must be constrained to consider closely the basic questions about man's relationship to God — but he should not try to answer them. For answers are to be found only in one's faith, and how faith should work for a given individual is manifestly not the subject matter of a course in the Bible at a secular university.

Approaching the Text: The Study of Midrash

HERBERT W. BASSER is Associate Professor of Religion, Queens University, Kingston, Ontario.

By the time the midrash unit is reached (in an introduction to Judaism course) students will be familiar with such terms as Pharisee, Halakha, Aggada and exegesis. To introduce the notion of Hakham, wise person, the teacher asks, "What do Joseph, the soothsayer in Shakespeare's *Julius Caesar* and Daniel have in common?" Having himself (herself) asked a riddle, the teacher elicits the answer: "Wise people solve riddles by spelling out the implications of mysterious, often apparently contradictory signs and symbols." Simple examples of midrashic techniques will demonstrate that the Rabbis function as "wise people." The teacher must stress that these techniques often involve the transformation of Biblical texts by means of acoustical shifts in the Hebrew wording. An ample example is supplied by the teacher who points out the salient features of the midrash. Then for homework, a midrash with at least five related forms is given in translation to the student and the student is asked to respond to a list of questions; some will be done for the next class, some for this topic's last class. These questions concern: comparing versions, finding problems in one version which are solved by another version, locating the specific problem in a Biblical text which generated the midrash, looking up the Biblical verses in the midrash and showing the exegetical technique used by the midrashist (students will often not succeed here if they lack Hebrew training and the teacher may want to provide the student with some hints), the artistic effect of the midrash, etc. Also, some well chosen secondary readings should be given which reinforce the discoveries made by the student in the first lesson. These techniques can be expanded to teach courses in "Midrash in Translation" over the period of a semester. The chapter concludes with general remarks about the study of midrashic texts in graduate studies.

Text and Context in Halevi's *"Hesiqatni Tesuqati Le'el Hai"*

HARRIS LENOWITZ, is Associate Professor of Hebrew, University of Utah.

The medieval Hebrew poem presents many problems to the student who is not native or near-native in his control of Hebrew. Among the most serious of these is the assemblage of two whole poems out of one. The first of these poems involves the understanding of the vocabulary as it works through the syntax of the "surface" text; the second of the poems is that formed by the connotations of that vocabulary. Discovering the sources, chiefly the biblical ones, from which the poet draws his vocabulary in a particular poem and then assembling these words (those of the present poem) with those biblical contexts permits the construction of this second poem, the "context text." Joining the two poems results in a proper reading of the whole poem with its tensions intact.

This paper guides the student (the teacher) in methods designed towards the construction of the "context text" taking the Halevi poem as a good case. The surface poem seems to be completely in favor of Halevi's abandonment of Spain for Israel. But it is tensed against the "context" poem which suggests Halevi's very real confusion and pain facing the experience. The basic principle suggested here for the research of contexts, so that meaningful ones may be found and meaningless ones left to themselves, is that the occurrence of a relatively rare word in the Bible with exactly the same form in our poem recalls the entirety of the biblical context. The method attempts to reconstruct, mechanically through the Even-Shoshan *Concordance* and *New Dictionary*, the tools for comprehension which the educated reader of Halevi's time, or the Israeli student brought up through the same traditional texts, used/uses automatically, aware of at least the original usage and context of the poem's words.

Teaching Modern Hebrew Literature to American Undergraduates

GILEAD MORAHG, is Associate Professor of Hebrew Literature, University of Wisconsin-Madison. He also serves as Administrative Secretary, National Association of Professors of Hebrew.

The chapter presents an integrated curricular approach to multilevel university teaching of modern Hebrew literature. It also offers an integrated instructional methodology designed to address the three major deficiencies characterizing most American undergraduates studying Hebrew literature. These deficiencies are: (a) insufficient competence in language skills necessary for deciphering Hebrew literary texts; (b) insufficient training in basic techniques of literary analysis and interpretation; (c) insufficient knowledge of the historical and cultural contexts of modern Hebrew literature.

The chapter offers methodological guidelines and specific techniques for overcoming these deficiencies while progressing through the various stages of a comprehensive curriculum. Basic principles for the selection and organization of the literary texts comprising such a curriculum, as well as for the structure, mode of presentation and learning activities of individual study units within this curriculum are provided.

Our approach is based on the pedagogical realities of teaching Hebrew literature to American undergraduates and is designed to enhance the students' knowledge and understanding of Jewish culture.

Against the Stream: Teaching Religious Ethics in Modern America

BARRY JAY SELTSER, is Assistant Professor of Religion, University of Southern California.

Efforts to teach religious ethics in modern secular colleges and universities must take into account several key factors:

(1) The instrumental orientation of most contemporary students makes the subject of religious ethics appear largely irrelevant.

(2) Most students have had some exposure to religion, and come to the course with preconceived (and usually highly incorrect) ideas.

(3) Students have ethical theories (however unexamined) from which they act.

(4) The American context makes it difficult to think of religion and ethics as mutually reinforcing.

After examining these factors and their effects upon the teaching of religious ethics, the chapter compares the methodologies appropriate to the teaching of Jewish and Christian ethics, noting both areas of agreement and disparity between the two fields. Attention is focused on Jewish ethics here, and the following topics are addressed:

(1) Students at "secular" institutions have particular stereotypes about Jews, stereotypes which must be confronted and discussed in class.

(2) Judaism must be approached primarily in historical terms, and this approach inevitably meets some resistance in an essentially ahistorical culture.

(3) Judaism, especially Jewish ethics, resists the search for easy answers, a fact which makes students very uncomfortable.

(4) In some respects, the idea of Jewish ethics is a Christian notion, and must be recognized as such.

The remainder of the chapter will discuss specific methods of dealing with (not — alas! — solving) these problems. Among the topics covered are:

(1) Teaching Jewish history — ways to excite, ways to bore;

(2) Confronting the relativism problem in ethics, and not succumbing to it;

(3) Convincing students of the distinctiveness of Jewish ethics, and particularly of the role of interpretation and the individual in the Jewish ethical tradition;

(4) Raising the level of ethical reasoning by asking students to confront traditional religious ethical dilemmas.

Teaching the Intertestamental Period to Christians Students

ELLIS RIVKIN, is Adolph S. Ochs Professor of Jewish History, Hebrew Union College-Jewish Institute of Religion, Cincinnati.

This paper reviews briefly the philosophy of Hebrew Union College-Jewish Institute of Religion in the training of rabbis for the Reform Movement and, in light of this rationale, it suggests why the Hebrew Union College Graduate School has successfully appealed to non-Jewish graduate students, many of whom are Christians affiliated with conservative denominations.

The collision of historical-critical principles with one's faith commitment is raised and analyzed in light of the writer's graduate elective course entitled "Reconstructing the History of the Intertestamental Period," which is divided into four segments spanning four semesters over a two-year period. The thrust of the paper discusses the first segment of the course, a segment which seeks to establish the structure of Judaism which emerged with the promulgation of the finalized Pentateuch and to set this structure off sharply from the structures of Judaism which both preceded the promulgation of the Pentateuch and which followed. The discussion casts aside secondary literature temporarily, and concentrates exclusively on the primary sources alone. The result is a form of

Jewish Studies which welcomes the findings of modern science as a mode of divine revelation and the scientific method as the most reliable instrument for the discovery of truth and for the building of knowledge.

Theological Education and Christian-Jewish Relations

EUGENE J. FISHER, is Executive Secretary of the Secretariat for Catholic-Jewish Relations of the National Conference of Catholic Bishops. He also serves as Consultor to the Holy See's Commission for Religious Relations with the Jews.

The question of the relationship of the Church to the Jewish people is integral to every area of the core theological curriculum, from sacred scripture and liturgy to systematics and Church History. Though the question challenges Christian theology "at the very level of the Church's own identity," to cite Pope John Paul II, it has seldom been surfaced, except in a negative way, in Christian theological curricula.

The idea raised in the present paper, then, is not so much an argument for the addition of electives on Judaism, rabbinic literature, etc., though these would prove very beneficial to existing programs. Rather, the point is made that each course as currently taught must face serious challenges raised by the contemporary reassessment of the relationship between the Church and the Jewish people.

The question of the relationship between the Old and New Testaments, for example, which is vital to any valid "theology of the Old Testament," is equally a question of how to articulate the relationship between Jews and Christians as peoples of God. It is equally fundamental to an understanding of ecclesiology and liturgy. Church history likewise must face not only its dark underside in the "teaching of contempt" against the Jews, but come to an enriched (and enriching) understanding of the continuing contributions of Jewish spirituality and religious thought to the development of Western theology.

Such a reassessment of the basic grounding of the Christian theological enterprise in the light of its Jewish origins and present dialogue with Jews and Judaism, it is maintained, is a necessary ingredient of the theological renewal called for "in our age."

Team Taught, In-Class Dialogue: A Limited but Promising Method in Teaching Judaism

JAMES F. MOORE, is Assistant Professor in the Department of Theology, Valparaiso University, Indiana.

One of the by-products of increased JewishChristian dialogue is a shifting picture of how Judaism is taught not only in public universities but also in private, Christian denominational colleges and universities. Departments of Religion or Theology that previously were entirely staffed by Christians are being expanded to include Jewish faculty. Thus, students have new opportunities to study Judaism from a more balanced perspective in classes taught by Jewish instructors. In addition, the added Jewish staff creates possibilities for new approaches to the teaching of Judaism both in terms of expanded curriculum and new styles (e.g., team-taught classes).

Valparaiso University has had the good fortune for various reasons to be in the vanguard of an experiment which has produced in our offerings a developing approach to the teaching of Judaism that is best called "Team Taught, In-Class dialogue." By this I mean a style of teaching that not only offers a balanced view on theological-traditional concerns but also the opportunity for a broadly conceived interchange between participating faculty. The proposed essay, first, sketches the dialogue approach not only to give a descriptive framework but also to provide a tool for assessment. Secondly, the essay surveys the actual course offerings over the last five years concentrating especially on our course on "suffering and evil." Thirdly, a general assessment of both the courses and the teaching style concludes with both a cataloging of possibilities and of limits to any dialogue approach. Finally, the essay will offer suggestions for the development of the dialogue style in a variety of teaching settings and in relation to a number of subject areas.

Surely, any approach as new as team taught interreligious dialogue classes is best understood as still in the experimental stage. There are certain unique factors that may contribute to either the success or failure of classes which have nothing to do with the actual method of dialogue teaching. In addition, an assessment of the impact upon students is often (as with other classes) partly guesswork. Still, there are ways (class evaluations, for example) that one can assess the experiment in process with a certain amount of confidence. Such assessments will be included in the context of the whole review not only to provide a realistic picture of this method but also to provide whatever information might be necessary to encourage others to join the experiment that has proved extraordinarily fruitful for our students and faculty.

Not By Words Alone

JO MILGROM, is Visiting Assistant Professor in Theology and The Arts at the Center for Judaic Studies of the Graduate Theological Union, Berkeley.

Distinct from the traditional concerns of art history, the visual arts have been largely neglected as *parshanut,* commentary on the Bible, and a powerful medium in the search for meaning. Visual art which responds to specific biblical passages evokes the unspoken language "written" between the lines, calling forth deeper symbolic meanings of the text and creating a personal bond between the individual and the text. Thus the age-old text becomes comprehensible and the individual life takes on perspective in light of the archetypal association.

The process of bonding between person and Bible can be called midrash, which is also the name of the genre of material thus created. Midrash-making is an art of creative metaphor, joining together different and apparently irrelevant elements. This essay will advance the use of creative visual midrash, a method which makes conscious use of the pre-conscious psychological mechanisms present in human creativity antecedent to verbal expression. Striking illustrations will demonstrate that the imagery behind established works of art is the common possession of the human unconscious and can be evoked from the ordinary human being untrained in art, through simple manipulation of paper, without tools or talent. These images are then linked as interface to the biblical text and to literary midrash as visual commentary, with its own verbal complement. Because this activity anticipates and first bypasses the normal verbal routes of midrash-making it calls up deeply personal associations, the processing of which effectively binds academic Bible study to ultimate religious concerns.

Wrestling with Torah, God, and Self

ARTHUR WASKOW, teaches on the faculty of the Reconstructionist Rabbinical College and is director of The Shalom Center at the College. He also is co-editor of New Menorah.

This article describes methods of using Torah study and the making of new midrash by the students themselves, as a way of teaching both the nature of Torah and the development of one's own ethical, moral, and esthetic worldview.

The main method to be explicated is the collective reading of passages of Torah by a group of students, under a teacher's guidance. The students may be asked to tell a story or improvise a drama that acts out a "missing" section of the story as it appears in the Torah text; or they may be asked to explain a seeming gap or contradiction in the text; or they may be asked to imagine a connection between two words, phrases, or passages that appear in different parts of Torah; or they may be asked to imagine the same story told from the standpoint of a different participant or a different tale-teller (e.g. — a woman? a Sh'chemite? Absalom?); etc. The teacher may introduce classical or modern Jewish midrash, Christian or Muslim interpretations, modern historical documentary or literary analysis or other genres of understanding the text, with the intentions of teaching students about these methods, teaching students about choosing among various understandings of Torah, and teaching students about themselves.

By Torah we mean here chiefly but not only the text of Chumash, the Pentateuch. Use of these or similar methods with Talmud and Kabbalah are also discussed.

The article also briefly explores the philosophical implications of this approach in regard to teaching "about" Torah and in regard to teaching the process of moral self-development.

The article is based on experience in teaching this way in courses in religion at Swarthmore College and Temple University, in courses at the Reconstructionist Rabbinical College, and in study sessions for adults and children among havurah members.

Reflections on a New Integrated and Interdisciplinary Approach to Undergraduate Studies: Jewish and Western Civilizations

STEVEN LOWENSTEIN, is Associate Professor of Jewish History, University of Judaism, Los Angeles.

JOEL E REMBAUM, former Dean of Undergraduate Studies and Associate Professor of Jewish History, University of Judaism, Los Angeles. Now Senior Rabbi, Temple Beth Am, Los Angeles.

DAVID STERN, is Assistant Professor of Medieval Hebrew Literature, University of Pennsylvania. Previously, he was the Norman and Sadie Lee Assistant Professor of Jewish and Western Civilization at the University of Judaism in Los Angeles.

A two-year Core Curriculum in Jewish and Western Civilization is the basis for lower division study in Lee College, the undergraduate program at the University of Judaism. Like its more famous counterparts in general education at other American universities — Columbia, The University of Chicago, and St. Johns — this Core Curriculum aims to educate its students in the intellectual traditions of our Jewish culture through the intensive study of the great classical texts in the humanities and the social sciences. It emphasizes the acquisition of basic skills: the critical reading of primary sources and written and oral expression.

Recent years have seen a revival of interest in general education, partly in response to the increasing professionalization of so much other higher education in America. With the growth of Jewish Studies in the past decades, there have also appeared courses and curricula that present the history of the Jewish people and of Judaism from different perspectives. The Lee Core program is the first curriculum to combine the study of Western civilization with the study of Jewish history and culture and to apply to both elements the methods and aims of general education. The program was conceived out of a commitment to general education and with the belief that Jewish history cannot be understood outside the context of world history. It thereby aims to educate students in the essential pluralism of Western intellectual and cultural traditions. In pursuing the comparative study of Jewish and Western civilizations, the Lee program tries to show how these two cultures developed, at once influencing each other — with the influences going both ways — and differing. Beyond the question of influence, though, the program's study of Western and Jewish civilizations in unison allows it to avoid the provincialism that so often attends the usual survey courses in Western Civilization — the lazy assumption that all civilization is Western; that the cultural values and intellectual axioms of the Western tradition are the right, if not the only, ones; that, indeed, in the study of human culture there exists a single line of truth. This is where the interdisciplinary side of the Lee Core program proves so crucial, for aside from studying the same problem from different cultural perspectives, it also tries to look at each civilization from the changing viewpoint of different intellectual disciplines — to see how, for instance, a historian might view his age and its dilemmas in contrast to a poet or a religious thinker, and then to show how these disciplines themselves developed in response to varying historical and intellectual circumstances.

Thus, three principles comprise the basic framework of the Lee College Core Curriculum: first, a commitment to general education, its methods and goals; second, the wish to apply those methods to the study of Jewish and Western civilization together; third, an interdisciplinary approach to the study of both civilizations and their institutions that introduces the student to intellectual and cultural pluralism.

This paper analyzes the structure of the Lee Core Curriculum and its rationale. It also examines how various components of the Core have been taught and the degree to which the program's goals and expectations were met and how effectively its underlying principles were realized.

Preface

At the invitation of Professor Jacob Neusner, I organized and chaired an annual session for the History of Judaism section of the American Academy of Religion entitled "Methodologies in Teaching about Judaism." The seminar stressed comparative methodologies, Jewish and non-Jewish, in teaching about Judaism, and ran successfully for three years, 1982-1984. The idea for the current volume grew out of the experiences from the seminar. Professor Neusner's ongoing concern and interest in both seminar and text are hereby acknowledged and appreciated.

Publication of *Methodology in the Academic Teaching of Judaism* was made possible by assistance from the following: Dr. Hal Barach, Ron and Sarah Dearmond, Dr. Gerald Glanz, Israel and Rose Gold, Rabbi Jim Kaufman of Temple Beth Hillel, Rabbi Gilbert Kollin of Hollywood Temple Beth El, Rabbi William Kramer of Temple Beth Emet of Burbank, Rabbi Norman Pauker of Mishkan Israel Congregation, Jack Roth-Bookseller, Rabbi Moshe Rothblum of Adat Ari El, Rabbi Moshe Rubinstein of Valley Beth Israel, Rabbi Eli Schohet of Beth Kodesh Congregation, Rabbi Harold Schulweis of Valley Beth Shalom, Dr. Auri and Deena Spiegelman, Lee Sporina, Joseph F. Stein Foundation, Dr. Myron and Pauline Stein, Dr. Herman and Gladys Sturman, Ben Sussman, Rabbi David Vorspan of Temple Beth Ami, Rabbi Shelomo Weltman of Temple Bnai Hayyim, and Rabbi Isaiah Zeldin of Stephen S. Wise Temple. Their support of this enterprise reflects a knowledgeable community's interest in the scholarly dissemination of Judaica. For this, I am thankful.

The key to this volume is the diverse talent and scholarship provided by the contributors. Their time and effort in providing the best volume possible is very much appreciated. The presentation and style of the original essays are kept in tact though editing was provided to ensure a degree of conformity.

The clerical work was provided by my student, MaryEllen Coker. I am deeply grateful for her word processing expertise and editing skills. Her conscientious devotion and cheerful disposition have made an otherwise laborious editing task a worthwhile and pleasurable experience. A special debt of gratitude to Professor David Ellenson of HUC-JIR, Los Angeles, who was kind enough to read the entire manuscript and offered a number of helpful comments. Finally, my wife, Susan, and my former students and now good friends, Fran Barach and Joyce Glanz, have assisted in a number of ways in the successful publication of this volume. Their contributions are gratefully remembered.

The volume is dedicated to my children, Asher and Dorit, who, in their adolescent way, are asking some of the questions to which this book is an attempted answer.

Zev Garber

Erev Rosh Hashanah 5747
October, 1986

Introduction

Thoughts on the Text, Teachers and *Talmidim*

Zev Garber

1. Introduction

Most research in the field of Jewish education is done with parochial departments of Jewish education, found in Hebrew Teacher Colleges and seminaries, in mind. Only a few have written on the state of the discipline at secular universities, reflecting the relation of the discipline of general education to a Jewish educational problem or issue. The goal of this text is to make college and university educators aware of the rich diversity of Jewish Studies, suggest ways Jewish Studies can successfully be integrated into humanities classes, and provide substantial and imaginative materials to assist them in that pursuit. The chapters of the book are free of institutional bias and "hand-me-down" methodologies; they are informed essays that combine theory and classroom management and teaching. Creating methodologies in thinking about Judaism rather than different conceptual and thematic educational models in enacting Judaism represent the forte of the book. The result is scholarship, analytically constructed, which enables the reader not to read about Jewish Studies but to confront the process itself.

Structurally, the work is divided into four sections. The first section raises questions of methodology within the *Wissenschaftlich* and university educational goals. The second section speaks on the teaching of Judaica in a variety of disciplines, including Bible, rabbinics, literature, ethics, and Hebrew language. The third section is concerned with the proper direction in teaching Judaism to non-Jewish students and touches, among others, the sensitive issue of how to educate and not indoctrinate. The final part is designed to be a "wild card" or "open end" section which includes personal ideologies and curricular issues involved in the integration of Jewish Studies and Western culture.

2. Learning

The *Methodology* text does not aspire to cover every phase of Jewish Studies at the university level nor does it claim to present a complete analysis of a subject under discussion. Rather its chapters speak of a "beginning" and not an "end" to a critical exchange of ideas and experiences. Each chapter takes seriously the four sequential steps of a learning experience:

Confrontation, where the student experiences the idea, behavior, or object superficially; *Analysis*, where the student seriously probes the occasion or text in light of previous experience and knowledge; *Interaction*, where the student's mutual or reciprocal communication with others helps him/her benefit from their feelings, ideas, and experiences with the reality under discussion; and *Internalization*, where by turning the new experience and sharing of ideas upon oneself, the student reacts meaningfully to the new reality as it relates to him/her as an individual and as a member of society as a whole. Some chapters deal with abstract philosophical and metaphysical discussions. Others deal in the main with real life situations and not theoretical abstractions. All emphasize a major pedagogical principle that students learn better and appreciate more their understanding of the subject matter if they are actively involved in learning rather than being passively taught. Learning involves not only information given but the recipient's discovery of what that knowledge means. A major concern of the text, therefore, is that the teacher be less of a knowledge-dispenser and more of a knowledge-facilitator, who leads the student to make discoveries and articulate values and conclusions.

Flexibility, innovation, implementation, enthusiasm, and relevancy are some characteristics of a good teaching methodology. The college classroom should not serve as a podium for intellectual exhibitionism or be a forum for undisciplined bull sessions. Some information and delight may result from such performances but little intellectual honesty and proper learning habits can develop. Emphasis on relevancy should be student-oriented so that students are involved in finding meaning on an individual basis. This may be achieved by the implementation of a teaching style that converses with the students as much as is possible and develops intellectual talents such as comprehension, application, analysis, synthesis, and evaluation rather than regurgitation of class notes as objectives of written assignments. The topics method for class lectures, discussion, and participation has proven to be for many of us a successful device in "thought" classes. Audio-visual aids are also important features which can successfully supplement course lectures.

3. Audio-visual Approach

In the teaching of Jewish Studies, one can draw on a number of experimental techniques (e.g., slides, tapes, music, drama, dance, motion picture, lifestyles, *realia*, etc.) which can create a three-dimensional appreciation of the subject under study. In the teaching of Jewish Martyrdom, for example, photographs from contemporary life are chosen for their emotional and aesthetic appeal. Selective readings from sacred and secular sources and impromptu dramatics by the instructor, complemented by relevant photographs of despair, exile, poverty, war, brotherhood, persecution, hunger, joy, etc., can illuminate in a more lasting fashion some of the wisdom of Judaism. The juxtaposition of readings/dramatics and photograph provide a vivid and intimate insight into life which does not suffer from the verbosity and technical jargon of a textbook or lecture, and underscores in a different and innovative way some of the universal appeal of Judaism.

The following steps may be taken in presenting a "photographic essay" on Jewish Martyrdom:

A. Select slides which are significant to unit objective and topic description.

B. Run through frames with commentary.

C. Repeat frames more slowly, stopping at each one or selective ones and inviting discussion, ideas, "what do you see?," role-playing, etc.

D. Show frames without verbal commentary, but accompanied by other multi-media, e.g., music, tape recording, etc.

E. Exhibit two viewings of the same photograph, but for different purposes. For example, one viewing for the historical or factual information given, and the second for a *midrash* on martyrdom, war, Holocaust, nuclear catastrophe, etc.

F. A silent run through of the frames is impressive once the student has been exposed to lectures, readings, discussions, activities, etc., on Jewish Martyrdom. Here the frames are shown with a half minute to a minute interlude, leaving an unspoken but dramatic message to be worked out by the viewer within him/herself and in the presence of other members of the group. The momentary silence experienced can last a lifetime.

By venturing into an excursus on a non-traditional method of teaching in an Introduction we are making two points. First, what is needed in the classroom is effective teaching and creative exposition in addition to critical textual evaluation. The teaching experience is incomplete if one without the other is to prevail. This is the excitement of learning and teaching alike. A prevalent myth in *Wissenschaft des Judentums* is that a Ph.D. is the guarantee of a good teacher and that the brilliant researcher is capable of communicating his/her scholarship in the classroom situation. The fact is — and student surveys bear this out time and time again — that a good researcher becomes a good teacher only if s/he works at it. This is not to say that the conventional way of research and publication are not important in a professor's total role on campus, but to stress that his/her first responsibility is to be a competent teacher, and good teaching does not necessarily mean minutiae-oriented scholarship. Second, while students may take in lectures in a passive TV watching state, they must be actively involved in the teacher's presentation. A painless way for this to be accomplished is by media impact. The audio-visual approach imprints learning on the mind and in the memory; the use of so many senses — kinesthetic when the students interpret in writing a shared experience, auditory as the students hear others and listen to their inner voice, and visual as they synthesize the graphic record before their eyes — all reinforce the concepts being learned. As a venture in human experience, it aids in fashioning meaningful, lasting ties in the appreciation of Judaism. It can provide a more vivid and intimate insight into life than does a textbook. A textbook must generalize but multi-media can contribute to a personal and sensitive presentation. In addition, by this alternative approach to teaching, the instructor gives a different dimension of what "human awareness" means than is found in the "heavy" findings of traditional scholarship.

4. Humanities and Hebrew Literature

Different disciplines have their own particular patterns of thinking, inquiry, or information processing. For example, scientific inquiry calls for classification, explanation of technical processes, detailed statements of fact often containing a definition or statement of principle, problemsolving, and experiment reporting which involves discriminating observation, careful explanation and considered conclusions. Jewish Studies exposes students to an appreciation of the Jewish heritage in all its aspects and helps students develop an understanding of the unique Jewish contribution to world civilization in general, and to western culture in particular. As such, Jewish Studies is an instructional form of the humanities and its emphasis is on reading, writing and reasoning.

What is the proper way of instructing these skills? So diversified is the answer, as the essays in this volume testify, that in this space we merely wish to observe what must not be done by quoting from an article by James Sloan Allen entitled "The Humanists are Guilty of Betraying Humanism" published in *The Wall Street Journal* of February 2, 1982 (reprinted in Douglas M. Astoli, ed., *Teaching the Ancient World,* Scholars Press, 1983, p.9):

> The humanists have betrayed humanism by converting education — and most egregiously the teaching of literature — into a pseudo-scientific labor over technical issues set forth in a jargon that baffles common understanding. One does not talk about novels or stories, poems or plays any more; one "decodes" or "deconstructs texts." One does not explore and evaluate an author's thoughts and perceptions for the purpose of strengthening mind and illuminating life; one seeks clues to "performative linguistic acts" for the purpose of achieving "critical enablement." Literature, after all, we are told, is "primarily about language, and not much else."

Substitute "professors of Jewish Studies" for "humanists" and you have a core problem in the instruction of Jewish Studies today: an obsession with the most trivial literary fragment or historical data as versus the finished product;

concern with esoteric questions, often archaic and arcane, as over the needs and interest of the present-day student.

A slogan of nineteenth-century *Wissenschaft* (Zunz, Scheinschneider, Jost) prevails in today's Jewish academe: Every writer must be a "digger," and all scholars antiquarians. The traditional methods of teaching modern Hebrew literature (as well as Bible, rabbinics, medieval literature) in the original, found in upper division and graduate courses, viz., translation, expounding of grammatical intricacies, lectures based on instructor's notes from research and graduate seminars, etc., prove less than adequate at an introductory level. In its place, we recommend an historical-critical method which emphasizes the contemporary literature as an interpretation of history and in light of other literary works in general, and contemporary Hebrew works in particular. A moderate number of readings from Hebrew poetry, prose and essay is suggested. One-third of the class time constitutes lectures on the socio-historical forces which motivated and shaped Jewish life in the last two centuries. Two-thirds of the class hour are devoted to a direct interpretation of the assigned texts in order to discern the major values and trends of modern Hebrew literature. A study of literature must not be confused with the history of literature, and thus a confrontation with textual sources more than histories and commentaries is of primary importance.

A deeper appreciation of Hebrew literature develops if the instructor plays more of a passive role than is traditionally assigned to him/her. By encouraging the student to do research at home in order to explicate the text in class, and answer questions of difficulty from a peer group, the instructor is planting in the students seeds of loyalty to some great literature, which otherwise would not grow from the total lecture method that often detaches the student from the material. Furthermore, the student gains self-respect from such an exposure, his/her own germane ideas are able to sprout, and a relaxed teacher-student relationship is created. The non-straight lecture method also enables the professor to grow in stature as an educator. By playing the role of a class catalyst, a professor has many opportunities to present his/her own contribution and to refine it in light of class feedback to a greater degree than one could by using the straight lecture method. An ideal educational experience is thus fulfilled since the goal of discovering provocative ideas of great men and women of letters is brought about by professor and student exploring together. This can penetrate, but alas not eliminate, what Mr. Allen rightly sees as a crisis in the humanities classroom: " ... proliferation of an ill-education in technical skills, ponderous analysis and pretentious jargon that feeds on self-doubts and intellectual dishonesty" (loc. cit.).

5. Notes on Teaching Jewish Religious Heritage

Eleven years ago I was invited to contribute to the pioneering *Study of Religion in Two-Year Colleges* (edited by C. Freeman Sleeper and Robert A.

Spivey; Scholars Press, 1975) and in the planning stage, the contributors asked themselves, "What do we want to accomplish with a typical student: (a) who may take only one religion course in his or her entire life, and (b) who is curious about the subject rather than highly motivated?" Permit me to answer this question by reflecting on a class in "The Jewish Religious Heritage" ("The Essentials of Judaism"), which I have introduced at a two-year public college (Los Angeles Valley College in 1971) and at a public university (University of California at Riverside in 1985), since it is being offered in so many colleges, and it is the most attractive course for a public institution which is about to initiate Jewish Studies for the first time.

An introductory class in "The Jewish Religious Heritage" is an invitation to study the Jewish religious civilization as one of western man's primary responses to the human predicament. The student is exposed to a brief historical background dealing with the development of Judaism as it is related to an exposition of its central affirmations. The goal is to familiarize the student with what the Jewish religious tradition regards as its essential genius and to provide an opportunity for an appreciation of the similarities and differences between Judaism and the other major religious groups of American culture. Among the class topics that can benefit an introductory student are the following: (a) the structure of faith: God, man, rites of passage, Jewish festivals, community, and (b) the dynamics of faith: religious commitment and social problems, contemporary values, and the present state of Jewish belief.

A required research project provides an opportunity for the student to examine in some depth one of the doctrines, practices, lifestyles, or institutions of contemporary Judaism which is of particular interest to him/her. Or the student may write on one of the topics developed during the class hour, e.g., the influence of a Jewish religious ethic on man's life, the nature of revelation, the "other" Jew (Jewish poor, Jewish feminist, Holocaust survivor, Jewish sectarian, gay Jew, etc.), God in the post-Holocaust age, etc. The student examines the topic in whatever manner s/he deems most productive (historically, theologically, philosophically, socially, Scripturally, rabbinically, direct interview, or any combination of several of these), evaluates the vital issues, points out the contradictions, weaknesses, tensions, etc., and makes constructive comments upon them. If the topic as represented is too broad, the student may refine it but only on the basis of a clear statement of what his/her delimitation is at the beginning of the paper, and only if it represents a valid context for investigation within the Jewish religious heritage.

The structure of the paper is constructed from the formal rules for writing for a research paper, using Kate L. Turabian's *A Manual for Writers of Term Papers, Theses and Dissertations* (4th Edition, 1973, University of Chicago Press) or the *MLA Style Sheet*. Since many of the students are new to college, this research project presents an excellent opportunity for them to do a structured paper as a model for future term papers. The research paper is viewed as a substantive research effort which demands a lot of reading in various sources, including books, journals and encyclopedias. To aid the student in the proper research technique, a critique of the term paper and a discussion session are provided by the instructor. Also, a select bibliography is affixed to the class syllabus as a guide to those individuals who wish to go further in their study of Jewish life and thought.

The prospectus of a course in "The Jewish Religious Heritage" is constructed to obtain the following goals:

A. To be aware that the Jewish religious tradition deals with peoplehood, worldview and lifestyle.

B. To realize that the culture, religion and history of the Jewish people are mutually interdependent.

C. To understand that the Jewish religious heritage is a vast reservoir of feelings, thoughts, values, concerns, and actions preserved by a people for close to four thousand years and manifested in artifacts, symbols, calendars, legal traditions, nature, history, persons, documents, codes, and ideas.

D. To feel the personal and the communal, the parochial and the universal, the legal and the mystic, the spiritual and the secular dimensions of Judaism.

E. To discover the change and development of Jewish religious experiences and expressions in the course of time.

F. To develop for the committed Jewish student a self-concept and self-pride in the relevancy and legitimacy of a Jewish content class, which encourages one to live openly and freely with one's own worldview and lifestyle; to develop by others empathy in appreciating the way of life, thought and faith of a vital, dynamic force in world culture.

G. To acquire the basic vocabulary for study of, and oral and written presentation in, a basic introduction to Judaism.

H. To be made aware of the laborious work involved in a critical, disciplined study of origins, sources and materials, and to obtain skills in oral and written presentations on a given problem of the Jewish religious heritage.

Humanistic concern, a nondogmatic approach, sensitivities, dialogue between teacher and student are some of the factors which can help weave a thread of continuity into material so complex and diversified, and make the learning of Judaism more particular and personal.

6. Professors and Programs

Previous sections have pointed out that the introductory student of Jewish Studies be exposed to a critical recognition of Jews and Judaism. The point is also made that Jewish Studies is not an attempt, however important, in discovering one's identity but laborious research and work involved in a disciplined study of origins, sources, materials, and methodology. This conclusion leads us to additional remarks about programs and professors of Jewish Studies.

A Jewish Studies program, in addition to its academic offerings, can serve as a medium where ideas are discussed and shared "*lishmah*," for their own sake. Committed to no specific Jewish preference or ideology, a Jewish Studies program entertains all ideas and opinions of Jewish concern. It is truly a market place of knowledge where no attitude, development, historical phase, or personality is above criticism be it the origins of Judaism, the impact of the Holocaust, the centrality of the State of Israel in Jewish existence today, dialogue with non-Jews, or the ideologues of Jewish Studies then and now.

It has been said more than once in this Introduction that a major *desideratum* of a Jewish Studies professor is that s/he be student-oriented. Since being student-oriented is largely a sharing of self, there are probably as many ways of being student-oriented as there are teachers. But the professor who perceives the material s/he teaches from the students' point of view, strives to make the learning experiences of the students personally meaningful, and believes in the worth and dignity of every human being and relates to his/her students on this basis has taken a giant step forward in accomplishing his/her obligation to teaching and learning, to the college, and to the community.

The ferment in Jewish Studies circles today regarding what constitutes Jewish Studies, how to teach it, and to whom, etc., is a natural product of the change that is sweeping the whole philosophy of American higher education. Like American colleges and universities, contemporary *Wissenschaft des Judentums* is being broadly transformed from an exclusive institution to an inclusive one. The once-narrow gates to higher Jewish education have been thrown wide to admit everyone, regardless of background, age, sex, and creed. In such a situation, the old structural lecture method, where the student sits back and absorbs like a sponge the knowledge of a professor's lecture, would simply not do by itself. The professor will have to innovate possibly along the lines mentioned in this Introduction and in a number of essays in this volume. One will have to teach the subject matter creatively and objectively without indoctrination. One must have the right to challenge students and to set and maintain scholarly standards but one is also responsible to respect the students' right to learn, to ask questions, to defend beliefs, to express opinions, or to disagree without repression or reprisal.

To motivate students to continue their Jewish Studies outside of the formal classroom we suggest thematic course offerings, probing the esoteric as well as the familiar Jewish topics, alongside the traditional courses in language, literature, history, civilization, etc. This type of class is not intended to be a permanent part of the Jewish Studies program. Rather, it is the kind of class responding to contemporary issues and may be offered several semesters (and if popular on a more permanent basis) under the heading "Selected Topics in Judaism." For example, the role of women in Judaism approached through *halakha,* ritual, or symbol; or examining traditional and modern writings to formulate a Jewish perspective on medical ethics; or understanding Jewish memory and the meaning of history after Bitburg; or the institutional structure of the American Jewish community, asking such questions as is there an American Jewish community in view of the diversity that is apparent among American Jews? How can the Jewish establishment better respond to individual Jewish needs? What are the current positions of the Jewish institutions in regard to such issues as public funds to parochial schools, the fourth R (religion) in schools and politics, quotas in universities, etc. If from the beginning, the introductory student learns to use his/her curiosity to make discoveries about Judaism and its culture and civilization, the chances are greater that s/he will continue to do so in the future. For if the student feels that one only has to learn what the teacher presents, one will have little or no motivation for future study, once one's formal education is completed.

Finally, a word about the commitment of a Jewish Studies professor. The professor of Jewish Studies should see his/her role beyond the normal academic one. Because of the goals involved, not the least of which is the continuity of a learned Jewish community of tomorrow, s/he is expected to invest much time out of the classroom with his/her charges. Ideally, one knows the students by name and is familiar with their entering characteristics, and reasons for taking Jewish Studies. One is available to students who seek help and guidance, both in and out of class. S/he answers questions in a "one to one" situation with the techniques of a skilled counselor. One cultivates open relationships with one's students upon which effective communication depends. Acknowledging that a major reason given by students in taking a Jewish Studies class is self-identification with their heritage, one is reasonably available outside of class as a source person for questions on Jewish life: *Kehillah, kashrut,* prayer, Israel, sense of time, language, continuity, conscience, etc., and helps to coordinate formal and informal student activities toward this objective. One makes a serious effort to establish a *havurah* among students and faculty which seeks to integrate the fragmented aspects of Jewishness on campus into a new communal framework. This fellowship can rediscover Jewish meaning through interpersonal dialogue and struggle, Torah and challenges, reassert the joy of living, and realize a transcendence from personal needs and bonds. Remaining in touch with Judaica from origins to contemporary interpretations becomes organic and natural in such an environment. Confronting Jewishness is an important task of a Jewish Studies professor; by varying the classroom procedure to a variety of learning experiences, one can help his/her students value and respect the rich tapestry of the Jewish heritage within the context of world civilization. This widening of the Jewish consciousness through intense awareness and pride of the Jewish psyche in all of its manifestations is surely one of the primary obligations of a teacher in Jewish Studies; and it is one which very few have successfully performed.

7. The Text

The underlying hopes of the Introduction are several: to offer a variety of observations for learning to happen effectively, to allow students to interact personally with course material, to make instructors aware of what students think, feel, and understand or fail to understand, to show the inseparable connection between writing and learning and thinking, and to create an atmosphere where individual student concerns and rigorous academic research complement each other. Our recommended teaching method advocates student-oriented and not fact-oriented curricula and that the instructor conceives of him/herself as a knowledge-facilitator rather than a knowledge-dispenser. Thereby the student is engaged in these learning/thinking operations: observing, recording, generalizing, summarizing, applying general to specific, integrating new ideas with old, inferring, critiquing, and questioning. In additional attempts to ensure student interest in Jewish Studies classes, we recommend the utilization of guest lecturers, library, theater and museum trips, slides and other audio-visual methods. We also suggest a topical approach to replace a chronological approach typically employed in introductory classes. Finally, contra the convenient Scantron sheet examination, we propose journals, reviews, personal projects and other written assignments which encourage exploration, originality, creativity and provide a vehicle for student-teacher communication in and outside of class that is comfortable, friendly, and non-threatening. As R. Eliazar ben Shammua might phrase it: honor and reverance are due both learners and teachers of Torah (*m. 'Avot* 4. 12). Isn't this what learning is all about?

The text embodies and goes beyond the Introduction. It suggests and hopefully contributes to an academic teaching of Judaism; the term "academic" makes the necessary distinction between university scholarship and proselytizing, intraconfessional, and other types of parochial instruction. The articles reflect specific theories, methods, and issues related to a scholarly teaching of Judaism. Thus Vernoff challenges fundamentally the subject/object dichotomy perpetrated by scholars who teach "about Judaism." Breslauer, Milgrom, and Waskow provide an introduction to often overlooked aspects of Jewish religiousness: imagination, consciousness, and literary/visual arts. Zuckerman, Basser, Lenowitz, Morahg, and Seltser discuss specific classes and teaching methodologies (theory and practice) which enable us to judge what can and cannot be done in the classroom. Fisher, Rivkin, and Moore focus on the importance of Judaism and how to teach contemporary Jewish concerns, ideas, and values to a primarily non-Jewish (Christian) audience. Bilgray surveys the field, scope, and future of the Hebrew teaching discipline in American colleges, universities, and seminaries. Lowenstein, Rembaum, and Stern analyze the first American curriculum to combine the study of western civilization with the study of Judaism and to apply to both branches of instruction the methods and aims of general education.

If successful, the book's agenda will provide opportunities for a critical exchange of ideas, intellectual stimulation, and, hopefully not least, stimulation of scholarly activity and productivity by others. Other volumes are suggested if and when warranted.

Part One

THEORY AND METHODOLOGY

Chapter One

The Contemporary Study of Religion and the Academic Teaching of Judaism

Charles Elliott Vernoff

How a subject matter is taught depends, in no small measure, on what it is conceived to be; and the basic conception of a subject area is established through its academically disciplined study. For several generations, accordingly, the prevailing norms for the academic study and teaching of Judaism have been dictated by the classical tradition of *Wissenschaft des Judentums,* the "science of Judaism," flourishing on a groundwork laid by Leopold Zunz and other giants of nineteenth century historical scholarship. This tradition has been well perpetuated in America within the contemporary Association for Jewish Studies. But Judaism, whatever else it may be, is a *religion.* And during the past generation, the academic study of religion has itself been swept up in a current of rapid and indeed revolutionary change. Since the early 1960's, departments of religious studies have proliferated within the secular university. Staffed by an interdisciplinary assemblage of scholars trained in areas as diverse as theology and sociology, these departments — spurred in part by their own graduate Ph.D.'s draped with the mantle of "religious studies" — have been under ever increasing practical pressure to define their academic mandate more precisely. And that entails delineating exactly what it is they study — presumably "religion." Circumstances have thus conspired to force, as never previously in the history of scholarship, engagement with the theoretical and methodological questions of just what religion is, why it should be studied and how it should be investigated and taught.[1]

To be sure, the crystallization of religious studies as an academic domain remains a process barely underway. Long established schools of historical scholarship within particular religious traditions can continue, for the most part, in easy disregard of a development which has yet to vindicate its full legitimacy. An exception to this state of affairs, however, is the case of Judaism. No scholar of the present generation has achieved greater renown for creative and sometimes controversial innovation within the tradition of *Wissenschaft des Judentums* than Jacob Neusner. Yet this same Jacob Neusner has not only assumed simultaneous leadership within the American Academy of Religion, nurturing bed for the new religious studies, but as Jonathan Z. Smith, himself a leading scholar of religion, has observed more than once, Neusner has increasingly diverted his own programmatic concerns and scholarly agenda toward the organic integration of Judaic studies into the broader conspectus of a nascent religious studies.[2] In 1983, this striking intersection of the contemporary study of Judaism with theoretical and methodological preoccupations of the newly emergent academic domain of religious studies embodied itself in a significant volume edited and partially authored by Neusner: *Take Judaism, for Example: Studies Toward the Comparison of Religions*.[3] For a scholar of Neusner's visibility to implant his work so firmly and deliberately within the vineyard of religious studies extends a peculiarly bracing challenge not only to other scholars but to all teachers of Judaica; a mandate to stretch their pedagogical horizons so as to incorporate the widest and most provocative insights and issues within the contemporary study of religion at large:

> The title of this book, then, is meant to lay down a challenge to the study of Judaism within the study of religions. *Take Judaism, for Example* — but to exemplify what? If we move *toward the comparison of religions,* what is it about religions that ... we wish to compare? Let me specify what I think we study when we study religion, and, even more specifically, what we study when we want to know about Judaism. I wish to know about Judaism. I wish further to explain why I regard the study of religion as urgent, not merely interesting — a necessity for society and a precondition for the future of humankind.[4]

The last sentence of this passage clearly, if implicitly, mediates between "study" as a scholarly activity in a research library and as a general classroom activity guided by an instructor. But tracing the potential impact of the contemporary scholarly ferment in religious studies upon the teaching of Judaism in the classroom is itself a task which can proceed only by way of example. We shall therefore examine one trajectory along which religious studies might in fact develop and consider how its theoretical insights and methodic principles may inform first the academic study and then, flowing from that, the teaching of Judaism.

An Emergent Direction in Religious Studies

During 1983, the same year *Take Judaism, for Example* appeared in print, a noted exponent of theory and method for the new religious studies, Ninian Smart, published a volume entitled *Worldviews: Cross-Cultural Explorations of Human Beliefs*.[5] Smart here proposes to identify the focal subject area for this emergent academic realm:

> Thus, the modern study of religion helps to illuminate worldviews, both traditional and secular, which are ... an engine of social and moral continuity and change; and therefore it explores beliefs and feelings, and

> tries to understand what exists inside the heads of people. What people believe is an important aspect of reality whether or not what they believe is true ... The English language does not have a term to refer to both traditional religions and ideologies; the best expression is perhaps *worldviews*.[6]

Other theoreticians of the study of religion had been converging for some time upon the notion of "worldview" that Smart in this book elevates to special prominence. The consensus of their thinking understands worldviews as arising in fulfillment of the constitutive need of self-conscious beings for some comprehensive and integral orientation to the conditions of their existence. Raimundo Panikkar, for example, insists that each person has ultimate presuppositions, i.e., some basic view of reality, and no one stands on "neutral ground".[7] Mircea Eliade implies that human consciousness cannot even coalesce without a structure of epistemological reference and orientation which organizes and interprets one's *Lebenswelt*.[8] Michael Novak observes that *mythos* basically means "story," and the irreducible domain of religious studies is that of the integrating "stories" that all self-conscious entities, individual or collective, must tell themselves to function within the environing reality of other selves and world.[9] Peter Berger, speaking as a sociologist of knowledge, situates religion at the generative center of "world-building" and maintenance.[10] And Ninian Smart himself proposes that the heart of the study of religion is simply "worldview analysis."[11]

Within the realm of Judaic studies itself, the category of worldview was particularly highlighted in 1979 when Jonathan Z. Smith delivered the first presentation in the History of Judaism section of the American Academy of Religion upon its reconstitution at the initiative of Jacob Neusner. Smith detects important anticipations of a theoretical model for the new religious studies in the often spurned notions of the "Pan-Babylonian school" of the history of religion, which paved the way for present usage of the term "worldview" within the field:

> ... what the Pan-Babylonian school introduced was the notion of a total system, to use their favorite word, a *Weltanschauung* [worldview] ... the object of religion, for them the most total expression of "world view," is man's cultural and intellectual world, not the world of nature. It is the inner relationships of the "elements," their system, their internal logic and coherence, that validates a "world view," not conformity to nature. Therefore, the "world view" may be articulated in a rigorously systematic manner.[12]

Smith goes on to question whether Neusner's narrow application of the concept of worldview to a literary "system," i.e., "the generative logic ... of a quite particular document," does not abandon the cardinal principle of *totality*.[13] In the epilogue to *Take Judaism, for Example,* Neusner responds to this critique:

> Our work then is to locate the logic of a given system and to relate that logic to the context of the system ... At this point I must digress to emphasize that when we speak of system, we mean only a social system ... The limits of the system are not literary but social, even though, in historical research, we tend to begin with literary evidence ... What I propose, therefore, is a way beyond the historicizing atomism which treats all things as unconnected to all others, and which therefore closes off the path to insight worth sharing, method worth repeating.[14]

Yet the "way beyond" Neusner proposes apparently can be neither that of the conventional *historian,* who seeks the particular above all, nor that of the conventional *philosopher,* who confines his interest to the universal:

> Historians treat events as singular ... But if there are patterns, they reduce the singularity, the givenness, of the singular. To historians, the search for insight is a task for philosophers, theologians, or social scientists — people who wish to bring things into relationship and to find out the universally useful truth in diverse things ... (yet) ... the theological construction of "Judaism" falls before the wrecking ball of historians, with their exceptions, their various examples, their particulars.[15]

Does the apparent clash Neusner discerns between the perspectives of history and philosophy imply, then, that the "way" toward understanding *religion as such* might lead "beyond" the horizon of the conventional academically disciplined historian, no less than that of the disciplined philosopher or theologian?

If something like "worldview" and its manifestations constitutes the object proper of the study of religion, it becomes evident that this study can indeed be neither history *nor* philosophy, yet it must have tangencies with both. First of all, from Jonathan Z. Smith's discussion of the Pan-Babylonian school may be derived, given the other theoretical concepts cited above, a working definition of "worldview": a view of "the world" as total system, by and large internally logical and coherent, which satisfies the elemental human need to *make sense of things* as the means of establishing basic sanity and maintaining a foundation for practical action. By this reckoning, any largely *self-conscious* and thus *choice-making* entity, collective or individual, will need *some* orientation to reality, which entails formation of a worldview; and worldviews accordingly provide the matrices for all group and individual systems of reality manifest in societies, cultures and persons. What evidences the presence of worldviews, then, is their empirically available molding of the thought and action of concrete human beings, not only in the texts they write and rituals they perform, but in their attitudes, character and general behavior. As custodian of the human past, it is surely the historian who furnishes the model for the initial gathering and assembling of such particular data. But what allows these data to be interpreted is an understanding of worldview as vehicle of the constitutive and universal human need for *orientation*, i.e., the demand to comprehend reality implicitly as a total system characterized by internal logic and coherence. It is the philosopher who furnishes the model for the purest and most self-conscious expression of this need, which itself is the most primal expression of self-consciousness.

At one extremity, therefore, the study of religion must certainly approach the historical disciplines with their skill at practical data gathering and primary interpretation. At the other extremity, though, the study of religion requires hypothetical mapping of the general structure of a worldview as embodying the need of self-consciousness for integral orientation to reality; and this mapping must be informed by awareness of philosophic consciousness as well as by philosophic disciplines with their skill at theoretical reflection. Yet the central arena within the study of religion is the study of *religions*, for example Judaism. To understand Judaism fully might require greater coordination of theory *and* empirical practice than has yet been achieved at institutions, such as the University of Chicago, which stress the former, and Harvard or Brown, which emphasize the latter. Hypotheses broaching the general nature of worldview must be brought into close critical relation with the substantive data of Judaism in its varied manifestations at different points in time and space. Through the mutual hermeneutic interplay of the data of the manifold concrete "Judaisms" with a developing hypothesis which seeks to formulate the generic aspects of "Judaism," a grasp of the Judaic worldview in its universality and particularity, its constancy and variation, its abiding similitude and ever novel empirical differentiations, should emerge. To achieve such genuine interplay, however, necessitates devising methods of hypothesis aimed not just at temporally unfolding historical configurations nor at eternal philosophic truths but at the diachronic and synchronic reality of *worldview as such*. Here lies a developmental frontier for the study of religion, visible beyond the clash discerned by Neusner.

Should successful methods of hypothesis yield deepening understanding of the Judaic worldview, the profound manner in which this worldview structures the society, culture and psychic makeup of its host group would certainly become more evident; conversely, an acquaintance with the dynamics of society, culture and the psyche could expedite a grasp of the functioning of a worldview within its milieu and thereby lead directly to essential insight into the worldview itself. Exploration of how religion functions within its milieu as a way toward understanding religion as such has provided much of the agenda for the study of religion at schools such as Syracuse University. Is the study of religion as worldview, then, perhaps a mere adjunct to the existing *social sciences?* The term "worldview" itself, after all, has achieved its widest currency in the field of anthropology.[16] The answer to such concerns is that methods of disciplined study in the existing social sciences appropriately urge an effort at the complete suppression and functional neutralization of the scholar's own worldview since it bears personal values which may distort *objectivity*. Fully understanding *worldviews themselves*, on the other hand, requires that a scholar become precisely and vividly *aware* of his or her own worldview *as* worldview — that is, as fulfilling the universal *subjective* human need for orientation — in order to have an empathic, cognitive and critical touchstone for fathoming the worldviews of others; and this is requisite even if one's personal worldview invokes the authority of science itself. For Western humanism, of which scientism is a variant, is very much a particular worldview with developmental roots extending as far back as ancient Mesopotamia where the original precursors of the Jewish people may have sought spiritual liberation from the slaveholding deities of old Sumer. Thus humanism itself may in principle have no less, but also no more, inherent claim to ultimacy than various other worldviews with differing yet coherent perspectives on the world as total system. In sum, then, it appears that "methodological self-consciousness" in the study of religion can be neither "objective" nor "subjective" in the conventional sense, but must remain faithfully transparent to the total character of the whole human person as a self-conscious entity requiring orientation to his or her environing reality.

What the academically disciplined study of religion actually necessitates methodologically may therefore best be described as a *probe of the limits* of scientific objectification, issuing in a kind of "self-transcendence" of the researcher's "objectivity" such that it cease to suppress the reality of that "subjectivity" which always accompanies it in any case. And this accommodation of subjectivity is demanded by the interests of *truth itself*, which likewise motivates the scientific ideal of objectivity as such. While not at all unscientific, then, the study of religion may stand at and delineate the *limits* of science, there admitting the rights of subjective consciousness — which is perhaps why the contemporary study of religion has evidenced notable affinity with the arts and humanities, among which it is often enumerated.

The foregoing characterization of an emergent direction in the study of religion depends, to be sure, on the assumption that the object of that study will increasingly be identified as *worldview*, in the fullest and most non-reductive sense. But granting this not implausible assumption suggests the likelihood of scholars' more and more recognizing that to study religion *as* religion is to venture forth into largely uncharted methodological terrain, moving in the direction not of any other study or studies but of a novel disciplinary perspective endowed with its own theoretical grounding, methodic arsenal and systematic agenda. What we wish to consider here are the consequences for teaching of this sort of a disciplinary perspective, committed to investigating religion in accordance with its own *logos* — i.e., its intrinsic nature, empirical characteristics, and inherent principles of intelligibility. To understand the pedagogical implications of such a *religiological* approach to the subject matter necessitates closer examination of scholarly method to determine how it might inform modes of classroom instruction.

An Exemplary Methodology in the Scholarly Study of Judaism

A religiological mode of studying religion as adumbrated above may seem at once novel, insofar as it still has few operational precedents, and familiar, to the extent that it retrospectively conforms with one's intuitive sense of what place the religious dimension occupies within the compass of human existence. Yet, in truth, the necessity for a new discipline which approaches religion in accordance with its own *logos* has already gained a measure of implicit recognition at the horizon of the historical, philosophic and social scientific investigation of religious phenomena and tradition. Nowhere is this more pointedly apparent than in *Take Judaism, for Example* where Jacob Neusner, in his summary reflections, brings the enterprise of the conventional historian of religion toward its limit and there glimpses the profile of an emergent religiology:

> Why do I wish to construct a system ... and to make sense of the whole by seeking other wholes, other systems? The answer is given in the question, in use of the language, "to make sense." ... It is only in discovering the choices, the contexts in which statements are made, in defining the persistent questions to which statements constitute answers, that the statements begin to make sense. Discovering similar patterns in a diversity of situations makes possible the juxtaposition for purposes of contrast and of comparison of the people who live in those circumstances and make their lives within them... These then are the decisive questions: What questions are answered and how are they answered, in the system of historical and social ecology framed and founded by a given group? How do others answer these same questions, within the same systematic structure of history and economy? And finally, what do we learn about both groups in the comparison and contrast of each with the other? These are the three exercises which respond to the questions of "Why?" and "So what?" For the answer to "so what" must be, so this is one way in which people made choices, and that is another way, and in the variables between the one and other lie rich insight even into how we are and might be.[17]

To move decisively beyond the self-limited horizon of the disciplined historian's framework, necessarily constrained to interpret "choices" solely in terms of such factors as "history and economy," no more is required than to consider afresh the *inward human substance* of those choices whose outward form the external environment of human life demonstrably conditions.

Anthropology has well understood that corporate human existence requires a coherent matrix that organizes all of life's activities into a systemic whole, and it investigates worldview chiefly as the "outer" collective form of this coherence. But human consciousness also demands an integral view of the world as the condition of *its own inner coherence*. As Peter Berger, among others, has shown, breakdown of one's "world," i.e., one's worldview, may lead directly, unless somehow mitigated, to a breakdown of self-consciousness as such into the fragmented state termed insanity.[18] Then those outward choices which determine the integral organization of one's world must conform with and reflect — constitute, as it were, the *outside of* — an inward "choice" of some *integrating focus for the organizing of conscious selfhood.* "Worldview" understood in a non-reductive way, that is, construed in its fullest and truest sense, thus not only organizes "the world" but *mediates* the coherence of the world and the coherence of the self, coordinating and thereby unifying outer and inner human reality.[19] Now, only that study which treats religion in its own terms, in its own total reality, is properly religiological. Accordingly, any religiological investigation of worldviews must take full cognizance of the inner matrix no less than the outer occasions of a given worldview; the choice of "how we are and might be" is in very truth a choice of modality for *total being,* inward as well as outward. No method for analyzing religion is yet religiological without evincing the power to probe, discriminate and compare such elemental human "choices" in their total and inclusive reality.

The choices of *modality for total being* which religiology scrutinizes perforce arise within the most encompassing context of the human situation, to whose outer *and* inner aspects alike self-consciousness must become oriented in order to negotiate the challenges of self-conscious existence. To pursue the study of Judaism religiologically therefore entails beginning with some theoretical understanding of the general "orientational needs" of human self-consciousness which give rise to *any* particular worldview. Here the relevant consideration is: What are the inescapable questions that *all* people, by virtue of their very humanness, must implicitly pose to their life situations — the primal bases of the "choices" to which Jacob Neusner refers? Or, to put it another way, what *are* the universal conditions of concrete human experience to which self-consciousness must coherently orient itself in order to make sense of "the world" and navigate a practical course through it on the journey from birth to death?

The outlines of an answer inhere in the query itself. To speak of "the world" conjures, in its most primary signification, the category of *space* and to speak of "birth and death" elicits the category of *time*. Within the framework of space and time, self-consciousness discovers itself *as* "self" in relation to "other selves." The experiencing of "self" and "others" unfolding within its spacio-temporal framework is universally conditioned by the presence and behavior of such spacial realities as the natural elements, whose behaviors are of course exhibited only in time, and such temporally encountered realities as pleasure or pain and birth, sexuality, sickness, death which conversely have their necessary spacial occasions. Each of these aforementioned factors, which universally condition human existence, poses the question to a newly crystallizing self-consciousness of that factor's integral *place* in the overall scheme of things — the question of its nature, structure, function, purpose and meaning within the totality of the world which, for "the world" to be recognized at all, must be presupposed by emergent self-consciousness to constitute a coherent whole.

Religiological theory faces, then, the crucial early task of constructing a foundational religiological epistemology which maps the parameters of any imaginable human *Lebenswelt*. As an exemplification of such an epistemology, it is at this time still difficult to surpass the classic basic texts of Mircea Eliade, notably *The Sacred and the Profane* and *Cosmos and History*.[20] But scholars, especially of Judaica, would do well to consider also the epistemological reflections of a thinker like Martin Buber, who with Eliade belongs to the extended Neo-Kantian tradition:

> We may characterize the act and the work of entering into relation with the world as such — and, therefore, not with parts of it, and not with the sum of its parts, but with it as the world — as synthesizing apperception, by which we establish that this pregnant use of the concept involves the function of unity: by synthesizing apperception I mean the apperception of a being as a whole and as a unity. Such a view is won, and won again and again, only by looking upon the world as a world ... He who turns to the realm which he has removed from himself, and which has been completed and transformed into a world ... becomes aware of wholeness and unity in such a way that from then on he is able to grasp being as a wholeness and a unity ... the single being has received the character of wholeness and the unity which is perceived in it from the wholeness and unity perceived in the world.[21]

The religiological study of Judaism must begin, then, by confronting the particular data of Judaism with the template of universal questions proffered by a religiological epistemology such as Eliade's. *How* precisely does Judaism deal with the nature of space, time, self, others and so forth? And *why* does it do it in this and not some other possible way? No very thorough and far-reaching investigation of Judaic source materials is required to mount initial hypotheses. For example, the uniquely Judaic understanding of time as "history" ubiquitously pervades virtually all particular instantiations of Judaism, even when retreating somewhat to the background as in Rabbinic Judaism, and distinguishes the Judaic worldview in respect to time from even so proximate and indeed conjugal a neighbor as Iranian Zoroastrianism. The integral complex of tentative answers to the fundamental epistemological questions effectively constitutes an initial hypothetical formulation of the Judaic worldview, which comparison with other worldviews may draw into sharper focus. But such a formulation can be preliminary at best. How might it be further ramified and modified through engagement with the multitudinous data of Judaism? Here begins the painstaking labor of a scholarship committed to understanding Judaic religion in its own terms.

The great philosopher of religion Rudolf Otto, in his classic work *Mysticism: East and West*, clearly anticipates a fundamental tenet of any interpretive approach to the study of religion which seeks to understand religion in its own terms and not as an aspect of something else:

> It is true that somehow or other the word "mysticism" must have *one identical meaning*, otherwise there could be no conception of mysticism, and the use of the expression as a general term would be impossible. For, logically, we can only use the same term for *several objects* when they are in some determinable aspect always "the same." This is true, for example, of the term "religion." ... But that does not exclude, it rather includes, the possibility of "religion" differing in each of these examples, and that within one and the same genus very diverse spiritual forms may be found. [italics mine][22]

Jacob Neusner illustrates this point in relation to Judaism:

> So there is no possibility of claiming there never was, nor is there now, such a thing as "Judaism" but only "Judaisms." For once we take that route, there will be no "Judaisms" either, but only this one and that one ...[23]

To speak of many historically concrete "Judaisms," in other words, is logically to presuppose certain similar characteristics of "Judaism" which they somehow share despite their differences. Differences and similarities, accordingly, must define *one another* and can only be grasped reciprocally in and through each other; the understanding of both can grow only conjointly. The Aristotelian method of hypothesis, which resides at the classic foundations of all empirical investigation, aims precisely to uncover generic similarity through the comparison and contrast of differential data: here is the primal root of "comparison and contrast" as a fundamental methodic element in the study of religion, as other empirical realities. On the basis of initial data samples, then, this method develops a hypothetical formulation of such generic "similarity" which is subsequently revised on the basis of additional data, even as the developing hypothesis in turn suggests what further data are required to test and refine it. All empirical thinking must, in one way or another, adapt hypothetical method. Historians, of course, utilize hypotheses in seeking the best explanation for a thoroughly particular configuration of human events. Yet philosophers, on the other hand, in their quest for the most universal understanding of the lawfulness behind all human events, likewise often devise reflective hypotheses which are submitted to tests by human reason, knowledge and experience.

A religiological approach to the understanding of "Judaism," however, really seeks to grasp neither the historical configurations of Judaism for their own sake nor the philosophic truths of Judaism but "Judaism" *as such,* i.e., the Judaic worldview and its expressions in concrete human life. Its application of the method of hypothesis must therefore begin with empirical data reflecting this worldview, assembled as much as possible into the concrete "Judaisms" of various texts, times and places, and move toward an ever more refined, complex and integral characterization of the "Judaism" they embody and express. As with any method of hypothesis, then, to depict such "Judaism" ever more precisely entails the use of *comparison and contrast* — in this case, not only internally but externally: comparison of the "Judaisms" internally to adumbrate "Judaism"; comparison of the rough emergent portrayal of "Judaism" externally with other worldviews — both more and less closely related — in order to bring its distinctive generic traits into clear relief. Working back and forth between empirical data gleaned from the history and texts of Judaism and an initially sketchy hypothetical formulation of the Judaic worldview, the religiologist thus traces patterns of coherence which with increasing degrees of exactitude specify that generic "Judaism" such that all particular "Judaisms" disclose themselves as varied instantiations of it.

Each of these particular Judaisms, it must be stressed, proffers a hermeneutic challenge to the generic portrait of "Judaism" insofar as it incorporates peculiarities demanding explanation or — more to the point — justification as a modality of "Judaism" not inconsistent, after all, with the generic portrait. The latter depiction will inevitably expand and deepen, not to say radically change, in the process of accommodating the peculiar "Judaisms" of the concrete historical tradition. On the other hand, features of these "Judaisms," perhaps otherwise unintelligible, will be illumined by the ideal-type model of "Judaism" itself. Some distinguishing characteristics of "Judaism" which this hermeneutic circle could elucidate might include: Judaic stress on the unique and irreducible value of the individual element, whether a component of natural creation, a human being, or a temporal event; unity, wholeness and integrity as central values with peculiar Judaic valences needing analysis; Judaism's affirmative attitude toward nature as divine creation, in contrast with a variety of "world-negating" religious traditions; creation, revelation and redemption as cardinal moments of Judaic temporality; justice and mercy, bearing their peculiarly Judaic valences, as essential attributes of authentic personhood. To fathom the signification of any such possible characteristic of "Judaism" necessitates tracing its manifold significations for the "Judaisms," striving to grasp the essential form systemically common to all of them in whatever permuted fashions. The viability of a crystallizing hypothetical formulation of "Judaism" is shown forth most persuasively in its capacity to distill some coherence even from apparently "exceptional" data, while such data in turn compel the hypothesis toward ever greater adequacy in explaining atypical or marginal Judaic phenomena.

What must continue above all, though, to monitor any such religiological investigation is a basic theoretical understanding of the nature of worldview in general, e.g., recognition that it is precisely through the development of worldviews that self-consciousness endeavors to construct its *Lebenswelt* into a coherent whole. The need of self-consciousness for coherence, which the religiologist comes to intuit in part by locating it at the dynamic motivational core of his or her own worldview, supplies a fundamental touchstone for searching out the coherence within each historical "Judaism" as well as the larger integrity of "Judaism" as such which each variant must in its own way reflect. But the profoundest comprehension of this larger coherence will come only through the uncovering of its relationship not only to *exterior* circumstance but to the *interior* coherence and structural characteristics of human personhood itself — only when the outer yields up direct insight into its veiled and innermost core. In principle, religiology's quest for the most illumining perception of any given worldview can cease only when its ground in some universal aspect of human being, providing an integral focus for orientation *from the inside,* discloses itself at last to the researcher's patiently alert, painstaking and meticulous attention — as it attends, way beyond all outward data, upon an *objectivated subjectivity* whose obscurer recesses the vision that sees within as without alone might pierce.[24]

An Exemplary Methodology for the Academic Teaching of Judaism

From this cursory description of a religiological approach to the study of Judaism, it may become evident that a peculiarly strong continuity must exist between the activity of the disciplined research scholar and the classroom instructor bringing religiological perspectives to their respective tasks. This is the case for two reasons. First, the religiologist ultimately works with higher-level data configurations, seeking the larger global patterns of coherence which reveal lineaments of worldview. For the practicing scholar involved with immediate gathering of data, a religiological perspective will assist in directing research toward corroborating suspected patterns of coherence within the materials of some particular textual-historical *Sitz-im-Leben.* The teacher, in contrast, will rely more upon data substantially gathered by others. Yet the quest for coherence within the data will be similar, whether conducted by a research scholar directly or implemented by a teacher reflecting upon primary and secondary texts. Since a conventional historian of Judaism need not employ a religiological hermeneutic at all, for example, it may well fall to the classroom instructor to discover how the writings of such a scholar advances understanding of the Judaic worldview.

A second reason for intimate connection between scholarship and teaching in religion is that the ultimate intellectual operations which produce religiological understanding resemble humanistic interpretation more than they do technical scientific analysis. The rubrics which guide these operations exist as fully in the classroom as in the research library or laboratory; e.g., the awareness of self-consciousness of its own innate need for coherence. The whole strategy of teaching religion from a religiological perspective must indeed be to catalyze the student's capacity for *experiencing the coherence of reality in a way different from that native to him or her.* To be sure, the teaching process must begin with the technically constructed empirical data carrying another worldview; but it achieves its ideal end only when the student is able to synthesize and internalize these data so that his or her own self-consciousness, through tutored empathy, can vicariously and temporarily — yet vividly — "inhabit" their configuration as a plausible view of the world in its wholeness. Though more radical, religiological understanding thus has manifest affinities with such classroom occupations as indepth literary appreciation through which a student "enters into" the vision of an author or a specific text; it is surely worth pondering that humanistic interpretation in general has a primary aim of analyzing and apprehending the internal coherence of what contemporary hermeneuts would call its "text," whether that text be literary, graphic or musical. The ultimate common ground shared by teacher and student exploring religion is indeed the ability of self-consciousness to intuit its own nature and especially its profound need for coherence, proceeding from a more conscious apprehension of its own overall worldview toward an educed skill at "entering into" the worldview of another.

In a significant sense, then, no firm boundary demarcates the practice of religiology in the research library from that in the instructional classroom. Scholar and teacher alike must gradually construct ever more adequate hypothetical formulations of a worldview on the basis of its peculiar characteristics and particular exemplifications. Each new exemplification tests and may modify the preexisting hypothesis. The hypothetical formulation of a worldview must be honed and sharpened through comparison and contrast with worldviews — their inward matrices no less than their outward occasions — originating in other religious traditions. A widening grasp of the peculiarities of a given worldview spurs, for scholar and teacher alike, the attempt to formulate a hypothesis which adequately explains and integrates them. And the common coinage which allows for transmission of understanding of a worldview, whether from source materials to a scholar's mind or from a teacher's informed awareness to a student's mind, is the universal characteristics and orientational needs of human self-consciousness. Elsewhere, in a provisional fashion, I have sought to exemplify both a genuinely religiological approach to adumbrating the Judaic worldview through comparative analysis of the Semitic monotheist traditions, and a more elaborated model of generic "Judaism."[25] How might a similar religiological perspective specifically inform the academic teaching of Judaism? Let us consider possible strategies for devising the four typical sorts of offerings in a basic Judaica curriculum: general and particular courses in Hebrew Bible, and general and particular courses in post-biblical Judaism.

1. General Course in Hebrew Bible

How would a religiological approach to surveying the Hebrew Bible differ in principle from other teaching strategies and how might such an approach be implemented in practice, utilizing currently available resources that for the most part reflect other methodological standpoints? These issues could themselves be addressed inductively by explicitly eliciting from students the range of conventional interests in this text, which might include:

A. *Historical* - The Hebrew Bible is a *source* for history, that of the ancient Near East, and as such belongs to archaeology, paleoentology, and the history of antiquity.

B. *Cultural* - The Hebrew Bible is the *basis* of a history, that of a corporate people, and as such falls within the specific purview of social and cultural anthropology, folklore and "Jewish studies" generally.

C. *Textual* - The Hebrew Bible *has* a history, that of its textual evolution, and as such is of interest to form criticism, redaction criticism and similar modes of purely textual scholarship.

D. *Literary* - The Hebrew Bible *portrays* a history, that of the Jews from their ancestral beginnings, and as such incorporates dramatic narratives worthy of purely literary analysis and appreciation, not to mention superb poetry and other prose.

E. *Theological* - The Hebrew Bible *explains* "history" as a divinely meaningful progression, and as such constitutes the religious foundation for the history-oriented faiths of Judaism, Christianity, Islam and humanism.

F. *Philosophical* - The Hebrew Bible is *based upon* "history" as a way of experiencing time and the human condition, and thus presents a modality of humanness of central import for the philosophy of religion, culture, time, and so forth, as well as for any general philosophical anthropology.

These characterizations highlight in assorted ways, of course, the centrality of *history* as a formative principle of Western humanity, consciousness, thought and academic enterprise. The religiological interest, then, resides in grasping the *worldview* of the Hebrew Bible as itself the fountainhead of this — and not only this — formative principle of the Western civilizational reality; apprehending that worldview entails considering the Hebrew Bible from all the above perspectives in order to fathom its worldview's influence in its entirety.

Through historical and cultural perspectives from the *social sciences* the formation and influence of the Hebrew Bible's worldview can be traced in an "objective" and external manner. The textual and literary concerns of the *humanities* permit entering into the substance of the worldview itself in a mediate aesthetic way which still admits of critical distance and phenomenological bracketing. In bringing to bear the theological and philosophical interests of *religious thought* proper, however, the Western student of the Hebrew Bible is apt to discover the extent to which his or her own very "subjective" identity and *Lebenswelt* have been hewn by the formative power of that text. With this awareness, the student has arrived at the threshold of a religiological understanding which transcends the dichotomy of "objective" and "subjective" to appropriate the Hebrew Bible in its operational relationship to immediately experienced "world" and worldview. To conduce toward such an understanding, a course structure must simultaneously apply social scientific, humanistic and religious perspectives to its encounter with the reality of the Hebrew Bible. Through the non-linear interaction of all three sorts of perception, a religiological grasp of the text will gradually crystallize.

For example, literary analysis of the biblical narrative might be framed by the historical scholarship of Yehezkel Kaufmann, on the one side, and the biblical theology of Martin Buber, on the other.[26] While both authors regularly advert to concepts such as freedom, unity and transcendence, Kaufmann's discussion is anchored in the realm of "objective" empirical research whereas Buber's penetrates the sphere of ultimate "subjective" meaningfulness. Situating the student between, obliged to wrestle with their relationship, will invite the efflorescence of an ever deeper consciousness of the Hebrew Bible as a living power organizing the student's "world" without and self within; the student may then come to recognize himself or herself as a virtual subject of the literary narrative he confronts at the mediate intersection between outer and inner, insofar as his very existence as concrete person has absorbed and been shaped by human modalities which first dynamically appear in biblical ethos, personalities and sociocultural milieu. Non-Western students will resonate to some extent with these modalities insofar as they have infused and molded global industrial society, which emanates from the West. Conversely, the inward sensibility of such students can provide a comparative foil to elicit general perception of the peculiar characteristics of Western sensibility which hearken back to biblical precedents.

2. Particular Course in Hebrew Bible

No axiom is more foundational to the religiological perspective developed herein than the inherent need of self-consciousness for coherence. This axiom governs, among other aspects of general religiological method, the analysis of particular elements within a whole: as hypothetical understanding of a coherent and systemic whole clarifies, it becomes possible to identify with increasing precision the logical function of each element within it. Applied to interpreting texts in the Hebrew Bible, this rubric likewise presumes that the quest for coherence shapes each element internally as well as determining their integral relation. Thus a religiological hermeneutic of the Hebrew Bible, although indebted to historical and linguistic scholarship for its critical preparation and corroboration, reposes its essential confidence in the need for coherence innate in the redactor's own self-consciousness and manifest in his conscious judgments. Its methodology recalls Franz Rosenzweig's famous avowal that he reads the "R" for redactor as "Rabbenu," implying that one must trust the wisdom of the canonizers as persons of inspired aesthetic and spiritual genius whose final product must be approached with the reverent attention accorded to any great and presumably unified work of art and spirit if one would probe its deeper strata.[27]

The interpretive power of such a hermeneutic might best be illustrated through application to a subsection of the Hebrew canon, itself arranged as a whole composed of parts. Teaching of the third section of the Bible, the *Ketuvim* (*Writings*), has not been salient as an especially rich area of pedagogy. With its axiomatic confidence in the redactor, though, a religiological hermeneutic would examine these texts in an attempt to identify their function within the Hebrew Bible in its totality, afterwards seeking to understand the view of reality each expresses individually and together as a possible subsystemic whole. An exemplary hypothetical formulation of the general function of the *Ketuvim* within the Bible overall might run as follows: *Torah* proper, the first section of the Bible, details the binding of God and the people of Israel *together* in a normative Covenant. Granting this much, the Bible's second section, *Nevi'im* (*Prophets*), evidently offers historically specific corrective guidance from *God* regarding violation of express provisions of the Covenant. But not every human situation is amenable to the intrusive witness of explicit covenantal norms. Most of the time, indeed, people must assuredly take counsel with *themselves* in order to determine their stance toward the situations with which life presents them — including those "metacovenantal" situations in which human relationship with God is itself vexed or otherwise at issue and in need of basic reconfiguration. Self-consciousness is, after all, prior even to consciousness of God. Does this mean that humanity shall be left to its own devices in confronting the manifold ambiguities and subtly shifting modalities of creaturely existence? From a biblical standpoint, the totality of God's concern would seem to preclude the likelihood of this. What is required alternatively is some sort of prudential wisdom capable of molding human awareness from within, insinuating itself so that guidance when needed might be forthcoming from persons, as it were, to themselves. Such guidance, then, would come from God not directly but indirectly, issued not by prophetic fiat at specific historical moments but rather taking the form of inspired tales, poems, object lessons and general nostrums always instantly ready to hand and also there to be gradually and freely absorbed into one's character as a transforming leaven. Whereas sporadic prophetic guidance descends, so to speak, transcendentally "from above," that is, from *without*, this abiding guidance by prudential wisdom could then arise mundanely "from below," that is, from *within*, in the consciousness of a person consulting a selfhood shaped by spiritually nurturing instruction. It is just this sort of companionable wisdom which the *Ketuvim* appear to embody — a wisdom for every typical human condition.

But the *Ketuvim* include not only such "wisdom texts"; they incorporate as well four texts of sequential narrative history, i.e., the two books of Chronicles, Ezra and Nehemiah. The presence of these generically distinct texts in the third part of the Hebrew Bible poses a special interpretive problem. By virtue of what organizational principles do they constitute an integral and coherent element of the *Ketuvim*? The basis for any answer may reside in two mutually supportive facts of the canon's organization: first, the books of Chronicles closely parallel the books of Kings, included in *Nevi'im*; second, the actual chronological span covered by other texts within *Nevi'im* and *Ketuvim* is similar, ranging from the time of the Judges to the Persian period. A final clue is that, despite the close parallel, the tone of Chronicles differs from that of Kings by virtue of an editorial tendency to extract moralizing wisdom from historical events, e.g., II Chron. 15-16. All this suggests that prophetic guidance "from above" and prudential wisdom "from below" are to be regarded as devolving in tandem after Torah was received and Israel had entered the Land. Moreover, each type of sacred knowledge implies a viewpoint of its own within which to perceive historical events, and the more mundanely oriented historical consciousness of the "wisdom" perspective shades directly into a scribal transition to the even more mundane consciousness of the Rabbinic period. Then the problem of historical narrative within the *Ketuvim* proper appears resolvable. But what of the integral design of the nine remaining texts which bear, in varying ways, the stamp of "wisdom" as such?

Scrutinized in the light of the foregoing hypotheses, the "wisdom books" of *Ketuvim* do indeed disclose themselves as subsisting within a coherent organizing matrix which may be diagrammed and explicated as follows:

	Closeness: Song of Songs *[THEORY]* Psalms *[PRACTICE]*	
	G	
Stability: Ecclesiastes *[T]* Proverbs *[P]*	W O R L D D	**Change:** Daniel *[T]* Esther/Ruth *[P]*
	Distance: Job *[T]* Lamentations *[P]*	

Human life transpires in a reality structured both by direct "vertical" relationship with God as well as by "horizontal" relationship with the world as such and its ongoing continuum of events. Within this ontological field, human beings require the help of prudential wisdom in four distinct modes to deal with the basic situational realities of (a) *closeness* to God; (b) *distance* from God; (c) *stability* in the world; (d) *change* in the world. The wisdom operative in each mode must furthermore be of two kinds: an orienting theoretical wisdom which describes the situational reality in its ultimate ideal dimensions and an instructive practical wisdom to guide action in the midst of that reality as it actually impinges. This system delineates a coherent hermeneutic framework which specifies eight functional niches that assign a meaningful order to all the texts of the *Ketuvim;* two texts occupy one niche, that of the "practical wisdom of change," insofar as the helping Providence which faith must affirm operates behind the scenes of challenging worldly circumstance may either show itself openly in the short range as with Esther, or remain hidden for the long range, as was the case with Ruth.

While space restrictions forbid additional analysis of individual texts in accordance with the hypothetically described hermeneutic framework, and only such analysis can buttress conviction that the framework completely "makes sense," it may at least be observed that this method has already modeled an internally logical and coherent system of prudential wisdom that may potentially clarify an area of biblical worldview — an area, moreover, which comparative analysis of the Hebrew Bible in its entirety could confirm is indeed a functionally requisite and textually instantiated component of that worldview. At any event, the present hermeneutic — as in every case where religiological analysis discerns a hypothetical configuration imbued with some inner logic — serves, even if merely plausible, the immediate pedagogical end of providing a natural heuristic through which a teacher may utilize socratic methods to engage students with the texts at hand.[28]

3. General Course in Judaism

Courses in Hebrew Bible exhibit a fundamental groundedness and finitude by virtue of their limited commitment to expound particular texts, however central. An introductory course in Judaism offers, in contrast, an arena of unlimited horizon within which the teacher may experiment both with presentation of the generic Judaic worldview — or more properly a current hypothetical formulation of it — and with the attempt to justify that formulation through appeal to the "Judaisms." Exigencies of practicability in an undergraduate survey course dictate that material be expounded deductively, working from "Judaism" to the "Judaisms," i.e., from abstract ideality toward concrete reality. Given this trajectory of exposition, three progressive levels of delineating the subject matter suggest themselves, corresponding to course subdivisions. First, the metaexperiential "core elements" of the generic Judaic worldview may be ideally laid out and these major structural components characterized individually and in relation. Secondly, this core in all its particularity may be situated within the universal framework of human experience by raising the question of how the Judaic worldview in principle structures existence in space and time. Thirdly, Judaism can be brought down to full concrete reality through investigating the specific actualities of Judaic experience within the context of a particular "spacio-temporal" community, whose modes of Judaic life and thought might — time permitting — be compared with those of other similarly concrete "Judaisms."

The core of Judaism, more precisely, is the freely committed or *covenantal* relation between the two "selves" or "persons" God and Israel, a relation defined by and subsisting in Torah. This relation becomes grounded within the framework of space and time through identification of components of space and time with the Covenant itself: the Land of Israel is that area of *space* especially designated for the full living out of the covenantal relation, and Israel may consequently occupy it only when enacting basic commitment to this relation; the Sabbath is that realm of *time* especially set aside to exemplify the quality of fully lived out covenantal relation and honoring it thus itself becomes the paradigmatic enactment of Israel's basic commitment to the Covenant. Because Israel's commitment to the Covenant is not in fact initially complete and must be deepened through learning experience, the wholeness of the covenantal relation can be actualized only gradually within the spacio-temporal framework of human life. Such defective progression toward eventual wholeness of relation imbues this framework with the character of "history," i.e., the developmental movement of events from a time in which Israel's hold on its designated space remains tenuous, continually threatened by the divinely ordained instrumentality of peoples hostile to Israel, toward a time at which Israel's residency in its appointed space has been fully consolidated and, as prerequisite, its relations with hostile peoples mended by virtue of Israel's completely actualized living out of its covenantal commitment. The Judaic worldview thus endows the common spacio-temporal framework of human life with a coordinated empirical *directionality* toward the Land of Israel in space and the period of consummated covenant relation in time; and it is this characteristic directionality, with the unique narrative significance it bestows upon the particular empirical realities of spacial locus, temporal occurrence and human person — individual and collective — that the Judaic sense of "history" properly entails. Awareness of this directionality, which constitutes the very career of the Covenant on earth, remains vivified through representation of its basic structure — creational beginning, revelatory middle, redemptive end — by the Judaic year's three seasonal pilgrimage festivals, whose pattern the three periods of the weekly Sabbath day — evening, morning, afternoon — itself replicate.

Specific observances which enact Sabbath and festivals are best reserved for the third unit of a course in Judaism, which may take up the details of Judaism in practice. An excellent vehicle for presenting such material, treating Judaic practices within living historical context, are anthropological studies like the classic *Life Is With People*,[29] a masterful tribute to the now extinct Eastern European Jewish *shtetl*. Its chapters at one point or another cover most of the significant Judaic teachings in regard to personal and communal behavior — both the dynamic moral substance and the ritual disciplines to promote acquisition of that substance. This presentation of "living Judaism" invites supplementation by source texts expounding religious doctrinal and ritual concepts and background reading in the history of Judaism. Elements of the Judaic worldview schematically explicated in the course's earlier units may be verified, exemplified and concretized by the witness of a concrete manifestation of Judaism. And the view of Judaism which emerges may be further tested and corroborated through selective examination of other representative historically embodied "Judaisms."

4. Particular Course in Judaism

A teacher or scholar approaching Judaism religiologically seeks to construct, over the long term, an ever more adequate model of generic Judaism. In its most compact and schematic form, the current state of such a model might be sketched out as prolegomenon to an introductory course in Judaism and ought to serve, on the other hand, as implicit context and foil for the presentation of more bounded topic areas within Judaism. A generic model of Judaism might, for example, discern a characteristic Judaic intention to relate transcendental unity, however conceived, to the unique particulars which become immanently unified into an integral whole by virtue of that transcendental unity. In the Hebrew Bible, this "logic of Judaic unity" governs both creation in space, resulting in the formation of an integral cosmos, and occurrences in time, guiding the unfolding of an integral history. The identical concern emerges in the methodic principle of the Rabbinic period that each element of Torah constitutes a unique and indispensable part of a unified whole. For Maimonides, contemplation of the integral role each element of the natural creation plays in the functioning of the whole discloses the unity of design within that whole, leading to awareness of the Unity of its Creator. In the Zohar, each *Sephirah* performs a unique function as an indispensable part of an integral whole unified immanently and transcendentally by the *Ein Sof*.

The most effective hermeneutic for a particular course in any such texts and periods of Judaism, it appears, may be furnished by the teacher's *own* currently revised model of generic Judaism. As the above example indicates, such a model should implicitly suggest deep structural relations between the designated topic area and many others throughout the sweep of the historical Judaic tradition, equipping the teacher to venture broadly based as well as narrow comparisons which draw upon various manifestations of Judaism. At the same time, any new course preparation becomes an opportunity to test, revise and embellish the model itself. The model functions throughout as a heuristic directing attention of teacher and student alike at underlying structural features of the Judaic worldview, perpetually raising questions not only as to why each feature is what it is and what constitute the parameters for its variant forms in different historical manifestations of Judaism, but also questions of elemental "choice" — e.g., what aspects of universal human existence or personhood the model most aligns with and how the model constellates within larger comparative frameworks. Thus, to pursue the above example a bit further, the religiological investigation of Judaism fairly swiftly confronts the scholar and teacher with the demand to specify exactly what "unity" means generically for Judaism in contrast with its root meaning for other religious traditions, as well as to account for variant significations of "unity" as understood within the manifold of the "Judaisms."[30]

One conspicuous way in which scholars of religion have been treating what many increasingly apprehend to be the distinctiveness of the domain they study, we have noted, is through the rubric of "worldview," a concept now being crafted into an ever more subtle and refined vehicle for insight into the nature and structure of religion. This concept has served as present basis for illustrating the impact recent developments in the scholarly study of religion might have upon the academic teaching of Judaism. Nonetheless, more primary than any such specific example stands the advancing understanding that the subject matter of religious studies may constitute an area of human reality no less distinctive nor any more reducible to some tangential realm than are other subject matters currently investigated within their own respective disciplines. The more that the most telling insights into this area prove to yield themselves only to *sui generis* methods conformed uniquely to the nature and structure of religion, the more the study of religion may acquire its own acknowledged status as a religiology. But "religiology" begins whenever a scholar or teacher is grasped by the awareness that religion has a *logos* of its own, an intrinsic mode of being that can be penetrated only when honored in its uniqueness, even though the methods of existing disciplines may enable partial access to it.

Most scholars and teachers of Judaism have been trained in the methods of extant disciplines within the humanities and social sciences, yet many have glimpsed the integrity peculiar to Judaism as a form of *religious* reality whose fullest disclosure may demand transcending standard disciplinary bounds. To this extent, many teachers of Judaism have already found their way to the threshold of incorporating a religiological perspective into the presentation of their subject matter, if only as ancillary to more conventional strategems for classroom instruction. To these, a view from the horizon of the contemporary study of religion encourages persistence in the endeavor to see Judaism whole and clear, in its own innate character, even when its reality can be captured only through a wholesale breaching of traditional intellectual frontiers which resorts to innovative procedures, exotic approaches, novel angles of vision. To others, content with established methods of teaching, the emergence of ever more articulated religiological perspectives for the study of Judaism may jostle complacency, stir fresh ideas, and issue a salutary challenge for more creative employment of proven instructional techniques. In the last analysis, though, the worth of any new perspective for examining Judaism will be judged by how compellingly, comprehensively and profoundly it reveals the lineaments of its object. From this standpoint, the contemporary study of religion may commend to all academic teachers of Judaism the possibility of unprecedentedly bold and stimulating experiments in determining and conveying that truth toward which all those pledged to the life of the mind aspire.

Indeed, the most bracing promise of such experimentation toward truth might be nothing less than a wider revitalizing of the life of the mind as such. Jacques Barzun, in a recent essay entitled "Scholarship Versus Culture," has eloquently decried the usurpation by a deadeningly analytic modern scholarship — its repercussions permeating even lay society — of a whole territory which human sensibility formerly allocated largely to that true cultivation of mind and spirit previously denoted by the term "culture":

> By the same human mind that has created science but the analytical method can work in an entirely different way ... The other use, direction, or bent, Pascal called the *espirit de finesse,* we would say "intuitive understanding." It goes about its business just the other way. It does not analyze, does not break things down into parts, but seizes upon the character of the whole altogether, by inspection short or long ... The objects that go to make up culture are designed to be understood and remembered and enjoyed by the operation of finesse; they are for inspection as wholes, not for analysis.[31]

Barzun fiercely indicts the negative impact of the modern academy and its procedures upon true cultural vitality:

> In the use of "method," whatever it be, the role of self-consciousness is evident. Here is a work of art: not *Let us read it* but *How do we deal with it?* Our jargon word *approach* is revealing: we creep up; we are on safari; we bring down the big game. The procedure naturally varies not only with the doctrine but also with the mental qualities of the practitioner ... But coping with a problem by analytic methods is the unquestioned aim.[32]

Yet religiological insight finds, at the primal core of that very self-consciousness to whose overextension Barzun unarguably ascribes much endemic alienation, precisely a drive toward *coherence* which knows no peace until it "seizes upon the character of the whole altogether ..." To follow the tracery of this impulse is to voyage toward overcoming the fragmentation of the human spirit at its crux to recover the wholeness of object and subject, of "outside" and "inside," itself. But if the quintessential rubric of religiological *method* is itself the elemental pursuit of *wholeness* or coherence, can it be that within its purview even the split between overspecialized scholarship and disenfranchised culture might find mediation and eventual healing? At the very least, an emerging ethos within the contemporary study of religion, far from being averse to the cultivation and hence true *education* of the whole human person, can perceive much of its own innermost soul in words that Barzun reserves to contrast culture with scholarship — and in this hopeful similitude the thoughtful teacher of religion might perhaps recognize the highest of pedagogical callings:

> Culture in whatever form — art, thought, history, religion — is for meditation and conversation ... As for a true meditation, it radiates in all directions, excludes nothing; its virtue is to comprehend — in both senses: to understand and to take in the fullest view. Both are actions of the mind *and spirit*, and therefore charged with the strongest relevant feelings. Indeed, both the interior monologue and the spoken dialogue aim at discerning which feelings and what degree of each belong to which idea or image. That is how culture reshapes the personality; it develops it by offering the vicarious experience of art and thought; it puts all experience in order gradually, through reflection, meditation, and conversation.[33]

Drawn into conversation with Martin Buber and Jacques Barzun, then, the words of Jacob Neusner may finally speak with even deeper resonance and issue a profounder summons to the exploration of religion than they could originally have intended, but which those learning to see religion fully will nonetheless be able truly to hear:

> Seeing the whole whole, finding out what makes it whole, establishing definitive context, discovering the questions to which systems constitute answers — this is the sort of description which makes possible the labor ...[34]

---

[1]Further analysis of the current state of religious studies may be found in the author's articles "Naming the Game: A Question of the Field," *Bulletin of the Counsel on the Study of Religion,* 14/4 (October, 1983), pp. 109-113; and "Response" to "Insiders and Outsiders in the Study of Religious Traditions," *Journal of the American Academy of Religion,* LI/3 (September, 1983), pp. 480-484. The latter more thoroughly treats the relationships of "objective"/"subjective" and "outside"/"inside" which figure crucially in this chapter, for which a companion article — emphasizing theory rather than pedagogical *praxis* — is now in preparation under the title "The Contemporary Emergence of Religiology from the History of Religion: An Example and Prolegomenon."

In regard to the current state of Jewish Studies a number of helpful bibliographical essays and surveys have been published within the past two decades. Notable among these are the following: Arnold J. Band, "Jewish Studies in American Liberal Arts Colleges and Universities," *American Jewish Yearbook,* 1966 (Volume 67), edited by Morris Fine and Milton Himmelfarb (New York and

Philadelphia: Jewish Publication Society of America, 1966), 3-30; Zev Garber, "Jewish Studies at a Two-Year Public College," ERIC, 1974 (ED 086 269); *idem*, "Alternative Teaching Methods in Teaching Introduction to Judaism," ERIC, 1976 (ED 114 151); *idem*, "Teaching the Holocaust at a Two-Year Public College," ERIC, 1983 (JC 830 218); Abraham I. Katsh, *The Biblical Heritage in American Democracy* (New York: Ktav, 1977); Jacob Neusner, *The Academic Study of Judaism: Essays and Reflections* (New York: Ktav, 1975, second edition, Chico: Scholars Press for Brown Judaic Studies, 1982; Second Series, New York: Ktav, 1977; Third Series, New York: Ktav, 1980); *idem, Judaism in the American Humanities* (Chico: Scholars Press for Brown Judaic Series, 1981; Second Series, Chico: Scholars Press for Brown Judaic Series, 1983); *idem*, ed., *New Humanities and Academic Discipline: The Case of Jewish Studies* (Madison: University of Wisconsin Press, 1984); *idem, Judaic Studies in Universities: Toward the Second Quarter-Century* (Durham: Duke University, 1984); *idem, Major Trends in Formative Judaism*, Second Series (Chico: Scholars Press for Brown Judaic Series, 1984), pp. 123-149.

[2]Jonathan Z. Smith, *Imagining Religion* (Chicago: The University of Chicago Press, 1982), pp. 19-20; and "No Need to Travel to the Indies: Judaism and the Study of Religion," *Take Judaism, for Example: Studies Toward the Comparison of Religions*, ed. Jacob Neusner (Chicago: The University of Chicago Press, 1983), p. 215.

[3]*Ibid.*

[4]*Ibid.*, p. xi.

[5]Ninian Smart, *Worldviews: Cross-cultural Exploration of Human Beliefs* (New York: Charles Scribner's Sons, 1983).

[6]*Ibid.*, pp. 1-2.

[7]Raimundo Panikkar, "*Aporias* in the Comparative Philosophy of Religion," *Man and World*, 13 (1980), pp. 357-383. *Man and World* is published in the Hague by Martinus Nijhoff.

[8]Mircea Eliade, *The Sacred and the Profane* ("Harvest Books"; New York: Harcourt, Brace & World, 1959), esp. Ch. I.

[9]Michael Novak, *Ascent of the Mountain, Flight of the Dove: An Invitation to Religious Studies* (New York: Harper & Row, 1971).

[10]Peter Berger, *The Sacred Canopy: Elements of a Sociological Theory of Religion* (New York: Doubleday & Co., 1967), Ch. 1 and Ch. 2.

[11]Smart, p. 5.

[12]Smith, *Imagining Religion*, p. 26.

[13]*Ibid.*, p. 34.

[14]Jacob Neusner, "Alike and Not Alike: A Grid for Comparison and Differentiation," *Take Judaism, for Example*, ed. J. Neusner, pp. 233, 235.

[15]*Ibid.*, p. 235.

[16]The most compendious anthropological theory of worldview to date was published just a year after Ninian Smart's volume of similar title; i.e., Michael Kearney, *World View* (Novato: Chandler & Sharp, 1984). Among the most

powerful influences upon theory of religion at the present time is the work of the anthropologists Clifford Geertz, Victor Turner and Mary Douglas.

[17]Neusner, pp. 234-5.

[18]Berger, pp. 16-17, 22-24, 44ff.

[19]That worldview mediates between external cultural "world" and internal integrity of the self suggests that the disciplinary niche for religiology may lie between anthropology and psychology (cf. Vernoff, "Naming the Game," p. 112). On the relation between external and internal human reality, "outside" and "inside," cf. Vernoff, "Response," pp. 482-83, and notes 24 and 29 below.

[20]Mircea Eliade, *Cosmos and History* ("Harper Torchbooks"; New York: Harper & Row, 1959).

[21]Martin Buber, *The Knowledge of Man*, ed. Maurice Friedman (New York: Harper & Row, 1965), pp. 62-63.

[22]Rudolf Otto, *Mysticism: East and West* (New York: Macmillan, 1970), pp. 157-58.

[23]Neusner, p. 235.

[24]For a specific example of experimental comparative method in what might be called "depth religiology," cf. the author's article "After the Holocaust: History and Being as Sources of Method within the Emerging Interreligious Hermeneutic," *Journal of Ecumenical Studies*, 21/4 (Fall, 1984), pp. 639-663. Utilizing this method allows tracing the interior, intrapsychic and intrasubjective grounding of the Judaic and Christian worldviews respectively within universal ontological structures of *personal identity* and *personal consciousness*. The resulting model of generic Judaism is further elaborated in the author's article "Unity," *Contemporary Jewish Religious Thought*, ed. Arthur A. Cohen and Paul Mendes-Flohr (New York: Charles Scribner's Sons, 1986). It should be noted that the present chapter intends to adumbrate religiological method only in the most general way; the horizon of this new disciplinary realm stands open for the development of many sophisticated methodic approaches toward penetrating the nature and structure of and systematic relations among modalities of religion.

[25]See note 24 above.

[26]Yehezkel Kaufmann, *The Religion of Israel*, trans. Moshe Greenberg (New York: Schocken, 1972). An excellent source of Martin Buber's biblical theology for teaching purposes is the essays in *Israel and the World: Essays in a Time of Crisis* (New York: Schocken, 1963).

[27]Cf. Nancy Fuchs-Kreimer, "Christian Old Testament Theology: A Time for New Beginnings," *Journal of Ecumenical Studies*, 18/1 (Winter, 1981), p. 86: "I would argue that the redaction which scholars cut through to find the 'acts of God' is, in itself, the evidence of God."

[28]I am indebted to discussion with Rabbi Ephraim Rottenberg and Mr. Natan David Seidel for insight into the historical consciousness of the *Ketuvim*. Further publications dealing with this hermeneutic of the *Ketuvim* and its application are in progress.

[29]Mark Zborowski and Elizabeth Herzog, *Life Is With People* (New York: Schocken, 1962). Part V, "As the Shtetl Sees the World," splendidly exemplifies

the anthropological rendering of Judaic worldview. It is particularly instructive to compare this with the exemplary rendering of Judaic worldview in a religiological mode found in the author's article "Unity." Although the two approaches are mutually complementary, the former understands worldview more limitedly, chiefly as the integrating matrix for a given culture; it stresses "view," as it were, rather than "world." In religiological perspective, on the other hand, worldview becomes situated in the context of *reality as a whole* in a way that bridges, transcends and finally abolishes the dichotomy of "object" and "subject." From this perspective worldview finds its place within the nested and interactive contexts of the ontoepistemological structure of *human personhood;* the perceptual *mediation* between human personhood "inside" and the reality "outside" which generates any "view" of the "world"; and the ontocosmological structure of that wider *reality itself* in its conditioning of all human existence and experience.

[30]Cf. Vernoff, "Unity," for an exemplary model of generic Judaism.

[31]Jacques Barzun, "Scholarship Versus Culture," *The Atlantic*, pp. 254/5 (November, 1984), p. 99.

[32]*Ibid.*, 100.

[33]*Ibid.*, 104.

[34]Neusner, p. 235. Compare the passage from Buber on p. 21 above.

Chapter Two

Jewish Literary Themes in the Teaching of Judaica

S. Daniel Breslauer

Narrative and the Jewish Tradition

Rabbi Nahman of Bratzlav in a well known section of his homiletical work *Liqqutei MoHoRaN* declares that when awakening people from their dogmatic slumbers stories are often indispensable. Such a use of stories for pedagogic purposes is, he contends, a legitimate "limud Torah," a study of Torah.[1] For Rabbi Nahman such study has a religious purpose, it awakens an awareness of the human condition, of the existential dilemma facing all people. The pedagogic nature of story telling is, according to Arthur Green, a means of providing different models with which individuals can identify. "Sooner or later," he suggests, "the hearer will recognize himself in one or another of the preacher's tales."[2] Narrative serves a religious purpose by providing a mirror in which the auditors can discover themselves.

This idea that a story is told for the purpose of self-recognition is found in a tale told about a disciple of the Baal Shem Tov.[3] When the Baal Shem Tov died he assigned his various disciples distinctive tasks. One was to become a cantor, another a butcher, and one, Rabbi Simon, became a storyteller. He had to go from place to place telling tales about the Baal Shem Tov. Finally he came to a place and forgot every story he had ever known. Try as he might he could not remember even one tale. Finally, in despair, he left, but as he went out the door he remembered one story. He returned and told how the Baal Shem Tov had once spoken with an anti-semitic bishop and thus prevented a pogrom. The auditor burst into tears and explained that he had been that bishop. He had once been a Jew but then abandoned his faith and converted to Christianity. He had ascended the power structure of the Church and was noted for hating Jews. The Baal Shem Tov, however, had appeared to him in dreams and convinced him to repent. When they met, on the day related by Rabbi Simon, the Baal Shem Tov had told him that he would know he was forgiven only when he heard his own story told by another. Now he knew that his sin had been erased.

In this story, tales serve a peculiarly religious function — they confront individuals with themselves. Studying a tale is, thus, a study of the self.

Stories provide self-understanding. The Baal Shem Tov insisted that until such a confrontation with the self, true repentance had not occurred. This aim of self-understanding has an important parallel in contemporary life — the teaching of what Jacob Neusner has called the "new Humanities" in American universities.[4] The rationale for learning about Black studies, Judaic studies, or Women's studies is to discover what is more generally human within each of us rather than looking for the exotic or eccentric. As Jewish studies are integrated into the general curriculum, it may be useful to look at Judaic narrative themes to see if they can fulfill the task assigned to Judaica as one of the new humanities. In order to fulfill that task, however, the narrow understanding of self and the particular view of the human condition that Rabbi Nahman urged is too limited. A full appreciation of the pedagogic value of narrative tradition in Judaism can come only by reviewing that tradition as a whole.

A Survey of Jewish Narrative

The development of the Hebrew story seems to parallel the various trends within Jewish thought — reflecting rabbinic piety, philosophical ethics, and mystical insight. Only in the final flourishing of the medieval tradition, in eighteenth and nineteenth century Polish Hasidism, a vibrant renewal and moralization of the Jewish mystical tradition, does the Hebrew story become an intrinsically important part of the Jewish literary expression.[5]

The pedagogic importance of the narrative style was shaped by the particular values being transmitted. In each case, however, certain common elements in narration remained constant. Storytelling has as its primary function the evocation of a mood. The storyteller seeks to awaken within the audience a response, a reaction to the tale. Sometimes tales are meant to evoke a sense of pragmatic reality; they bring a person up short against the harsh truths of life. Sometimes tales provide spiritual inspiration. They evoke the ideals of community and the values of society. They forge the bonds of socialization that tie members of one community to each other. Sometimes tales penetrate the deepest mysteries of life. They are mythic evocations of realities that cannot be captured in any other way, they are intimations of a knowledge that cannot be expressed in concrete and mundane words. Philosophers, rabbis, and mystics of the past as well as modern authors, whether in Israel or in exile, use stories in different ways in order to achieve different ends.

The philosophical approach is basically prudential. Drawing on Arabic and Greek resources, thinkers like Sa'adyah, Bachya Ibn Pakuda, Moses Maimonides, and Judah Halevi emphasized the value of following Jewish practices. Through ethical behavior an individual becomes worthy of God's blessing, develops self-perfection, and advances toward spiritual goals. Illustrative stories show how an individual progresses through the stages of self-improvement. The prudential message of, say, Bachya's use of stories is characteristic. He uses tales to point to the condition of humanity and to encourage a spiritual approach to life. He tells, for example, in *Hovot Halvavot III* a tale about a man suddenly crowned king in a strange land. Only later he learns that after a year he will be left on a deserted island. He spends his year as king preparing for the time when he will be dethroned. The story clearly points to the human situation. It does so, however, from a philosophical standpoint. The major themes of Jewish philosophy from Sa'adyah through Crescas are echoed in this didactic tale. A human being is king in this world only for a while. When that time is over, the soul enters its future abode. Unless a person has made preparation here for that future, the time on earth will have been wasted. The basic lesson of the story is pragmatic; philosophical knowledge is essential training if a human being is to succeed in this world and in the next. Various other such tales emphasize the same point. The philosophical strand in Jewish teachings uses tales to show how philosophic training is essential to successful human existence.

Rabbinic morality is more communally oriented and less focused on the individual, as noted earlier. Tales from the Talmud evoke a sense of communal solidarity and social order. Stories tell of rewards for obeying the norms of the social group — obeying the Sabbath, honoring one's parents, and the giving of charity (See Shabbat 119a, Kiddushin 31a, Ta'anit 24a). One characteristic category of rabbinic ethics is *zedakah,* the giving of charity. Certainly prudential considerations enter into rabbinic lessons about the need to donate one's wealth to the poor. Tales are told of how individuals who make sacrifices in order to contribute to charity are rewarded. These rewards, however, are not primarily those of spiritual achievement. Giving *zedakah* demonstrates a sense of concern for the society as a whole. The tales illustrate the possibility that by helping others one is in fact helping oneself. Stories that point to the social dimension of morality are expressions of rabbinic ethical thought.

The Hebrew story received its widest premodern treatment in Jewish mystical writings. The German Hasidism and the Spanish mystics used the tales they had inherited, transformed them, and integrated their content with mystical themes. Jewish mysticism, the kabbalah, was also a major force shaping Jewish moral literature. In the sixteenth and seventeenth centuries a type of moral instruction arose which integrated mystical and rabbinic teachings. The hallmark of this later mystical moralism was its use of the cosmic myth developed in Lurianic Kabbalah. This myth understood the world as the product of a cataclysm which had occurred at the beginning of creation. This myth, hinted at in chapter one, needs to be fully explored here. When God created the world, the material vessels which were the structure of the universe were too weak to hold the powerful sparks of holiness which were the animating force of life. The vessels shattered and trapped in their midst the scattered sparks of God's life force. The disorder and chaos characterizing the present age is but a symbol of the catastrophe, the effects of which are still being felt. The purpose of human beings in general, the Jews in particular, is to redeem these sparks from their imprisonment in matter and return them to their proper source in God. When that is accomplished, the universe will return to its former order.

The mystic tale seeks to emphasize the cosmic purpose of being human. It captures the sense of disorder which perplexes people when they begin to seek the meaning of life. It validates the human struggle against the obstacles which block the path of personal and social improvement. This is a myth that seeks to encourage human striving and acting. It is a myth with a moral meaning. The purpose of being human is to redeem sparks of holiness; the path to being human is found by fulfilling that task. The way in which that task is fulfilled unites the two themes of the rabbinical and philosophical approach to Jewish morality. On the one hand, an individual must seek self-perfection as the philosophers suggest; on the other hand, the community of others with whom one interacts is the appropriate arena in which redemption takes place; the rabbis, thus, were right to stress community. The unification of the two themes of classical Jewish morality is caught in the metaphor of redeeming the sparks of holiness that have been scattered throughout the world. The way to their redemption occurs through two means — as an individual soul is perfected, the sparks within that soul are brought to their perfection, and when an individual interacts with the social world correctly sparks are also redeemed. The two aspects of Jewish morality emphasized by the rabbis and philosophers are brought into harmony through the mystical myth. That harmonization through the telling of a story represents a major contribution made by Jewish mysticism to the moral literature of Judaism.

The modern stage of Hebrew narrative begins in the eighteenth century with the Haskalah writers who self-consciously utilized Hebrew as a polemic and modernizing tool of literary liberation. It provides as Robert Alter declares "a luminous mirror both of the creative elan and of the deep perplexities of Jews trying to define some relationship to an age-old heritage in a radically unfamiliar new world."[6] Stories of tradition dislocated and of uneasy modernism run through the tales of writers like Shumel Yosef Agnon, Yosef Hayyim Brenner, and Hayyim Nahman Bialik. Alter calls the latter's essay "Revealment and Concealment in Language" a "negative Kabbalah" in which the "void" becomes the life-giving divinity. Although Alter does not mention him, Richard Rubenstein utilizes a similar mythology both in his own theological work and in his exegesis of rabbinic narrative. The theme of narrative in the modern period seems to be the confrontation of the Jew with the terrors of a modern, secular and demonic world.

The themes and motifs found in Hebrew literature since the eighteenth century are echoed in English and European Jewish writing as well. The works of Elie Wiesel are testimonies to such themes as are the varied writings of such people as Saul Bellow, Brian Glanville, and Leslie Fiedler. The symbiosis of secular literary traditions and Jewish experience in modernity is a common foundation for Jewish writing both in Hebrew and in diaspora languages.

Cynthia Ozick provides a terrifying parable in "The Pagan Rabbi" that illustrates this point.[7] A traditional rabbi is seduced into a worship of nature and the pagan deities of the natural world. He is slowly destroyed, and his wife is witness to that destruction. Creation takes on a power of its own, freed of its links to the creator. Contemporary Jewish literature presents a picture of a chaotic world swirling freely without a direction or director.

What is the significance of this development for the teaching of Jewish studies? The first implication is that narrative can be used to convey different elements within the Jewish tradition. The dimensions of Jewish philosophy, its themes, concerns, and place in religious life can be communicated through the narratives and motifs derived from the philosophical tradition. The morality and ethical values of Judaism can also be taught through the medium of story. Rabbinic tales and their modifications in subsequent narratives provide clues as to the developing and changing values affirmed in different Jewish communities. Students can also be introduced to Jewish cosmology and abstract theology through the dynamic and fascinating use of stories, narrative and lore. Finally the complexities of modernity, the questions facing the Jew who seeks to conjoin traditional values and contemporary experience are dramatically communicated through the use of modern Jewish narratives.

Approaches to Jewish Narrative: History, Myth, and Psychology

In decoding Jewish narrative to understand its implications, a variety of techniques are helpful. On the most elementary level, students can be led to appreciate the images and ceremonies of Jewish life through a study of literature. Thus Agnon's "The Kerchief," for example, can provide an opportunity to discuss Jewish holidays — the Sabbath, Tisha b'Av, Bar Mitzvah — and concepts — messianism, redemption, exile, compassion. A deeper study of narrative, however, is needed; students should be taught to look beneath the surface of a narrative to see its structure, its effect upon the reader, and its theological value. The work of three authors — Yoav Elstein, Richard Rubenstein, and Elie Wiesel — can illustrate how narrative can be used to teach students to discern hidden layers in religious texts. Elstein uses a structural approach in order to discover the transformations through which a story has passed before reaching a final version. His studies of hasidic legends illuminate both the narrative process and the way in which ideas are transmitted through them. He has shown how hasidic stories in general and Rabbi Nahman's tales in particular may be the transformation of concepts into a narrative form.[8] In one study he traces the way in which a story is shaped in order to express a deep seated social need that can find no other appropriate outlet.[9] From the first rabbinic exegetes onward, biblical stories, for example, were understood as expressions of the Jewish ethos. They became structural clues to the nature of God, Israel, and the relationship between them. It might be said that the essence of both God and Israel are contained in stories. Attention to detail and the transformation of stories show a change in the effective theology governing Jewish life and thought.

A well-known and often used hasidic tale provides an example of this development. The tale relates how when the Baal Shem Tov was presented with a certain problem he would light a fire, go to a special place in the woods, say particular prayers, and the problem would be solved. In each successive generation one element in this ritual was lost — the fire, the place, the prayers, and finally Rabbi Moses Lev of Sassov declared that just telling the story would be sufficient. Elstein compares this tale as presented in the sources with its rendition by Gershom Scholem in *Major Trends in Jewish Mysticism.* He suggests that the story appears to be charting the decline of the generations. When looked at in context, however, it is a reaction against such thinking. The former generations are richer only in their metaphysical tools, not in their actual success. When compared with the midrashic material, the story shows interesting similarities to a tale told in *Midrash Lamentations Rabba.* The social problems facing the Jews in the diaspora period were close to those of fourth generation Hasidism: how to maintain continuity of tradition despite tragedies of experience. The tales are told to emphasize the quality of generations despite apparent decline. Although the midrash and the hasidic tale have different details and the stories are not similar externally, they have common themes. This is what Elstein means by structural continuity.

This type of analysis can teach students to look for more than the surface story being told in a narrative. They are directed to the contextual meaning, the hidden implications, the social dimensions of a tale. Another dimension to a story is its psychological resonance. Tales appeal to the reader because they touch a subconscious nerve, a suppressed instinct within the self. Richard L. Rubenstein investigates Jewish tales with a keen psychological sensitivity. The power of the *'aggada* of the folklore and narrative tradition is, he finds, related to its ability to address suppressed desires. The *'aggada,* he contends, "comprehended and exposed mankind's darkest temptation."[10]

One example of the aggadic tradition which Rubenstein uses is that of Korah and his rebellion against Moses.[11] The biblical story is rather straightforward. Korah was a priest who envied the levitical perogatives of Aaron and, by extension, Moses. For the Rabbis, however, the case was more complicated. Korah represented the deficiencies which they well understood in rabbinic Jewish tradition. From this perspective Korah launched a rational and persuasive campaign against the restrictions of traditional Jewish law and claims of authority. He raised all the questions and problems that they knew were unanswerable. According to Rubenstein, the portrait of Korah was an objectification of the evil they saw within themselves. They identified with the sinner and thus their criticism of Korah was ironic and actually self-directed. Students can be led to see how an apparent defense of tradition is actually a criticism of it. Criticism can be disguised, but nevertheless powerful. Such a psychological reading of narratives can breed an awareness of and sensitivity to irony. When students turn from Rubenstein on the *'aggada* to Agnon's apparently naive tales they are prepared to recognize his ironic vision. A psychological sophistication about how fiction draws upon hidden and repressed desires is needed for both a general understanding of literature and more particularly for a comprehension of the subterranean but ever present tensions within Judaism itself.

Structural analysis and psychological deduction applied to narratives often tends to reduce them to preconceived schemas or paradigms. Stories express more than the analyst can discover. The value of Elie Wiesel as a commentator on stories and not merely as a storyteller is that he makes the reader "feel the pitiful inadequacy of all our common sense categories of reality."[12] Storytelling is a sacramental act for him, one that he associates with his Rebbe. When he protests to the Rebbe against giving a Bar Mitzvah talk in his presence, the Rebbe understands but declares, "I don't ask the storyteller to play the role of master; all I ask is that he fulfill his duty as messenger and witness."[13] It is that task which Wiesel is trying to fulfill through his various works.

Telling stories is transforming experience into legend, according to Wiesel. This is the technique which he says he has learned from other storytellers and which Robert Alter says Wiesel has drawn from Hasidism in which "the concise tale is typically used as a revelation of spiritual truth."[14] An example of such an understanding of stories is Wiesel's retelling of the paradise story. He is fascinated by Adam, a man who at first has everything but is nothing and then has nothing but can become everything. Wiesel sees Adam in the beginning as far from the mythological hero. He is passive, he is merely an instrument of the divine, his life is ultimately boring. After he has left the garden, however, Adam becomes a true self. He not only experiences life but can give life meaning. Wiesel comments that only on leaving the garden did human beings discover a purpose to their existence "to perfect the world ... to use the experience that had been theirs. To transmit, to communicate by deed and word. To safeguard. To tell a tale, omitting nothing, forgetting nothing."[15] The telling of stories may involve the invention of legend, the creation of a vehicle for conveying the inexpressible. Wiesel teaches students to look beyond what a story says to what it cannot say, to its allusive quality. Stories are myth as well as a means of communicating facts. Using the sensitivity to mythic themes that Wiesel provides, a student can read Jewish narratives to gain a sense of the mythic structure undergirding much of Jewish religious thought.

As a method for teaching Judaic studies, narratives have, thus, a particular advantage and a particular technique of exegesis. The advantage is that they offer a broad and fascinating introduction to Judaism in its full variety; the technique is that of sensitizing students to the many levels of meaning found in stories — their social, psychological, and mythic dimensions. An example may clarify how a story can increase an understanding of Judaism. Rabbi Nahman of

Bratzlav, as indicated earlier, was a master in the use of tales. The final part of this essay will look at one such tale — that of the Master of Prayer — and see how it might be decoded as an introduction to Jewish religious life.

The Tale of the Master of Prayer as a Complex Story

Rabbi Nahman considers stories a means of awakening an awareness of religious concerns. Through hearing stories, an individual learns how to progress morally and spiritually. Perhaps most importantly, the hearing of a tale will stimulate a person to seek out a leader, a *zaddik*. The "Tale of the Master of Prayer," the twelfth in his thirteen major stories, provides an example of how a story functions on a number of levels in order to fulfill its primary task — that of arousing the hearer to moral development. The tale is clearly a mixture of moral concerns, social awareness, and mystical myth.[16] The plot is easily told, but even such a telling cannot obscure its complexity. The plot contains a number of subthemes and subplots which indicate the variety of meanings in the tale.

On one level the story is concerned with the moral development of a particular country. The people of this country have taken the acquisition of wealth as their highest value and built a society based upon that value. The story traces the development of that society, its progress towards reform, and its final healing. The people of that society develop from their original misperception of the value of money to one social problem after another. Finally, however, they begin an ascent in ethical living. They move from pragmatic wisdom to social consciousness to spiritual living. At the end of the tale they, and the kingdom of which they are a part, find that perfection of social and private life for which humanity seeks.

On another level the story reflects the cosmic myth of Lurianic Kabbalah. Certain central characters emerge in the course of the narrative — a Master of Prayer, a Warrior, a Treasurer, a Sage, a Queen, A Crown Prince, and finally a King. The tale relates that originally all these were members of a single royal court. A catastrophic whirlwind scattered them. Finally, at the end of the story, all are reunited and the perfect order that had been at the beginning is restored. Here is a variation of the Lurianic tale of the broken vessels and the restoration of the sparks of holiness. The final section of the tale is concerned with a ritual described by the King. The King himself tells a story — the story of a mysterious mountain that is completely of fire, of a lion who ravages the sheep and cannot be stopped, and of a miraculous kitchen which has food which will cure the people of the country deluded by wealth. Only the last element in the King's story is relevant to the story at hand. The reader is left perplexed as to the reason for the extraneous details. Methodologically this complexity introduces the student to the problem of looking for the structure and hidden meaning in a tale.

The structural meaning of this story is difficult to decode. Because the story is complex it has been read in different ways by different interpreters. One set of interpreters believes that the choice of the love of money as the moral vice in question is not fortuitous. Money corrupts beyond any other false value that a person can choose. The essential thrust of the story, according to this interpretation, is on moral self-improvement. A person must strive to find release from that most tenacious of vices — the desire for possessions. Adin Steinsaltz interprets the tale this way, stressing that of all vices only the desire for money cannot be elevated to a moral stage and must be exterminated by a Master who can transform a person. The highest level of moral growth is the tutelage of a Master.[17] Other interpreters suggest that the love of money is only an arbitrary vice, taken as one example, of the chaos of an unredeemed world. The important lesson of the story, from this standpoint, is that human beings are under a dire misconception of their purpose in the world. They must be awakened to their true nature and need the guidance of such figures as the Master of Prayer. The vice of loving money "is the cardinal example of misperception, but other examples are strewn throughout the story."[18]

The variety of literary techniques Rabbi Nahman employs may be one cause of this variety of interpretations of the story. Arnold Band, in his study of this tale, remarks on the way in which the story is told. He notes that "while the story of the Land of Riches and the Master of Prayer is told straightforwardly, the cosmic myth is told in fragments."[19] This literary device may be the clue needed in order to unravel the complexities of the story. Perhaps Rabbi Nahman is using different literary styles in order to achieve different pedagogical ends. If that is the case then he is following in the Jewish moral tradition and adapting the medium to the message, choosing the appropriate literary form for the moral lesson being taught. Various statements by Rabbi Nahman himself suggest that this may be the case.[20]

Looking at the story from the perspective of a structural analysis, the reader can be led to consider the themes of moral living, the place of money in religious life, and the meaning of redemption in Judaism. The variation in interpretations can demonstrate that there is no one Jewish ethical system, that no one mythology of redemption is uniformly accepted in Judaism, and that the relationship between master and disciple is a complex one in various Jewish communal structures. The student can be led to compare the story presented here with other messianic-tales — some of Agnon's tales, some midrashic legends, and the messianic Zionism of the Haskalah period can provide useful parallels and contrasts to the way these themes are developed. The tale introduces students into a variety of Jewish themes and to the variety of Jewish reflection on those themes.

Psychological Dimensions in Rabbi Nahman's Tale

There are a number of psychological insights which the student can derive from, or on the other hand bring to, the study of this tale. On an elementary level, the story can be understood by reference to Rubenstein's insight that villains often portray the hidden desires of the storyteller. The city devoted to riches provides a convenient mirror image of mystic asceticism. The suppressed desires of the hasidic ascetic are given imaginative play, but also ridiculed through the picture drawn of the country enslaved by its passion for wealth. Rubenstein's psychological insight helps students to see how the tale might have resonated to a hassid identifying with but suspicious of the motivations of the materialistic fools satirized in the story. This insight by itself, however, is not enough to decode the psychological resonance of the tale. Three stages of psychological development are present in the structure of the story. At first the reader is led to ridicule the people enslaved to money. The burlesque and mocking description of that country leads the reader through identifications with the victims to greater perspective on self. The desires and temptations of material life can be mocked, placed in perspective through ridicule, and thus a person can cope with them. The first stage of development occurs through identification with the victims and, through laughter, placing their temptations in perspective.

As the tale develops, however, this ridicule is replaced by more serious concerns. The people in the community learn to recognize danger when it threatens them all; they curb their selfishness and band together, first against an outside threat: the King's Warrior stands against them. Although he eventually becomes their leader, his original function is as a catalyst to social solidarity. Secondly, as the people from the country enslaved to gold go forth on a pilgrimage for help, they abandon some of their idolatrous practices — they refuse to practice human sacrifice since that would decimate the community. This second stage of development is, from a Jewish standpoint, that of *zedakah*, of communal awareness. Psychologically, however, it can be identified as the stage in which a "superego" develops, in which identity is extended beyond self alone to include all of society. This new stage of psychological resonance in the tale is accompanied by a change in the literary form itself.

The first part of the tale is focused on the Master of Prayer; he is the foil through which the folly of the worship of gold is made clear. In the second part of the story, however, he recedes into the background. Pilgrimage rather than ridicule becomes the paradigm and the people find the King's Treasurer who leads them on their way, bringing them along in the search for the King who, when found, commissions the Warrior to take them through a strange ritual which finally brings them to a perfect cure. Students can be led to see how the Master of Prayer is only the focal point of the first part of the tale. Through the analysis of the structure of the story they can learn to see the different psychological dimensions in the tale.

The third part of the tale demonstrates another dramatic shift in style. The ritual which the warrior performs is described using images drawn from the prophet Isaiah and is rich in symbolic meaning. Students can recognize in this transformation of style a new psychological device coming into play. In this ritual the Warrior initiates the people devoted to wealth into a new stage of existence. He brings them to a kitchen whose foods are warmed by the heat of the firey mountain; they eat the food and then find that they themselves stink with the stench of feces. Realizing that it is the money that gives off the odor, they dig pits and throw themselves into them. They are buried alive until the Warrior reveals to them who he is and tells them to arise and go back to their country in peace. Here images from Isaiah are used to symbolize the sense of shame that comes when a person recognizes the need for external help and assistance.

This reaction can be recognized as what anthropologists have called a ritual of passage, a symbolization of the experience of "liminality." That experience occurs when an individual is between stages — neither fully out of one stage nor into another. Rituals enable people to bridge the gap between their stages of development. In this story Rabbi Nahman is describing the stages of human moral development. He shows the difficult transition from moral ignorance to ethical achievement to mystical dedication. From this perspective, acknowledging one's ignorance is a means whereby an individual gains perspective on the self. It has pragmatic value in personal development.

Once students have become sensitive to these shifting psychological levels in the story they can be shown how various aspects of Jewish life in general parallel them. The *'aggada*, as Rubenstin has shown, is a normative channel into which antisocial instincts can be directed. The halakhic structure of Judaism can be explained as a means of developing a social identity, of stimulating *zedakah*, and of creating a mature superego. Various questions central to any discussion of Judaism — the nature of guilt, anxiety, legalism, communal solidarity — can be addressed through focusing on this second stage in the tale. Finally Jewish ritual can be explained in sociological and anthropological categories. While the tale has its own idiosyncratic ritual, students can apply their study of ritualism in the story to an analysis of Bar Mitzvah, Passover, Yom Kippur, and other traditional Jewish celebrations. The variety of religious expressions in Judaism can be correlated with a variety of psychological stages in human life.

Ignorance, Halakha, and Religious Authority in Nahman's Tale

A central concern in Jewish religious thought, from Philo through the medievals and including modern thinkers like Martin Buber, is that of discovering the limits of knowledge. Jewish thinkers have wrestled with the philosophical problem of epistemology, and students can be introduced to it through the study of Rabbi Nahman's works. The cosmic myth of Lurianic

Kabbalah stresses the confusion of this mundane world. Rabbi Nahman's tales point to the hiddenness of God as do stories attributed to the Baal Shem Tov. Students focusing on the tale of the Master of Prayer can be initiated into a philosophical debate. A key phrase in the narrative, repeated as the members of the King's court are discovered, declares, "indeed all the factions are misled and confused and all need to be returned from their folly and restored to their true purpose."[21] Rabbi Nahman is insisting upon the ignorance of all human beings, the lack of knowledge that is inherent in being part of a chaotic, unredeemed, created world. In such a situation guidance is needed. Students can be taught to recognize how philosophers turned to philosophy, rabbis to techniques of Torah interpretation, and mystics to their spiritual mentors in the face of intrinsic ignorance. Each Jewish thinker offered a different solution to the error of humanity, each provided a type of guidance for those inevitably misled by the illusions of reality. The search for religious and moral guidance in Judaism can be illustrated by a look at historical figures from Yohanan Ben Zaccai through Rashi and Maimonides. Students looking at Rabbi Nahman's tale, taught to understand the social and contextual elements in hasidic leadership controversies, can nevertheless be led to see in his claim of human ignorance a religious statement about human nature and its needs and not merely as a sociopolitical ploy.

Human beings, Jews in particular, Rabbi Nahman's tale suggests, need supernal guidance. For the country deluded by riches the King provided that guidance. A symbol of the King's power is a "hand" which was a map upon which was inscribed all the events of the world. By looking at that hand it was possible to see all the events of the world, past, present, future. The King's use of this hand is symbolic of the power of the *zaddik*. The *zaddik* can guide his followers in their personal and social development because he has all of human life and history at his command. The *zaddik* is the symbol not merely of arcane knowledge but of the communal reality which is the true repository of that knowledge. The *zaddik* stands for all of human history, for the total plan which God has for humanity as a whole. Thus later Bratzlaver writers explain that this "hand" was the means by which the great biblical leaders — Adam, Noah, Abraham, Moses — and the late *zaddikim* could know all of the history at a glance.[22]

Looked at from the perspective of traditional Judaism, this symbolism is a justification of *halakha* and the regulation of behavior through acceptance of divine authority. The student can be led to appreciate the structure of Jewish law and the theology of revelation which animates Judaism through Rabbi Nahman's tale. Jews need the guidance of Torah and the scholars who can interpret Torah truly because human ignorance is radical. A discussion of the narrative in the story "The Master of Prayer" can lead into a consideration of the meaning of authority, religious obedience, and piety in Jewish life. Students may be led to consider whether authority may not be necessary given the nature of human beings, whether pragmatic or ideal legislation is preferable, and the relevance of a "heavenly" ethic for mundane human life. The philosophy of Judaism is a natural outgrowth of the themes found in Rabbi Nahman's tale.

Conclusions

The value of using an analysis of narrative as an introduction to Judaism should be clear from the previous discussion. The complexities and multidimensional aspects of literature present an opportunity to inculcate care, caution, and ingenuity in reading a religious document. The specific concerns of Jewish life — philosophical questions, practical issues of religious practice and the authority of *halakha* — find symbolic expression in Jewish Stories. The psychological resonance of such stories also helps students understand the appeal and human attractiveness of religious ideas, practices, and morality. A general introduction to Judaism often suffers from the dilemma of having too much to offer and students with too little a background to assimilate everything. As part of the new humanities, Judaic studies should concentrate less on the communication of detailed facts for their own sake. Facts should be introduced as they illuminate the human side of Jewish religiousness. Narratives provide a framework for such illumination. They offer a structure upon which facts can be built as part of the process of decoding the contextual, psychological, and religious dynamics of a particular text. Because the Jewish literary tradition encapsulates so many of the elements with Judaism itself and has a direct relationship to the human experience of religious life, the study of that literature provides a valuable look in introducing Judaic studies to students in the humanities.

---

[1]See his *Liqqutei MoHaRaN*, section 60-67. (New York: 1969). For good background material on Rabbi Nahman and his approach to story telling, see Arthur Green, *Tormented Master: A Life of Rabbi Nahman of Bratzlav* (New York: 1981), Yehudit Kuk, *Rabbi Nahman of Bratzlav: Comments on His Stories* (Jerusalem: Gerst Institute, 1973); Adin Steinsaltz, *Beggars and Prayers*, edited by Jonathan Omer-man, translated by Yehudah Hanegbi, Herzlia Dobkin, Deborah French, and Freema Gottleib (New York: 1979); Joseph Weiss, *Studies in Bratzlav Hassidism*, edited by M. *Piercaz* (Jerusalem: 1974), Mendel Piekarz, *Studies in Braslav Hassidism* (Jerusalem: 1972).

[2]Green, *Tormented Master*, p. 346.

[3]Martin Buber, *The Legend of the Baal Shem*, translated by Martice Friedman (New York: 1969), pp. 107-120; see also Jacob Kadaner, *Sippurim Noraim* (Munkacs: 1912), pp. 11a-13a.

[4]Jacob Neusner, *Judaism in the American Humanities II: Jewish Learning and the New Humanities*, Brown Judaica Series 42. (Chico, California: Scholars Press, 1983).

[5]See Joseph Dan, *Hebrew Ethical and Homiletical Literature* (Jerusalem: 1975); *idem.*, *The Hasidic Story* (Jerusalem: 1975); *idem.*, *The Hebrew Story in the Middle Ages* (Jerusalem: 1974); see particularly the first two chapters which are

general considerations, and chapter 16 which focuses on the story in philosophical and mystical writing. In *The Teaching of Hassidism,* edited with an introduction and notes by Joseph Dan, with the assistance of Robert J. Milch (New York: 1983), Dan suggests that the Hasidic story was not an early or necessarily characteristic part of Hasidism. He claims that its "place in Hadisism has been exaggerated to the point of distorting the historical picture." (p. 4). The association of story and homiletical moral teachings, however cannot be disputed.

[6]Robert Alter, *Modern Hebrew Literature,* edited with introductions and notes by Robert Alter. (New York: Behrman House, 1975). p. xi.

[7]Ozick, Cynthia. "The Pagan Rabbi," *In The Pagan Rabbi and Other Stories.* (New York: Alfred A. Knopf. 1971), pp. 3-37.

[8]Yoav Elstein, *Structuralism in Literary Criticism: The Transformation of Two Hasidic Tales* (Los Angeles, 1974); *idem.,* "The Metaphysical Element in the Making of the First Story by Rabbi Nahman of Bratzlav," *Da'at* 9 (1980), pp. 39-52, and *idem.,* "The Hasidic Tale: The Transformation of Conceptual Systems Into Narrative Sequences," *Da'at* 9 (1982), pp. 26-38; Elstein's theoretical approach and its application to modern Hebrew literature are demonstrated in his earlier work in *Hebrew Structures of Recurrence in Literature,* Tel Aviv: Elef, 1970.

[9]Elstein, "The Hasidic Tale."

[10]Richard Rubenstein, *The Religious Imagination: A Study in Psychoanalysis and Jewish Theology.* (Boston: Beacon Press, 1968).

[11]*Ibid.,* pp. 85-86; 117-126; 130-131; 136-137.

[12]Robert Alter, *After the Tradition: Essays on Modern Jewish Writing* . (New York: E. P. Dutton and Company, 1969), p. 151.

[13]Elie Wiesel, *One Generation After.* Translated by Lilly Edelman and the author. (New York: Random House, 1972), p. 90.

[14]Alter, *After the Tradition,* p. 155.

[15]Elie Wiesel, *Messengers of God.* (New York: Random House, 1976), p. 28.

[16]See Arnold Band, *Rabbi Nahman: The Tales* (New York: 1978) and Kuk, *Rabbi Nahman,* pp. 110-164.

[17]Steinsaltz, *Beggars and Prayers,* p. 111.

[18]Band, *Tales,* p. 318.

[19]Band, *Tales,* p. 317.

[20]See Nahman of Bratzlav, *Leqqutei MoHoRaN I,* pp. 60:9, 5:2,5.

[21]Band, *Tales,* p. 243.

[22]Gedalyahu Kenig, *Kuntres Haye Nefesh* (Tel Aviv: 1967) pp. 34-39.

Chapter Three

The Methodology of Hebrew Language and Literature: Some Basic Needs

Albert T. Bilgray

General Introduction

This volume includes a number of other discussions relating to Hebrew. These devote themselves specifically to methodological techniques for teaching the language, as well as Biblical, midrashic and modern Hebrew literature. We make general references to various techniques and aids but do not attempt to recommend any specific approach. Our primary purpose here is to set up the basic premises and point up the *needs* that confront us.

This chapter is far too brief to permit a thorough or complete analysis. We begin with a quick preview of today's environment as well as the professional dilemma confronting young instructors. We discuss also the Hebrew language survey of a decade ago and the two track approach in teaching Hebrew. We lay down the premises that point toward a possible numerical decline of Hebrew students in the foreseeable future. We then proceed to delineate the most essential current needs and follow these up with further research *desiderata*. We conclude with brief summaries of the roles of the campus, the professional association, and the foundations in meeting our challenge. It is not our concern here to unveil world shaking *hidushim* but it is our fervent hope that this volume and follow up efforts in this field will lead to a significant breakthrough that will help establish one or more workable methodologies in the broad realm of Hebrew language and literature.

A brief note concerning terminology is in order. To avoid redundancy, we shall use the less cumbersome term "Hebrew methodology" to refer specifically to the "methodology of teaching Hebrew language and literature in American institutions of higher learning." Our survey here covers instruction of Hebrew at theological seminaries and church-oriented institutions as well as secular colleges and universities. When we use the adjective "American," we refer to North American institutions, including, of course, the fine programs available on Canadian campuses. When we mention "older" programs, we allude to Hebrew programs that were already established at the beginning of this century. Our term "newer" programs refers to the vast body of Hebrew study introduced during this century, largely in the post World War II era.

The Present Academic Environment

We begin with a brief survey of the present academic environment. The proliferation of Hebrew programs at American universities and colleges during the quarter century following World War II was truly remarkable. This was the era that witnessed the introduction of Hebrew at more than 300 campuses. At most institutions, this expansion was either checked or reversed during the 1970's, an era of austerity within academe.

Our last official figures, incorporating the autumn enrollments for 1983, reveal that for the first time in more than a decade the study of foreign languages rose somewhat. Despite the hopeful statistics of 4.5% increase between 1980 and 1983, the total number of students pursuing foreign language study at American colleges and universities remains under one million.[1] 1968-1974 was the peak era for foreign language study. Our latest figures, despite the increase since 1980, in some of the foreign languages, do not match the halcyon days of 1968-1974. In the case of Hebrew, the decline since that era has been consistent. Between 1960 and 1974 Hebrew enrollment increased seven-fold, an exceptionally spectacular growth. Since 1974, however, the number of Hebrew students has dropped steadily, a decline of 18% in nine years. This drop constitutes a serious hemorrhage.[2]

Let us pause briefly now to reflect on the impact of the past decade upon the study of foreign languages in general and more specifically on Hebrew. Five obvious factors can be discerned in characterizing our current situation:

1. *Decline in Enrollment:* The recession of 1982 affected individual students as well as the institutions. Academe did not bounce back fully after the general economic condition improved. The situation has been compounded by the decline in the birth rate. These are among the factors that led to a lower general enrollment. Foreign language as well as Hebrew studies have been affected.

2. *Retreat from the Humanities*: The situation is aggravated further by the fact that college students of the 1980's are abandoning the humanities and turning toward pragmatic fields such as engineering and business administration.[3] This affects all foreign language studies and has an obvious impact on Hebrew studies as well.

3. *Resistance to Foreign Language Study:* The American resistance to the study of foreign language persists. On many campuses the foreign language requirement was relaxed or eliminated altogether during the 1970's.[4] The decline since 1975 is not quite as precipitous as it was between 1971 and 1975.[5]

Nevertheless, this continuing trend has clearly weakened many, probably most of the foreign language programs in the land. We assume that Hebrew suffered from this general trend, also.

4. *Decline of National Grants*: Government and foundation grants to colleges and universities are declining.[6] Some campuses have turned to local communities, alumni and other support groups for additional funding. The general response has been negligible except from business corporations that usually earmark their funds almost exclusively for programs of business administration, engineering and mining.[7]

5. *Retrenchment*: Faced with a continuing austerity and a decline in funds from student tuition and other sources, colleges have been compelled to retrench. Applying the pragmatic principle of "last hired, first fired" they are cutting back or eliminating some of their *newest* offerings as well as those programs that are *not large* enough or sufficiently *entrenched* to resist the axe. On most campuses the study of Hebrew belongs, unfortunately, to all three vulnerable categories.

In the light of these five factors, we can understand why few programs of foreign language studies are growing in momentum. On most campuses of the 1980's Hebrew studies is content to hold on to the level of the early 1970's.[8] This reality contrasts significantly with the situation that prevailed a decade ago.

To help achieve perspective we take a look at the foreign language situation of a decade ago. Under the impetus of the expanding college programs and the financial support of the National Defence Education Act of 1958, Title VI (NDEA), foreign language study kept moving ahead steadily during the 1960's. Although the study of Hebrew was not subsidized under the terms of NDEA, Hebrew progressed amazingly. For some years it was the fastest growing foreign language study on the American campus.[9]

Hebrew Language Study a Decade Ago

The last thorough study of Hebrew studies was done in the early 1970's. Back in 1972, I observed the need to survey the status of Hebrew studies. A preliminary exploration pointed toward the desirability of two parallel studies, one limited to so-called secular or general colleges and universities and the other concentrating on church-oriented institutions. After some careful deliberation, it was decided to use the *identical* questionnaire for both types of institutions so that a more exact comparative analysis could be made. The research and analysis took four years, the first devoted to preliminary exploration followed by the three phases of the study. The results of each phase were presented at NAPH sessions in 1974, 1975, and 1976.

The first phase, which we call the "University Study," limited itself to private and state colleges and universities.[10] The second phase, which we call the "Church-Oriented School Study," concentrated on four types of institutions, church-oriented colleges, church-oriented universities, undergraduate theological schools (previously known as "Bible Colleges") and graduate divinity schools.[11] The third phase, which we call the "Comparative Study," summarized the total conclusions and proceeded to compare and contrast the study of Hebrew at secular and church-oriented institutions.[12] It also analyzed some of the difficulties involved in a comparative study.

The basis for this study was an extensive questionnaire of 144 questions which was mailed out in January, 1973 to 200 teachers of Hebrew who were members of NAPH. In our two basic surveys the information we sought and the data we endeavored to gather followed similar lines, since we used the same questionnaire. At each institution we sought to find out whether the study of Hebrew is growing or declining. We considered the factors influencing the trend, including the presence or absence of foreign language requirements. As we viewed the variety of Hebrew programs offered, we explored the relationship of Hebrew programs to Judaic study courses where these were available. We gathered statistical information concerning the Hebrew program, the courses, the professors, the textbooks, and other materials as well as the assorted methods used, including language laboratories and conversation techniques. We probed carefully the characteristic difficulties and innovative ideas. We collated all this information separately for first year Hebrew, second year Hebrew and advanced Hebrew studies so that the professor or researcher who specializes in one area of instruction will have data related to his or her field of interest. We supplemented our survey of methodology with an effort to understand the motivation and philosophy that governs the teaching of Hebrew at each institution.

At first we found it difficult to make comparisons because it appeared that we were comparing apples with oranges. Eventually, we realized that we were dealing with two kinds of *apple orchards*, the first type of orchard (the general or secular college) cultivates its apples for the general market and grows virtually all of its apples early in the season (during the undergraduate years).[13] At the second type of orchard, there was a greater variety of apple growth procedures. Some are grown early (undergraduate students). Others are grown late in the season (graduate students). To complicate our analysis, this second orchard also cultivates a special type of apple for the restaurant trade (i.e., professional ministers). This specialized restaurant apple is usually grown late (graduate divinity students). Sometimes, however, it is grown early (undergraduate "Bible College" students who enter the ministry without any follow up graduate study).

There were other difficulties which the interested researcher will want to explore. Comparisons of the two categories of Hebrew study were complicated further because they varied in their degree of success. At the general colleges and universities, the Hebrew program proliferated tremendously during the post war era of 1945-1970. At church-oriented schools, Hebrew study (as well as Greek study) had been declining steadily during that period. Despite the internal variations within each of the categories, there are some generalizations that can be made for the state of Hebrew studies in 1973. There was a pronounced contrast in philosophy, motivation and methodology.

Hebrew studies at the general universities and colleges are patterned to parallel the other foreign language disciplines such as French, German, or Spanish which start with an undergraduate non-professional offering. They begin with a modern Hebrew language introduction and usually concern themselves, after the second year, with contemporary as well as classical literature. A few graduate students then proceed to earn professional degrees in language and literature study (the MA requirement for high school teaching and the Ph.D. for college instruction).

The church-centered schools pursue what is primarily a professional motivation, preparing for the ministry. They follow a classical methodology concerned almost exclusively with an understanding of the Biblical text. Their rationale is summarized in the following statement:

1. "We study classical Hebrew to be able to read the Hebrew Bible.
2. We read the Hebrew Bible to understand Hebrew history and Hebrew theology.
3. Once we understand Hebrew history and Hebrew theology, we are better equipped to understand the New Testament and Christian theology.
4. When we understand the New Testament and Christian theology, we are prepared to interpret the text of the Hebrew Bible."

This makes the circle complete. The philosophy that undergirds this pattern of Hebrew study is theological. The program is largely professional and pre-professional. It is frequently associated with graduate divinity school studies but as already noted, it is also available to undergraduate "Bible College" students who do not pursue any graduate study.

The five factors listed above characterizing the current campus situation at secular colleges and universities apply also to church-oriented schools where the situation is even *less promising* . In 1973, as already noted, Hebrew study was already declining. We have no reason to believe that this decline has been checked *except* at the schools *where* Hebrew instruction is *required*. The reasons are clear. More and more students who are preparing for the ministry are avoiding the discipline of foreign language study. Furthermore, they are seeking electives that appear to them more relevant for the minister of the future such as public relations, business administration, computer science, audio-visual techniques, and counseling procedures.

A Numerical Decline of Hebrew Students?

In what appears to be a future in which less students will pursue Hebrew studies, it becomes even more imperative for professors of Hebrew to seek out the best possible teaching procedures. Conscientious teachers of Hebrew have always been concerned with methodology, particularly at the schools where the program was limited to one professor or a part-time instructor. They have endeavored to keep the classroom activities varied, interesting and meaningful; they have experimented with creative and innovative ideas; they have tried to understand their students and their needs. This has been done on an individual basis, each professor generalizing from personal experience what direction to follow or techniques to use at his or her particular institution. Through the 1970's, good teachers tried to be effective and efficient because this led to better teaching. This is still true today. Now there is an additional incentive. Hebrew studies programs, like most offerings in the humanities, are facing a fierce competition in the academic market place. At the many schools where the program is small or poorly rooted, Hebrew study offerings will *not* survive unless the teaching becomes far more effective.

Two Hebrew Language Tracks

Every student of Hebrew methodology is aware of the two distinct language tracks. At most American institutions the term "classical" Hebrew refers to Biblical Hebrew, a body of literature clearly defined for centuries.[14] At church oriented colleges and seminaries, Biblical Hebrew is usually the primary and only study of Hebrew. Biblical Hebrew is also well established at some old American universities, particularly the institutions that came into being before the nineteenth century.[15]

"Classical" Hebrew must, by definition, include Rabbinic Hebrew which also embraces a specialized body of literature, much more extensive than Biblical literature, incorporating a body of commentaries and super-commentaries, composed and written in a unique style and usually set apart from Biblical studies.[16] Text study of Rabbinic literature is not a primary concern at most American institutions of higher learning.[17] Nevertheless, there is a growing awareness in the church-oriented as well as secular institutions that Rabbinic literature must be viewed as an essential historic ally of Biblical literature.

At secular American colleges and universities the proliferation of Hebrew studies during the post war era has concentrated on modern and contemporary Hebrew. Most of the programs were established to meet a student demand.[18] In the relatively few institutions where "older" programs existed, modern Hebrew was introduced, usually after some resistance, as a separate second track in another department or a distinctly separate program. In a relatively short time the newer programs became the primary or "standard" track in terms of student involvement although they were not nearly as well entrenched historically and politically as the older established programs of Biblical Hebrew.[19]

What is the current status of the two track approach on campuses where it is available? At the universities which have the *older* programs, the long established departments initiate beginners into a study of Biblical Hebrew.[20] These courses were at one time restricted to graduate students in "Semitic" or "Ancient Near Eastern" studies. Since Hebrew is no longer considered exotic, some of the older programs now permit undergraduates to take these courses.

Students participating in the *newer* programs receive their grounding as undergraduates in the "standard" track that usually consists of two years of modern Hebrew.[21] At this point a second track of Biblical Hebrew becomes available to those who seek it. The vast majority of students who remain in the program continue studying modern Hebrew literature. Eventually, but rarely before the fourth year, a few students may elect to specialize in Rabbinic Hebrew literature.[22]

The pragmatic realities of student demand and academic austerity have decreed the current pattern of language tracks. We may assume that the current pattern is acceptable or deemed reasonable by most faculty and students. It would be desirable, however, to inaugurate some research on the subject of two tracks and the general question of when and under what circumstances they should be coordinated. This is essential because educational philosophy helps determine the curriculum while the curriculum dictates which courses are offered. We will refer briefly to the subject of two track research later.[23]

The Young Instructor's Dilemma

Conscientious professors strive toward two significant goals. They want to enhance their competency within their specialization. They also seek to improve their skill in the classroom. Most college instructors have not taken even an elementary general course in the principles of education or teaching techniques or a special methods approach to their field of concentration. Usually this is not the fault of the individuals. The very nature of graduate study specialization frequently leaves no room for a comprehensive course in methodology.[24] Young instructors, as they pursue the two goals of subject competency and classroom skill, find themselves pressured for time. It becomes essential for them to budget their energy and time efficiently. During the early years of the instructor's career when lifestyle and work patterns are being established, most professors are compelled to neglect methodological competency. They devote themselves primarily to scholarly research. The reasons are clear:

1. *Prerequisite for progress in the profession*: Upward mobility in one's career and the achievement of tenure is dependent largely on publications. Universities give lip service to "teaching skill" and "related community service" but the dictum of "publish or perish" prevails at all major institutions. An impressive list of publications will compensate fully for an absence of community service and an abysmally poor teaching ability.

The most superb and inspiring teaching skill and an extensive devotion of time and energy to relevant community activities will avail not if the professor does not have a minimum requisite of publications. Facing these circumstances, the typical young teacher has no choice but to concentrate on scholarly research and publication. Unless he or she is exceptionally capable, creative and conscientious, the usual instructor is compelled to forego methodological skill and concentrate on scholarly research.

2. *Ready paths toward traditional scholarly research*: The young teacher who has earned an academic doctorate has learned to use the tools of scholarship. Further research and resultant publications will demonstrate whether he or she can make a contribution to the literature in the field without the guidance of a senior advisor. Professors discover early that the *paths* of scholarship within their specialization are wide open. The fields to be explored are usually outlined clearly. Everyone who has been trained adequately possesses the potential for a career of research scholarship.[25]

3. *Obstacles on the road of methodology* : Unfortunately, one cannot become an inspiring teacher through an impulsive decision to be one.[26] Even the so-called "natural" teacher must be informed, organized and disciplined. He or she must begin with a perfect mastery of the subject. There must follow a careful organization of the most relevant items to be presented or clarified. The presentation or discussion should not be cluttered with an excess of verbiage or supplementary information. The student should be able to recognize vividly the salient principle being developed. Even then, devoted teachers persist in disciplining themselves continually to find new illustrations or novel approaches that will make the presentation even more graphic and effective. The task requires patience and time. Since most of us are not natural teachers and have received little or no instruction in methodology, we need to supplement our class experience with relevant technical information. In my judgment, every conscientious instructor will want to read in his or her field of foreign language instruction methodology. The situation is compounded, however, by the fact that there is no bibliography of materials relating to the teaching of Hebrew on the American campus, a serious need we will discuss later.[27] When professors discover the prevailing situation they frequently give up. They are not prepared to participate in the lonesome task of ploughing new ground continually. They settle for a few aids and techniques and decide to concentrate exclusively on the scholarly research which their career demands.[28]

At this juncture we speak farewell to the teachers who have given up toiling in the vineyard of methodology and related areas. We wish them well as they concentrate exclusively within their limited area of scholarly research. This essay now addresses itself to the few professors who endeavor to combine the pursuit of specialization with a desire to develop a teaching skill. It is unfortunate that too many of us view this matter as an either-or dilemma that cannot be reconciled. A number of distinguished scholars who have left their mark in various areas of Hebrew scholarship have supplemented their achievements with a continuing concern for the promotion of Hebrew study as well as historical analyses,[29] and evaluative critiques,[30] of current Hebrew and Judaic studies on the American campus. Others have penetrated more deeply into the realm of methodology. They have devoted considerable energy to explore new methods, develop teaching aids and compose new textbooks.[31] I believe it is possible for all of us to meet the challenge of Hebrew language methodology. Even those of us who are not "g'dolim" in our generation can coordinate classroom teaching skill with a growing competency in our field of concentration. The purpose of this essay is to help remove the roadblocks and make the path of teaching skill more accessible to an even larger number of dedicated professors of Hebrew.

Some Current Basic Needs

As mentioned previously, the literature in the field of Hebrew methodology has not been gathered or organized. As a result, every instructor seeking information relating to teaching skill confronts new ground, dry and barren in a process repeated by countless others. It is an effort of needless duplication contributing little or nothing to the knowledge already possessed by others. Ironically, however, there *is* a serious need for an organized, *integrated* exploration. We cannot leave the resolution of this challenge to the well meaning but misdirected efforts of scattered teachers responding instinctively in a hit or miss fashion. The time has come to establish a *coordinated* national effort that will collate the accumulated experience on the campuses of our land and give our professors an opportunity to share their observations, experience and skill. In addition, we must pinpoint the specific problems confronting us and mount an integrated, coordinated effort to resolve this situation.

A Bibliography of Methodological Materials

We realize, of course, that every instructor must go through the experience of mastering classroom teaching skills. But the task would be far more satisfying for the individual if he or she were equipped with a basic knowledge of how to proceed. We need to begin by gathering and organizing the information already recorded in this field. Our effort should be initiated with the creation of a bibliography of methodological materials that can be useful to the professor of Hebrew language and literature on the American campus. We should seek a trained research librarian to attempt this project. One of the national foundations concerned with research in the humanities may subsidize a trained librarian to pursue this task.[32] A valuable resource that has not been analyzed or indexed is the body of articles of briefer references to be found in the 24 volumes of *Hebrew*

Abstracts and *Hebrew Studies*.[33] A similar effort should be made to explore the back files of the seven volumes of the *Hebrew Annual Review* and the *Association for Jewish Studies Review* . The careful researcher will explore the extensive methodology literature relating to foreign languages. It will probably uncover some articles that deal specifically with Hebrew methodology or are relevant to it.

In addition to the easily identified published articles, an experienced library researcher will seek to track down many unpublished papers presented to a variety of conferences, regional and local.[34] Particular mention should be made of the methodological conferences inaugurated by Edna Amir Coffin, Michigan, and Gilead Morahg, Wisconsin, held at Ann Arbor in 1983 and Madison in 1984. These were comprehensive three-day institutes that have been eminently successful. A third conference is projected for May, 1985. The papers presented at such conferences should certainly be annotated and indexed. It can now be said that Hebrew methodology is a concept whose time has arrived.[35]

The diligent researcher will not be content with published articles and unpublished papers. Another possible resource is the file of many years of *Iggeret*, a newsletter of the National Association of Professors of Hebrew which contains brief but promising references to Hebrew teaching innovations and other aspects of methodology.[36] A similar search should be made of the *AJS Newsletter*. We are positive that there are other bibliographic materials which the disciplined researcher can discover.

An Updated Survey of Hebrew Instruction

The findings of 1973 must be brought up to date with a new comprehensive survey of Hebrew instruction. We must now ask:

1. How has the financial austerity that pervades among educational institutions affected Hebrew studies?
2. How many campus programs of Hebrew study have been strengthened in recent years? What strategies and tactics are required, in the present environment, to achieve this goal?
3. How many programs of Hebrew study have maintained the level of 1973 or held their own in recent years? What are the positive factors that led to this successful result?
4. Are programs of Hebrew study being cut back? Are programs that are holding their own also being cut? If so, why?
5. How has the drop in college enrollment influenced Hebrew studies?
6. To what degree have lower enrollments in the humanities affected Hebrew studies?

7. What impact have reduced foreign language requirements or their elimination had on programs of Hebrew studies?

8. Have the local community, college alumni or other constituents been invited to help support Hebrew studies? What has been the result of such efforts?

9. What are the motivations that lead students to enroll for the various offerings of classical or modern Hebrew. To what degree can this information be applied to specific institutions so that they can tailor appropriate courses to meet specific student needs?

10. How many church-oriented institutions have been able to check the decline of Hebrew studies? What are their effective strategies and tactics?

The updated survey should be more sophisticated and detailed than our 1973 project. Computer science now comes to our rescue. A study using computer techniques can achieve much more valuable information. Yet, it will likely require considerably less effort than our 1973 project which was analyzed and executed in the old fashioned manual manner. We will want to analyze textbook materials, particularly those published or re-edited since 1970 and explore the degree to which they meet the needs or motivations of the various categories of students. Finally, we will want to explore the explosion of innovative techniques and experimental approaches developed during the past decade. To what extent can these techniques and experiments stand on their own feet and be used as *independent* approaches that may replace the traditional methods of "textbook-classroom" teaching? If so, where or when are these novel methods and procedures most effective? In instances where these new techniques cannot replace traditional teaching, how can we use the new approaches to *reinforce* or *supplement* traditional methods? The findings in this area could certainly lead to a very lively debate.

Fostering Workshops in Methodology

As pointed out above, occasional papers and mini-workshops relating to Hebrew language and literature methodology have been presented over the years at various professional conferences.[37] Since 1983 we have had conferences devoted specifically to Hebrew methodology.[38] This is a positive step forward that should be encouraged and expanded. The values are obvious. In their most elementary form such specialized institutes serve an important function in the sharing of disparate individual experiences. Most specialized workshops go far beyond individual experience sessions. They reach group conclusions that may develop cohesive principles. The careful analysis of collective conclusions as well as the interaction of specialists concentrating on methodology publishing their findings may well lead eventually to an accepted methodology or a series of methodologies.

Further Research Needs

Motivations

One of the most pressing research needs is a study of the motivations that lead students toward Hebrew. In the years ahead, academic administrators will call upon us to be more efficient in our teaching. As professors we have known that we can be more effective if we understand the motivations that impel students to enroll for our courses. We know that if we can meet our students' needs we will be eminently more successful. It has been established firmly that different motivations separate the student at the church-oriented school from the general university student. It is just as clear that the student of classical Hebrew, whether it be the Biblical text or the medieval Rabbinic text, has far different interests from the student of modern Hebrew. But we need to go beyond these obvious motivations and pinpoint all the factors that influence students to enroll for Hebrew study and analyze which elements may be relevant on our particular campus.

It would certainly be convenient if a comprehensive Hebrew program could be offered on every campus just as it would be convenient for the food manager in our home to supply us with an extensive smorgasbord of daily offerings. Such variety is, however, unnecessary, even wasteful. We know that the well fed family can have a wholesome diet despite the limited choice available at each sitting. The realities of the 1980's tell us that very few campuses will be able to offer a wide smorgasbord of Hebrew studies. The challenge that confronts us now is to discover the intellectual diet that is best suited for each of our campuses. A study of student motivation of the local and national level will help guide decisions for the individual campus.

It would be most desirable to have an in-depth study of the many factors that motivate Hebrew. The conclusion of such a study should incorporate a do-it-yourself guide that professors can apply to their own campus Hebrew program. It might include a simple test that could be given to prospective students. Such a test would help the program chairperson tailor the essential Hebrew curriculum that is most suitable for the particular campus. In an era of academic austerity, such a procedure can help preserve a viable Hebrew program while meeting the needs of the students.[39]

Exploring Innovative Aids and Techniques

The search for innovative aids and techniques will never end.[40] Circumstances change, attitudes vary with each wave of students, good classroom teachers continue to grow and develop insights of greater maturity. Some obvious areas for independent research include:

1. An analysis of the use of language laboratories for teaching Hebrew. The practice is well established but will benefit from novel use and further refinement.[41]
2. An analysis of the variety of conversation approaches being used to teach college Hebrew.[42]
3. A survey of recent computer aids for the teaching of Hebrew.[43]
4. An exploration of the use of the drama technique as an aid for the study of Hebrew.[44]
5. A survey of television techniques for the study of Hebrew.[45]
6. An exploration of the field of "Do-it-yourself" study.[46]
7. A survey of miscellaneous innovations and promotional efforts.[47]
8. An objective analysis of the literature relating to Hebrew textbooks[48]

Such a survey might lead to a specialized conference devoted primarily to the clarification of the premises and philosophies that motivated the composition of the newer textbooks since 1970. The publication of these proceedings would stimulate further publications that could be most productive.

Coping with Student Differences and other Specialized Problems

As one considers research needs, certain characteristic difficulties in teaching Hebrew language and literature come to mind. Every teacher of first year Hebrew has faced the challenge of a small number of students who are bright and conscientious. Yet, they have a peculiar difficulty in mastering foreign languages regardless of methodology.[49] To what extent is the inability to master Hebrew a unique phenomenon? It would be valuable to have research done on first year Hebrew study problems. Such a study would be particularly helpful to the revisers of current textbooks or the authors of new ones.

A totally different type of challenge faces us in the teaching of third year Hebrew literature. Most students have basic difficulties in making the transition from language instruction to literature study.[50] No adequate answer has been given to the poor adjustment at this juncture. It may stem from the absence of second year textbooks geared to the needs of the American student.[51] Underlying the overall problem is the task of making the proper transition to a different culture while pursuing the mechanics of mastering linguistic details.[52] If the new culture is long in years and rich in content, as in the case of Hebrew literature, it reflects a multiplicity of nuances and a vast variety of form and expression. Extensive research in this area is essential. The problem of teaching third year modern Hebrew is complicated further by the presence of Israeli students who frequently take literature courses. The mix creates a difficult stew. The American students lack the linguistic facility and cultural background to make the transition. Their Israeli counterparts are woefully deficient in grammatical insight.

Miscellaneous Research Needs

The updating of the 1973 survey may reveal that retrenchment in academe as well as other factors may have led to the serious decline in Hebrew studies during the past decade. Statistical information, uninterpreted, cannot answer our questions. It would be most desirable to mount a research project exploring the diagnosis as well as the prognosis. Foundation funds may be available for such a study.

Also desirable but not nearly as urgent would be a research study of the two track system and the various recommendations for its most effective utilization.[53]

Meeting the Challenge

The Role of the Campus

The key question is whether the American campus is prepared to meet the challenge of methodology. I believe the answer is in the affirmative.[54] There is clear evidence of a growing interest. We are no longer content with occasional papers by scattered individuals concerned with an isolated aspect of Hebrew methodology. There are now professors deeply committed to the full challenge, prepared to explore methodology research.

As they publish their findings, academic recognition will come to research devoted primarily to Hebrew methodology. Such acceptance will give Hebrew methodology a tremendous boost.[55] There are other obvious responsibilities an individual campus can undertake such as sponsoring bibliography research and an updating of the 1973 survey of Hebrew instruction. Other possible campus activities are the sponsorship of specialized conferences on motivation research, innovative aids, individual differences, etc.[56]

The Role of Professional Associations

For the time being, the primary responsibility for promoting methodology will remain with the professional associations, NAPH[57] and AJS[58] and, to a lesser degree, AAR-SBL[59] and AAJR.[60] NAPH should expand and strengthen the foothold it has established. AJS should be encouraged to initiate a panel devoted to Hebrew methodology.[61] As their programs develop further, both associations should create and implement national committees on Hebrew teaching methodology that will coordinate the gathering and dissemination of methodology literature and bibliography, foster presentations at conferences and encourage the publication of research papers relating to Hebrew methodology.[62] Once the two associations have implemented their national committees, informal cooperative communication should be initiated for the interchange of useful information. Eventually the two national committees may be able to sponsor a joint conference devoted primarily to Hebrew methodology and establish a national joint commission on Hebrew methodology.

Assistance from Foundations

As pointed out above, there are various projects that can be sponsored or developed without too much difficulty by an individual campus or one of the professional associations. Some efforts such as the bibliography project and the updating of the 1973 survey would certainly be accelerated by a grant from one of the national foundations dedicated to research in the humanities.

The pursuit of grants is a specialized art.[63] It can be generalized that most foundations avoid supporting an established entity even though it is deemed most meritorious or may be facing a temporary financial crisis.[64] They are more likely to be persuaded by a proposal that appears to respond to an unmet need or involves a new area of research for which funding is not available.[65]

Occasionally there are exceptions to the formula that foundations limit themselves largely to innovative and complex research requests. A possible proposal that is relatively simple and requires little research would be a *one time advisory service* for the "small or medium sized" Hebrew programs. Such a proposal might attract a foundation because it answers an essential unmet need that would be most helpful to most of the Hebrew programs in our land. This proposal possesses special merit. It might well be sponsored by one or all of our national professional associations.[66]

Concluding Observations

The agenda before us is clear. Aware of the environment in which we operate during the 1980's, we must now proceed expeditiously to gather a working bibliography and complete a survey of the present state of Hebrew instruction. We must continue to foster specialized methodological conferences and establish a series of research studies on motivation, unique student problems, curricular and textbook philosophy as well as a host of innovative aids and novel techniques that will continue to flow from our creative teachers. The task will move ahead through the joint efforts of dedicated professors and cooperative campuses, committed professional associations and friendly foundations. The fine beginnings apparent since 1980 reveal that individuals as well as institutions recognize the need for serious research in the field of Hebrew methodology. "If we will it, it need not be a dream."

APPENDIX A

Conference on the Teaching of Hebrew Language and Literature

Sponsored by the National Association of Professors of Hebrew
University of Michigan, Ann Arbor
May 22-24, 1983

PROGRAM

May 22, Sunday Afternoon

1:30-2:30 Registration, Anderson Room A & B, Michigan Union

2:30 **Welcome and Introductions:**
Prof. C. Windfuhr & Conference Organizers

The Role of the Dialogue in Language Instruction
Professor Moshe Nahir, University of Manitoba, Canada

Text and Context: Teaching Hebrew Literature
Professor Gilead Morahg, University of Wisconsin, Madison

Break

6:30 Light supper and evening lecture, Anderson Room D

Problems in Teaching Literature as Language and Language as Literature in Universities Abroad
Professor Gershon Shaked, Hebrew University, Jerusalem

May 23, Monday West Conference Room, Fourth Floor, Rackham Building

9:00-10:00 **Teaching the Hebrew Verbs**
Miri Kubovy, Yale University, New Haven

10:00-11:00 **Common Errors in Hebrew of Native English Speakers**
Nava Scharf, Cornell University, Ithaca

Break

11:15-12:15 **Using Teaching Aids in Language Instruction**
Dr. Ziona Kopelovich-Hanash, University of Michigan, Ann Arbor

Lunch Break

2:00-3:00 **Development of Language Skills — Level II of Teaching Hebrew**
Dr. Edna Grad, Northwestern University, Evanston

3:00-3:30 Break

3:30-4:30 **Transition to Reading Extensive Text in Hebrew**
Rina Donchin, University of Illinois, Urbana

Dinner Break

8:00 Public Lecture (in English)

The Meaning of Secular Jewish Culture — Linguistic and Literary Issues
Professor Gershon Shaked, Hebrew University, Jerusalem

May 24, Tuesday Morning Lab A, Modern Language Building

8:30-9:15 **The Use of Language Laboratory** (in English)
James Yzenbaard, Director, University of Michigan Language Laboratory, and staff

9:15-10:15 **Teaching Hebrew of the Media: Radio Broadcasts**
Professor Edna Amir Coffin, University of Michigan, Ann Arbor

10:15-10:45 **Video Use — Demonstration**

10:45-11:15 Break

11:15 Concluding Lecture: **Language and Culture**
(in English)
Professor Alton L. Becker, Linguistics, University of Michigan

12:30 Lunch. Michigan League cafeteria line, then Michigan Room on second floor. Discussion and suggestions for 1984 workshop.

HOST DEPARTMENTS: Program in Judaic Studies, Department of Near Eastern Studies, Center for Near Eastern and East African Studies

APPENDIX B

National Association of Professors of Hebrew
Central Region Conference

Teaching Hebrew: Art and Technology

May 20-22, 1984
University of Wisconsin, Madison

PROGRAM

May 20, Sunday Afternoon Lowell Hall, 702 Langdon Street

1:00-3:00 Registration and Reception: Lower Lobby

3:00-5:00 **Integrating Biblical Texts into a Modern Hebrew Curriculum**
Yair Mazor, University of Wisconsin

Syntactic and Semantic Clues to Reading Hebrew Newspapers
Sara Rubenstein, University of Colorado

5:00-6:00 Light Supper, Lower Dining Room

6:00-8:30 **Feature Films: Cultural Enrichment for Hebrew Classes**
Edna Amir Coffin and Tsila Evers, University of Michigan

May 21, Monday: Room 118

9:00-10:00 **Plays as Reading Texts for Hebrew Language Learning**
Rina Donchin, University of Illinois

10:00-11:00 **Acting in the Classroom as a Tool for Teaching Hebrew**
Oded Borowski, Emory University

11:15-12:15 **Dramatic Production for Foreign Language Instructions** (Video Applications)
Judith Miller, University of Wisconsin

Lunch Break

2:00-3:00 **Using Videotaped Dialogues in a Basic Hebrew Course**
Jeffrey Knisbacher, U.S. Department of Defense

3:00-4:00 **Utilizing Native Speakers to Promote Communicative Skills**
Nili Sharon, University of Minnesota

Break

4:15-5:15 **Oral Presentations and Student-Led Discussions**
Bilha Mirkin, University of Wisconsin

May 22, Tuesday Room 118

9:00-10:00 **Using Computers for Hebrew Instruction**
Hannah Sharon, University of Michigan

10:00-11:00 **The Electronic Ben Yehuda: Can the Computer Replace the Pocket Dictionary?**
Jonathan Paradise, University of Minnesota

Break

11:15-12:15 **Teaching Culture: A Group Work Approach**
Robert Didonato, University of Wisconsin

---

[1]*Chronicles of Higher Education*, August 29, 1984. These figures cover a survey of 850 two year colleges and 1,521 four year colleges and universities. The statistics were compiled by MLA, the first such study since 1980. Among the 12 most commonly taught languages, 7 registered gains, the most significant being Japanese (40.2%) and Russian (26.7%) followed by Chinese (15.9%), Italian (11.2%) and French (8.8%). Spanish (1.8%) and German (1.0%) scored the lowest gains. Miscellaneous languages gained 1.1%. Of the 5 foreign languages that declined the most marked were Ancient Greek (13.7%) and Portuguese (9.1%). These were followed by HEBREW (6.3%) and Latin (3.2%). The smallest decline was sustained by Arabic (.9%).

It may be helpful to note the *current ranking* of the 12 most commonly taught foreign languages. Rounding out the numbers in thousands, the big three are Spanish (385), French (270) and German (126). Far behind are Italian (under 39) and Russian (30). Listed sixth and seventh are Latin (24) and Ancient Greek (19). HEBREW (18) ranks eighth. Japanese (16) and Chinese (13) are ninth and tenth. Portuguese (4) and Arabic (3) are eleventh and twelfth. All *the other* miscellaneous languages total less than 14,000. (If banded together as a category, they would be ranked between ninth and tenth place). The total number of students of foreign languages was 966,013.

[2]Thanks to Monica S. Devens, Assistant Director, MLA, we now have some pre-publication statistics compiled by MLA that give us a picture of the entire sweep of foreign language study since 1960 as well as a more analytical picture of what happened between 1974 and 1983. We can now make some observations concerning general trends but the directions of specific languages puzzle us. Two languages are doing very well, a third is hanging on. Italian is doing better than it did in 1968. Spanish has almost regained its peak position of 1970. Ancient Greek reached its high point in 1977 but it is still doing better than it did in 1968, despite a sharp recent decline. The statistics for Hebrew are also confusing.

In 1960 Hebrew registration was 3,831. By 1974 it had climbed to 22,371. The 1983 figure was 18,199.

[3]Between 1972 and 1983 the number of American high school students scoring more than 650 (in a possible 800 points) of the verbal portion of the Scholastic Aptitude Test fell from 53,794 to 27,408, a decline of 49%. We must assume that the vast majority of students who did poorly in their verbal score did not opt for the humanities.

More concrete documentation of the retreat from the humanities is found in the 1984 report, "To Reclaim A Legacy," by William J. Bennett, Chairman to the National Endowment for the Humanities. In his study, he points out that the number of majors in modern languages has declined 50% since 1970.

[4]Albert T. Bilgray, *The Foreign Language Requirement at Western Universities* , unpublished documented study prepared at the request of Hermann Bleibtreu, Dean, College of Liberal Arts, University of Arizona, 1976.

[5]See Richard I. Brod and Carl B. Lovitt, "The MLA Survey of Foreign Language Entrance and Degree Requirements, 1982-3, *ADFL Bulletin*, Vol. 15, No. 3, March 1984, pp. 40-1, and Richard I. Brod and Jeffrey Meyerson, "The Foreign Language Requirement - Report on the 1974-5 Survey," *ADFL Bulletin*, Vol. 7, No. 1, pp. 43-8. The MLA 1982-3 survey was the first such study since the 1974-5 survey. It covers 1,260 four year colleges and universities, *all* of whom *responded*. (The study was made possible by a grant from the U.S. Department of Education). The figures indicate that the number of institutions that abolished foreign language degree requirements declined by 5% between 1975 and 1983 in contrast to the 24% decline from 1971 to 1975.

For a broader picture of the last 20 years it is well to note that during the peak period of foreign language study, from the early through the mid sixties, nine of the ten college institutions required a foreign language toward an undergraduate degree. A foreign language is now required at approximately half the institutions that reported such requirements in 1966.

[6]Foreign language study during the 1960's was influenced strongly by the NDEA of 1958. The 1980-3 rise of enrollment in Japanese, Chinese and Russian (see [1]) is related to renewed support from the Department of Defense. For a comprehensive analysis of the entire, broad field of language and area studies, see Richard D. Lambert, *Language and Area Studies Review* , (sponsored by the Social Science Research Council, Monograph 17, American Academy of Political and Social Science) Philadelphia, October 1973, xix +490p. and his updated survey, *Beyond Growth: The Next Stage in Language and Area Studies*, Association of American Universities, Washington, D.C., April 1984, xiii +436p. In his 1973 study (p. 157), Lambert makes the observation that "the growth of Hebrew represents a different pattern. NDEA has had little to do with it. In fact, most modernist Middle East programs are determinedly Arabic oriented ... Nevertheless ... Hebrew enrollments have had a steady, relatively high enrollment growth of about 25% per year." Lambert thus confirms the frequent observation that although many Hebrew programs are affiliated with Middle East area studies, their progress has proceeded not because of this fact but in spite of it! This lack of interest or concern with Hebrew seems to affect even supposedly neutral researchers of Middle Eastern area languages. In Lambert's 1984 update volume, one of his collaborators, A. B. Winder, in his summary of the special needs of the "Middle East Area Studies Group" mentions Hebrew (p. 413) as one of the four major Middle Eastern languages and then proceeds to limit his discussion to the

specific problems of Arabic study. He also refers to the Yom Kippur War as "the October/Ramadan Arab-Israeli War of 1973." (p. 412).

[7]It should be noted, however, that Hebrew studies have benefitted from the assistance given by some local communities to support college programs of Judaic Studies. Also significant are endowment funds for Judaic Studies such as those raised by a variety of communities as well as the alumni of Harvard and Yale.

[8]See [1] above.

[9]This was particularly true between 1960 and 1974. See [2].

[10]"University Study," *Hebrew Abstracts*, Vol. XV, 1974, pp. 170-2.

[11]"Church-Oriented School Study," *Hebrew Abstracts* , Vol. XVI, 1975, pp. 84-9.

[12]"Comparative Study," *Hebrew Studies*, Vol. XVII, 1976, pp. 146-54.

[13]It should be noted that at the first orchard we did *not* include in our survey the limited number of very specialized apples that were permitted to ripen and mature fully before they were plucked from the trees, i.e., MA and Ph.D candidates. When our 1973 study is brought up to date, we should include a survey of graduate Hebrew programs at general universities

[14]This literary field has been ploughed thoroughly; concordances and dictionaries for Biblical literature are virtually complete and student aids have multiplied. The area of scholarly research can be delineated clearly since the literary corpus is established. Specialization and concentration in this realm is often motivated by religious convictions and affinities.

[15]"At Harvard and Yale, from the very origin Hebrew ranked with Latin and Greek" (Abraham I. Katsh, *Hebrew in American Higher Education*, N.Y.U. Bookstore, N.Y., 1941, pp. 18-19). Preparation for the ministry was a significant factor in the creation of American colonial universities. For other historical reasons and further documentation see two other works by Katsh, *Hebrew Language, Literature and Culture in American Institutions of Higher Learning*, Payne Educational Sociology Foundation, Monograph No. 2, 1950, N.Y.. and his very comprehensive updated study, *The Biblical Heritage in American Democracy*, N.Y. Ktav, 1977.

In addition to programs for divinity students, Biblical Hebrew was offered routinely in departments of classics along with Greek and Latin. In programs of classics, however, Hebrew was abandoned gradually during the nineteenth century. By the beginning of this century it was available largely as an exotic or esoteric offering in some graduate programs (such as Semitic Studies, Oriental Studies or Ancient Near Eastern Studies) at a few established universities. At some of the older universities it was offered also as a professional prerequisite in their graduate divinity schools.

[16]The student of Rabbinic literature cannot be isolated from Biblical study. Many Biblical scholars, however, do not concern themselves with Rabbinic studies, particularly if they concentrate in a very limited area. For this and other historical reasons, Rabbinic Hebrew literature is usually unexplored and, at times, disregarded at most church-oriented institutions.

[17]For students who seek this concentration of text study there are two possible avenues. Those who seek the traditional approach (or an understanding of that

methodology) turn to the traditional *yeshivot*. Those who desire a more analytical pursuit of Rabbinic literature turn to the well established graduate rabbinical seminaries. The net result is that there is very little demand for such text studies on the typical university campus.

[18]For an historic explanation of this phenomenon, see Arnold J. Band, "Jewish Studies in American Liberal Arts Colleges and Universities" in *American Jewish Year Book,* 1966 (Volume 67), edited by Morris Fine and Milton Himmelfarb, N.Y. & Philadelphia, Jewish Publication Society of America, pp. 3-30 which summarized concisely but effectively the status of 92 programs in 1965 and pointed up the growth of Jewish studies, largely from 1945-1965. We need a similar study for the very significant progress since 1965.

The "newer" Hebrew programs, despite their emphasis on Modern Hebrew, were often housed in the department of "Classics" or in a program of "Religious Studies" or "Ancient Near East." In the course of time, as the newer Hebrew programs grew, many of them established their individual identity or became affiliated with a developing program of Judaic studies.

[19]At times the rivalry between two parallel listings of Hebrew offerings reflected an unfortunate academic struggle for control of the turf. Enlightened participants in both corners now realize that time is clearly on the side of the newer programs. At most institutions, academic acrimony has diminished or has been resolved.

Students of academe are familiar with the customary resistance toward the introduction of related or similar programs as "new offerings." Departmentalization and specialization within the various colleges of a university campus often lead to the development of a variety of similar courses in a specific discipline, such as chemistry, that may be scattered all around the campus).

[20]In this respect they pursue a pattern similar to the typical program in the church-oriented schools and seminaries. (It should be pointed out, however, that my 1973 study revealed that even a decade ago there were a few seminaries that experimented with the study of *modern* Hebrew as an introduction to the Hebrew Bible.)

[21]This is the usual pattern for the newer programs at American colleges and universities. It should be pointed out, however, that at some campuses the introductory grounding, before one can depart from the standard Hebrew track, is three years rather than two. On the other hand, there are some instances where recommended students may pursue Biblical Hebrew after only one year of modern Hebrew. There are a few campuses, however, where the newer programs do offer their students the option of beginning the study of Biblical Hebrew without any introduction to modern Hebrew.

[22]Many of these options are frequently restricted for purely technical reasons. Since most students prefer modern Hebrew, the number of offerings in Biblical Hebrew is necessarily limited. For similar reasons, there are virtually no opportunities to pursue a specialization in Rabbinic Hebrew except at a few major university programs. (See [17] above).

[23]See discussion on "Miscellaneous Research Needs."

[24]Wilga Rivers, Coordinator of Language Instruction at Harvard, has devoted more than a decade to this challenge. She has continually reiterated the urgent need for a wide ranging course in methods of teaching language, literature and

culture for graduate students in foreign languages. She declares that such preparation still "remains a dream" at this time. In a survey of graduate students which she conducted she reports that the vast majority felt that courses in the methodology of language and literature teaching should be regular features of the graduate study program. The most frequent request was for "a thorough training in the teaching of language, literature and culture and for experience in innovative teaching and course development with sympathetic supervisory help in the early teaching years." (Wilga Rivers, "Preparing College and University Instructors for a Lifetime of Teaching: A Luxury or a Necessity?", *ADFL Bulletin*, Vol. 15, No. 2, Nov. 1983, p. 25).

In his 1984 Chairman's Report to the National Endowment for the Humanities, William J. Bennett faults the graduate schools for turning out "narrow research specialists" instead of good teachers. (See also [3] above).

[25]In most instances there are some local resources for scholarly research. Regional libraries are usually accessible or cooperative. Even the books and documents found only in national or international collections are available to the isolated researcher. There are, at times, personality conflicts, local academic traditions or unique circumstances that may block the progress of the young instructor but in most instances, if he or she is not indolent and pursues scholarly research with patience and diligence, there should be no barrier to scholarly growth and professional progress. A journey of a thousand miles always begins with the first step.

[26]In my judgment there are no "born" teachers but there are some "natural" teachers who feel more at home in the classroom than most of us. No beginning teacher is "fully" prepared. For most of us skillful teaching, if it is achieved, is the result of "on the job training," a painstaking process of trial and error.

[27]See discussion on "A Bibliography of Methodological Materials."

[28]As they make progress in the scholarly research, they find personal satisfaction in the approbation of colleagues. Skill in the classroom is rarely recognized or appreciated, even by fellow professors on the campus since they are not present to witness it. But the visible listing of publications stemming from scholarly research does elicit appreciation and approval. Finally there is the reward that flows in the form of professional progress and the ultimate recognition of one's peers everywhere.

[29]A significant example is Abraham I. Katsh, President Emeritus of Dropsie University and Distinguished Professor Emeritus, N.Y.U. He is the author of 20 books and more than 300 learned articles in a broad concentration which includes jurisprudence, Islamic studies as well as Hebraica. At N.Y.U., where he spent most of his academic career, he founded the Jewish Cultural Foundation, established the N.Y.U Library of Judaica and Hebraica and chaired the Department of Hebrew Studies. He rendered the scholarly community a special service in that he was able to visit the Soviet Union, Poland and Hungary five times during a score of years and succeeded in microfilming many rare manuscripts and valuable documents relating to Hebraica and Judaica. This was the only successful cultural effort behind the Iron Curtain of a Western scholar pursuing research in Hebraica.

Paralleling his very successful academic tenure, Professor Katsh pursued a very vigorous career devoted to the promotion of Hebrew. He was fired by a zeal to foster the study of Hebrew at *all* levels. He was the pioneer of the "newer" programs, having established the first offering of modern Hebrew in 1933. He also instituted the first teachers' college program for the training of high school and college teachers of Hebrew. In 1940 and in 1949 he made national surveys of Hebrew instruction at American institutions of higher learning. He wrote a series of historical studies detailing the significant role of Hebrew learning at American universities since the creation of Harvard. In 1950 he founded NAPH, the National Association of Professors of Hebrew, which brought together, for the first time, the professors teaching at Christian seminaries as well as teachers at secular colleges and universities (see also [57] below). He brought into being and edited for a score of years, *Hebrew Abstracts*, the precursor of the current journal, *Hebrew Studies*. He established the first university program involved in a continuing educational program in Israel, a project he directed for 18 years. The American-N.Y.U. Student and Professorial Workshop in Israel was carried on in conjunction with the U.S. Department of State and Office of Education. It was unique in that it attracted to Israel professors as well as students, from universities, colleges and seminaries distributed all over America. The record reveals clearly that Abraham Katsh represents an excellent example of scholarly distinction combined with an active career promoting the growth of Hebrew learning. See [15] above for a listing of some of his writings devoted to an *historical analysis* of Hebrew study and influence in America.

[30]Jacob Neusner is a significant example of an established scholar who supplements achievement and recognition within his own specialization to devote much of his time and energy to a *critical analysis* of the nature of Jewish studies on the American campus. Neusner, University Professor, Professor of Religious Studies and Ungerleider Distinguished Scholar of Judaic Studies at Brown University is the recognized author of more than two score volumes dealing with the significant formative period of late ancient Judaism. His *History of the Jews in Babylonia* uses the technique of the history of religions in dealing with the locale and era that produced the Babylonian Talmud. He brings a similarly novel approach to the Pharisees in his *Rabbinic Traditions about the Pharisees*. His emphasis on comparative study and form criticism has given scholars a new insight into rabbinic sources. In his endeavor to open up the world of the Talmud, he has completed a new translation of the mishnah and is editing and contributing toward the ambitious efforts to translate the Jerusalem Talmud (University of Chicago Press) and the Babylonian Talmud (Scholars Press). Neusner developed a remarkable program of Judaic Studies at Brown University and has written prolifically. He established the fine Brown University series of scholarly studies in Judaica which now numbers more than 60 volumes. Despite his forthright expressions of opinion, frequently iconoclastic, Neusner has received the recognition of his colleagues. He was still in his thirties when he was elected to the presidency of the American Academy of Religion and has rendered the academic world significant service serving on the National Endowment for the Humanities.

In addition to his contributions to the world of scholarship Neusner has concerned himself with the writing of non-technical, even popular, literature that would make rabbinic sources accessible to interested laymen. Neusner has had a special continuing concern with the state of Jewish studies at American universities. Of particular interest to us, here, is his ongoing interest in the improvement of methodology in all aspects of Judaic studies, including Hebrew language and literature. This very volume of essays is a further outgrowth of his concern with methodology.

Many of his most significant essays relating to the state of Judaic studies have been compiled and republished in *The Academic Study of Judaism: Essays and Reflections* (First Series, New York, Ktav, 1975, second edition, Chico, Scholars Press, 1982; Second Series, N.Y., Ktav, 1977, and Third Series, N.Y., Ktav, 1980). The papers and essays are published as originally issued. He frequently invites respondents to react to his theses and then appends his own comments. In these essays Neusner characteristically critiques other scholars and the whole field of Judaic Studies but he applies the same critical analysis, also, to his own previously held positions.

Judaism in the American Humanities: Essays and Reflections, (Chico, Scholars Press, Brown Judaic Studies #28, 1981) developed out of his experience on the board of the National Endowment for the Humanities. In the Second series of this collection (Chico, Scholars Press, Brown Judaic Studies #42, 1983), he deals largely with the new humanities on the campus, the academic study of religion and the exploration of countries, regions and peoples (such as Russia, Eastern Europe, Latin America and Judaic Studies) which previously were largely ignored. It also includes a number of his items not published previously. Neusner feels very strongly that academe is far too polite. Much more can be accomplished by speaking out. He quotes his teacher, Harry A. Wolfson of Harvard, who said, "If you want to be *accepted* ... do not disagree with anyone ... (and) be a great scholar in the *eyes of the world*. On the other hand, if you want to be *a great scholar do things your own way*. People will get used to you." (Those of us who knew Wolfson will recognize this statement). Neusner is willing to wait till people get used to him. In this volume he republishes an item that appeared in the *Brown Daily Herald* on Friday, May 1, 1981 ("To the Senior Class: Go Unlearn the Lies We Taught You - A Commencement Speech You'll Never Hear"). Portraying rare intellectual honesty, Neusner persists in republishing this piece while admitting candidly that by Monday morning the *Brown Daily Herald* had received more than 100 vigorous responses, *all* of them angry.

His *New Humanities and Academic Discipline: The Case of Jewish Studies* (U. of Wisconsin Press, 1984) collects a group of papers dealing with graduate Jewish study. In addition to the presentations by Neusner, this volume includes three essays by Robert Alter, U.C. Berkeley, Arnold J. Band, U.C.L.A. and Baruch A. Levine, N.Y.U., all dealing with graduate training in Hebrew language and literature.

In his *Judaic Studies in Universities: Toward the Second Quarter-Century* (Durham, Duke University, 1984) Neusner makes the observation that Judaic Studies has arrived as a recognized field of concentration, particularly on those campuses where professors are no longer the lone representatives of their discipline. He tackles the sad state of curriculum and makes the observation that except for the first year of Hebrew language instruction there is no theory of "how a course should take shape" or find its place among other courses. Since Judaic Studies is far too fragmented, it is necessary for professors to work more closely with colleagues on their individual campuses even as they must diversify in their specializations. They must interpret, particularly for their students, how the different specializations and varied interpretations of historic and literary phenomena are all related. See also Neusner's *Major Trends in Formative Judaism* (Second Series: Texts, Contents and Contexts), Chico, Scholars Press, 1984 (Brown Judaic Studies #61), particularly Chapter 7 "American Study of Judaism," pp. 123-49.

[31]Menahem Mansoor, Joseph L. Baron Professor and Chairman Emeritus of the Department of Hebrew and Semitics, University of Wisconsin at Madison is the author of more than a dozen works and countless scholarly articles. His pioneering study of the Dead Sea Scrolls, particularly *The Thanksgiving Hymns*, is recognized universally. His diplomatic experience in the British Foreign Service and his thorough understanding of Arab civilization led to the writing of his "Political and Diplomatic History of the Arab World, 1900-1967," a monumental study embracing 16 volumes of texts and notes.

He came to Madison to introduce a one person program which he built up into one of the outstanding departments of Hebrew and Semitic Studies in our country. He also edited the annual journal, *Hebrew Studies*, for a number of years. Not content with personal scholarly research and academic administrative skill, Menahem Mansoor recognized the need to compose, out of his experience and research, half a dozen textbooks in Biblical, Modern, Conversational and Journalistic Hebrew. In addition, he has written a number of textbooks devoted to literary and conversational Arabic.

His pioneering vision extended beyond the classroom. He saw the need to reach potential students who are not on the campus. He proceeded to create the only program of correspondence courses relating to Hebrew and Arabic now comprising more than two dozen offerings. He has supplemented the usual pattern of such courses with an additional library of sound recordings (see [46] below). His love for Hebrew learning and the desire to promote it led him to expand the scope of the Wisconsin Society for Jewish Learning. He created the Wisconsin Archaeology Society and the summertime "Lands of the Bible Seminars" which he conducted for 19 years. He developed major public exhibitions on "Archaeology and the Bible" which attracted 100,000 visitors. Another exhibit on the "Origins of the Alphabet" is currently on tour. Menahem Mansoor combines diplomatic experience, sound scholarship in Semitics with a determination to pioneer in the specific realm of Hebrew methodology.

[32]It is also possible that a candidate for a master's or Ph.D degree at a graduate library school, a college of education or a theological seminary may undertake this effort. In that case, either an academic institution or one of the professional associations could be the official sponsor of such a project.

[33]In doing research for a paper on "The Methodology of Hebrew; A Preliminary Statement" presented at the NAPH methodology mini-conference on December 20, 1982, I explored the written articles and references in past files of *Hebrew Abstracts*, *Hebrew Studies* and *Iggeret* and was pleasantly surprised to find considerable methodological resource material there.

[34]Supplementing the occasional presentation of papers on methodology, NAPH has recently made provision for mini-workshops on methodology within its regular annual program.

[35]See Appendix A and Appendix B for a listing of the papers presented at the first two institutes. What may have been the first effort to sponsor a conference limited to methodology was attempted in 1975. It was scheduled for February 1976 at U. Mass., Amherst. An impressive list of speakers was lined up and brochures mailed to the NAPH membership. The conference was cancelled for reasons unclear, presumably lack of funds or lack of response. That situation has now, fortunately, changed.

[36]See [33].

[37]See [34].

[38]See [35].

[39]If such an in depth study of motivation cannot be launched in the reasonable future, it is urgent that we have at least a quantitative statistical study of the reasons offered by students for their involvement in Hebrew studies. Even a moderate selective study limited to a dozen well sampled campuses would be significant.

As suggested above in our discussion of "An Updated Survey of Hebrew Instruction," a more elementary appraisal of student motivations can also be incorporated in the new survey updating the findings of 1973. Such conclusions would be helpful until we have the findings of a comprehensive or a moderately selective study.

[40]See Ziona Kopelvich-Hanash, Michigan, "Using Teaching Aids in Language Instruction" (See Appendix A). In any consideration of innovative aids, we should keep in mind the specialized techniques and mnemonics that teachers have developed for teaching a particular aspect of a language. See, for instance, Miri Kubovy, Yale, "Teaching the Hebrew Verbs" (See Appendix A).

[41]If available, the presentation by James Yzenbaard, Director, University of Michigan Language Laboratory on "The Use of the Language Laboratory" may be a helpful introduction. (See Appendix A).

Operating on the principle that foreign language labs are more likely to be used if they are readily accessible, additional terminals open twenty four hours a day, were established in dormitories and other campus buildings of a midwestern university. A description of this arrangement was detailed at a program sponsored by NAPH some years ago. How successful was this experiment? Has it been imitated elsewhere? If successful, has this project suffered, or been eliminated, because of urgent cutbacks?

We noted in our 1973 study that language labs, featuring modern Hebrew conversation, were being used at a few church-oriented campuses to facilitate a comprehension of Biblical Hebrew. Has this experiment persisted? Biblical tapes in Israeli Hebrew have been available for a number of years. In a 1983 announcement, Weston W. Fields, Grace Theological Seminary, Winona Lake, Indiana, reports that, during a recent sabbatical in Israel, he arranged to have a Hebrew University ulpan instructor tape all the exercises in Lambden's *Introduction to Biblical Hebrew*. The tapes, officially approved by the author and publisher, are available on four cassettes. A survey summarizing and analyzing the many uses of language labs for classical as well as modern Hebrew would be most helpful.

[42]Specialists may disagree as to how audio-visual techniques are to be classified. Should recordings of dialogue or radio broadcasts be subsumed under language labs, in its traditional pattern, or should they be used as a supplement for class conversation? Should films be categorized with conversation techniques or with drama or independently? Should television be designated with drama or have its own unique classification? I am not concerned here with establishing or justifying a neat new system of classification. My primary purpose is to point up a limited and most incomplete number of examples of possible resources and to emphasize, one again, the vital need for further experimentation and research.

A number of presentations listed in Appendix A and B are in the category of conversational techniques. See Moshe Nahir, Manitoba, "the Role of Dialogue in Language Instruction"; Nava Scharf, Cornell, "Common Errors in Hebrew of Native English Speakers"; Nili Sharon, Minnesota, "Utilizing Native Speakers to Promote Communicative Skills" and Bilha Mirkin, Wisconsin, "Oral Presentations and Student-Led Discussions." Back issues of *Iggeret* make a number of references to the direct person to person ulpan conversational technique initiated in Israel and used in the United States and elsewhere, even in the USSR.

Recordings of dialogues or live radio broadcasts can also be very helpful in supplementing direct conversation. See Edna Amir Coffin, Michigan, "Teaching Hebrew of the Media: Radio Broadcasts," listed in Appendix A. David Salczer, Ohio State, expands the thesis that it is urgent for the student to absorb the feeling of non-verbal communication. He recommends current Israeli movies as a medium to achieve this goal. See "the Teaching of Non-verbal Communication in Modern Hebrew" In *Hebrew Studies*, Volume XVII, 1976, pp. 154-160. See also Edna Coffin and Tsila Evers, Michigan, "Feature Films: Cultural Enrichment for Hebrew Classes," (see Appendix B). It would be most helpful to have a survey that would summarize and analyze *all* of the conversational and oral techniques for teaching Hebrew on the college level.

[43]Two presentations listed in Appendix B deal with the use of computers. See Hannah Sharon, Michigan, "Using Computers for Hebrew Instruction" and Jonathan Paradise, Minnesota, "the Electronic Ben Yehuda: Can the Computer Replace the Pocket Dictionary?"

Students of Biblical Hebrew have used computer science effectively, beginning with the compilation of concordances and the organization of grammatical studies. At the 1981 NAPH national session, H. Van Dyke Parunak, Michigan, made a presentation on "The Electronic Card File: Using a Computer for Grammatical Analysis of Biblical Hebrew." Those present were cautioned to remember that the computer cannot "produce instantaneous scholarship" nor is it a substitute for old fashioned study. It requires a considerable amount of desk work before one approaches the machine as well as very precise problem descriptions and instructions. Parunak made no reference to GIGO ("Garbage in, Garbage out"), the computer code phrase denoting that the computer is only a tool. Its effectiveness depends on how it is used. When this caveat is kept in mind, the computer can become a very useful aid to the scholar, eliminating the use of the traditional hand written card file.

The Council on the Study of Religion Bulletin publishes a regular section entitled "Offline: Computer Research for Religious Studies," edited by Robert A. Kraft, Pennsylvania. A recent issue (Vol. 15, No. 4, Oct. 1984) reports that an ambitious exhibit of computer-related displays would supplement the usual publishers book exhibit at the annual session of AAR-SBL at Chicago in December 1984. Housed in its own special exhibit hall, it would include multi-lingual word processers and emphasize "systems and products of special use for humanists who have special requirements such as foreign language display printing ... working with foreign characters on various computer systems including ... (DAVKA for Hebrew) ... and a new Hebrew Bible research system called MIKRAH ..." The same informative article refers to a revision of the work done by Parunak, now more accurately noted as the "ParunakWhitaker" Hebrew Consonantal text coding. Pointing up the obverse side of GIGO, Editor Kraft reports that he had conveyed incorrect information on Parunak-Whitaker in a previous column because he had apparently punched the wrong buttons and "called up the wrong file from" ... (his) "computer director." It would be most helpful to have a presentation or written record that would survey and summarize all the current uses of computer science to enhance teaching and research methodology in Biblical and modern Hebrew.

[44]Students interested in drama can be reached in a variety of ways. They can be encouraged to read Hebrew plays, intensively or extensively, for language familiarity (See Rina Donchin, Illinois, "Plays as Reading Tests for Hebrew Language Learning" in Appendix B). They can be motivated further to attempt their own acting out patterns in the classroom (See Oded Barowski, Emory, "Acting in the Classroom as a Tool for Teaching Hebrew" also in Appendix B).

[45]The television technique can be used as a unique specialization. It may have special appeal for some students because of its contemporary flavor and cinematic approach. Appendix B lists two video applications. See Judith Miller, Wisconsin, "Dramatic Production for Foreign Language Instruction (Video Applications) and Jeffrey Knisbacher, U.S. Department of Defense, "Using Videotaped Dialogues in a Basic Hebrew Course."

The late Zvi Abbo, S.U.N.Y., Albany, pioneered in the realm of television techniques when he introduced a TV beginner's course in Hebrew in the early 1970's. His interesting presentation at the 1973 national session of NAPH was summarized in *Hebrew Abstracts*, Vol. XV, 1974, pp. 123-5. Fortunately, his fine work was preserved. At the 1981 NAPH national session, Daniel Grossberg presented a follow-up paper entitled "Hebrew Learning Center-TV-and Individualized Language Instruction" which updated the progress at S.U.N.Y. since 1974. It would be helpful to have someone survey and summarize for us what is being done with television throughout North America.

[46]We are familiar with the host of aids published over the centuries, and beamed directly at students who seek to read and understand the Bible in the original Hebrew or Greek. At Madison, Wisconsin, Menaham Mansoor has made an historic contribution through his development of correspondence courses in Hebrew, Aramaic and Yiddish as well as non-linguistic cultural subjects. In recent years these have been supplemented further by recordings and videotapes. *Hebrew Studies*, Vol. XXII, 1981, pp. 152-3, has a highly laudatory review by Geoffrey Wigoder, of Jerusalem, concerning Mansoor's *Hebrew Course Audio Visual Approach* issued by the Linguaphone Institute of London. It makes use of a variety of techniques and consists of four cassette tapes (or 16 records) plus five volumes of text. It would be most desirable to have someone undertake a detailed analysis of the full series of language courses by correspondence sponsored by the Department of Hebrew and Semitic Studies at Wisconsin. Most Hebrew professors would want to know what proportion of the correspondence students enroll as absolute beginners. They would also seek to know when and under what circumstances Hebrew instructors at Wisconsin encourage their students to supplement their classroom study with correspondence courses. (See also [31] above.)

[47]Language labs and conversational approaches are no longer considered innovative. A decade ago most programs of modern Hebrew made some use of these two techniques. We can assume that resourceful professors will expand the use of the computer and that there will be further experimentation with the drama and television approach as well as other aspects of the audio-visual technique. Campuses that cannot offer a full smorgasbord of courses each year may encourage some of their students to enroll for correspondence courses available through the

University of Wisconsin. We can be sure that refinements will be made in these established patterns. We must continue to look, however, for new approaches and creative ideas.

In addition, it would be interesting to note what programs of Hebrew study are doing to enhance their offerings. How many are involving their students in an officially sponsored summer program in Israel, perhaps in the form of a Biblical archeological dig which is particularly attractive to the college generation? How many programs are encouraging their students to spend a full academic year in Israel, thereby deepening their feeling for contemporary Hebrew, as spoken in the street and expressed in the media? It would be interesting to know how many colleges are experimenting with *intensive courses* that telescope a year of Hebrew into a summer session or an academic semester or a quarter How many schools which have an intercession period between the fall and spring semester offer their students the opportunity to do "catch up" or "make up" work in Hebrew? It would be helpful to have a survey of the current pattern of innovative ideas and promotional efforts. The realities of the 1980's demand it.

[48]This comprehensive study should include critical, laudatory and defensive articles and statements by reviews and authors. It might begin by exploring the older debates dealing with such topics as the merits of the inductive and deductive approaches.

See the vigorous defense of the inductive method by William S. LaSor, Fuller theological Seminary, an approach he has used to teach Hebrew, Greek, and Japanese, *Hebrew Abstracts*, Vol. XV, 1974, ppg. 108-19). The discussion could then proceed to explore in depth some of the newer concepts that influence the textbooks that have appeared since 1970.

[49]We know, of course, that some very bright students cannot cope with the regimen of foreign language study. In some instances, it has been necessary for university administrators to release excellent students from the foreign language requirement so that they might be permitted to graduate.

[50]Gilead Morahg, Wisconsin at Madison, has given considerable attention to this challenge. See his essay in this volume. This problem is not limited to the study of Hebrew. Wilga Rivers, in her study of foreign language graduate students, reminds us that many of them refer to the "unhealthy gap" between language and literature for which they were not ready although they were well motivated to pursue language study. See her "Preparing College and University Instructors for a Lifetime of Teaching" cited above [24].

[51]See Edna Grad, Northwestern, "Development of Language Skills - Level II of Teaching Hebrew" (See Appendix A). If the transition from language to literature is to be effective, the student must be exposed, no later than the second year of study, to examples of literature taken from the Bible, mishnah, rabbinics, medieval and contemporary Israeli life. (See Yair Mazor, Wisconsin at Madison, "Integrating Biblical Texts into a Modern Hebrew Curriculum" in Appendix B). Because of the lack of an acceptable anthology suitable for the second year study, most professors improvise, experimenting with their own collections of readings reflecting their own subjective predilections. Too often these cannot approximate a scientifically measured selection of the various literary styles the student requires for third year literature comprehension. The individually chosen selections are usually duplicated and studied intensively as class texts. In some instances they are supplemented with extensive reading of established literature and contemporary newspapers. (See Rina Donchin, Illinois, "Transition to Reading Extensive Text

in Hebrew," Appendix A and Sara Rubenstein, Colorado, "Syntactic and Semantic Clues to Reading Hebrew Newspapers" in Appendix B). Much more experimentation and serious research in second year Hebrew instruction is essential!

[52]A number of items in Appendix A and B deal with this challenge. Note the listing of the lectures by Gershon Shaked, Hebrew University, "Problems in Teaching Literature as Language and Language as Literature in Universities Abroad" and "The Meaning of Secular Jewish Culture - Linguistic and Literary Issues." See also Alton L. Becker, Linguistics, Michigan, "Language and Culture" as well as Robert Didonato, Wisconsin, "Teaching Culture: A Group Work Approach."

[53]See discussion on "Two Hebrew Language Tracks," above.

[54]I stressed this theme in a key presentation on "The Methodology of Teaching Hebrew: A Preliminary Statement," before NAPH at its mini-workshop on Hebrew methodology, December 20, 1982 (cited above, [33]). Zev Garber, Los Angeles Valley College and Elmer B. Smick, Gordon-Conwell Theological Seminary were the respondents. In that paper I made a number of specific proposals for the involvement of NAPH. The respondents were most positive and the participants in the group discussion that followed emphasized the need for further organized activity. In the two years that followed I made the fostering of Hebrew methodology one of the main goals of my NAPH administration, reiterating this theme in presidential messages and other NAPH literature. The response has been positive.

[55]A pattern of academic acceptance will not be unique. Colleges of education and departments of psychology, particularly programs of educational psychology, have placed considerable emphasis on educational methodology. Professors in colleges of medicine submit their experience in teaching medicine and the experimental work done in developing new medical techniques as legitimate medical research that is accepted universally as a contribution to the literature in the field. Such research, monitored properly, is recognized even when the key collaborators are medical students or lay technical assistants hired for the specific research. Many distinguished professors of medicine have established their full academic reputation on the basis of such publications. To a more limited degree, research of this nature is done also in other professional colleges, such as engineering, mining, business, government and law.

[56]Jacob Neusner, Brown, makes the observation and cites examples of how universities are beginning to supplement the role of professional associations in sponsoring various programs relating to Judaic studies. See *Major Trends in Formative Judaism* (Second Series: *Texts, Contents and Contexts*) Scholars Press, Chico, 1984 (Brown Judaic Studies #61), p. 133, note #26.

[57]The National Association of Professors of Hebrew (NAPH) was founded in 1950 by Abraham I. Katsh, Dropsie and N.Y.U., who pioneered in the "newer programs" (See [29]). He recognized the need to establish an academic professional group that would concentrate on Hebrew. His second goal was to bring together the two categories of professors, those teaching at universities and colleges as well as the ones teaching at church-oriented institutions and professional seminaries. Its membership of 250 is divided almost evenly between the two categories. The two groups of teachers, at one time isolated geographically as well as philosophically, have formed a fine symbiotic relationship, working together to resolve mutual problems and attaining a keener understanding of their

unique orientations and challenges. NAPH meets annually in conjunction with the fall meetings of AAR-SBL. It also holds regional conferences in the spring. It publishes an annual journal, *Hebrew Studies* and the semi-annual *Iggeret*, a helpful professional information bulletin. In 1983, NAPH announced the inauguration of the Monograph Series, as yet unsubsidized. NAPH has a strong interest in Hebrew methodology. In 1983 and 1984 it sponsored comprehensive three-day conferences devoted exclusively to methodology (See Appendix A and B and [35]) and is contemplating a special information bulletin limited to the methodology of teaching.

[58]The Association for Jewish Studies (AJS) is by far the largest professional association devoted to Judaic Studies. It came into being in 1967 to meet the need for a more open organization serving the rapid expansion of Hebrew and Jewish studies. Its membership of 900 welcomes professors and graduate students. It is estimated that at least half of its membership consists of professors who devote *full-time* to teaching some aspect of Judaic Studies. It is reasonable to assume that 250 or more devote at least part of their professional activity to Hebrew language and literature. The AJS meets annually during December in Boston. It offers fine panels of scholarly presentations in a variety of areas.

Tentative program for the 16the annual conference, December 1984, lists 35 groupings of discussions of which 10 appear to be in Hebrew literature and 10 in history; 6 in the social sciences; 4 in philosophy and 5 in miscellaneous categories. There is a strong concentration on the modern period. In the history panels, 8 of 10 deal with the modern scene. In Hebrew literature, half of the presentations are related to modern and current Hebrew literature. A similar trend is apparent in the social study topics.

AJS publishes an annual scholarly volume, *The Association for Jewish Studies Review*. The *AJS Newsletter* carries some fine book reviews and excellent editorial observations. It is clear that Hebrew language and literature play a very significant role in the program of AJS. As far as I know, AJS has done very little, if anything, in the field of teaching methodology relating to institutions of higher learning. (It is interesting to note, however, that the 1984 program does carry a scheduled session devoted largely to the problem of developing teaching staffs for Jewish day schools).

[59]The American Academy of Religion (AAR) which observed its 75th anniversary in 1984 and the Society of Biblical Literature (SBL), which recently passed the century mark, are two giant umbrella organizations that meet annually in the fall. NAPH and ASOR (American Schools of Oriental Research) usually join AAR/SBL in their autumn conventions. As a result, the fall conference reflects an elaborate smorgasbord of offerings. The 1984 schedule included approximately 250 different panels of papers as well as specialized discussions and meetings. It featured also an exhibition of approximately 100 book publishers and groups of publishers. In 1984 they sponsored a special display of computer equipment to meet the needs of humanists and religionists concerned with multi-lingual research. AAR/SBL also sponsor ambitious programs of regional activity and special conferences, held in the spring.

Both AAR and SBL follow a very open approach toward research in Hebrew and Judaic Studies. Christians and Jews cooperate on many levels. AAR has a standing section on "History of Judaism." It usually runs an annual session devoted to the academic study of Judaism. SBL extends its interest beyond the Hebrew scriptures. It acknowledges officially its special affiliation with three associations, of which NAPH is one. It lists a program on the "Literary Study of Rabbinic Literature."

In 1982 it set a significant precedent when it elected Lou H. Silberman, Vanderbilt and Arizona, a specialist in Rabbinics, as its national president. In 1984 it held a specific scholarly program as well as a special reception in memory of Samuel Sandmel.

[60]The American Academy for Jewish Research (AAJR) was organized in 1920 and incorporated in 1929. It is the oldest and most prestigious professional association devoted to Jewish study. Its membership includes distinguished scholars who have achieved universal recognition for their research. It is self-limiting in its pattern of selection and has been labeled as "exclusive" and "elitist." This perception led to the creation, in 1967, of the more open professional association, AJS. Since its leadership is not concerned with the organizational trappings of a professional association, AAJR limits itself largely to the presentation of learned papers and some publications. It has never concerned itself with the techniques of teaching methodology.

[61]In my judgment, a permanent AJS section devoted to Hebrew methodology and supported by committed leadership carries the promise of a tremendous potential for the future of Hebrew teaching methodology on the American campus.

[62]NAPH is currently organizing a national committee that hopes to implement these goals. I recommend two parallel committees for NAPH and AJS because I am persuaded that this approach is more practical. In trying to sell a new idea to professors scattered all over North America, it is easier to work internally within each organization. Since national associations do not meet frequently and attract only a fraction of their constituents when they do hold sessions, the general membership must be reached through mailings, newsletters and occasional discussions at regional or national meetings. No organization can proceed with a new project or program until it has sufficiently loyal adherents to give it firm support.

Even when an issue is most laudable or non-controversial, organizational sovereignty and the slow mobility of widespread national associations may be barriers. By way of example, the national conventions of AJS and NAPH were held on identical weekends but in different communities, from 1980 through 1983, an unfortunate conflict that caused considerable frustration to members of both associations. Advance commitments made by both organizations caused a three-year delay in reconciling this regrettable conflict.

[63]It can be handled best by those who have developed that fine skill and are prepared to give it adequate time and effort. Each foundation has its own rationale and tradition in making its decisions, a formula that is rarely revealed. A familiarity with a particular foundation, the gradual development of personal contacts and the building up of a mutual confidence can be significant factors.

[64]An established entity, such as a professional association, a scholarly journal or an academic program can, however, be the *sponsor* of a new program that may receive a grant.

[65]Since foundations prefer innovative, creative and experimental programs or research projects *not being paralleled* elsewhere, they are likely to reject fledgling programs not yet established, i.e., the support of methodology conferences. Fortunately, this particular project need not suffer. The very successful Ann Arbor

and Madison methodology conferences of 1983 and 1984 were largely self-sustaining except for minimal support from the host campuses. (See [35] and Appendix A and B).

More promising areas for foundation assistance might be the in-depth study of motivation for Hebrew studies or the various probes coping with persistent student problems in the first and third years. The exploration of the efficacy of specific aids and techniques may draw "a bite" if it can be demonstrated that it may solve a serious problem or has a promising potential.

[66]A decade ago the National Endowment for the Humanities subsidized a national survey of Classics departments that had five or less professors teaching Latin and Greek. It involved an intensive two-week institute at Beloit, Wisconsin, followed by a consultative three-day review of the departmental program by visiting specialists. Most college departments of Classics became eligible for this survey and many took advantage of the opportunity. I explored the possibility of initiating a fund request for a similar institute and consultative service for Hebrew language programs. The project required extensive paperwork and a knowledge of how to deal with foundation grants which I did not possess. I was compelled to abandon this effort when I became preoccupied with other pressing responsibilities. I believe this possibility should be explored.

Part Two

SOME CLASSES IN CURRICULA

Chapter Four

Choosing Among the Strands: Teaching Old Testament Survey to Undergraduates at a Secular University

Bruce Zuckerman

Each time I start my one semester "Old Testament" [1] survey course, I focus the class' attention on the word "Bible"[2] and its derivation from the Greek. After all, this is an obvious point of departure. If one is going to study "the Bible," or at least a major part of it, one should know from whence the term comes: namely from *ta biblia*, neuter plural of *to biblion*, "book": Hence, "the books" or, more properly, "the Books" *par excellence*.[3] Indeed, the other common designation of the Bible as "the Holy Scriptures" is most appropriate, since "Scriptures" (note the plural) is a good rendering of the sense of *biblia* while "Holy" captures the nuance of specialness which makes these writings venerated above all others in the western world.

But I also begin my survey course with the derivation of "Bible" for another reason: because the term *biblia* can serve as an effective metaphor that catches the sense of biblical study as I think it should be conveyed to an undergraduate class. For *biblion* also means a strip or strand of *biblos* — the inner bark of the papyrus plant from which the first paper was made.[4] Thus, the plural *biblia* can also be taken as the aggregate of many such strips laid (as was the practice) warp and woof to form an ancient papyrus scroll. Seen in this light, *ta biblia* is revealed to be a very complex grouping of strands — no two of which are precisely the same — in a labyrinthian web as individual and multifarious as the whorls of a human fingerprint.

Utilization of this metaphor allows one to draw an appropriate analogy: for the Bible is very much like the papyrus scroll on which it often must have been written in ancient times. It too is a maze of strands of many types and kinds: so many that we can hardly hope to identify, let alone keep track of all of them. The central problem that faces any teacher of Old Testament, especially one who must teach a course that purports to "cover" the Old Testament in a one semester time span (approximately 15 weeks or so of lecture and discussion) is how to handle such a welter of material in a responsible fashion, how to choose among the strands of ancient materials and modern interpretations in order to convey to one's students a sense of the fabric that makes up this complicated weave.

There is, of course, no definitive answer or set of answers to this question. Teaching, much like acting, is an individual art; each teacher will and should approach so commanding a subject as the Old Testament in his or her own particular way. I certainly have no intention of issuing to my fellow "OT" teachers anything resembling detailed pedagogical pronouncements. Instead, I will only offer my particular midrash on the subject with the *proviso* that there is always "another interpretation" equally valid, perhaps more so. In light of this, the following discussion of teaching Old Testament will be limited to a consideration of selected broader issues of method and approach and how I perceive them.

At the outset of this discussion, we should perhaps define our terms: among the essential considerations for teaching any course are an awareness of what one's target audience needs to learn, the environment in which the learning experience is taking place and, not least of all, the precise nature of that audience. Our working assumptions will be first, that the target group needs to learn what is concomitant with the goals of a liberal arts education; second, that the educational environment is secular; and finally, that the audience is undergraduate. In teaching Old Testament, one must be self-consciously sensitive to the implications that go with each of these classifications; for they inevitably shape the manner in which one constructs the course of study.

As regards the "liberal arts"[5] classification, a teacher must recognize that there are certain responsibilities that go with teaching Old Testament as part of a liberal arts education. Of course, there was a time when a liberal arts education and knowledge of the Bible were considered essentially synonymous. That is, it was assumed that knowledge of the Bible was, along with knowledge of the classics, *the* essential foundation of the Humanities. While this is hardly true today, a teacher of Old Testament must nonetheless recognize that his or her role has not really changed that much. Granted, the OT teacher can no longer claim that one must learn the Bible because it is the source of all essential truth in the universe (a claim that might have been made from a university podium in earlier times and which remains viable in non-secular contexts). Still, he or she can maintain that knowledge of the Bible is basic; for, whether one believes its worldview or not, that worldview has largely molded the context of modern western civilization. Moreover, students enroll in a course in Old Testament today for essentially the same reason they did so in the past. As a rule, there are few undergraduates who seek out an OT survey course because they are majoring in Religion or even because they are interested in the Bible *per se*. Rather, the vast majority of one's students (whether they have thought this out or not) have elected to take Old Testament survey because they wish to grasp some sense of why western civilization has developed in the manner that it has. Consciously or unconsciously, they have recognized that it is impossible to do this without taking into account the informing influence of the Bible. Thus, the appeal of an Old Testament course to undergraduates is very much in line with the old liberal arts assumption: that one simply cannot be considered properly educated without a decent comprehension of the Bible.

Because the study of the Bible therefore remains one of the traditional bastions of a liberal arts education (at least for those who have sought out a course thereon), the teacher of Old Testament has the responsibility to cover *all* the essentials of the material. That is, he or she should begin in Genesis (or wherever else one wishes to begin) at the outset of the course, end in Daniel (or wherever else one wishes to end) some 15 weeks later and move through the main body of the Old Testament writings during the intervening weeks.

The need to move comprehensively through the material in any survey course may seem so self-evident as to not require mention. Certainly, a vast majority of OT teachers would ascribe to this viewpoint in principle. However, as is also often the case in survey courses, the practice does not necessarily hold to this ideal. There is a strong temptation for a university teacher to follow his scholarly instinct to dwell extensively upon the details of the subject matter. But this instinct, however motivated by one's honest desire to give a full presentation of the issues at hand, ultimately can result in too little material being covered too well. In the particular case of Old Testament study, the result can be a full-blown picture of Genesis and/or Exodus at the beginning of a course, while the Wisdom literature or the post-exilic writings get short shrift (or perhaps no meaningful discussion at all) at its end.

In other survey courses in the Humanities, the truncation of the coverage, while not to be condoned, can perhaps be at least tolerated. However, this is not so in an Old Testament survey course. Because the material in all its major forms and types is such a formative influence on western civilization, it should be broadly covered and not under-represented in any of its major aspects. To give less than a full presentation of the Old Testament can only serve to undermine its importance as a basic point of reference in a liberal arts education.

On the other hand, one cannot hope to cover the Old Testament in any significant depth during a 15 week period. A rigorous selectivity is absolutely essential. Indeed, I strongly feel that an OT teacher must be more-or-less ruthless in cutting down the breadth of the material in recognition of the serious time constraints imposed by a survey course. I do not even try to touch upon every Old Testament book during the course of study. Rather, I try to rely on a textbook to expose one's students to supplemental biblical texts which have not been specifically focused upon in class. Overall, one must be willing to sacrifice material that is highly important in order to give full coverage to the absolutely essential.

One might well claim that the cases I have just made above, first in favor of comprehensiveness and subsequently in favor of rigorous selectivity, are contradictory. However, while the demands of these competing interests manifest an inevitable tension, they should not be seen as necessarily at odds. An educator must try to strike an appropriate balance between them: He or she should aim to give students a full sense of the variety of biblical material while at the same time allowing them the opportunity for selective concentration, even on occasion detailed text analysis of the salient features of the Old Testament.

There is yet another important aspect of teaching Old Testament survey as part of a liberal arts education that a teacher should carefully consider: exactly *what* should be the dominant emphasis in the course? To put this another way, ten years after a student has taken one's survey of the Old Testament, what (if nothing else) should the teacher want his or her students to remember?

To judge from the titles and course descriptions of Old Testament commonly found in college bulletins, this question has often been answered in a manner that I, at least, feel is incorrect. Thus, for example, when I first began teaching the Old Testament in a university context, I inherited a course entitled "Old Testament Literature and History." Such a title is typical for OT survey and, in this respect, highlights what I think is the problem. For I strongly believe that, although a teacher should neither ignore the literate nor the historical aspects of the Bible, he or she should also not allow either one to be the dominant emphasis in an OT course.

These days, the "Bible as literature" type course has had particular prominence on the college campus, stimulated no doubt by the recent influx of literary critical studies of biblical texts in the scholarly literature. Yet even the designation, "Bible as literature," has about it a sense of "special pleading" that should alert one to consider the implications of teaching the Old Testament from this standpoint. One never hears of other courses taught in an analogous manner. For example, one can look in vain for college course offerings on "physics as mathematics" or "social science as statistics." Obviously, this does not mean that mathematics is less than essential for the study of physics or that statistics are unimportant for explaining social phenomena. Nor would I wish to argue that the Bible is not "literate" and that literary analysis of the Old Testament is a fruitless endeavor. Far from it. But to isolate this particular "literary" side of biblical study largely to the exclusion of other aspects is both misguided and wrongheaded. To put it more bluntly, to see the biblical texts solely as literary documents to be interpreted as one would a novel or a sonnet, completely misrepresents the Bible to an OT survey class.

At best, an approach of this sort is simplistic. The Bible is not "literature" or, at least, not literature in the sense we usually understand that term. Generally speaking, modern literary criticism looks at a given piece of writing as "the work of an individual who determines its final form and publishes it under copyright at a particular date."[6] More to the point, the "literary" approach to the Bible assumes one can take a given biblical text in a manner consistent with this view of literature. Thus, a biblical text is seen as a unified work presented from a consistent perspective — as though written by the hand of a single author. As Simon Parker has noted:

> The new literary criticism of the Bible treats the texts as ahistorical, as removed from all aspects of historical existence except as the object of the present critic's reading. They are simply literary objects in our world, not avenues to or messages from an ancient world.[7]

I would argue that such a literary-critical approach to the Bible is seriously in error under any circumstances. However, whether or not this modern literary approach to the Bible can be defended as a valid scholarly endeavor, I believe it is quite impossible to countenance as the dominant viewpoint in an Old Testament survey class. Certainly, one may be tempted to approach the biblical writings as though they were ahistorical. One can then "short-circuit" all of the technical problems involved with analyzing an ancient collection of texts with long text traditions (both at the oral and written stages of composition) which emerged from a culture quite distinct and remote from our own. But that is just the point. Simply by pretending that these problems are irrelevant to a "literary" understanding of the Old Testament does not make them go away. The biblical texts are historical documents — very complex historical documents indeed. Their concomitant historical-critical problems are always present and do affect interpretation in decisive ways on virtually every page of the Old Testament. More often than not, these issues rise as awesome barriers that impair interpretation — making all approaches to some extent uncertain.

A teacher of Old Testament must be sure that his or her students are not directed to find the sort of "easy" interpretations sanctioned by the literary-critical approach. The problems inherent in gaining confident insight into the Bible should be continually highlighted: especially the most basic issues of text and language. In my own Old Testament course I spend the first two sessions solely on these issues. At the outset, I want to make sure that my students understand that what constitutes the biblical canon is and has always been under dispute, that the texts of the Bible (rather than "The Text") are impossible to establish based upon the evidence of the ancient manuscripts, and that the biblical languages are inherently ambiguous due to their consonantal orthography as well as a grammar and vocabulary that are far from well understood. Only after these difficult historical problems have been brought to the forefront do I feel that my students are sufficiently sensitized to the limits of biblical interpretation and thus can proceed with appropriate caution.

The literary-critical approach, because it does not recognize the limits of what one can actually *know* about a biblical text and because it essentially throws caution to the winds, delivers the wrong message to one's class. In fact, there is a cultural chauvinism, if not arrogance, underlying the "Bible as literature" perspective — as if to say that this (and presumably all "literate" works) can be seen as though they were products of western civilization and a western mind-set. Fostering this approach in class can therefore only aid in skewing students' views of the roles of the Bible in western civilization. It ignores what I think is a fundamental principle in teaching Old Testament: that before one can properly speak of the formative influence of this book on the western world, one must see it first in the context of the Ancient Near Eastern world and its culture.

Despite the obvious weaknesses in a teaching approach which confines study to the "literary" approach to the Bible, this type of course has remained (and probably will remain) popular in many college curricula. I think there are subtle but largely unstated reasons why this is so, and they bear looking at critically. In fact, there is quite often a hidden agenda involved in teaching the "Bible as literature." Not only is this type of course easier to teach because of its ability to side-step the technical problems inherent in biblical interpretation, it is also the avenue of least resistance for a teacher who wishes to avoid confronting the religious sensibilities of his or her class. In particular, the "Bible as literature" course is very serviceable as a means of avoiding dealing seriously with students of a traditional or conservative background who take for granted a "fundamentalist" interpretation of Scripture.

This is true for essentially two reasons. First, the "literary" approach largely can be seen to fall closely in line with the basic fundamentalist assumption that biblical books are unified literary works, composed or rather inspired by a single author, namely, God. The literary-critical assumptions, as applied to the Bible, actually constitute a secularized fundamentalism which "true" fundamentalists can happily embrace. Thus they remain content; and, as a consequence, the teacher need not deal with the delicate and difficult issues that necessarily arise when the Bible and its historical/cultural background are *both* focused upon. Second, the "Bible as literature" course not only ignores the historical context of the Bible, but also completely avoids any consideration of the Bible as a religious document written for explicitly religious purposes. A typical stance of a teacher who presents the "Bible as literature" is that his or her "literary" analysis has "nothing to do" with religion, that issues inherent with a discussion of the Bible as religious record "are not relevant" to the course. With this credo stated at the outset, the teacher can remain insulated from the controversies that naturally occur when the Bible's religious perspective is fully explored. Once again, this would seem a secularized manner of teaching the Bible; but, on a more subtle level, it again offers an easy way to keep fundamentalists content (or at least at bay). For this approach really never considers the validity of the fundamentalist interpretive assumptions, or, for that matter, any others outside the literary-critical purview. Thus a "truce" can be effected between teacher and conservatively religious student. The teacher agrees to avoid seriously considering the fundamentalist interpretation because it is "not relevant," and the student agrees to pursue his viewpoint — but outside of the classroom. Since, as previously discussed, the mechanics of the literary approach are very much akin to the fundamentalist assumptions in any case, the educator can proceed to teach the Bible as a completely non-controversial subject. He or she can pretend that the mode of presentation is completely academic and has nothing to do with religion — even though a desire to avoid religious controversy has played a major role in shaping the way the course is presented.

Such a hidden agenda comes very close to being a type of masquerade; for it purports to be one thing while in fact it is quite another. The "Bible as literature" pretends to have nothing to do with religion while it is precisely the fear of religious controversy that makes this the avenue of choice in so many instances. In fact, there is very little that separates this teaching strategy from other approaches that stand in the shadow of religious sensibilities. One is reminded, for example, of the so-called "creationist" approach to teaching biology. The creationist teacher pretends to present a strictly scientific theory based solely on empirical evidence regarding the origin of life. But, as above, there is a hidden agenda to this pseudo-scientific theory of evolution. Creationism exists solely for the purpose of coordinating "science" with Genesis — even though Genesis itself is not usually mentioned explicitly in creationist theory. While the literary approach to the Bible is not as blatant as creationism in the manner it accommodates to religious sensibilities, it nonetheless shares with it a kind of tunnel vision that borders on self-censorship. In this regard, the "Bible as literature" approach runs entirely counter to a fundamental tenet of a liberal arts education: that the university is an open market place in which all aspects of a subject are to be pursued, tested and judged against the full range of evidence.

Another factor also plays a role in the fostering of the "Bible as literature" course on the college campus. Because the literary-critical assumptions give one license to shunt aside the technical aspects of biblical study, teachers without training in biblical languages or serious knowledge of Ancient Near Eastern culture feel free to teach Old Testament, usually offering the course as part of the curriculum of an English or a Literature department. The Bible, after all, is integrally tied up with literature in the western world. It is therefore only natural for literature teachers to turn to this seminal influence — much as they would turn to *Beowulf* or other early antecedents of writing in the West.

I do not want to suggest that only someone with a Ph.D. in biblical studies and/or Ancient Near Eastern languages and cultures is qualified to teach the Old Testament. In fact, there can be no doubt that scholars with a critical background in the study of literature can offer insightful perspectives on the Old Testament. But rarely do teachers, who received their professional training outside the field of Ancient Near Eastern studies, make the effort (or even feel the need) to master the technicalities of biblical studies or, lacking that, seek assistance from scholars in the field who can give them advice and guidance. Instead, they present the Old Testament as another book alongside other works on the Western Literature bookshelf. We have already noted the inherent chauvinism that sanctions such an approach; but beyond this, there are, in my view, serious academic questions involved in the fostering of courses in a university environment taught by personnel who really are not expert in a given field. Of course, it would also be an error to draw the lines between fields too strictly — an overly rigorous academic territoriality can only inhibit academic freedom and stifle cross-pollenization among scholarly disciplines. Nonetheless, in the specific case of the "Bible as literature" there is not generally a serious recognition that a line *does* exist — that a teacher who presents such a course has a responsibility to set the Bible within its own environment. Once again, one can only question the appropriateness of such a course as part of a liberal arts education.

Finally, there is one other aspect of the "Bible as literature" course that helps to keep it popular and which merits consideration. The fact is, the inclusion of the "literature" designation in the course description helps significantly to "sell" the course on the undergraduate marketplace. For a number of reasons, students are attracted to a course that purports to present the literary aspects of biblical study. The more conservatively religious student, as already noted, will see in this designation a signal that his own belief system will not come under scrutiny or challenge. A non-religious student, on the other hand, will see in the "literature" label an indication that the class will be concentrating on "Bible stories" rather than more intimidating technical biblical material (like laws or genealogies) or the drier tenets of theology. A biblical literature course of this sort is thus generally seen as being both fun and safe; it usually also has a reputation of being easy — in any case, easier than a "regular" Bible course.

Teachers of Old Testament are fully aware of the salability of the "literature" label; they also are often under subtle pressure from their colleagues or university administrators to fill as many seats in their class as possible. Religion departments, after all, generally do not live by their majors; they are service departments that are expected to attract a broad clientele of elective students. There is thus a temptation to work the word "literature" into the title of an Old Testament course because it will deliver a better body count. There is even the possibility that teachers will simply use the "literature" label without any serious intention of discussing the "Bible as literature" at all. The designation simply functions as attractive advertising, and much like advertising, tends to mislead.

One might argue that there is nothing wrong in offering students a course they can more easily relate to which will attract them to biblical study when a course perceived to be more intimidating will not. However, the "sugar-coating" of a course of study (or advertising to this effect) is not an appropriate goal for an Old Testament survey offering — nor should it be tacitly encouraged or condoned in a university setting. Granted, it is a teacher's job to impart knowledge in a manner that is sufficiently entertaining as to be effective; still, the primary stress must be kept on education, not on entertainment or, for that matter, marketability.

This excursus on the problems of the "Bible as literature" approach to Old Testament survey might seem to lead to an obvious conclusion: that the only appropriate way to teach the Old Testament is as a record of history. This is, in fact, a common approach utilized by scholars who concentrate in Ancient Near Eastern and/or biblical studies. Yet the "Bible as history" also needs to be examined critically in terms of its appropriateness as an integral part of a liberal arts education.

The historical-critical approach to the Old Testament basically seeks specific, factual information about the times and cultures in which the biblical texts evolved, the individuals and groups that were instrumental in their composition and the parties and forces that shaped the manner in which the texts were edited and preserved. To put this more succinctly (although somewhat tautologically), the historian seeks truth in the Old Testament in what it reveals about the objective reality of Ancient Near Eastern history. Since the historian inevitably must look at the Old Testament writings as far from objective in presentation, he or she therefore focuses upon extricating the history embedded within the biblical text. Naturally, at the same time the historian also endeavors to classify what is historically unreliable and formulates criteria by which to distinguish fact from tradition.

Because the hard evidence required for historical analysis of the Old Testament is so limited, the historical-critical approach to the Bible has developed a number of means by which to reclaim or, if need be, reconstruct the factual record. On the practical side, the historian has taken full advantage of the accumulating evidence about the Ancient Near East that archaeologists have uncovered. Also, the discovery and collation of ancient biblical manuscripts and related written works from libraries and other repositories worldwide have again offered the historian significant insights into the biblical tradition and how it was formulated and passed on. On the theoretical side, the historical-critical approach has developed powerful analytical tools by which to gain insight into the Old Testament based on internal evidence alone, among them, source and form criticism being, of course, the most prominent and broadly accepted.

Overall, there can be no question that the various disciplines within the historical-critical purview have proven successful in delineating the record of history in the Old Testament. In fact, the historical-critical approach has accomplished so much and the prospects for continued advances look so bright that it is only natural that the historian of the Bible and/or the Ancient Near East should wish to showcase the success of the methodologies in the classroom. The "Bible as history" type course is a frequent result.

Obviously, I do not wish to suggest that biblical history should be ignored; my remarks above in connection with the literary-critical approach to the Old Testament have already made this quite clear. What concerns me is a course of study in which the history in the Bible becomes an end unto itself rather than a means towards Old Testament analysis. The problem here is that the historical-critical approach actually tends to look past the Bible towards its antecedents and to make those antecedents the object of minute study. If, as I suggested at the outset of this discussion, the Old Testament is a complicated weave of many strands, then the general intent of the "Bible as history" is to disentangle (to the extent that this is possible) each and every strand and appraise each respectively in its own right. The historical-critical approach to the Old Testament thus tends to be a process of fragmentization more concerned with the component parts of the Bible than with what resulted when the parts came together.

Granted, this is not entirely the case, especially in light of the recent interest in canon criticism or criticism of the Bible as Scriptures. Still, the focus predominantly remains on the delineation of subtle clues within the biblical text which show the historical process acting upon the Old Testament. Such a focus is quite appropriate in graduate level course work or even in the context of an advanced Old Testament offering for undergraduates. But this is the wrong emphasis in an Old Testament survey course. For if the course of study becomes too deeply embroiled in the nuances of historical-critical study — for example, too caught up in distinguishing the subtle differences between one editorially distinct fragment and another or too embroiled in considering the pros-and-cons of competing historical chronologies or too preoccupied with the complicated picture of settlement and resettlement that the archaeological record indicates — then the larger picture will become submerged in detail and thus less well depicted. Certainly, there is something laudable in a course of study that uses the Bible as a means to open a window on an ancient world; every Old Testament survey class should do this to some extent. But if an Old Testament survey *only* ends up directing students' attention backwards, then I think the course has failed in large part to fulfill its function as part of a liberal arts education. Rather, the ultimate goal should be to look forward from the biblical times to our own. The historical perspective on the Bible must be kept subservient to this aim in an Old Testament survey course.

One has to query whether there is not as much of an hidden agenda involved in teaching the "Bible as history" as there is in the "Bible as literature" approach. There is a strong desire among scholars involved in Ancient Near Eastern studies to disengage, one might even say emancipate, the study of that time and culture from the Bible and especially to bring the discipline out from under the overarching shadow of biblical religion. This may best be seen as an effort to secularize the field of study, indeed, to defend it as a legitimate academic endeavor, alongside similar secular approaches to the study of history. The field of Ancient Near Eastern history is thus affirmed to be intrinsically important, not merely important because of the light it throws upon the Bible and its theology.

The discussion that has arisen recently regarding the appropriateness of the designation "Biblical Archaeology" is illustrative of this tendency. Some archaeologists and historians feel compelled to eschew this label since it clearly implies that their excavations and concomitant analyses of Ancient Near Eastern sites are only important because they teach us more about the "Holy Land." Likewise, in my own educational experience, I can recall a teacher of Mesopotamian History and Akkadian Languages who would severely reprimand any student that dared to draw a biblical parallel to the culture and literature of the Eastern Semitic world during his class. In cases like these, scholars are by no means denying the relevance of their work to an understanding of the Bible; rather, they are simply "defending their turf" lest it be taken over and perhaps even drastically distorted by interpreters whose sole interest is to exploit the biblical perspective on the Ancient Near Eastern world.

One can only be sympathetic to this desire to defend the integrity of Ancient Near Eastern history as a field academically important in its own right. Certainly it is appropriate to question a designation like "Biblical Archaeology" within a specifically academic context [8]— after all, one is not excavating the Bible but rather the civilizations of the Ancient Near Eastern world. However, in one's zeal to preserve the academic integrity of the field, one should take care not to distort the way the Bible itself should be taught in a liberal arts survey course.

In fact, consciously or unconsciously, an historian may tend to feel that *any* Old Testament survey course inherently depicts a slanted view of the Ancient Near East. After all, from a contemporary standpoint, the Israelite and Jewish civilizations were only of minor importance. An historian may thus feel that to portray this world from a biblical standpoint is essentially to portray it "inside-out" — rather like looking through the wrong end of a telescope. This feeling can be significantly exacerbated when, as is sometimes the case, an historian is compelled to teach the Old Testament more-or-less against his or her will. Obviously, there are far fewer academic positions in Ancient Near Eastern History and/or Archaeology than there are in biblical studies; and, in today's constricted academic job market, a scholar takes what he or she can get. The result can therefore be a situation where an historian is teaching the Bible instead of what he or she would prefer to teach: Ancient Near Eastern History. Given such a set of circumstances, an historian's sense of the unfairness of the biblical perspective may shade into a genuine resentment of the Old Testament worldview. Couple this with the chauvinism for the field of Ancient Near Eastern studies already mentioned above, and the result can be a "Bible as history" course that tends to depict the Old Testament as but one faint voice amidst a cacophony of voices — many of which well anticipated salient biblical ideas and concepts.

Of course, this is a legitimate way to view the Old Testament. Indeed, if one were teaching a survey course in Ancient Near Eastern History, it would be quite correct to portray the civilization that produced the Bible as essentially a socio-political backwater. It would also be appropriate to consider the Old Testament mainly in terms of the contribution it makes to Ancient Near Eastern history and further to examine in detail the complex of critical theories and comparative evidence by which one may determine the dimensions of this contribution. But in an Old Testament survey course, this approach is as wrongheaded as was the "Bible as literature" approach discussed above. Once again, the guiding principle should be the role of Old Testament survey as part of a liberal arts education. Regardless of how unimportant the Bible was in its contemporary surroundings, it is vitally important in terms of its influence on western civilization. It is this influence that must be underlined if an Old Testament survey course is to fulfill its proper function within a liberal arts curriculum. To the extent that the hidden agenda in teaching "Bible as history" turns students away from a full-scale encounter with the Bible as a primary shaper of western consciousness, it is a wrong approach.

But if neither the "Bible as literature" nor the "Bible as history" properly portrays the Old Testament in a survey course, then precisely how should it be portrayed? One answers this question by posing another one: Precisely in what manner does the Bible in general and the Old Testament in particular penetrate and mold western civilization? The answer, of course, is obvious: it does so as a *religious* influence. Thus, the emphasis in an Old Testament survey course should be first and foremost on the Bible as a religious document. Obviously, the historical and literary aspects of the Bible must play an important role in any Old Testament survey course; but they must be kept in their place: they must primarily be used to lay a foundation for the presentation of the major ideas and concepts that are at the core of biblical religion.

Let us consider several examples to illustrate the point: One should not bring in comparative evidence of the Ancient Near Eastern flood stories of Gilgamesh or Atra-hasis simply to set the Bible's Noah story in a broader cultural setting. It is far more important to use this comparative material to show how the biblical writers/editors both assimilated an ancient narrative tradition from the wider culture and simultaneously reacted against it. Thus, if in Mesopotamia the flood hero is portrayed as stoic, responsible and completely moral while the gods, in contrast, are shown to be childish and frivolous, without any sense of morals at all, then in the Bible just the opposite will be so: God in the biblical flood story will be shown to be completely responsible and moral in action — it is mankind, whose make-up is wicked from youth, who acts immorally and thus rightly brings upon his race a drastic punishment. Indeed, it is only God's mercy and love that saves him from being utterly destroyed. In teaching about the Flood, one must clearly mark the contrasts between the Mesopotamian and biblical perspectives, not because they are intrinsically interesting, but rather because this allows significant insight into the biblical view of God and mankind and their relation to one another. Thus, the excursus on the Flood serves its correct purpose in Old Testament survey: to clarify concepts at the foundation of biblical religion.

To take another case, one does not present the theory of the Deuteronomic Redaction of the Former Prophets merely to place the editing of this material within a proper historical-critical framework. Instead, one analyzes the nature of Deuteronomy because this is the decisive theological viewpoint in the Old Testament. Its presentation of God's action in history, its justification of God's punishment of His chosen people as a direct consequence of covenental violations demonstrate why one properly calls the account from Joshua through Kings prophecy rather than history.

Another example: One does not present the so-called "Court History," the story of David as king until his death and the succession of Solomon, solely as a great literary masterpiece, indeed, the consummate prose work in the Old Testament. The portrait of David presented by the Court Historian can stand alongside the greatest tragic depictions in Shakespeare (indeed, probably played a role in shaping Shakespeare's flawed heroes); and certainly one should spend time showing a class how the greatest of biblical prose writers used his spare but elegant narrative art to depict the great king, his children, his court and his enemies. However, ultimately one must draw back from mere literary analysis to consider how important this portrait of David is to the concept of kingship in the Old Testament. For David is one of the Bible's greatest paradoxes: the most promising hope as king, the most terrible disappointment as human being. Indeed, he functions as the very embodiment of what makes kingship in the Bible an institution with so tragic a dimension. For the establishment of kingship is seen in the Old Testament as both a great evil and a great good: a great evil because it is a pagan office in which a man takes on the role of God; a great good because it intensifies the relationship of God to his people by focusing it through the intermediary of a single man and office, and no less because it points towards God's promise of rescue from despair through the agency of a king-to-come. All these conflicting ideas are wrapped up in the figure of David as he is shown to us in the Court History. He is not simply a literary figure but a religious focal point in a climatic position in the Former Prophets, and so he must be presented in an Old Testament survey class.

Finally, let us consider the Book of Job. Job has many editorial layers — the Prologue/Epilogue, the Poem, the Hymn to Wisdom (chapter 28) and the Elihu speeches, to name the most widely accepted.[9] Also, the end of the dialogue between Job and his three friends has been textually disturbed (or censored) and thus has become somewhat mixed-up and garbled. Moreover, the language of the Poem itself bristles with grammatical problems that inhibit interpretation of many individual passages. One cannot, I think, ignore these problems and complexities in Job and then pretend that it is a unified literary work to be interpreted and taught accordingly. Job is a document with a complicated history, and one's class must be made aware of this history if they are to understand Job properly.

Job is also a masterful work of literature. The Prologue/ Epilogue is a finely crafted but simply developed retelling of an old story, a superb example of the folktale genre. The Poem, in contrast, is a highly sophisticated and complicated work that draws upon literary forms (e.g., the dialogue form one finds attested in Mesopotamian Wisdom contexts) and literary antecedents (e.g., the rich Canaanite mythology which we now know from Ugarit) to produce the most clearly "literary" work in the Bible. This aspect of the work must also be conveyed to a class that would properly understand the Book of Job.

But neither the historical-critical nor the literary aspects of Job should be allowed to take over when one presents Job (in the one or two lectures available) in an Old Testament survey course. Rather, it is its function as a specifically religious inquiry into the nature of God that must be concentrated on. The Book of Job, in all its layers, centers on this basic issue; and depending on how one sees Job resolving it (if the issue is in fact resolved), so one understands its writers' grasp of the human condition. One must recall that Job is not in the Bible because it is a great literary masterpiece, nor is it there because it is an important historical artifact. Job became a part of the biblical canon because it has something important to say about God and Man; the questions it raises are *religious* questions and thus it is as a religious document that it should be explored in Old Testament survey.

Obviously, each teacher of Old Testament will take his or her own particular line on how to present the Noah story, the Deuteronomic Redaction, the Court History and Job; and I certainly do not wish to imply that the way I discuss these sections of the Old Testament (or other sections) is the only serious way in which to do so before an undergraduate audience. But I do believe that the priorities reflected in my examples are correct. However far afield one goes into the comparative evidence, the critical theories, the grammatical problems, the archaeological record or the art of literature in order to interpret the Bible, one must begin with religious ideas and end with them: they must always be the point of reference if one's survey course is to achieve its ends as part of a liberal arts education.

But if it is the religious perspective that a teacher must emphasize, another question then must be raised: How does one properly present the Bible as a religious document in Old Testament survey? Regarding this issue, I once had the parent of one of my students query me: Why should not Jews teach the Old Testament from a Jewish perspective, Christians teach New Testament from a Christian perspective, and, for that matter, Buddhists teach Buddhism from a Buddhist perspective, etc.? I could only reply that a university's stance is and must remain *academic* and that, at least ideally, the academic perspective is dispassionate. To the extent that a teacher would allow his or her podium to become a position of advocacy, religious or otherwise, to that extent the teacher has exceeded his or her mandate. For a university is not a church, a synagogue or even a divinity school but rather a secular institution whose educational aims must also be secular. Thus, although a teacher should focus the class' attention on biblical religion, he or she should not do so *from* a religious standpoint. The only responsible position for a teacher to take, in presenting Old Testament survey, is an uncompromisingly *secular* position.

However, it is not easy to present a secular view of biblical religion to a class of undergraduates. In particular, it is difficult to guide one's students to perceive that there are definitive, if subtle, distinctions between the religious concepts in the Old Testament, the teacher's secular presentation of same, the teacher's personal religious commitment (or lack thereof) *vis à vis* the Bible and especially the individual student's own religious stance regarding the truth of the biblical message. For most students these distinctions tend to blur together; and, however dispassionate the teacher's stance in teaching about religion in the Bible, the typical student will nonetheless react passionately, not academically, to what he or she encounters in the course of study. In particular, two common reactions are to be expected. First, when the student sees the teacher presenting biblical religion from a secular instead of a religious position (as would one's minister or rabbi), he or she assumes that the teacher must not be personally religious. Second, the student will interpret the teacher's secular presentation, not as religiously neutral, but in terms of the student's own religious commitment. If the student is not particularly religious, he or she will assume that the teacher is "just like me," someone who does not take "this religious mumbo-jumbo" seriously. On the other hand, if the student has a strong religious commitment, he or she will assume that the teacher wishes to challenge if not attack that commitment and therefore is someone not to be trusted.

A teacher of Old Testament survey should go to considerable lengths to combat problems of this sort that are the product of teaching the Bible and biblical religion from a secular viewpoint. In my own experience, I have found several strategies to be effective. First of all, I believe the teacher should not reveal the nature of his or her religious commitment to an undergraduate class; at least, I have found that my position as a dispassionate educator is easier to maintain when my students have no certain grounds by which to judge my own religious convictions. Such personal information is simply too prejudicial. For no matter what you say about your religious belief, your students will incline towards the conclusion that what you are teaching must fall in line with that belief system. That is, they will conclude that you are only highlighting a given line of interpretation of biblical religion because you are a Jew or a Catholic or an atheist, etc. Such a circumstance can only hinder one's ability to present the Bible in a proper fashion.

Of course, eventually (usually sooner than later), someone will ask the teacher in class "what do you believe, anyway?" When this happens, the teacher should make an emphatic point of refusing to answer and then proceed to give a full-scale justification for that refusal. I have often used what I call the "Dan Rather" (it used to be "Walter Cronkite") defense at such a juncture. That is, I will query the class as to why the newscaster does not make clear to the public his political persuasion? The answer, of course, is that, if he did so, everyone would then inevitably tend to look at his presentation of the news as either Democratic, Republican or whatever. More to the point, the newscaster refrains from revealing his own politics because he wishes to underscore his intention to give a depiction of the day's events that is independent of politics — neither Republican nor Democratic, only fair-minded. Thus, in making no statement about his position on the political spectrum, Dan Rather is making a strong statement about his commitment to the aims of journalism — to bring before the public a non-prejudiced and honest interpretation of the news. One then proceeds to note that an exactly analogous situation applies to the position of a teacher of Old Testament to his or her class and are thus appropriate grounds for keeping the teacher's religion out of the classroom. Laying out a position of this nature can be most beneficial. Not only does it preserve one's neutrality as a teacher of religious ideas in the Bible, but it also makes a prominent issue of that neutrality. One's students come to recognize that the teacher is trying to avoid any hint of religious advocacy and instead desires to keep the discussion on a strictly academic and secular level.

But a teacher cannot simply stake out a position of academic neutrality and assume that his or her students are sophisticated enough to grasp the full implications of such a stance. Beyond this, one should also take pains to articulate carefully what the secular role of a teacher should be, especially in contradistinction to the theological advocacy role of a person holding a religious office. To put this in more philosophical terms, the teacher of Old Testament survey must try to make sure that his or her students understand the difference between knowledge and faith as applied to biblical interpretation.

I often develop this issue with my OT class by noting the different manner in which Old Testament should be taught in the context of a university and a divinity school. A university and a divinity school teacher begin on common ground by discussing and analyzing the evidence and theories that characterize the current state of academic knowledge *vis à vis* the Bible. But a divinity school teacher can and should go further. He or she is speaking within the framework of a religious community to a student body who, by their very presence at the school, have signaled their willingness to accept a given theological viewpoint. Thus, the teacher can rightly proceed to note that beyond what, academically speaking, one can know or speculate about a given aspect of the Bible, his or her religious community further believes in a particular doctrinal position based upon faith.

A teacher of Old Testament in a university setting does not operate under the same theological umbrella. Certainly, the teacher has the responsibility to present the full academic context of biblical study and, in doing so, to consider the specific tenets upon which religious doctrines, biblical or otherwise, are built. However, he or she has no right to take the further step that the divinity teacher must take. Indeed, I believe it would be unethical for a teacher in a secular context to endorse a doctrinal position of any sort or to make any value judgment regarding a given student's faith commitment, even in terms of how it relates to the Bible.

Using this or a similar line of classroom discussion as a springboard, a teacher of Old Testament should further emphasize that, while academic knowledge and religious faith are not necessarily at odds with one another, they are quite different in the scope of biblical interpretation that they respectively allow. The academic viewpoint is circumscribed, tied to the empirical evidence available. To the extent it theorizes, going beyond what the evidence clearly shows, it does so in relationship to and with allegiance toward the empirical evidence. Hence, if one's theories are demonstrated to contravene the evidence (or new evidence appears which compromises one's theories), then they are restructured or abandoned accordingly.

The religious viewpoint is far more wide-ranging. It is not confined by the evidence available but rather transcends it. To the extent that what one knows confirms what one believes, well and good; but faith, virtually by definition, leads to interpretations that cannot be empirically established. Indeed, faith can lead one to take religious positions which appear — on strictly empirical grounds — dubious in light of the preponderance of the evidence.

In light of these distinctions, a teacher should therefore note that the kinds of answers pursued in a secular Old Testament survey course must be different than the answers to which one is guided through one's religious faith. In fact, in the final analysis, an academic pursuit of religious concepts in the Old Testament, when taken to its logical limit, leads inevitably to questions rather than answers. Indeed, if there is one overriding concept that I try to establish in my own Old Testament survey course, it is this: that the Bible is not an "Answer Book." That is, one will never be able to look into the Bible, rationally analyze its depictions of God and His actions towards mankind and *make complete sense* of them. Secular, academic inquiry is simply not up to that task. Only through a given faith commitment can one find the inspiration to answer the sort of rationally unanswerable questions that the Bible poses. But it is not the job of a university teacher to articulate this faith or to supply this inspiration. As I often have told my students: Everyone of you has the choice to make "a leap of faith" (or not). My role is not to tell you when or how to do so; rather, my role is to show you where you are standing before you come to a decision to jump. Only when the role of a teacher of Old Testament survey is thus defined in this or similar ways to one's class, can an educator hope that his or her academically secular presentation will be properly understood.

The discussion, above, of the secular context of an Old Testament survey course highlights what every Old Testament teacher knows, in any case: that this is a very sensitive subject matter — a subject matter that tends to affect people's lives in a more direct and personal manner than most courses in the college curriculum do. Thus we must turn, finally, to a consideration of this issue: How does a secular presentation of biblical religion impact upon undergraduates, especially undergraduates who come into class with a strong religious commitment? In my opinion, this is the aspect of teaching Old Testament that a teacher should be most concerned about. For one cannot simply assume that this impact will be ultimately beneficial instead of detrimental.

When faced with the issue of how an OT course personally affects students, a teacher may have a tendency to take an academically aloof position. It might even be argued that such an aloof position is the only one possible for a teacher to espouse if he or she wishes to maintain the academically dispassionate stance discussed above. Such a line of reasoning would lead a teacher to conclude that one must "let the chips fall where they may" during the presentation of an OT course, that one must go where the empirical evidence leads and never duck the hard religious issues and implications that will therefore arise — even if students become upset as a result.

To a large extent, this is a correct way to approach an Old Testament survey course. One must never short-change the academic ideals of a liberal arts education by compromising the pursuit and exposition of knowledge that is at its heart. But in practice this idealistic stance must be tempered by the recognition that one is teaching undergraduates — students who are not necessarily as well armed for the academic fray as the teacher is and whose developing intellects are both impressionable and fragile. One should be acutely aware that undergraduates, by-and-large, have not developed the maturity and intellectual self-confidence required for independent judgment. This potentially leaves them psychologically vulnerable, and a teacher of Old Testament should be sensitive to and sympathetic towards this vulnerability.

No type of student is more vulnerable in this respect than the one with a strong, traditional religious background and training. Such a student, generally speaking, has an extensive knowledge of the Bible, but that knowledge has been nurtured within a religious environment which reinforces a particular viewpoint of the Scriptures which is more-or-less taken as a "given." Faced suddenly with an entirely different approach, one which examines all biblical issues critically and accepts none as self-evident, the traditionally religious student may feel that he or she has gone "through the looking glass": The territory may look familiar but it all seems twisted around wrong.

Moreover, this "Looking Glass" world will almost certainly be viewed by such a student as a hostile environment, and this in turn often triggers a hostile reaction towards the teacher. Thus, it is to be expected that an OT teacher will be faced with encounters, often of a vociferous nature, with students who are bent upon advocating their conservative religious understanding of the Bible, an understanding which they perceive to be under attack.

It is just at such a juncture that the teacher of Old Testament must take special care. The temptation to react combatively to the traditional student's challenge, though often hard to resist, should nonetheless be resisted at all costs. Of course, there are good reasons why a teacher of Old Testament may tend to lose patience with students who insist upon injecting their conservative biblical interpretations into the middle of his or her survey course. The traditional student's comments can often come close to being derogatory, implicitly challenging not only the teacher's authority but even his or her competence. Moreover, the remarks can also be ill-timed and distracting, coming in the middle of lecture, for example, and thus upsetting one's momentum and throwing off a carefully plotted and timed presentation. Also, the issues raised by a conservative student are often couched in a naive, even an unthinking manner. Thus, the teacher may be irritated that he or she has had to stop everything in order to answer "another silly question."

All of these factors can join together to lead a teacher to respond in kind to a student's belligerent advocacy of a traditional religious viewpoint. Moreover, in general, it is easy to do so with considerable success. After all, the teacher has an arsenal of knowledge — especially technical knowledge of languages and cultures — with which the student can rarely compete. The teacher also has both the weight of professorial authority as well as parliamentary control of the class. Thus, a skillful teacher can use his or her considerable advantages to outmaneuver and out-debate a traditionally religious student, deftly undercutting the less sophisticated arguments — indeed, "skewering" the student before a class that, in such circumstances, inclines to side with the teacher, in any case.

One can hardly expect a traditional student, counterattacked in this manner, to react positively. More likely, he or she will respond in one of two manners: retreat or surrender. If the student retreats, he or she withdraws from further serious academic discussion and turns a deaf ear to what the teacher is saying about the Old Testament. In such an instance, the educational process essentially ceases to operate; in the most extreme cases, the student simply drops out of the class. This is bad enough, but the alternate response is far more serious. When the student is suddenly exposed to heretofore unconsidered critical interpretations of the Bible, especially under "battle-conditions," he or she can be deeply affected, perhaps even traumatized. After all, it is often the case that a student's traditional faith, while strong, is also both inflexibly brittle or untried. If the traditional interpretations that have served as the armor for this faith are perceived by the student to be in any way penetrated, then his or her faith commitment itself can also be shattered. The student is then left like Humpty Dumpty — and none may be able to put his fragmented psyche back together again.

A teacher of Old Testament survey must therefore recognize that he or she has tremendous power — and that the power is double-edged: one may educate but one may also do damage. To be sure, the teacher of any course has a similar power to affect his or her students' lives. But I believe the capability to do damage is particularly acute in a survey course on the Bible. Students, like most people, have a tendency to compartmentalize what they know. If a conservatively religious student takes a course in Physics or even Biology, he or she can usually isolate that type of knowledge from religious knowledge, guided by faith. Science and Religion can be perceived as simply not being relevant to one another. If the fallacy of such a position is suggested, the traditional student can always take the viewpoint that Physics and Biology are wrong — that their teachers, after all, do not really know and understand the truth of the biblical message.

Even other courses in religion or philosophy that challenge a traditional student's faith can be effectively parried in a similar manner. Religious and philosophical ideas are usually presented as abstract concepts open to interpretation and challenge. Thus the traditionally religious student can conclude that what Plato, Buddha, Zoroaster or even Kierkegaard has to say, though interesting, is also misguided. The theologians and philosophers can be dismissed because they either did not know or they misunderstood the text of the Bible. And it is the text of the Bible itself upon which all faith hinges in most conservative circles.

However, it is precisely the text of the Bible that is a central focus in any Old Testament survey course. Thus, when an OT teacher raises issues about basic interpretation of the Bible — chapter and verse — he or she is shaking the rock upon which much conservative religious belief has been built. The shocks to a traditional student's religious faith are not so easily cushioned in such a circumstance, and the results can sometimes be no less than devastating. Indeed, I know of cases where students have spent years recovering from the trauma of being exposed to a critical inquiry into the Bible — and most OT teachers, who know their students well, can recall similar situations.

The students who worry me most are not the ones who make their traditional viewpoints known in one's course but rather the silent conservatives, who, either out of shyness or fear of ridicule and/or retaliation, keep their religious faith under wraps. They too can be traumatized by an Old Testament survey course; but their trauma can be far more intense because it stays beneath the surface, unarticulated by the student, unknown to the teacher. Nonetheless, one must always be aware that the silent ones also are out there in the classroom. An educator must recognize that in teaching about the Bible he or she is doing more than teach: lives are being affected, sometimes seriously, and even if the teacher does not always know whose or how, he or she should care enough to be self-consciously concerned.

So, in light of these concerns, how should one handle undergraduates in an Old Testament survey course? For one thing, a teacher should not seek out confrontation. Recently, a student told me about a teacher of Bible whose lecture strategy each week was always the same: According to this student, the teacher would focus upon the lecture topic of the day (labeled by the teacher as a "cherished belief") and then challenge the class in these terms: "You believe such-and-such? You're wrong!" Such an approach has the obvious advantage of being dramatic and thus riveting to a student's attention. However, in my opinion, the price is too high. One should recall that exposure to critical knowledge of the Bible is a potent and dramatic enough experience for many in one's class. One should not indulge in confrontational overkill; for, in doing so, one may end up running rough-shod over students' sensibilities.

Secondly, one should be patient with even the most vociferous of traditional students. The teacher must not look upon such students' comments as challenges to his or her authority or as silly distractions from the issues at hand. Students are raising questions because they are seriously concerned about the answers. While the ramifications of these questions should be fully explored with nothing held back, this should be done in a sensitive manner. Students should not be made to feel foolish; if their questions are obviously naive, then an issue should not be made of this naiveté. Rather the teacher should always try to frame a response to a particular question so that the question itself appears intelligent. Beyond this, the student must never be dismissed as an inferior opponent. Instead of isolating the student in this manner, the teacher should rather take pains to reinforce the collegial teacher-to-student relationship that encourages the broadening of intellectual perspectives rather than their diminishment. Such a non-hostile and open attitude may even have the effect of drawing a response from the silent conservatives, alluded to above. Once such students feel that they will not be made to look foolish or that they will not be penalized (in terms of their grade) for taking a traditionally religious stance, they too may become engaged actively in the issues raised by Old Testament survey rather than staying on the sidelines, perhaps suffering silently.

Finally and most importantly, the teacher should respect students' religious beliefs and leave them room for their faith. Students should not be made to feel that they are intellectually inferior or ignorant simply because they hold to their own religious convictions during the course of an Old Testament survey class. Indeed, any teacher should recognize and make clear to his or her class that the academic, secular worldview has its own credo, its own dogmatic positions and its own axioms which ultimately depend as much upon faith (invoked in the guise of "common sense") as anything else. While it is certainly appropriate for an educator to act as defender of the academic faith in the classroom, he or she should not further proselytize students into believing that this is the only possible way for "right-thinking" people to look at things. It may be true that the secular worldview has the high ground within the confines of a university, but one must admit at least the possibility that there are more things on heaven and earth than are dreamed of in its philosophy. One's students certainly have the right to believe so, and a teacher should not only respect that right but also not discourage its exercise.

Of course, in teaching an Old Testament survey course, one must consider not only its effect upon students with a strong religious commitment but also its influence upon the wide range of other students who find their way into such a course. A most challenging aspect of teaching the Bible is that it tends to attract all kinds — not only undergraduates who read the Bible everyday, but also those who have never opened it even once; not only students at home in the Humanities but also those who have chosen this course as the one diversion from their study in the hard sciences. Overall, the vast majority of one's students will be those who have never looked at biblical religion seriously, and one must be just as sensitive to their concerns as to the concerns of the religiously committed student.

The fact is that the field of Old Testament study can appear most intimidating to those unfamiliar with the Bible. There is so much material to assimilate, so many different types of writing for the student to encounter, such a lot of technical issues with the inevitable technical jargon to take in, that it is normal for students to feel overwhelmed. A common reaction that many students have is that the teacher expects them to be familiar with the Bible even before they have entered the classroom. Moreover, as the teacher begins to engage in dialogue with the religious students who know their way around the biblical text, the sense that many students develop of being uninitiated outsiders can be further intensified.

In my own OT classes I have found that the best way to redress this sort of alienation is through the establishment of an easy and open procedure by which students may ask questions at any time. Questions tend to open up an Old Testament class; individuals discover that they are not the only ones who are feeling both isolated and confused. Moreover, if the teacher makes it unmistakably clear that questions are not only expected but a *necessary* aspect of the class, then the question periods and the dialogues that develop as their result can turn out to be the most educationally beneficial parts of the entire course.

Obviously, questions are always an integral part of most courses of all types; however, I believe that students' need to pose questions to the teacher is especially pronounced and therefore of crucial importance in an Old Testament course. In my own class I have noticed that there is a revealing pattern to the way questions come. Over the period of four to five lectures the class will have little to ask; and then in a subsequent lecture period, an outpouring of questions will occur, so many that not infrequently I find myself spending most of the class hour answering them. Moreover, in such a question period there is an "edge" to the way the questions are posed, as if the class is using questions as a therapeutic means by which to come to terms collectively with the larger issues inherent in the study of biblical religion. For in such a question period, however picayune the questions begin, they almost inevitably turn towards issues of a much broader nature.

In the best of such question periods, everyone becomes engaged: teacher, religiously committed student, the student without religious background and all the shades in between. Together, like Jacob wrestling with the angel, they struggle with the basic questions which the Bible poses; and, if like Jacob, they no more succeed in gaining the answers sought, perhaps they too are changed by the process. I personally feel that no OT class of mine has been worthwhile if it does not have moments of this sort. They represent the best of what an Old Testament survey can offer to undergraduates.

In the final analysis, one has to consider what is the most important thing that a teacher of Old Testament has to offer his or her undergraduates. As I mentioned before, a characteristic of the undergraduate intellect is that it has generally yet to gain the capacity for confident, independent judgment. The most important aim that an OT teacher should try to achieve is to give students the tools by which they can further formulate this capacity for independent judgment, the ability to look at the Bible intelligently and knowledgeably, but also in their own terms, independent of the teacher's viewpoints. A teacher's efforts and methods should ultimately tend towards this final end: After all, there are far too many strands in the biblical weave, and one can only pass the fabric quickly before one's students' eyes during an Old Testament survey course. At the beginning of an Old Testament course, the teacher must do all the choosing among the strands, but by its end it is the students' ability to choose for themselves that is of decisive importance.

Each time I conclude my one semester Old Testament survey course, I do so with a strong feeling of discouragement and failure. By its very nature, a survey course dramatically abridges and therefore distorts its given subject matter. Such a course ultimately never can succeed in conveying to one's students anything approaching a genuine grasp of the subtleties of a particular field. Survey courses are the blunt instruments in a college curriculum — they achieve their ends in the broadest sense, but with little fine detail and less finesse.

Teaching the Old Testament within the framework of a survey course can be a difficult enterprise, full of frustrations and small defeats. The process of communication between teacher and class is always tenuous and, by the time my OT course has reached its end, I am always acutely aware that far too many of my students have failed to grasp even the most basic of concepts that I wished to convey.

Yet teaching Old Testament survey can also prove to be more than simply a necessary evil. For even as OT survey fulfills its role for students as part of their liberal arts education, it can serve as a valuable experience for the teacher as well. Such a course compels the teacher to step back from his or her more myopic scholarly endeavors and reconsider the larger picture of biblical studies, reviewing the broader issues and asking again the essential questions. This experience of rethinking the Old Testament is, at least for me, not a repetitive exercise but rather an evolving process. As I choose among the strands of biblical ideas that I wish to present to my class, I find that each semester they are somewhat different strands that entail different approaches and fresh conclusions. By watching how students react to their encounter with biblical ideas, I find myself getting back in touch with those intangible attractions that brought me into the field of biblical studies in the first place. And, of course, there will always be more strands in the biblical web to encounter and new ways to look at them. Because this is so, teaching the Old Testament to undergraduates at a secular university will remain for me the difficult pleasure that it has always proven to be.

---

[1]There is, of course, the question of whether one should use the term "Old Testament," since it is potentially offensive to Jewish sensibilities. Certainly, if one is lecturing or teaching to an audience under specifically Jewish auspices (for example, in an adult education class at a synagogue), one should use a more diplomatic usage: the common ones being "Hebrew Bible" (a slight misnomer since a small percentage of the "Hebrew" Bible is written in Aramaic) or the traditional "Tanak" (the acronym for Torah-Nevi'im-Ketuvim=Law/Teaching, Prophets and Writings), designating the three fold division of Scripture. However, in a secular environment I believe that it is appropriate and sensible to use "Old Testament," since it is the clearest, most widely understood designation for the biblical writings outside of the Christian canon or New Testament. One simply qualifies the term as a common *secular* label that is not meant to imply any manner of theological value judgment.

Of course, it could be objected that "Old Testament" is too prejudicial a term to be used as a secular label. Still, one could also raise the same objection to the use of the terms "Bible" or "Scriptures." After all, in labeling the Judaeo-Christian Canon (or part thereof) as the Book or the Writings *par excellence,* as one implicitly does when in using these labels (see the discussion immediately following), could we not be accused of being insensitive to Moslems or Buddhists or any other religious group — each of which has their own holy scriptures and religious books *par excellence* in contradistinction to our (that is the western world's) Bible? Indeed, if we follow this argument to its logical conclusion, do we dare employ labels like "the Law" or "the Teachings" for the Torah or "the Prophets" for Nevi'im, considering that these too are chauvinistic designations which imply a religious authority for these writings which not all the world's people grant and accept?

In fact, perhaps the best byproduct of using a label like "Old Testament" as a specifically designated *secular* term, is that one can then initiate a discussion in the classroom on the pros and cons of using this or other labels that imply a certain religious prejudice. At the same time one can also use this discussion of terminology as a means of making an undergraduate class confront a basic fact of life: that the western world is a Judaeo-Christian world, and whether one is Christian, Jew, Moslem, athiest or whatever, the dimensions of modern western civlization are to a large extent defined by religious terms — whether we choose to ignore them, circumvent them or label them as secular.

[2]Although this study specifically focuses upon teaching the Old Testament, many of the issues discussed are inevitably more broad and thus relevant to

teaching "the Bible" in general or, better, texts of a biblical nature (including not only New Testament books but also those in the Apocrypha and Pseudepigrapha). It is in fact quite impossible entirely to isolate issues unique to teaching Old Testament from those relevant to teaching the Bible. In any case, this will be the working assumption in the discussion that follows, and the terms "Old Testament" and "Bible" will be used interchangeably throughout.

[3]Cf. *A Greek-English Lexicon*, ed., H. G. Liddel, R. Scott (Oxford, Clarendon: 1968) *s.v. biblion*, p. 315; also *The Oxford English Dictionary*, vol. 1, ed., J. A. Murray *et al.* (Oxford, Clarendon: 1933; rpt., 1970) *s.v.* "Bible," p. 846.

[4]Cf. Liddel and Scott, *ibid.*, *s.v. biblion*, p. 315 and *bublos*, p. 333.

[5]*Webster's* defines "liberal arts" in the following manner: "the studies (as language, philosophy, history, literature, abstract science) in a college or university intended to provide chiefly general knowledge and to develop the general intellectual capacities (as reason and judgment) as opposed to professional or vocational skills;" cf. *Webster's Ninth New Collegiate Dictionary* (Springfield, MA: Merriam-Webster, 1983) p. 688 *s.v.* "liberal arts." This definition seems to me quite adequate to cover in the broadest sense what the aims of a liberal arts education entail. As will be seen, I believe that it is especially the aim of a liberal arts education to broaden one's general knowledge and to give one the tools to judge the progress of civiliation in the context of its history and thought.

[6]The quotation comes from an unpublished paper, "What has Literary Criticism to do with History?" read by Simon B. Parker at the annual convention of the Society of Biblical Literature, December, 1984. I am very grateful to Dr. Parker for furnishing me with a draft copy of that paper. Much of the following comment on the difficulties of reading and interpreting the Bible simply as "literature" rely heavily on the insights of Parker's paper, and my debt to him is acknowledged forthwith.

[7]*Ibid.*

[8]One must recognize, however, that Ancient Near Eastern history and especially archaeology in the Near East do not function solely within an academic environment. Cognizance must be taken of the public's interest in and support of research in these fields, and by-and-large the public is interested in what history and archaeology have to say about the Bible and "biblical times." Thus if historians and archaeologists (not to mention linguists and philologists) wish to keep the public's interest and thereby attract the funding that will keep their research and excavation efforts viable, they will have to continue to focus some of their attention towards the relevance of their fields to the Bible. Thus, labels like "Biblical Archaeology" will and should remain in a scholar's arsenal of public lecture titles.

[9]Many would also divide the poem into further discrete editorial layers, e.g., viewing the Theophany as an addition to the rest of the Poem or seeing the Behemoth/Leviathan speech as an interpolation at the end of the Theophany.

Chapter Five

Approaching the Text: The Study of Midrash

Herbert W. Basser

In this chapter we offer methods to teach Midrash to students who have no background in the subject and also to students who have some such background. Being teachers we need to reflect upon the precise task our subject demands. In the ancient curricula of the Rabbis, the terms "Scripture" and "Midrash" appear side by side. Here Scripture referred to the teaching of the pronunciation and punctuation of Holy Writ (according to received tradition) and the literal meanings of texts (according to the understanding of the Bible-School master). On the other hand, Midrash referred to the more advanced teaching of the Rabbinic understanding of the Scriptures. This understanding was hidden beneath layers of intricate associations and structures. The very first words of the great *Genesis Rabba Midrash* tell us that the Holy Torah was a work of art which a first tutor could introduce to a child but which also had veiled meanings and hidden secrets. Some said it also contained "Alexandrian" allegories. This initial passage received due attention from the commentators who used these interpretive notions in their writings. The first century historian, Josephus, also introduces his *Antiquities* with similar notions as to how Scripture was written. Some of us may also be familiar with how Jesus began his Sermon on the Mount in Matthew's Gospel by saying he was coming to fill in Scripture; not to destroy it in the least. He then contrasted the way the teachers of tradition pronounced Scripture with his alternate (antithetical) pronunciations. For instance, "Love thy *rei'acha*" could mean *love thy friend*, implying that one could hate his/her enemy. Yet, read differently (but keeping the same Hebrew letters) the verse could say "*ra'echa,*" your enemy too. The reported conclusion must be that both "friend" and "enemy" are to be loved; so *rei'acha* here must mean "your fellow human." In religious Jewish communities Midrash functioned as the uncovering of the intended message of the "divine writings." It was to be separated from the reading of Scripture only in this: the rote reading of Scripture *(miqra)* was a learned skill, not an intellectual exercise; Midrash was not only a skill and an intellectual exercise, but also the only conduit to the knowledge of God and His will.

For the professor, the question of how to teach Midrash arises with a peculiar set of problems at hand. The academic setting of the university will not permit the subject to be taught as the definitive sense of Scripture as it has been taught for millenia in the religious academy. It must be addressed as a subject in its own right. Yet the student must never lose sight of the intent of Midrash to uncover the truest senses of Scripture. The student must be taught first to see midrashic literature from the community's perspective and then to view it from an outside perspective. The student should attain some appreciation of the mystery inherent in Midrash by reflecting upon and analyzing some specimens of Midrash. This is a very difficult task. Properly it involves mastery of languages and literatures, an appreciation of the appropriate rabbinic mind-set, and an ability to solve obtuse problems.

The professor who teaches beginning survey courses in Judaism will be faced with introducing students to this very difficult subject matter. The professor will have only a few hours to excite the imaginations of the students. To grasp the nature of Midrash is important for the students of Judaism (Rabbinic) Judaism being a religious tradition developed by midrashic imaginations).

Students find their ways into the classes for a variety of reasons. Their life situations have little in common with the scholars who produced Midrash or the modern interpreters of Midrash. The only way I know of dealing with this situation is to plunge the student into translated texts. Which texts? Assuredly, some texts work better than others to introduce students to the genre of midrashic literature. The suggestions which follow are based on one professor's personal experience. The first text was selected, not because it is typical, but because it can engender discussion. I prefer to use a simple Yerushalmi text and ignore a more elaborate parallel in the *Midrash Rabba*. Why select the simpler text to start? I propose that students initially should tackle material that they can appreciate readily. This approach builds confidence in the students' own abilities. The students, unhampered by a plethora of unfamiliar material, can engage in immediate analysis. However, it is important to move quickly along to more sophisticated and normative examples of Midrash. Good teachers try to prevent those barriers which will hinder the student in grasping the rich texture of the material. The intrigue of midrashic puzzle must be transmitted to the students. The religious genius behind the flow of the texts must be allowed to provoke wonder in the imaginations of the students. The instructor who shares this excitement will have solved much of the difficulty involved in teaching the pursuit of this stimulating literature.

I. Introductory Courses

Students sign up for the Introductory Judaism course for a variety of reasons; not the least of which is convenience. Some may find that the hour, location, or subject matter seems "convenient." These students generally have unrealistic expectations, thinking that the course is probably some "Old Testament through Jewish eyes" kind of course. Although these students, for the most part, drop the course after failing an initial test (designed to discourage such types), it is not unusual to receive final papers in which students are still trying to prove that the New Testament is the proper fulfillment of the Old Testament as opposed to the non-Christian view. While this in itself is not a bad beginning point to approach Midrash (with apologies to those NT scholars who see the Gospels as Midrash and may even see one Gospel as Midrash on another Gospel), survey courses in Judaism engender a wider scope of view and the Gospel measuring stick, if left unchecked proves counterproductive. The typical survey course covers the main Jewish political and intellectual movements (perhaps phenomena is a more apt word) from Biblical times to the present.

Four weeks into this course we encounter a topic termed "Rabbinic Judaism." For me this term connotes an ideology whose adherents see and saw their world in definitive structures which are recorded in Mishnaic, Midrashic, Talmudic, Gaonic, Rishonic, and Aharonic literatures. Although the unit follows the unit on the destruction of the Second Temple, no attempt is made to convince students that the ideology of the Rabbis originated after the Destruction in 70. Indeed, the arguments that this ideology in general is as ancient as, or in some cases even more ancient than Scripture, seem to me persuasive.[1] Be that as it may, I refrain from looking at the historical problems and questions in the Introductory course and instead concentrate on an appropriate sampling of the literatures. To cover the Midrash unit we have three one-hour periods. Although students will, at this point, be familiar with selected passages from Philo and Josephus, here too, I generally refrain from speculating on historical connections between various writers. I adopt the attitude that whatever information any piece of Jewish literature produces could be known through some other tradition and that Midrash is not a unique means to derive the new but a creative way to confirm the old. Thus it is not the "what" that is exciting (although it will be new for my students) but the "how."

The teaching plan is drawn up and the game is afoot.

Lesson Plan, Day One:

I introduce the class to the notion of "the wise person," by asking a question like, "What do Joseph, the Soothsayer in Shakespeare's *Julius Caesar* and Daniel have in common? (The answer I want is "the sage solves riddles, turns the cryptic into the mundane and the curious into the obvious.")

I always plan to stress that the classic riddle is formed by the juxtaposition of items which seem to be so disparate that their mere presence on a given list seems unintelligible.[2] "What is black and white and red all over?" etc., etc. Solutions always find a common thread, and often times the common thread makes use of a pun or paranomasic play. The sage is the one who perceives the intelligible progression in the puzzle and continues it, spelling out the implications of the mysterious, baffling signs and symbols which are being interpreted. In sum, the question I ask concerning commonality between a number of names is fine for opening questions as it, too, is phrased as a riddle.

Next, I put on the board a sample of a riddle found in Rabbinic Literature. This riddle is a "solution" to a cryptic list. The list is given in the Talmud. But the "solution" also has to be explained:

> *"From Mandator to mandator*
> *From Notable to notable*
> *From Zealot to zealot*
> *From Parole to parole*
> *From the Clutch of the Hand of the Holy One, blessed*
> *be He, to the clutch of Moses' hand."*[3]

I show the students that the key to the little verse is found in the last line which identifies the scene of the verse as the *Giving of the Torah at Sinai from God to Moses.* Each line then identifies *God the Giver* and *Moses the receiver* by the same terms to show that Moses was the perfect representative for God. This is so because the same epithets apply to both God and Moses. But what was the list that spawned this verse. It was the list of the letters of the alphabet (Hebrew) which have dual forms and are always stated in a peculiarly unalphabetical order: m, n, z, p, c.[4] The names of the letters are made to yield epithets that can apply to both God and Moses: mem-mem (ma'amar-ma'-amar), nun-nun (ne'eman-ne'eman), zadi-zadi (zadik-zadik), peh-peh (peh-peh), caf-caf (caf-caf). The list in English reads: Mandator, Notable, Zealot, Parole, Clutch. Why does Hebrew have dual forms for these letters? Because they represent the twin terms which identify God and Moses as Divine and human counterparts. The Talmud notes that the children who composed this verse from the list were destined to become great Rabbinic sages.

I keep notes like the above in front of me while I teach. Sometimes I present the list first (as does the Talmud) and then the interpretive poem, and sometimes vice versa. I have found that, at times, one way is more effective and at other times, the other way is more effective. At any rate, by showing that the Hebrew letter *nun* is read as *ne'eman* (notable) or *mem* as *ma'amar* (mandator), I have begun to draw attention to the technique of paranomasia as an exegetical tool in Midrash. There will be not time for further discussion in this class. I give out copies of the following Midrashim on a prepared sheet and ask the student to work at half the questions on the sheets for the next class.

HOMEWORK SHEET - MIDRASH

A. Let the beloved come
The son of the beloved

And build the beloved
For the beloved
In the portion of the beloved
That the beloveds may be purified there (B.T. Menachot 53a).

B. Let the beloved come
And build the beloved House
For the beloved (Sifrei Deut. 352)

1. Let the beloved come — this refers to King Solomon as it is written, ... (the reference is to 2 Sam. 12:__)

   The son of the beloved — this refers to Abraham as it is written, ... (the reference is to Jer. 11:__)

   And build the beloved — this refers to the Holy Temple as it is written, ... (the reference is to Psalm 84:__)

   For the beloved — this refers to the Holy One, blessed be He, as it is written, ... (the reference is to Isaiah 5:__)

   In the portion of the beloved — this refers to Benjamin as it is written, ... (the reference is to Deut. 33:__)

   That the beloveds may be purified there — this refers to Israel, as it is written, ... (the reference is to Jer. 12:__) (B.T. Menachot 53a)

2. Then let Israel come who are called the beloveds
   The son of Father (Abraham) who is called "beloved"
   and build the Holy Temple which is called "beloved"
   In the portion of Benjamin who is called "beloved," thus is
   it written, ... (the reference is to Deut. 33:__).
   For the Holy One, blessed be He, who is called "beloved" (Sifrei Deut. 352)

3. Let the beloved come — Let Israel come who are called beloveds"
   The son of the beloved — the children of Abraham who is called "beloved"
   And build the beloved — and build the Holy Temple which is called "beloved"
   For the beloved(s) — in the portion of Benjamin who is called "beloved"
   In the portion of the beloved — for the Holy One, blessed be He.
   (Yalkut Shimoni Deut. B'racha 955 and compare Sifrei Deut. 352)

a. Match "A" with one of 1., 2., or 3., match "B" with one of 1., 2., or 3.

b. Which version do you think is the most original version?

c. Compare 2. and 3. Which text seems corrupt? What is the nature of the corruption?

d. In version "B," who do you think "beloved" refers to: Solomon or Israel?

e. What is the problem in identifying Solomon as the son of Abraham? What is the problem in identifying Israel as the builders of the Temple?

f. Do you think version "B" is the earliest or latest version of all versions given here? Argue the merits of its being the earliest version, of its being the latest version.

g. Three looks like the solution to a riddle. Reconstruct the riddle.

h. Which versions are riddles and which solutions?

i. What unstated list of words has generated this cycle of midrashim?

j. In what ways are these midrashim like the verse about the dual letters? In which ways are they different?

k. Fill in the numbers of the verses in the references by consulting a Bible. Why are these verses suitable verses? Describe the exegetical principles involved in each case.

l. Why do some versions omit the verse?

m. In what ways do these versions address Israel's past history, her future history?

n. Are these versions Midrashim or poems? What do you think the best setting for expounding these verse-like Midrashim was: synagogue, temple, school?

o. Who is the supposed speaker of these riddles and when in history would our midrashist think these words were spoken?

p. What is the effect of having God, Israel, the Temple, Abraham, etc. identified by a common, single term?

q. Which text is introduced by the phrase "six are called beloveds"?

Do a. through i. for next class and j. through q. for the following class.

In every section of Midrash that I teach, I try to point out three things: (a) the Rabbinic viewpoint that is being reinforced, (b) how this view is read out of a scripture that seems indifferent to the particular point, and (c) the literary form that identifies the teaching as Rabbinic. In the case at hand I offer the view that #2 provides the best clue to the original, Palestinian formulation which I reconstruct as follows:

Let the beloved come, the son of the beloved.
And build the beloved, in the portion of the beloved.
For the beloved.

Thus "the son of the beloved" and "in the portion of the beloved" simply modify Israel and the Temple respectively and do not function as separate units. "B" illustrates the essential teaching of the Palestinian tradition: Israel, Temple, and God function as a unit, as a single term. Even when Israel is castigated, these terms — beloved, beloved, beloved — function. The Palestinian tradition centers upon the renewal of Zion and the Temple and may not necessarily only reflect past history. On the other hand, the Babylonian tradition "A" adds a sixth line such that the builder of the Temple is now identified as Solomon. This forces the focus of the passage to refer to past history and also moves around the lines so that the "purification" line follows immediately after the "portion" line. Thus the "for the beloved" and "in the portion of the beloved" trade places in "A". In Yalkut Shimoni we find the Palestinian text as in Sifre, the explanations of the last two lines are in the Palestinian order, i.e., *Benjamin*, followed by *the Holy One*. However, the beginnings of the lines "for the beloved" and "in the portion of the beloved" are in the reversed, Babylonian Talmud position such that the two halves of each sentence do not match. Sifre texts actually read "Six are called *beloved*" as does the Babylonian tradition. Even so, Sifre lists only five *beloveds* unlike the Babylonian Talmud which lists six *beloveds*. It would appear that copyists have confused the two traditions somewhat. However, it is remotely possible that the Babylonian Talmud actually preserves the oldest of the traditions, dating back to Second Temple times and that the traditions in the Palestinian sources are later (looking to the restoration of Temple). The point is not to solve these issues but to discuss them by using the selected texts in some coherent system of explanation. This is all I distribute for this unit. I know some teachers who give their students lists of the various critical editions of Midrashim and bibliographies concerning Midrash. But I think any survey course becomes entangled in thorny detail if too much is attempted. The teacher must clearly recognize his/her goal and not let any other issues cloud the presentation. I therefore concentrate on these seventeen questions.

Lesson Plan, Day Two:

I expect some students have done work and others have not. I read the question, ask a student to respond, if the answer is what I wanted, I write it on the board, if not, I give my answer and ask who has similar answers and we discuss them for a few minutes pointing out their merits or problems. I spend no more than 5 minutes on each question and at the end of the period I have my answers on the board which represent my opinions and I let the class know this. Next, I assign the reading of the English translation of Bialik's article on "Halakhah and Aggadah" and let the class know that I will take up the remaining nine questions on the last day of this unit, the next class.[5]

The last class requires no specific plan. The class is simply a continuation of day two. If the presentation seems cursory and rushed, it is. Introductory courses are meant to introduce topics for further study, not to settle issues. By following the regimen I have outlined, more or less, I intend to prepare students to respect the study of Midrash as an academic inquiry. One should always aim for intelligent discussion on a limited topic. Examinations and papers reflecting these discussions are necessary to challenge students, to keep them actively engaged in the course, and to insure honest feedback on the effectiveness of the teaching methods utilized by the instructor.

II. The Teaching of a Course in Midrash Translation

Such a course presents unique challenges. The selection of materials is important and each teacher may decide upon some personal cluster of Midrashim which he/she senses can be shaped into keys to unravel the corpus in general. Here, I will offer my suggestions, but it must be understood that my preferences hinge upon a personal predilection for Midrashim which bear upon halachic teachings. I like such traditions because they present an added problem for the reader: the question of which halachic text is, in fact, being commented upon.

If Bialik is correct in that *Aggadah*, unrestrained by the practical considerations of *Halakhah*, may give rise to outlandish notions in shaping hope, courage and aspiration, the reverse is also true. Halakhah is a vast literature, each sentence of which interconnects with every other sentence, reaching every nook and corner of possible human behavior. It is an enterprise which has united Jews as a whole, set them apart from others, and led to schisms within Judaism itself. But the student of Halachah without Aggadah would lack social memory and religious impetus. To follow the dictates of Halachah, people need story, comprehension, art. We must feel the imperative from within, know its justice and experience its "perfect fit."

I generally begin the first week of a course in midrash in translation by doing just the thing I do in the survey course. However, in the survey course, there is no time to discuss Bailik's essay. After the initial week, in the "translation" course, I discuss Bialik's essay.[6] I then introduce the students to Mishnah Shabbat 2:6 in translation, which presents a list of three items. The relationship amongst these items is not clear and therefore calls for interpretation.

Let us look at this Mishnah in Shabbat (2:6): "Women die in childbirth for the commission of three sins: taking laxities in regard to menstrual laws, dough-offerings and candle lightings." Here we encounter an excellent example of a troublesome statement in the Mishnah. By careful questioning, the teacher will be able to show the students that the statement cannot be lightly dismissed for the simple reason that it is Mishnah (and thus "canonical"). Let us see some midrashic literature on these themes.

(Selection: Tannu Rabbanan, etc., Appendix)

After some discussion as to why the Rabbis understood "delight" to refer to having candles lit, the teacher focuses on the word *man* (*Adam*). Does this mean only man? Does it refer to any Jew (man or woman)? Can it refer to a non-Jew? After some discussion of the materials within the context they are found, one may decide that we are dealing here probably with the notion of a *man*, but that the term could possibly refer to a woman. We then turn our attention to how Lam. 3:17 implies an obligation for candle lighting.[7] Rashi explains B.T. Shab. 25b to mean that a meal is not a delight without light and to mean that Lam. 3:17 suggests that light is a delight since one can see to eat or avoid injury through falling. But we have no source showing that the obligation was given to women (the verse is phrased in the masculine form). An early midrashic poem confirms that candle lighting (dough offerings and blood laws) were meant for all, men and women. B.T. Shabbat 31b reads:

(See selection from B.T. Shabbat, Appendix)

Is there anything at all in this poem which suggests that these commandments of blood, offerings, candles apply specifically to women? The poem itself is phrased in the masculine. Let us now examine the poem in detail. What can be said about its use of repetition of sounds, which is apparent even in English translation? What is the significance of the grouping of items in Mishnah which this poem alludes to? Notice the progression of the poem which follows the progression of the Mishnah but here takes on fuller shape: (a) physical life blood, (b) covenantal election, and (c) spiritual life. Body, election and soul are tied together with the obligations outlined in the Mishnah. The Mishnah's grouping is not merely explained, it is given cosmic significance which revolves around human creation, Israel's election, and spiritual existence. Note how the unity of these obligations is stressed by the repetitive cadence of the lines, and half-lines.

The following Midrashim know that some traditions did not speak of these obligations in terms of woman solely and contain the query, "Why were these commandments given to women as implied in the Mishnah (and similar literatures)?"

(See selections from Tanhuma Noah I, Tanhuma Buber Noah 1, Appendix)

These two texts above should be compared, their differences noted and discussed. Students should be asked to compare these traditions with the text in Gen. R. 17 (end) which omits proof texts (or were they later added to the above traditions?). The teacher may wish to compare the texts with those found in Printed Tanhuma Mezora 9 and Buber Mezora 17. The quotation of the Mishnah Shabbat which is found in many of these sources may or may not be the original source for these traditions and that question should also be discussed. Gen. R. 17:13 reads:

(See selection from Gen. R. 17, Appendix)

These texts should be read and discussed thoroughly by the students and teacher. It is important in each case to see:

(a) what problems the texts answer,

(b) how the texts make their points,

(c) what problems these texts create.

The salient points for discussion here touch upon such issues as the source texts upon which these Midrashim are based (Mishnah, Toseftah, other) and the nature of the recording and the transmission of these Midrashim.

Without too much of a lapse the teacher can now introduce two versions of the Midrash found in Avot de Rabbi Nathan B, ch. 9. These texts do not supply proof texts. Is this because the versions with the proof texts were so well known or is it because these texts represent an older version which did not have proof texts? Is the rhyme and meter of the poetic versions (of which the proof texts break the rhythm) necessarily proof that these texts were originally promulgated without proof texts?

The text of Avot de R. Nathan contains Mishnah Shabbat 2:6, and presently functions as a commentary upon it much as the Tanhuma and Yerushalmi texts appeared to. Whether or not these texts are actually based upon our Mishnah or upon some related tradition, not connected with childbirth, is a moot point. David Halivni, *Mekorot Umessorot* (vol. 3, p. 94), suggests that the more original traditions of the Mishnaic teaching did not mention death in childbirth, but only death. What can be said in support or in contradiction to his thesis in regard to our Midrashim? Avot de Rabbi Nathan B, ch. 9:

(See text in Appendix)

The teacher should then present the Talmud Yerushalmi Shabbat to Mishnah 2:6. The passage bears an obvious relationship to the Midrashim we have just looked at. This Midrash seems to have been cast in rhymed form (perhaps the first line should be amended so that it ends with *haya* — was). The Toseftah is uniquely presented as a rhyme so that it ends with "*hadlakah* (lighting)" and omits the mention of "*ner* (candle)" found throughout the other legal and homiletic traditions. It thereby completes the rhyme.

(See text of Talmud Yerushalmi Shabbat, Appendix)

Now that the student has had a wide view of the texts, a number of pertinent issues can be addressed. The students may be asked to prepare a short essay discussing the philosophic thrust of the various Midrashim. The theology inherent in B.T. Shabbat seems more towards the maintenance of the world through *imatatio dei*. Through specific commandments, e.g., the list found in traditions like Mishnah Shabbat 2:6, Israel preserves, by imitation, the divine act of creation and election. The marked, balanced cadence of the tradition and its poetic phrasing make it especially apt for this message.

The other Midrashim and the Yerushalmi tradition, in the spirit of measure for measure, present the Tannaitic list of commandments given to women as a benevolent remedy for the collective sins against Adam which Eve had originally committed. The form of these Midrashim, with their balanced rhymes of "crime and atonement," is suited for the message.

Whether one likes the one tradition, or another, the artistic interpretations of the apparently incongruent list of female obligations on the Mishnah, cannot fail to make its impression. Some students may feel that these "solution" traditions were created for women and children, the poetic quality not suiting the serious tone of the study halls, but such conjectures (while worthwhile making) cannot be proven or disproven.

A central question must now be asked. Do these "solution" Midrashim explain, in reality, the rationale for Mishnah Shabbat and its related traditions, or were they promulgated after the fact to explain the seemingly incongruent list found in these traditions. Maimonides, Mishnah Torah *Yad* Sabbath Laws 5:1, tells us that the list, in the Mishnah which mentions the sins for which women die, reflects the sociological pattern that women customarily did these commandments because they were the ones who were home. It is worthwhile discussing Maimonides' view and asking on what basis he dismissed the reasons cited in the midrashim we have looked at. What would Maimonides have thought about these midrashim?

The students should be encouraged to compare the proof texts of the various sources and note their differences. For example, the Yerushalmi text uses a Biblical verse to show that Adam was the blood of the world ("And a mist went up ... ") while this very verse is used to show that he was the dough offering of the world in other versions. Do we simply have a scribally misplaced text here, or has something else happened?

Once students begin working with the texts and familiarize themselves with the variations in the sources, they will concoct theories as to why one text differs from another. The wise professor is one who will place obstacles in the path of his students as they proceed, the idea being to get them to study by refining and testing ideas, not to discourage them from offering suggestions (no matter how outlandish).

Other texts can now be looked at and prepared by students.[8] The students will now know to ask standard questions and should be allowed to expound upon pre-selected texts themselves. Thus seminars can be arranged, with a different student every week presenting a text which is then collectively discussed by the class. Since many texts will not work in translation, the teacher, whose class is reading in translation only, will need carefully selected texts where detailed knowledge of Hebrew is not basic to the comprehension of the Midrash.

Occasionally, the teacher will have to explain a word play but generally one can either select Midrashim which are not dependent upon such devices or find English editions where the plays are explained in notes. For classes which read Hebrew, it is recommended that they use a scientific edition, if available. What should students read for such a course? Such authors as Alon, Bloch, Bowker, Daube, Finkelstein, Gerhardsson, Ginzberg, Heinemann, Herford, Kadushin, Lieberman, Marmorstein, Moore, and Urbach have done ample work in the field. For those who read Hebrew, two excellent works are: *Darkei Ha'aggadah* and *Toledot Ha'aggadah.*

Such courses in Midrash are more than useful for students who wish to study theology, medieval Judaism, Church Fathers, Dead Sea Scrolls, literature, Hebrew language, comparative religion, modern Hebrew literature. It goes without saying that any student who wishes to proceed to do work in Rabbinic Judaism must be well-grounded in Midrashic texts.

III. Graduate Studies

Finally, a word should be said about students in graduate courses. Graduate students require very careful training. It is not advisable to accept students into a graduate program in Rabbinic literature unless they have demonstrated excellent language facilities and an intense working knowledge of Talmudic literature, medieval commentaries on Talmud, and halachic process. It is, in my opinion, far easier to teach such a student Hellenistic Jewish Literature than to teach Talmud to one already adept in Hellenistic Jewish literature. The process of studying a Talmudic sentence involves much more technical knowledge than reading even the most difficult passage of Philo. Once the typology of Philo's system is understood, one can read with relative ease. Talmudic literature assumes a detailed knowledge of Halakhic constructs on the part of the reader and much of it eludes interpretation even after many readings. The goal of graduate education in Midrash is to expose the student to various types of Midrash, to discuss their theologies and their worldviews.

No less important is the critical study of the text itself. Teachers have to teach the proper approach, by example, to the selection of better readings amongst variants, the use and misuse of parallels in deciphering texts, and notions of development of textual traditions. Students should be well read in the secondary literature, but they must also develop the skills and intuitions necessary to make decisions concerning the meaning of the texts they study. I think it advisable that students be asked to submit work in both Hebrew and English. Students will be more inclined to read and contribute to the Hebrew specialty journals in Midrash if they have experience with producing this type of material in its own idiom.

Finally, if there is any specific advice that can be offered it is this: classes should reflect concern with texts but also concern for people's feelings. Education at any level is not concerned with progress in a limited area but in the general intellectual development of a student. Students cannot develop properly if they bear hostility toward a subject area, a particular professor, or themselves. The cultivation of proper attitudes in the student, towards his/her own self, colleagues and teachers, and the discipline as a whole is what we mean by good education. A congenial atmosphere, a pleasant emotional climate in the classroom, and the mutual respect of achievements is necessary to promote high standards and excellence without resentment. It is amazing what students will do if they want to and what they will not do if they do not want to.

APPENDIX

Mishnah Shabbat (2:6):

Women die in childbirth for the commission of three sins: Taking laxities in regard to menstrual laws, dough-offerings and candle-lightings.

Tannu Rabbanan (the Rabbis studied as official tradition):

From whence do we know that a man (adam) is obligated to be extremely punctilious in the obligation of candle lighting? From the verse which states, "And thou shalt declare the Sabbath a delight" (Is. 58:13), which refers to the obligation of candle lighting.

(See Tanhuma Buber Mezora 17, Printed Tanhuma Noah 1 and Midrash Leqah Tob Beshallah 16:8)

B. T. Shabbat 3lb reads:

A "measure of blood" I have given you
    Concerning blood I have commanded you
The "first of all" I have declared you
    Concerning first offerings I have commanded you
The soul which I gave you was called a "candle"
    Concerning candles I have commanded you.

Printed Tanhuma Noah I:

Says the Holy one:
First Adam at the head of my creatures had breath
And received the order about the Tree of Knowledge
But the Scripture says of Eve
That the woman saw the tree ... and gave to her man to whom she did cleave (Gen. 3:6)
And since Scripture says, "Whoever spills the blood of Adam (man) so within man shall his blood be spilled" (Gen. 9:6)
Her blood is spilled as punishment in surety
And she observes the blood of menstrual purity
That it may atone, for the spilling of Adam's blood in perpetuity.

Why was the commandment of the dough offering given to them?

Since she defiled the dough offering of the world

As Rabbi Yosi ben Kezarta said just as when the dough becomes wet the woman takes her dough offering so did God act in creating first Adam, as it is said, "And a mist rose from the earth and watered ... " (Gen. 2:6)

and afterwards it states,

And the Lord God created Adam of the dust . . ."

Printed Tanhuma Noah I (continued):

Why was the commandment of candle lighting given them?

She extinguished the candle of Adam (other texts: the world) as it is written, "God's candle is Adam's soul" (Prov. 20-27). Thus shall she be obligated to observe the candle lightings.

Tanhuma Buber Noah I:

Since Adam was the head of His creation of the world and Eve deceived him bringing upon him that which was said, "for thou art dust and to dust thou shalt return"

So the Holy One said:

May there be given to her, the commandment of menstrual purity

That there may be atonement, for that blood which she spilled, in perpetuity.

And why was the commandment of dough offering given to her:

Since Adam was the dough offering of the world.

And Eve came and defiled him

So the Holy One said,

May there be given her the commandment of dough offerings that will atone for her for the dough offering of the world which she defiled.

And from whence do we know that Adam was the dough offering of the world? Thus did our Rabbis teach: Rabbi Yosi ben Kezarta said just as when the dough becomes wet the woman takes her dough offering so as soon as the Holy One wet the earth he took Adam as the dough offering from it. This is as Scripture states,

And a mist rose from the earth ... (Gen 2:6) and afterwards it states, "And the Lord God created Adam of the dust ... "

And why was the commandment of candle lighting given them?
Since Adam was the candle of the world (of the Holy One)
And Scripture states, "God's candle is Adam's soul" (Prov. 20:27)
And Eve came and extinguished him
The Holy One said,
Let the commandment of the candle be given to her
In order to atone for the candle which she extinguished.

Gen. R. 17:13 reads:

And why was the commandment of menstrual purity given to her?
Since she spilled the blood of first Adam
Therefore the commandment of menstrual purity was given to her.

And why was the commandment of the dough offering given to her?
Since she defiled first Adam who was the completion of the dough offering of the world
Therefore the commandment of dough offering was given to her.

And why was the commandment of Sabbath candle lighting given to her?
Since she extinguished the soul of first Adam
Therefore the commandment of Sabbath candles was given to her.

Avot de Rabbi Nathan B, ch 9:

For three sins women die in childbirth, because they do not observe carefully the commandment of menstrual purity or the commandment of dough offerings or the commandment of candle lighting.

Why was the commandment of menstrual purity given to women and not to man?
For Adam was the blood of the Holy One Blessed be He
Eve came and shed it
Therefore she was given the commandment of menstrual purity
In order to atone for the blood which she had spilled.

Why was the commandment of dough offering given to woman and not to man?

For Adam was the pure dough offering of the Holy One blessed be He,

And she defiled it

Therefore she was given the commandment of dough offerings

In order to atone for the dough offering she had defiled.

Why was the commandment of candle-lighting given to woman and not to man?

For Adam was the candle of the Holy One blessed be He who lit the way for all who would be born

And she extinguished it.

Therefore she was given the commandment of candlelighting

In order to atone for the candle she extinguished.

Talmud Yerushalmi Shabbat to Mishnah 2:6:

"When they are not careful about the laws of menstrual purity . . ."

First Adam, the blood of the world (he was)

As it is written, "and a mist went up from the earth. . ."

Eve, of his death, was the cause

Thus was given to woman the menstrual laws.

And about the law of the dough offering:

Adam, the pure dough offering, for the world he was

As it is written, "And the Lord God formed Adam of the dust of the earth..."
And the tradition accords with what Rabbi Yosi ben Kezarta said: "as soon as the dough becomes wet the woman takes her dough offering."

Eve of his death, was the cause

Thus was given to woman the dough offering laws.

And about the law of candle lighting:

First Adam the candle of the world he was

As it is written, "God's candle is Adam's soul."

Eve, of his death, was the cause

Thus was given to woman the candle lighting laws.

We learn: Rabbi Yosi says

Three tentacles, which death do cause

There are

And the group of three to woman given was

And these they are

Menstrual laws, dough offering laws, and lighting laws.

---

[1]See Ch. Tchernowitz, *Toledoth Hahalaka* (New York, 1934), pp. 197-223.

[2]See A. Wünsche, *Die Rätselweisheit bei den Hebräern* (Leipzig, 1883) and G. Nador, *Jüdische Rätsel aus Talmud und Midrasch* (Köln, 1967).

[3]Palestinian Talmud Megillah 1:9.

[4]See Babylonian Talmud Megillah 2b.

[5]See *Law and Legend* (Tr. J.L. Segal, New York, 1932) and *Halachah and Aggadah* (Tr. L. Simon, London, 1944). The Hebrew text can be found in *kol kitve H. N. Bialik* (Tel Aviv, 5725, reprinted from 5698 edition), p. 216. See also "Halakhah and Aggadah," published anonymously in *Contemporary Jewish Record VII,* 1944, pp. 663-67, 677-80 (copyright 1944 by Commentary); an abridged version of "H and A" is found in *Modern Jewish Thought: A Source Reader*, ed. by Nahum N. Glatzer (N.Y.: Schocken Books, 1977; pp. 55-64).

[6]The purpose of assigning this reading is to introduce students to the genre of Midrash through the writings of one of the century's ablest students of the genre. Bialik treats concerns of the artist by showing what the artistic impulse, if left unchecked by the sobering *Halakhah*, could lead to. He thus glorifies the balance of these two enterprises which largely define the Jewish worldview. Bialik's essay provides a focal point for H. Slonimsky's perceptive work, *Essays* (Cincinnati, 1967).

[7]The Hebrew of Lamentations 3:17 reads "shalom nafshi". The Rabbis took "Nafshi" in the sense of "vayinafash" as in Exodus 31:17: "On the seventh day He ceased (*shavat*) and rested (*vayinafash*)". The Rabbis understood Lamentations 3:17 to mean that there should be a peaceful atmosphere and safe surroundings for Sabbath repose. This, they claimed, implied that there had to be Sabbath lights.

[8]My purpose in presenting this paper is to offer some samples for study. I have, therefore, kept the texts together to facilitate comparisons. Having presented these texts to a number of different college audiences and Synagogue study groups, I must caution the reader that these texts require much more analysis and introduction than have been provided here. The teacher must supply that approach from his/her own experience and views. It is also advisable to have more texts available if these texts fail to sustain interest. The pace must not be allowed to slacken. Generally speaking, the approach provided here is a good skeletal one which can provide all with fun and insight no matter how many times the material is presented to various groups.

Chapter Six

Text And Context in Halevi's *"Hesiqatni Teshuqati Le'el Hai"*

"הֱצִיקַתְנִי תְשׁוּקָתִי לְאֵל חַי"

Harris Lenowitz

Though Medieval Hebrew poetry has been an essential part of the Israeli educational experience, the same cannot be said for the typical American Hebrew student. This poetry joins the flow of Hebrew — from Biblical to modern slang — in which the Israeli student is immersed and in which he swims easily *(mutatis mutandis)*. The Diaspora student of Hebrew language and literature tends to see the entirety of the language as disjointed segments. This tendency in American Hebrew students is a negative result of the heuristic necessity of defining the character of the several historical varieties of Hebrew. A recapitulation of the Israeli experience in the Diaspora environment is not really possible in the area of language and literature. Yet this poetry is inextricably bound into Jewish culture. It constitutes some of the most powerful prayers of the *siddur* and *mahzor*; essential social records are found in it, and so on. In short, the poems are a basic reference for the educated Jew; and for the scholar, *a fortiori*. Whether our students need to understand the poems in order to grasp fully the nature of the several different Judaisms that have been the audience for this literature, through the poems themselves as well as by attending to the audience responses; or to gain some illumination into the history of Jewish language and literary forms, the problems of the language of the texts may seem to him insurmountable. This is especially true as concerns a sympathetic response by the student to the text. While diverse aspects of the poems may be taught and understood, it is rarely the case that the student integrates them successfully and thereby achieves a whole relationship with the work. He cannot identify with the poem or the poet.

The problems are typically of two sorts: the language itself is not readily comprehensible but requires analysis, especially given the poets' innovating tendencies; the second: even though the major texts are published with references to important sources (Bible, Mishna, Talmud, Midrash), the annotations are limited to formulae. The student is not persuaded thereby to seek the reference, having no idea of its import; moreover, it is at least as important that the student read the context of the quotation and this is never presented in notes. These problems of reference are exacerbated for the student in his initial studies of the language and literature by his having to research the context in Hebrew, for none of the translations of the sources is ambiguous enough to enable the student to catch the turn, the surprising nuance, which the poet finds useful in the context of the poem he is writing. Only the Hebrew will serve.

In order to demonstrate the utility of some pedagogic devices in pursuit of a sympathetic understanding of poems where the function of context (and of language innovation) is so high it will be useful to demonstrate the value of the suggestion through a close reading of one poem. Excellent work is proceeding in just such close readings in Israel. The scholarship into medieval Hebrew poetry and poetics flourishes there now in a rich growth stemming from a previous period of painstaking work establishing texts. Whereas in the past the text-work has done by non-native speakers of Hebrew, this new work of interpretation is being produced by people constantly speaking Hebrew; and many of them sabras (Mirsky, Fleischer, Levin, Pagis, J. Schirmann, Yarden, *inter alia*). The close reading here will focus on a single subtext of one poem, the one produced by replacing the poem's language in its original contexts.

Before leaving for Eretz-Israel, Yehuda Halevi writes a poem in which he shares with us his feelings on leaving Spain. This theme of parting is an aspect of the genre of sea-songs (a group of which this poem introduces) occasioned by Halevi's departure for Israel. Likewise, there are many poems by many poets of the period written on the occasion of leaving one place for another (other than Eretz-Israel). Both genres play a part here, but this poem is essentially different from the first sort in not being written during the voyage (or imagining it in retrospect); and from the second, in the holiness of its destination. Even so, a count of the lines focussed on departing Spain versus those focussed on the venerable destination shows the former to equal the latter. Moreover, we have an early critical note to contend with: the Arabic inscription on the reverse of the manuscript H. Schirmann uses reads, "He said the following concerning his longings for his family and birthplace." (Schirmann, *The Hebrew Poem in Spain and Provence* (Hebrew) vol. I, p. 501 is most convenient for a good text and typical notes). The relevance of these facts to the understanding of this poem will become clearer as we proceed.

For the most part, Schirmann's notes are very convenient and written simply enough for an advanced Hebrew student. But if it may be granted that the reader of the poem in its proper milieu operated with a complete concordance of the literature mentioned at his disposal — and this is certainly the case with the prime audience of the poem, the poet — then one might be well-advised not to trust Schirmann alone but to research complete concordances of the literature mentioned. This discussion will restrict itself — and this has proven to be about enough for the student in general — to the Even-Shoshan, *Qonqordansia hadasha le-tanakh* and *Ha-milon he-hadash*. The first is sufficient for the Bible;

the historical notes and examples in the second open some other doors. The poem is short enough for us to research every word.

1. My longing for the living God has so driven me to seek the site of the thrones of my annointed princes
2. that it has not even permitted me to embrace in farewell my household, friends and brothers.
3. And I will not weep for the garden I have planted and watered and whose growths have done well,
4. nor will I recall Yehuda and Azarel, two dear blossoms, the choicest of my blooms.
5. nor Yitzhak who was like a son to me, the yield of my sun, the finest produce of my months;
6. and I will almost forget the house of prayer in whose studies were my restful joys;
7. and shall forget the pleasures of my Sabbaths, the splendor of my holidays and the glory of my Passovers,
8. and will pass my honor on to others and leave my praises to idols.
9. I have exchanged my rooms for the shade of shrubs and the security of my walls for a briar,
10. and my soul has wearied of the best of spices; I have made a thorny odor my perfume.
11. I have left off walking on my hands and head and set my path through the ocean depths,
12 so I might reach the footstool of my God, and there spill out my soul and speech,
13. and lay myself at the doorstep of His Holy Mountain and set my "openings" opposite the openings of the gates of Heaven
14. and raise my spikenard by the Jordan's waters and send my shoots into Shiloh.
15. God is my aid — How could I fear anything? with his merciful angel bearing my supplications.
16. I will sing praise to His name while I live and confess Him eternally.

Of course some research guides that will take account of relevant data and reject those irrelevant are necessary. Before discovering seven, or thirteen or forty-three hermeneutic principles, though, one principle must be established: the occurrence of a relatively rare word in the Bible with exactly the same form in our text is important (the less rare, the less precisely the same form, the less important; perhaps).

"הֱצִיקַתְנִי," our first word is highly restricted in its biblical occurrences: the verb occurs 12 times in only two *binyanim*, only four times in the *hif'il* perfect, only twice with accusative suffixes, once with the first person, singular accusative suffix: in Job 32:18. (Schirmann does not note this.) Whether this is an important datum should not be made to depend on the answer to a difficult set of questions which would attempt to explore the frequency the verb had during the period concerned; its frequency with accusative suffixes; its frequency in the genres to which the poem belongs in part; not even its frequency in Halevi's Hebrew. Most of those questions are doomed to be unanswered by the student unless the teacher cares to inform him; and in either case tend to remove the student from an active relationship with the poem to a passive role. A second principle then: the co-occurrence of the word in this text and in Job is important if the *student* finds the fact significant and useful. Halevi uses the reference for the motif of "impatience to speak the truth" which it brings with it from Job.

Rather than go through the whole poem here, word by word, all the "occurrences of whole words or phrases, of some rarity in the Bible, and one in the Mishna, which occur in the poem as well; and whose traditional contexts seem significant or useful to a reading of the poem" follow:

"לְאֵל חַי," Ps. 42:3; Given that the preposition is the commoner of the two used with the noun "תְּשׁוּקָה" and that it alternates with "לְאֵל" the following potential occurrences need also be considered: Ps. 84:3; Josh. 3:10; Hos. 2:1. These occurrences in their original contexts suggest: a longing ("thirst") for El-hai; El-hai as the object of poetry; El-hai in the midst of Israel just before crossing the Jordan into Eretz-Israel; the promised redemption of Israel, no longer "not-my-people," but as "Sons of El-hai." In this case, even though a composite understanding of the word in all these contexts enriches any reading of the poem (stressing the liveliness, vitality of the God; His possession by Israel as it were; the end of exile; the poet's function in singing these), neither the occurrence of the same precise word in Ps. 42:3, nor the powerful significance of the composite suffices for any certainty in our selection of reference. Rather the opposite. In this search we have encountered an expansion and a greater precision for what might otherwise seem an empty, decorative term in spite of having no single, exclusively significant context in the Bible.

As Bialik is reported to have said (M. Ovadyahu, *Bialik Speaks*, p. 51):

> The secret of the contemporary writer's use of the Biblical "sentence" (pasuk) or quotation is to open with the quotation but, instead of completing it, to weave it into an original sentence of his own. This redeems the quotation of its age and adapts it truly to modern creation.

> I fight against the Biblical (pasuk) wherever our writers use it to embellish an empty rhetorical phrase, wherever it gives off a musty, archaic smell ... However, I fight with all my heart in favor of the Biblical (pasuk) wherever it is used to redeem the old for the sake of the new.

The contemporary writer is that of any age, not just the modern. And it is necessary to emphasize here that the proper use of the *pasuk* may be lost not only on the poet who misuses it; and on the Diaspora Hebraist who is not sensitive to its contexts; but also on the native speaker of Hebrew who does not see the word or phrase as having a certain history.

"לְשַׁחֵר," Prv. 7:15; where the immediate context is that of a lover accosting her beloved ("I have had a sacrifice, an offering to make, and I have paid my vows today; that is why I have come out to meet you, to watch for you and find you." NEB). However, the larger context of Proverbs 7 displays the speaker as a harlot and the lad as a fool for allowing himself to be beguiled by her. If this biblical context brings meaning to the poem, it must be ambiguous: while stating his desire to seek out the place where the kings' throne stood Halevi may begin here to present the motif of his desires to remain in Spain, such as they are, as wise and those to leave for Israel as imprudent. There is some support for the view that the Proverbs text is significant to the Halevi poem: both phrases additionally include locatives as objects. Moreover, some of this ambivalence continues into the next verse.

"מְשִׁחַי" Although the phrase (כִּסְאוֹת-X) occurs several times, the occurrences, if they export any significance, are overwhelmed by the word "my annointed ones" and its appearance in Ps. 105:15 (and in I Chron. 16:22) in the context of God's mercy and protection of Israel: "Touch not my annointed servants, do my prophets no harm." While the protection was sufficient then (in the patriarchal period), it has not proven so for Halevi's Eretz-Israel and the single word with its biblical context, a well-known one, is freighted with a glorious past and a dismal present for that topos.

All the second line is a paraphrase of Gen. 31:28, the cue to which is given by the word "נְטָשְׁתְּנִי." (The biblical word is "נְטַשְׁתַּנִי," Halevi having made the necessary adjustments so that the verb might be in concord with the subject here). It may be translated here, "You have (not) permitted me." But the general meaning of the root נטש has everywhere else a suggestion of abandonment, discarding; and the ambiguity seems a fruitful one here: a punishment from which Halevi gains merit.

This general meaning is not nearly so fruitful as the plot and characters of the incident recalled from Genesis. Laban says these words, crocodile tears, to Jacob for having escaped his clutches (with a good deal of his wealth): it is Halevi's longing for Eretz-Israel which has not permitted Halevi to make the (impossible) farewells to Spain and his family and friends. Can it be that Halevi intends the comparison between himself and Laban? Probably not, since the situations of the two men are inverted (Laban staying; Halevi leaving). But there is again, as mentioned earlier, the suggestion of the two Halevi's: one desiring the sick comfort of rest and ease in Spain; the other the hard road to Eretz-Israel and atonement.

"רֵעַי וְאַחַי" inverts the formula of Ps. 122:8, where the psalmist seeks permission to pray for the peace of his brothers and friends. Those Halevi is leaving behind in this part of the verse are then primarily his companions in prayer and study, a group he turns to in the following three verses.

"פִּרְחֵי יָקָר" Schirmann notes that this phrase is modeled on פִּרְחֵי כְהוּנָּה. This phrase occurs in the Mishna (Yoma 1:7) and describes something like young or apprentice priests. The phrase has proven generative and modern Hebrew shows both פִּרְחֵי טַיִּס and פִּרְחֵי קְצִינִים with the sense "novice, apprentice aviators; officer cadets." The mishnaic context would, through Halevi's cueing of it, signal his tender love for what are probably his best students (so principally Sh. D. Luzzato) and the very high importance he placed on their function, in the Diaspora to be sure.

"וְבוּל שִׁמְשִׁי וְטוּב גֶּרֶשׁ יְרָחַי" deepens the motif of the great value Halevi places on the endeavor to fulfill whatever can be fulfilled of Jewish value outside Eretz Israel. These words are a reworking of Deuteronomy 33:14. This verse opens the promise of the good, rich land to Joseph in Jacob's filial blessing. The fruits of this promised land are specifically due, the best and first of them, to be offerings at the Temple. But Halevi's produce, his students, will not reach Eretz-Israel or the ruined Temple. On the other hand, Halevi seems to say, their service in the Diaspora can be conceived as in some way the equivalent of that they might have fulfilled in Eretz-Israel in an earlier time.

Perhaps it will be well to pause here for a moment and restate the second principle as a way of limiting this focus on biblical (or mishnaic) contexts. The next two lines extend the motif of the rich and largely satisfactory, in *almost* every way, religious life Halevi lived in Spain. There do not seem to be important or useful references to biblical language or contexts in them. While it is true that אֶשְׁכָּחָה figures importantly in a number of biblical contexts which have to do with mutual obligations, the God and people of Israel owe each other mutual dependencies; and that, in only a slightly different form it appears as a key word in the psalmist's oath (Ps. 137:5). The language around the word in the Halevi poem is turned away from the poetic towards the prosaic and from the contextual towards the direct and simple statement. The tone of slightly inflated praise which has preceded these lines has here quieted, as if the poet for the first time seriously considers his loss. For irony as concerns what he will lose has been, until these lines, at least one aspect of the ambivalent feelings the subtext (the text composed through a reading of the poem's references) has been presenting. The word כִּמְעַט likewise strikes a quiet, careful note. It too has its places in the Bible and elsewhere; but here, with this word, Halevi for the first time admits clearly that there are values in Spain he will not forget, for which he will weep. The three successive, certain, negations of lines 2, 3, and 4 give way to Halevi's sympathy and nostalgia, as it were, for the life he is leaving and its very real values. Halevi has allowed this emotion to develop in the poem and reader as if it has been slowly dawning on him as he itemizes what he will abandon. One may learn hereby that "not everything that glitters is gold." That is, that a departure from the world of tradition and context in the language may occur; that nothing is served by insisting on consistency of an absolute sort where the poetry, of its nature, requires variety.

Some things that glitter may indeed be fool's gold. While it is of interest to philologists that Halevi uses a pattern derived from Ps. 116:7 as a source for the form of his word מְנוּחַי, that context plays, in spite of the word's rareness, no part here, given the heavy freight it bears in the psalm of "returning" to resting places. The contribution a reference makes to the poem, in terms of the poem's structures of thought-and-form, must be reckoned as a *sine qua non* for the history of its morphology to be significant.

The air of firm rejection of the blandishments of Spanish life returns along with quite an extensive biblical reference in verse 8, a reworking of Isaiah 42:8. The context there is an auto-doxology wherein YHWH defines His being as omnipotent. Halevi's verse might then be paraphrased: "As ludicrous as the notion of YHWH's surrendering His eternity and omnipotence to weak and empty symbols or other gods, just so worthless has been the homage paid me; empty homage is appropriate to those, my vain and misguided rivals for the dead garland and the meaningless offering of praise." This statement of absolute rejection of that which is eternally worthless in Spain should not be taken as a rejection of Spain altogether. While the following four verses make the point that the least desert bush of Eretz-Israel is preferable to the security of oaken-barred doors in Spain; the least shade, a chamber; the most unsophisticated wild and natural odor of Eretz-Israel, the superior of Spain's fanciest perfumes; at least there is some way of comparing the objects. What cannot be compared in speaking of the Diaspora and Eretz-Israel is the Holy Presence and the impropriety of a Jew worshipping not the true God but idols, whether by choice (as the rivals of v. 8) or to a degree at least by force (as in the implication of the phrase עַל כַּף וְעַל אַף in v. 9). (Brody supports Kempf's interpretation of this phrase in this fashion, whether based on an Arabic locution or not; Schirmann is not entirely clear in his notes, but is at least somewhat of the same opinion). Halevi seeks to leave off the feckless and evil worship of patrons and princes absolutely and to go wandering to worship the proper Patron and Prince in the ruins of the Proper Court.

"הֲדוֹם רַגְלֵי אֱלֹהַי" The phrase comes from Lamentations 2:1. God is figured as sitting or standing with his head in the heavens and his feet resting in Jerusalem and spurning the comfort of that city. That abandoned ruin is precisely what Halevi seeks, there being no higher place on Earth.

"אֶשְׁפְּכָה נַפְשִׁי וְשִׂיחַי" This phrase comes to the poem from a continuation of Ps. 142:3 "אֶשְׁפֹּךְ לְפָנָיו שִׂחִי" or Ps. 102:1 "וְלִפְנֵי הי יִשְׁפֹּךְ שִׂיחוֹ," 1 S. 1:15 "וָאֶשְׁפֹּךְ אֶת נַפְשִׁי לִפְנֵי הי יִשְׁפֹּךְ שִׂיחוֹ." The line in the poem creates a cluster of emotion through a combination of the contexts: of anguished sorrow and a longing for atonement and fulfillment (Hannah's response and Ps. 142), together with the fear of a continued lack of response from God (Ps. 102).

"אֶסְתּוֹפֵף" The word (in another form) appears once in the Bible, "בָּחַרְתִּי הִסְתּוֹפֵף בְּבֵית אֱלֹהַי" (Ps. 84:11) and the idea of choosing indeed dominates this whole poem. In fact, here at least, the biblical context to the quotation is more important than the quoted word itself. Halevi *has* chosen Eretz-Israel over Spain; but there *has* been a process of weighing out and balancing of contrasting urges.

"אַקְבִּיל" The *hif'il* of this root occurs twice in the Bible and continues to be used in the later literature primarily with the meaning "to set, stand in a proper and precisely opposing position." (See Ex. 26:5; 36:12: the arrangement of the opposed fasteners of the hangings of the *mishkan*; and *Sifrei* to Numbers, 59, where the arrangement of lights and parts of the menorah is required to be such that each illumines the other; and the common use as "come to meet, greet"). Against Schirmann's interpretation, that the meaning here is "(to pray) in the place where my prayers will be received," the contexts argue for "... where my prayers will be properly positioned." The very handsome image of a proper place for prayer, a temple without walls or a tent is lost in Schirmann's interpretation.

"פִּתְחֵי שַׁעֲרֵי שַׁחַק" This phrase rings with Ps. 24:7, 9 "שְׂאוּ שְׁעָרִים רָאשֵׁיכֶם וְהִנָּשְׂאוּ פִּתְחֵי עוֹלָם" the precise topos envisioned for Halevi's prayer offering. "פִּתְחֵי" precedes "שַׁעֲרֵי" for, although the gates themselves are broken and gone, the openings to Heaven remain.

"פְּתָחַי" Set precisely opposite these unique openings, these pores into the upper Jerusalem, the poet will open his soul through his own prayers and will have begun his own ascent into the spiritual world.

"וְאַשְׁלִיחַ בְּשִׁלֹחַ שְׁלָחַי" Here the poet, in ecstasy, states that he will henceforth dwell in this spiritual garden. The watercourse and pool of the Holy City will become his own garden plot. Into it he will send his shoots. The "shoots" here come from the same place the spikenard did: Song of Songs 4:13 f. The Shiloh has not ceased to fill, in Heaven as on Earth; even though the mortals for whom it was meant are gone, its quiet flow runs on (Isa. 8:6). Growing there, his shoots "sent out" into the constant flow (Jer. 17:8), the poet will have *eternally* secure existence (as opposed to the temporary security offered in Spain). He will never see heat; be ever green, fearless of the drought and ceaselessly fruitful (the continuation of that same verse). Whatever may befall his mortal frame, his spirit, with God, is eternally secure. His messages, offerings (a play on "shoots" as "sendings forth"), will be carried directly and certainly by an angel and his thanks and confession thus be unending, immortal.

The text of this poem, its words and their very divinity and biblicality, appears quiet, assertive, dogmatic. The poet is certain of the worthlessness of his life in Spain and of the redemption of his life in Eretz-Israel. The subtext of the poem is far from quiet or still. This subtext is the one composed by reading of the poem *as* its references and their contexts. In this text the words are far from dead, are vital, in the pristine appearances in the language. Each, in all its original clothing, with all the context intact, leads us on the path not of quiet acceptance of the unique worth of the Holy Land but on the road of struggle to accept the loss as well as the gain. The regard in which Halevi holds his mission outside Eretz-Israel is scarcely less than that in which he holds his life in that sacred space. No matter his being in the Heavenly City he will not forget the synagogues of his own offerings in Toledo. This strong hold on material beauty and pleasure, an eternal hold, is opposed by a longing for eternal worth but not defeated by it, and differs from the drought of the spirit by the pool of Shiloh (above, Jer. 17:8; the inverted comparison).

Halevi loves what he leaves and his leaving what he loves makes a greater offering than his abiding by it; but it is made clear also in the subtext that there are in it values of eternal worth that cannot be left. Elsewhere, in the philosophy, we can find absolute statements on the incomparable merit of Eretz-Israel. In the *Kuzari* (II, 9:24) Halevi gives a scientific demonstration of the natural superiority of Eretz-Israel as well as demonstrating the historical truth of the proposition. But here we have a poem, not an argument; a reflection on his deepest feelings by an explorer and a lover of this world.

This paper was done to demonstrate a potentially useful strategy approaching the encounter between a Diaspora student of Hebrew of intermediate-to-advanced competence and an important medieval poem. The need for such a strategy derives from differences observed in the training of Israeli students and that of non-Israeli students in Hebrew literature. The Israeli's Hebrew is inclusive, from biblical Hebrew to current usage, as is not the case for a non-Israeli. The gap between these two groups is perhaps widest in their grasp of medieval Hebrew poetry. Even though this gap is all but erased in cases where the Diaspora student is the recipient of traditional training in religious texts it is yet worthwhile to use medieval Hebrew poetry as a demonstration since religious Jewish youth do not constitute more than a significant minority of Diaspora students in Hebrew language and literature. After a few presentations of the approach have been made to and with the class the case should have been made, so that the student will be persuaded to follow the strategy in his own preparations.

The initial step the student of intermediate level will take is simple: checking the entry for a single word (usually) in a bilingual dictionary. This step defines the rough area for further research and is particularly important in cases where homographic roots are involved. The second step involves an examination of the proper entry in the Even-Shoshan *Ha-milon he-hadash* in order to determine the historical period in which the word arises. Although the intermediate student will struggle with the problems of Hebrew definitions of Hebrew words the major concern here is not the meaning of the word but its contexts in traditional literature. These are indicated by the sigla dedicated to that function in that dictionary. Moreover, the student is persuaded, to a degree at least, that the use of a Hebrew-Hebrew dictionary is not always strenuous and may be quite useful. Having determined the rough historical period, and here we might say the textual origin, of the word the student turns to concordances. If the item is biblical in its first appearance, as most of those dealt with here were, the student checks the Even-Shoshan *Qonqordansia hadasha le-tanakh* to determine if the word/form he is looking into occurs and, if it does, turns to the particular site where it does occur to learn the contextual associations of the item on the assumption that they are important. (If the item is post-biblical in its first appearances use can be made of the Kossowsky concordances or perhaps the Ben-Yehuda *Thesaurus*, although, given the excellent work done by Even-Shoshan it is not unlikely that the student at this level will encounter the very item in the dictionary entry.) Having done this for all important items in the poem being examined the student needs to construct an assemblage of the "meanings-in-their-contexts" in order to detect attitudes towards his subject which the author has decided to place in the context-text rather than in one of the other texts of the poem. Finally the students will compare the context-text of the poem with other texts, particularly the surface-text, to detect tensions among them.

Ultimately, using such a simple, mechanistic method the student arrives, perhaps, at rather deep conclusions. Not only are the conclusions he reaches unavailable to him from standard notes (if they exist) or from bilingual dictionaries; the student has learned as well the cheering news that he can do interesting original research and that the tools for doing so are not so daunting as they might seem to him at first glance and are of great value.

Chapter Seven

Teaching Hebrew Literature to American Undergraduates

Gilead Morahg

In memory of my mother, who taught.

Anyone who has attempted to teach Hebrew literature to American undergraduates knows that this undertaking involves an encounter with a wide variety of problems which often hamper the success of the enterprise. An analysis of the instructional process of teaching Hebrew literature to students who are not Israelis shows that the many difficulties this process must overcome stem from a multi-faceted clash between two divergent contextual frameworks: the cultural context in which the literary text was written and the cultural context in which the literary text is being read. The numerous disparities between these cultural matrixes inhibit the learning process and their range must be significantly reduced if the targeted literary works are to be effectively taught.

Reading a literary text constitutes a communicative act between its sender (the writer) and its recipient (the reader) who are often widely separated by time and place. Like all acts of human communication, successful reading depends on a productive interaction between a basic set of presuppositions held by the sender and a corresponding set of relevant presuppositions held by the recipient. These essential presuppositions fall into three broad categories: (1) presuppositions concerning the *language* in which the message is communicated; (2) presuppositions concerning the *genre* (i.e., the novel, the newspaper item, the business letter) which gives the message its form and enables much of its meaning; (3) presuppositions concerning *previous knowledg*e that is shared by the sender and the recipient and thus constitutes the referential context within which the message becomes meaningful. If we apply these concepts to the actual conditions of teaching Hebrew literature outside of Israel, we will find a great gap between the presuppositions of the sender (the Hebrew writer) and the recipient (the American learner) in every one of the critical categories.

The most obvious disparity between writer and reader is in the area of language. This is more apparent in the introductory level of a literature program, when the students first encounter authentic Hebrew literary texts. But the disparity persists through the most advanced levels of undergraduate instruction. The linguistic presuppositions of the Hebrew writer concerning his or her intended reader are radically different from those of the American Hebrew learner who attempts to read the writer's work. The writer assumes a reader with the language competence of a fully educated native speaker of Hebrew. Few American students entering a Hebrew literature course fit this description. Their elementary and intermediate level language courses accustom them to reading the simplified and artificial language of Hebrew textbooks and of the newspapers that are written specially for beginners. But these courses can usually do little to prepare students for meeting the linguistic demands of Hebrew literary texts. Consequently, students find it very difficult to decipher the complex sentence structures of most literary works and their vocabulary falls far short of enabling them to engage the richness and intricacy of Hebrew literary style. Their attempts to comprehend even a short work of Hebrew literature prove to be an extremely difficult, time-consuming and often highly frustrating undertaking.

Presuppositions concerning genre are equally problematic. The literary writer presupposes a reader who is not only proficient in the language but is also truly literate. This intended reader is expected to have at least a basic understanding of the forms and functions of literature as well as a clear grasp of what distinguishes literary art from other forms of human discourse. It is an unfortunate aspect of the American educational system that many students may graduate from high school — and often even from college — without acquiring this necessary knowledge. Having never been taught how to read a work of literature analytically and critically, these students do not know how to approach a story, a novel or a poem. For such naive readers the encounter with a sophisticated literary text is often a bewildering experience that bears little relationship to the intended impact of the work.

The most formidable obstacle in the way of effective learning of Hebrew literature is presented by the disparity in presuppositions concerning previous knowledge that is created when the writer and the learner come from different cultural backgrounds. It is important to recognize that in addition to being a singular act of personal expression, a work of literary art is usually also a product of the immediate historical, cultural and social surroundings of its author. Explicit and implicit references to the world that lies outside the text are a major communicative device which few writers can do without. The effectiveness of almost every work of literature is largely dependent upon the familiarity of its readers with characteristic facets of the time and place in which the work was written. Most writers presuppose such a familiarity and draw upon it as they go about shaping and developing their works. Thus Bialik, in writing his poem "Levadi" [Alone], presupposes readers whose previous knowledge includes a familiarity with the concept of the "Shekhina" to which he can assign a central role in his poem without having to explain what it is. Likewise, Tschernichowski, in writing his "'Ani ma'amin" [I Believe], can include such verses as:

For my soul still yearns for freedom,
I have not sold it to a golden calf,
For I still believe in man,
And in his spirit, his vigorous soul.

His soul will cast off petty chains,
Will uplift us to the heights sublime,
No worker shall in hunger die,
Freedom — for the soul, bread — for the hungry.

with the assumption that his readers' previous knowledge will include sufficient familiarity with Marxist doctrine to enable an understanding that the poem embodies a defiant repudiation of this doctrine.

The ironic construction of Brenner's story "'Avlah" [The Slander], to give one final example, is predicated on the reader's presupposed knowledge of the values and ideals of the Second Aliyah pioneers. Without such knowledge, the ironic intent that underlies the development of the narrative may be easily overlooked, causing its thematic signification to be entirely misconstrued. And this, indeed, is what often happens when American undergraduates are required to respond to this story without having been sufficiently prepared. The teaching of literature outside of its natural cultural context makes one intensely aware of the extent to which each work of literature is, indeed, an intertextual construct — a product of various cultural discourses on which it relies for its intelligibility. Learners cannot truly comprehend the works of such poets as Judah Halevi, Bialik and Yehuda Amichai, or the fiction of Peretz, Agnon and Yehoshua without a basic understanding of the cultural context from which these works emerged. Yet the typical student enrolling in a Hebrew literature course at an American college will not have acquired such an understanding. The detrimental effects of this lack of historical and cultural background are often compounded by the natural inclination of naive readers to impose presuppositions derived from their own cultural context upon works that have little affinity with this context. All of this results in an all too familiar sense of confusion, misunderstanding and even disrespect for the material that is being studied. In view of the impediments that exist at each level of essential interaction between the American learner and the Hebrew text, it seems evident that without systematic corrective action the encounter of the learner with the text will inevitably result in a dismal failure of communication.

The above analysis of the existing disparities between the presuppositions of the writer and the learner may serve to explain many of the difficulties that hamper the teaching of Hebrew literature. But it may also provide us with a useful point of departure for seeking ways to overcome these difficulties. The first obvious step in this direction is the introduction of a mediating figure into the communicative transaction. This, of course, is the figure of the teacher whose role is to facilitate learning by devising and implementing appropriate means of bridging the gaps that exist on each essential level of interaction between the reader and the text. In order to fulfill this role successfully, the teacher must regard the teaching of a specific text as the end-product of a sequence of preparatory stages that precede the actual classroom presentation.

Effective classroom instruction is always preceded by a process of selection and organization which determines the content and structure of the complete schedule of study, or *syllabus*, designated for a particular course. Each of the texts that are selected and arranged within the syllabus should be regarded as an interactive component of a larger pedagogical design. This process of selection and organization should, in turn, be guided by a clear conception of the instructional objectives that are to be pursued within the general framework, or *curriculum*, of an integrated, multi-level program of Hebrew language and literature courses. The notion of an integrated, comprehensive curriculum that encompasses all the courses in the program and determines the substance and organization of each individual course is the mainstay of the approach to the teaching of Hebrew literature that I am about to propose.

The first stage in designing a functional program for teaching Hebrew literature is the determination of a set of basic principles that define the didactic objectives of this program and the methodological means of attaining these objectives. These principles should serve to determine the content and sequencing of all the courses within the program. They should guide the selection and organization of texts in each course and generate the most fitting and productive methods of teaching the selected texts. The primary structural principle for creating an integrated curriculum is the *principle of coherent continuity.* This principle stipulates that a viable curriculum is a sequence of courses in which each course constitutes a direct continuation of the preceding course and a controlled foundation for the course that is to follow. The principle of coherent continuity also applies to the organization of the instructional units within an individual course and it must be sustained on each of the three levels of essential interaction that have been discussed.

The Language of Literature: A Coordinated Curriculum

Coherent continuity of required language competence is an absolute necessity for the creation of a cohesive sequence of interlocking Hebrew language and literature courses. In order to ensure a smooth transition from one course to another, the linguistic starting point of each course must coincide with the level of language competence attained in the preceding course. The previously acquired language skills of students entering a new course should be a critical consideration in determining the textual content of this course. We should never confront students with texts written on a linguistic level that exceed the limits of their previous knowledge of Hebrew. But since the language of the designated texts must become increasingly difficult and complex, the language skills of the students must be continuously enhanced. As their learning of literature progresses, the students must also continue to acquire language skills that will enable them to meet the increasing linguistic demand of more advanced literary texts. This correlation must be maintained on all levels of instruction. At no point in the literature curriculum should the teacher abandon the systematic effort to enhance the students' semantic and syntactic accommodation to the Hebrew literary text by designing and implementing exercises, activities and instructional aids that serve to diminish the disparities between the linguistic presuppositions of the learners of Hebrew literature and those of the Hebrew writer.

The need for linguistic continuity exists on all levels of instruction, but it is particularly apparent at the point of transition from the last course in the language sequence to the first literature course, which is the weakest link in many undergraduate Hebrew programs. The materials incorporated into the lowest level literature course all too often consist of texts that are far too advanced for students who have completed the usual four semesters of elementary and intermediate college Hebrew language courses. This qualitative leap has significant quantitative consequences. Most students who complete the Hebrew language program do not continue into the Hebrew literature program. The majority of the relatively few undergraduates who enter the literature program are not drawn from the ranks of the learners in the elementary and intermediate language courses. They are usually students who have acquired Hebrew competence outside the university — in Jewish day schools, in high schools that offer Hebrew as a foreign language, in various programs of study in Israel, in homes where Hebrew is spoken and, on rare occasions, in parochial afternoon schools — and whose superior command of the language qualifies them for entering directly into the more advanced levels of the literature courses.

The break in linguistic continuity between the Hebrew language and literature programs causes the sharp decrease in advanced enrollments and accounts for the radical discontinuity between the students completing the language program and those entering the literature program. A curriculum that denies its language students access to its literature courses undermines its viability by stemming the flow from an important pool of potential learners who, with appropriate action, could have been directed to the study of Hebrew literature. The characteristic incompatibility of Hebrew language and literature programs is usually not the result of a calculated policy but rather of a lapse in planning and coordination. The key to redressing this unfortunate situation is a conception of the *entire* Hebrew curriculum as an integrated continuum which maintains constant contact and coordination among all its courses. Maintaining a coordinated continuity is particularly important to the integration of the Hebrew language and literature courses which all too often operate independently of one another and sometimes actually work at cross purposes. One of the more typical instances of such detrimental lack of continuity occurs in the area of reading acquisition.

Many language programs favor an extensive approach to reading. They train and encourage students to combine their previous knowledge of the language with the contextual hints provided by the text in order to arrive at an approximate understanding of the general content of this text. Translation and detailed paraphrasing in the target language are discouraged. Dictionary use is held at an absolute minimum. This approach may have merit in the reading of textbook passages and newspaper items, but it is inadequate and often counterproductive when applied to all but the simplest literary texts. The complicated and often irregular sentence structures of most Hebrew literary works, combined with their tendency towards idiomatic and allusive language, will quickly frustrate attempts at extensive reading by all but the most advanced Hebrew learners. Moreover, the true study of literature will benefit very little from a learner's tenuous grasp of the "general content" of important works of poetry and fiction in which both words and sentences are carefully measured, deliberately shaped and heavily loaded with signifying implications. The competencies that are required for the study of such texts include an array of *intensive* reading skills that will enable the learner to decipher difficult semantic elements and complex syntactic structures.

Prospective students of Hebrew literature must be taught to read intensively and analytically — as well as extensively and intuitively — from the earliest stages of their instruction. A Hebrew language curriculum that is oblivious to the specific language skills that are necessary for the study of literature and does not provide for their systematic development will either disqualify many students from making a successful transition to a more advanced literature program or, as is often the case, make it impossible to establish such a program. Ongoing coordination between the language and literature components of a Hebrew curriculum is an essential means of ensuring that the instructional objectives of the language program will take into account the specific competencies required in the literature courses. It will also ensure that the level of instruction in the first course of the literature sequence will be based on the attainments of the prerequisite language course.

The Meaning of Literature: A Supplementary Learning Sequence

Diminishing the disparities between the presuppositions concerning genre that separate the American learner from the Hebrew text involves a second area of instruction in which continuity must be maintained. The typical American undergraduate does not possess the conceptual knowledge and analytical tools that are necessary for progressing beyond the surface content of a literary text to its deeper levels of structure, meaning and aesthetic expression. Consequently, an effective Hebrew literature curriculum must be supplemented with a clearly defined sequence of instructional activities that will integrate basic concepts of literary analysis into the general progression of targeted texts. From the earliest stages to the most advanced levels, the teaching of Hebrew literary texts must be accompanied by a corresponding development of the students' analytical and interpretative skills. The objective of this curricular component is not to instruct the students in the latest permutations of the prevailing critical theories but rather to familiarize them with the distinctive features and fundamental structures of the literary genre.

The topics of genre-specific instruction that are to supplement the learning of individual texts should include such basic concepts as the inherent relationship between form and meaning, the elemental structural and prosodic components of poetry and fiction, the distinction between subject and theme, as well as author, narrator and character in fiction. They should also include an active understanding of the more common rhetorical devices in literature such as metaphor, irony and ambiguity. A comprehension of the nature and function of plot development and narrative point of view in fiction is as essential as the familiarity with the role of image, contrast and analogy in poetry. While this list of suggested topics is not definitive, it does offer a general guideline for designing an appropriate supplementary learning sequence.

Since the structural and conceptual elements that are required for effective learning constitute the characteristic attributes of the literary genre, they can be found in many individual works of literary art. Consequently, this aspect of curriculum planning is of secondary importance in the selection and organization of the particular texts that are to be included in a given course or sequence of courses. It should be subordinate to more crucial considerations that are yet to be discussed. But one should never lose sight of the needs that the supplementary learning sequence is meant to serve. Once the appropriate texts for a particular course are collected and the general framework for their organization is determined, consideration must be given to the manner in which the final selection and organization of these texts in the syllabus will advance the acquisition of analytical and interpretative skills. In addition to serving all other objectives of the integrated curriculum, each text must be examined for the opportunities it provides for enhancing the students' cumulative knowledge of basic critical concepts and techniques.

Every Hebrew literature course should include a schedule for introducing relevant generic concepts and activities designed to apply these concepts to the assigned texts. This necessary interaction between concept and text can begin at the earliest stages of instruction, for even the simplest story will lend itself to introducing such concepts as the distinction between subject and theme or the differences between author, narrator and character. The most modest of poems will provide opportunities for learning some basic elements of prosody or the essential characteristics of a metaphor. Once such concepts are learned they can be readily reinforced by systematic application to future texts which, in turn, should serve to introduce additional literary concepts and critical skills. Thus, as the texts become more difficult and complex, the learners become more adept at addressing themselves to the deeper structures and underlying meanings of these texts.

The Reason for Literature: A Humanistic Perspective

The principles I have been discussing so far constitute a merely structural framework for a program of study that is yet to be filled with appropriate content. A determination of the specific literary content of each course requires recourse to yet another set of normative principles that will guide us in the appropriate selection and organization of the target texts. The need for a definitive answer to the question of "What should we teach?" may appear to be self-evident, but an informal survey of various Hebrew literature programs in American universities shows that this question has not always been thoroughly and systematically addressed. Many of these programs operate on a catch-as-catch-can basis. Text selection is determined by a teacher's familiarity with and fondness for certain works, or by considerations of the works' accessibility and appeal to the students, or by what is available in the few existing textbook anthologies of Hebrew literature, none of which are effectively designed to meet the needs of American undergraduates. In some cases texts are grouped into topical or thematic units (i.e., parents and children; friendship and love; childhood; war; kibbutz life; etc.) which are internally cohesive but are not related to other units in the course or to the materials studied in other courses. The transformation of this haphazard manner of teaching Hebrew literature into a cohesive, fully integrated curriculum requires the extension of the principle of coherent continuity to the textual content of the entire literature program.

The practical planning of an integrated curriculum must be preceded by a clear formulation of the ultimate instructional objectives of the literature program as a whole. We must begin designing the means of instruction by questioning their desired ends: Why do we wish to teach Hebrew literature? What are the benefits we intend our students to gain by studying it? What is the purpose of the enterprise? Definitive answers to these cardinal questions will provide an overriding rationale for our program and generate the criteria for selecting our texts, assigning them to functional locations upon the continuum and devising effective methods of teaching them to our students. Of the various possible answers to these fundamental questions, I would like to propose an approach that seems most relevant to the pedagogical realities of teaching Hebrew literature to American undergraduates.

Most American undergraduates who choose to study Hebrew literature have no intention of pursuing a more advanced course of studies that will train them to be professional Hebrew scholars. While our curriculum should certainly provide for the few who may seek a professional career in this field, it must take into account that it is directed primarily towards the education of people who are headed in other directions and whose future contact with Hebrew literature will be, at best, very limited. This is also true of their ongoing contact with the Hebrew language itself. Most of our students will not be going into fields of professional endeavour that require a knowledge of Hebrew language and literature. Even fewer will end up making a life for themselves in Israel. Our curriculum should clearly encourage the former and provide for the latter. But it should not be designed as a teacher-training program or as a preparatory program for prospective immigrants. With few exceptions, a Hebrew literature curriculum should be designed to contribute to the general experience of an education in the humanities which most America undergraduate programs aspire to provide.

A sharper definition of the overriding objective of a viable Hebrew literature curriculum may be arrived at by eliminating some of the more common misconceptions as to what this objective may be. Perhaps the most common misconception in this regard is approaching the study of literature as yet another means of enhancing competence in the language. Such an approach vitiates the very essence of the learning experience that an encounter with literature can provide. The primary objective of a Hebrew literature curriculum should, therefore, not be the advancement of the students' mastery of the Hebrew language. It should also not be providing instruction in the methods and disciplines of literary criticism. It should not even be the pursuit of the singular aesthetic experience offered by select works of literary art. Let there be no mistake: all of these objectives are extremely important. They should be integrated as essential components into every curriculum. But, as such, they must be subordinated to an overriding objective which is to create a broad and dynamic encounter between the American learner and Hebrew culture.

The dynamics of literature are often generated by the encounter of an individual sensibility with the forces of circumstance and, in many cases, the nature of this encounter is defined by the circumstances of a specific historical reality. Of all the humanistic disciplines, literature is unique in its capacity to merge individual experience with cultural context so as to reflect the human dimensions of historical occurrences. An effective undergraduate literature curriculum should be geared towards drawing upon the genre's unique properties of deepening our understanding of human experiences while illuminating the historical and cultural realities that almost invariably contribute to the shaping of these experiences. Expanding the students' knowledge of the historical circumstances, social dynamics and intellectual trends that have shaped the destiny of the Jewish nation, while deepening their understanding of the effects of this destiny upon the lives of individuals and communities within the nation, is the principle purpose of the humanistic approach to a viable Hebrew literature curriculum. This purpose also serves as the primary criterion for selecting the culturally significant materials that are to be incorporated into the curriculum.

The proposed approach assumes a reciprocal relationship between history and literature. It requires that the works selected for inclusion in the curriculum be representative of the historical and cultural contexts to which they belong. Each of these texts should be regarded both as a unique work of individual expression and as a literary reflection of a writer's reaction to a specific social reality. In addition to establishing a normative touchstone for text selection, this approach provides a conceptual framework for relating the selected texts to one another and an orienting perspective for the manner in which each text should be taught. The resulting curriculum will comprise a literary continuum that reflects clear historical and cultural patterns in the life of the Jewish people. Among the guiding criteria for selecting the texts that will comprise the culturally oriented Hebrew literature curriculum are the topical and thematic aspects of these texts. Every work must be considered on the basis of the degree to which its topical concerns and thematic significations reflect a representative range of the central historical characteristics and human issues of the period in which it is set. The selected texts should be drawn from a variety of literary genres. They should gradually cohere into a thematically integrated historical framework, although they need not be taught in strict chronological order or arranged in tight thematic clusters. A modern Hebrew literature curriculum, for example, should contain works that range from the Haskalah, or post-Haskalah period through the pioneering settlement period to the present time of Israeli statehood. The sequencing of these works within the curriculum is determined largely by their ascending levels of difficulty.

Introductory-level courses may consist of simple texts representing a variety of genres, periods and thematic concerns. As instruction progresses, the connections between the various literary aspects will begin to emerge and will serve as a basis for a systematic presentation in the more advanced survey courses. A strictly topical or thematic grouping of texts is appropriate only in the most advanced levels of instruction, after the general contextual framework has been firmly established. The process of establishing this framework begins at the earliest stages of instruction and is made possible by continuously involving the learners with the salient thematic elements in different periods of Hebrew literature as they occur and recur in the designated works.

A critical step in planning a curriculum is the formulation of explicit thematic guidelines for selecting texts and relating them to one another. These guidelines are, to a large extent, subjective and may vary from program to program, but, in all cases, they must be clearly defined and consistently applied. By way of example, it might be useful to present the thematic designations that have been providing coherence and continuity to the modern Hebrew literature program in which I teach:

1. *Modern revolutions in Jewish life: Hassidism, Haskalah, Zionism.*
2. *Diaspora and Zion: A crises of values.*
3. *Experiences of the pioneers: The ideal and the real.*
4. *Holocaust: The human dimensions of a national tragedy.*

5. *Israeli society at war: Consequences and implications.*
6. *Literary perspectives on Israel myths.*
7. *Living in a realized dream: Literary perspectives on social issues.*
8. *Israel and the Israeli: Harmony or conflict?*

Every text included in the curriculum should have a direct bearing on at least one, but usually several, of the predetermined themes and should be taught in relation to other, similarly oriented works.

After they are gradually introduced at the introductory level, these themes will accompany the curriculum through all its stages. As they progress from level to level, the students encounter these themes in different variations, combinations and contexts. They approach them from different perspectives and perceive their interrelations as interlocking manifestations of a dynamic social, historical and cultural reality. The more we involve our students in the deeper levels of works by representative writers, the better they will be able to perceive the human dimensions of the ongoing encounter with the various historical and cultural contexts that these writers represent. Once our students complete the Hebrew literature program they will have acquired a body of humanistic knowledge that may well accompany and enrich their lives in the years to come. An example from one of the learning units in an Introduction to Hebrew Literature course will serve to illustrate this dynamic:

The figure of Hannah Senesh serves as a focus for an instructional unit in our introductory-level course. This unit consists of the following texts: a biographical chapter in simple Hebrew;[1] selections from the diary of Hannah Senesh,[2] two poems by Hannah Senesh,[3] selections from Aharon Megged's play, *Hannah Senesh.* The topical and thematic considerations for this selection should be evident. The events surrounding the life of Hannah Senesh, her prominent place in the pantheon of Israeli heroes, the things that she wrote and those that were written about her, all lend themselves naturally to many of the thematic underpinnings of the extended curriculum. They provide opportunities for addressing such prevalent aspects as the dichotomy between Zion and the Diaspora, the ambivalencies of the pioneering experience, reactions to the Holocaust and to war, the distinctions between literature and myth, the disparities and tensions between the needs of the individual and the demands of society. This selection also satisfies the requirement for generic diversity by presenting elements of essay, confessional writing, poetry and drama. Effectively taught, these texts will enhance the students' knowledge of an important historical period as well as their understanding of some characteristics of the literary response to historical reality.

The biographical text which opens the learning sequence provides the necessary factual context for the later readings. It also provides an example of didactic writing that selects and organizes its factual material in accordance to ulterior ideological motives. A comparison of this text to the selections from

Hannah Senesh's diary will reveal the extent to which the didactic text simplifies her character and ignores the complexities of her motives. In addition to illuminating the disparities between popular myth and subjective reality, the diary selections introduce a variety of relevant thematic aspects and constitute a useful transition from the nonliterary writing of the biographical text to the literary characteristics of the poetry and the play. Much of what is learned in this unit will be used to inform subsequent stages of the integrated curriculum.

A curriculum based on coherent thematic continuity creates the necessary conditions for diminishing the disparities in communicative presuppositions that separate the reader from the text. But it does not constitute a definitive solution to all the problems that are created by the fundamental incongruity between the essential aspects of the cultural context in which a Hebrew text was written and the different cultural context in which this text is being read by the American learner. The actualization of the learning potential that is inherent in the integrated curriculum must take place within the day-to-day process of overcoming the cultural, linguistic and generic barriers presented by each individual text.

Teaching the Text: Aids and Means

Providing a Context

The relevant meanings that are to be communicated by almost every work selected to serve the objectives of the culturally oriented curriculum are often the function of explicit or implicit references to an extra-textual context with which the writer assumes his reader to be familiar. It is impossible to grasp the meaning of the opening lines of Bialik's "Alone," for example, (they were all carried away by the wind,/ The light has swept them away,/ Thrilling to a new song of their dawning life;) let alone of the entire poem, without being aware of the conflict between the convictions of traditional Jewish orthodoxy and the new spirit of Enlightenent in which Bialik's generation was caught up and to which his poem was responding. Such knowledge is necessary for the effective learning of all other texts related to the theme of Modern Revolutions in Jewish Life, be they the poems of Saul Tschernichowski, the fiction of David Frishman or the essays of Ahad Ha'am. A general knowledge of different historical and cultural contexts is similarly necessary for the effective learning of texts related to the other thematic components of the curriculum. Since the knowledge presumed by the writers is typically lacking in many of our students, the teaching of the selected texts must be accompanied by a systematic enhancement of the learners' historical and cultural knowledge. This may be accomplished by a variety of means.

Brief periodic background lectures by the teacher are most useful in placing a text, or group of texts, in the appropriate historical and cultural context. The text itself can serve as a valuable source of historical and cultural knowledge. Preparation for teaching each text should include a search for internal contextual indicators that are most relevant to the period and thematic features this text is intended to represent. A discussion of these contextual references should be incorporated into the teaching plan in such a manner that will enable the teacher to expand upon them and to lead the learners to an understanding of the particular relation of the specific text to its general context.

Another means of bringing American learners into the contextual framework of the assigned works involves the use of visual and audio-visual aids. Occasional in-class viewings of slides and video programs that present salient aspects of the period in which the assigned texts are set provide a valuable visual link between the world of the reader and the unfamiliar world of the text. They create natural opportunities for a discussion of the contextual dimensions that are most relevant to the intended thematic orientation and constitute valuable points of reference for future discussions as well. They also add diversity and texture to the learning process. Such materials are readily available from a variety of sources, many of which are still virtually untapped.[4]

The objectives of an ambitious curriculum must always contend with the constraints of actual time available for classroom learning. Given the diversity of activities that must be carried out during the usual three weekly contact hours, the time devoted to contextual enhancement in class must be rigorously controlled. But this essential aspect of knowledge may be further expanded outside the classroom by assigning background readings (in English and/or Hebrew) that are to be carried out independently by the students. Brief historical background readings in simple Hebrew may be assigned in the early stages of instruction.[5] In the more advanced stages of learning, these basic Hebrew texts may be supplemented by more extensive and more sophisticated background readings in English. The best single source for such readings that I have found is Meyer Waxman's *A History of Jewish Literature*.[6] This comprehensive work is particularly suited for undergraduates. The introductory chapters to each of the historical periods, as well as the biographical and critical discussions of individual writers are lucid, informative, and pleasingly free of jargon. Relevant background readings should routinely accompany the learning process. Students should be expected to demonstrate their knowledge of this supplementary material in class discussions, in their papers and on their exams.

Efficient management of instructional time requires that all learning activities that can be carried out outside the classroom should be assigned as homework. In addition to reading the background materials, these activities include the initial readings of each designated literary text and a systematic preparation for its discussion. In-class instruction should begin only after the students have contended with the linguistic difficulties of the text and addressed themselves to its relevant contextual, structural and thematic dimensions on their own. Yet, in reality, most students need help with each of these textual aspects. If we are to make good use of valuable class time, we must devise effective means of facilitating the students' independent encounter with the linguistic, generic and contextual aspects of the text. These means consist of instructional aids and conceptual guidelines that will orient the learners in their initial readings and assist in their preparation for the class discussions that are to follow.

Guides for the Perplexed

One of the most effective methods of enabling students to accomplish the required preliminary readings of a difficult Hebrew text involves the preparation of a detailed Reading Guide that will accompany every assigned work of literature. The Reading Guide should be written in Hebrew and will typically consist of a brief introductory statement concerning the contextual and circumstantial setting of the work, followed by several sets of questions, each addressing a different aspect of the text. It will also contain a glossary of selected lexical items.

More often than not, the most difficult part of a literary work from a different time and place are its opening passages which thrust the reader into an alien environment of obscure references and disorienting authorial presuppositions. The opening to Brenner's "The Slander" may serve as a case in point:

> It happened at the end of that winter, when you on the other side were already under the British while we here continued under the Turks. I will not pause to describe the nervous tension in which we lived day after day. Newspapers and telegrams never came to our commune, and we had no inkling whatever of what was happening in the rest of the world. We were fed by rumors, and by the sound of firing which came from the direction of Kfar Saba. Of one thing we were sure — that things were in a sorry mess. Our liberators were stuck midway between Jerusalem and Nablus, and were not moving. Why didn't they march straight ahead, northwards? The general opinion was that they did not want to pass through our settlements for fear of provoking the Turks, who in their retreat might destroy us.

This passage presupposes a reader who is familiar with the political, social and ideological realities in Palestine during the First World War. A reader who does not possess the presupposed knowledge will quickly become disoriented and have great difficulty in comprehending the Hebrew text. The Introductory Statement that opens the Reading Guide is intended to alleviate some of this difficulty by placing the work in its historical context and providing some essential information concerning the immediate setting and circumstances to which the work refers. In the case of "The Slander" this statement may read as follows [in Hebrew]:

> The story takes place during the First World War. The turks ruled Palestine and the British were trying to conquer the land. The Jewish inhabitants wanted the British to succeed because they believed that

British rule would be better for them. At the time of the story the British had succeeded in conquering only the southern part of the country.

The narrator of the story is a member of a small commune of Jewish farmers, not far from a larger Jewish colony in the central part of the country. This area was still in the hands of the Turks and their allies, the Germans. The members of the group are waiting for the British army to reach them, but the British advance has been stopped.

The situation in the commune and in the colonies around it is not good. They are suffering from hunger and are also afraid of the Turks.

The Introductory Statement is followed by two sets of guiding questions. The students are instructed to read all the questions before they begin reading the text itself and to refer back to them as their reading proceeds. The first set consists of Content and Context Questions that are designed to assist the learners in understanding the surface meaning of the text and to alert them to the various contextual references that are embedded in it. These questions will usually follow the linear progression of the text and address each textual block — a stanza in a poem, a paragraph in a prose work — in the order of its appearance. The Content and Context Questions for the opening paragraphs of "The Slander," for example, may read as follows [in Hebrew]:

1. What are the reasons for the settlers' "nervous tension"?
2. Why was it difficult for the settlers to know what was happening on the front and how did they get their information?
3. Who is being referred to as "our liberators" and why?
4. What was the general opinion about the British reasons for not advancing straight to the north?

A preliminary reading of these questions, as well as those that follow, will provide the students with considerable information and necessary orientation concerning the story they are about to read. Once they begin reading, they can continuously check their comprehension of each textual block by attempting to answer all of the questions that are related to it. They may consider their initial reading of a given textual block as being complete only when they can answer all of these questions. The Content and Context Questions also serve the teacher as a quick and effective means of verifying student comprehension without resorting to translation or line-by-line reading and elucidation in class. This allows for the larger portion of the instructional time allocated to each textual unit to be devoted to a more wide-ranging, in-depth discussion based on the second set of questions that accompany the text. These are Discussion

Questions that are designed to relate the surface of the text to its underlying structures and significations.

The Discussion Questions included in the Reading Guide for each text are intended to orient the learner towards the interrelated contextual, structural and thematic aspects of the texts that have been targeted for discussion. They provide an informed common basis for such a discussion by requiring a preparatory consideration of predetermined textual elements that are most relevant to this particular juncture in the learning sequence. Once again Brenner's "The Slander" may serve as an example.

"The Slander" is an appropriate textual selection because of Brenner's importance as a writer and because of this story's affinities with several of the curriculum's central themes: Modern Revolutions in Jewish Life; Diaspora and Zion; Experiences of the Pioneers. By the time they encounter this story, the students will have already acquired a basic knowledge of the circumstances, problems and ideals of the Second Aliyah. They will have also been introduced to some of the rudimentary formal attributes of narrative fiction. Our objectives in teaching this story may include:

1. Enhancing the student's knowledge of the social issues and human dimensions of the Second Aliyah period by identifying the most relevant contextual references.
2. Enhancing the students' awareness of the nature of a literary work's thematic response to a given historical reality by viewing Brenner's work as a realistic antithesis to the then prevailing "Israeli genre" of writing which tended to idealize the pioneering experience.
3. Introducing the function of irony in communicating meaning and advancing thematic signification.

The Discussion Questions that will accompany "The Slander" should be designed to orient the readers towards the designated instructional objectives and to lead them towards discoveries of the interrelationships among the relevant contextual, structural and thematic aspects of the story. They may include the following clusters:

1. When the officer first arrives at the kvutza and encounters the narrator, the following exchange takes place: "He addressed me in fluent German: 'Who lives here? Jews, I presume.'

   "'Jewish workers,' I stressed in a Germanic Yiddish."

   A. The narrator's answer reveals an important set of values that he shares with the other members of the group. What are these values and how are they expressed in this brief exchange?

B. Find three other instances in the story in which these and other related values are expressed.

2. In "The Slander," as in many of Brenner's other works, the values of the pioneers are put to the test of reality. Where do we see this testing taking place and what are its outcomes in:

   A. The relationships among the members of the group.

   B. The attitudes and actions of the group towards the officer.

3. The members of the group feel very badly about what they did to the officer, but at the end of the story their feeling changes. All of them, including the narrator, feel good.

   A. What were the reasons for their bad feelings?

   B. What caused the change in their feelings?

   C. Does the author expect the readers to share in the good feelings of the group, or is the ending of the story ironic?

   D. Irony involves a contrast between an expectation and its fulfillment, or between the appearance of a situation and the reality that underlies it. Do you agree that there is irony in the first exchange between the officer and the narrator?

   E. Can you find any other instances of irony in the story?

   F. How is the author's use of irony related to the central themes of the story?

It may be argued that such a structured approach to the teaching of a text curtails the spontaneity of the reader's response. Eliciting highly subjective responses to the designated texts is not a primary objective of the proposed curriculum. But experience shows that proper direction actually enhances the learners' capacity for engagement, discovery and pleasure in what may otherwise be difficult and frustrating material.

Breaching the Lexical Barrier

The suggested Discussion Questions are a most effective means of involving learners with the text, orienting them towards the designated instructional objectives and generally enhancing the learning process. But they do not serve to remove the numerous lexical obstacles that usually hamper, and often subvert, this process. Most significant Hebrew literary texts contain numerous lexical items that are not part of the typical student's acquired vocabulary. Many of these are simply words that are unknown to the students and may be found in their dictionaries. But the paperback dictionaries that are most commonly used offer little help in deciphering idiomatic phrases and culture-specific terms. They also omit many words that are infrequently used in all but literary texts. Even students who are very skilled in using their dictionaries will quickly become confused and frustrated when attempting to read a Hebrew literary text which will typically contain key lexical items that are not to be found in their dictionaries. Since we cannot expect undergraduate students to invest in R. Alcalay's expensive *Complete Hebrew English Dictionary,* we must find an alternative way of providing the necessary lexical aid.

One way of closing the gap between the lexical presuppositions of a Hebrew text and the American learner's previous knowledge of Hebrew is to explain the unfamiliar items in class. This is highly undesirable since it requires devoting a considerable amount of valuable class time to a tedious, non-participatory process of translation and/or lexical explication. It also denies the advantages of having the learners do the initial readings of the text on their own. A far more advantageous way of providing the necessary lexical assistance is the preparation of a selected glossary for each of the assigned texts.

The Reading Guide for every text should include a Glossary that is designed to provide learners with immediate access to difficult Hebrew texts without undercutting the ongoing development of general language skills. The Glossary should contain selected lexical items in the order of their appearance in the text for which Hebrew explanations or, when necessary, English definitions are provided. The items selected for glossing are to be drawn from four distinct categories: cultural and contextual references with which the learners are assumed to be unfamiliar; difficult idiomatic constructs; key words that do not appear in the students' dictionaries; randomly selected words that are unknown to the students but may be found in their dictionaries. The reasons for including the first three categories should be evident. The fourth may require further explanation.

A successful Hebrew literature curriculum cannot exclude all but the simplest literary texts. The objectives of the comprehensive curriculum require a continuous introduction of works with increasing degrees of linguistic difficulty. At every level of instruction the students will be confronted with texts that contain numerous words that are unknown to them. Requiring students to look up every new word, or even every unknown word that is essential for their understanding of the test is counterproductive. It involves tedious hours of largely mechanical dictionary work in which little actual learning takes place. Much of this time could be better used for other learning activities. The value of looking up words in a dictionary cannot be wholly discounted since it enhances the learners' grasp of Hebrew morphology and may contribute to increasing their vocabulary. But these benefits are amply provided for by the many lexical items that are not included in the glossary. By incorporating a portion of the unfamiliar words into the glossary, we enhance its effectiveness as a means of facilitating reading comprehension without detracting from the desired learning objectives.

A Concluding Note From the Field

The principles and practices delineated above evolved from the experience gained over the past eight years in the Hebrew literature program at the University of Wisconsin-Madison. This program was established in 1955 as part of the undergraduate course offerings of the Department of Hebrew and Semitic Studies. Twenty years later the literature program, which had long consisted of three amorphous course sequences, was in serious trouble due to consistently diminishing enrollments. In 1977 enrollments dropped to an all-time low. There were only eleven students taking Third Year Hebrew. Of the seven students who entered Fourth Year Hebrew only four continued into the second semester of this course. The most advanced course, Readings in Contemporary Hebrew Literature, consisted of two students who spent an entire semester struggling through Agnon's "Tehila."

Spurred by the evidence that its Hebrew literature program was heading towards oblivion, the Department undertook a critical review and radical revision of its modern Hebrew curriculum. The purpose of this revision was to improve the quality of instruction by integrating all the modern Hebrew language and literature courses into a coherent program with clearly defined instructional objectives for every level of learning. The Hebrew literature program was entirely restructured. A new, culturally oriented and thematically integrated curriculum was designed and implemented according to the principles outlined above. Higher and more carefully controlled academic standards were set. A variety of teaching techniques, learning activities and instructional aids aimed at facilitating the students' encounter with the linguistic, generic and contextual aspects of the literature were tested. Those that were found to be most effective were incorporated into the curriculum. Once the Hebrew literature began to change, it was infused with a new sense of vitality and purpose. Student enrollments increased steadily and the rate of student retention within the program improved quite dramatically.

Restructuring the Hebrew literature program was a long-term project which often progressed through a painful process of trial and error. It is still far from being complete and perhaps never will be, for improvement is a perpetual undertaking. But eight years after embarking on this enterprise, its benefits have become tangible and illuminating. At present the Hebrew literature program consists of a six-semester learning sequence which is divided into three integrated yearly courses. In the first semester of the 1984-85 academic year close to seventy students were enrolled in this program. The third-year level "Introduction to Hebrew Literature" course had thirty students. Twenty-five students enrolled in the fourth-year level "Survey of Modern Hebrew Literature." Thirteen students participated in the most advanced level course, an undergraduate seminar in contemporary Israeli literature. The rate of student retention within the program is particularly satisfying. Of the twenty students who completed the third-year level course in 1983-84, seventeen continued their studies in the fourth-year level course in the following year. Eight of the thirteen students who enrolled in the 1984-85 undergraduate seminar had previously completed the fourth-year level courses. The growing strength and effectiveness of this program, the scope of knowledge it provides and the enthusiasm it generates, lead me to believe that the principles and practices on which it is founded constitute a viable basis for a successful approach to the problems of teaching Hebrew literature to American undergraduates.

---

[1]"Hannah Senesh," *Pirkei keri'ah betoldot ha'am veha'arets: 'ishim* [Readings in the history of the nation and the land: major figures] ed. Nira Sha'anan. Ministry of Education, Department for Adult Education (Jerusalem, 1979), pp. 131-134.

[2]*Hannah Senesh* [Includes diaries and other writings] (Tel Aviv, 1959). Some selections may be found in *Sha'ar lesifrut* [Gateway to literature: readings for Hebrew learners] ed. Michal Homsky (Tel Aviv, 1968), pp. 168-171.

[3]*Ibid.*

[4]The slide Archives of the Shazar Institute in Jerusalem, for example, offer a wide selection of authentic slide programs on various aspects of the modern Jewish experience, i.e., The First Colonies; "Hashomer"; The Second Aliyah; Illegal Immigration 1938-1948; The Holocaust; the Jews of North Africa; Benjamin Ze'ev Herzl; David Ben Gurion; the Jewish Underground. These programs may be obtained from: Slide Archives of Jewish History, Zalman Shazar Institute, 4 Hovevey Zion St., P.O. Box 4179, Jerusalem, Israel. The PBS television series "Heritage: Civilization and the Jews" which covers a much wider span of Jewish history is available on video cassettes from: Films Incorporated, 1213 Wilmette Ave., Wilmette, IL 60091. Additional information about available visual and audio-visual materials may be obtained from: The Pedagogic Centre for Jewish Education in the Diaspora, The Melton Centre for Jewish Education, Hebrew University of Jerusalem, Jerusalem, Israel.

[5]See, for example, Reuven Bar-Sever *Perakim betoldot 'am yisrael laulpanim* [Chapters in Jewish History for the Ulpan], Ministry of Education, Department for Adult Education (Jerusalem, 1965).

[6]Meyer Waxman, *A History of Jewish Literature* (New York, 1960).

Chapter Eight

Against the Stream? Teaching Religious Ethics in Modern America

Barry Jay Seltser

Teaching is an inherently challenging task. Students presumably know less than their teachers (although this claim may not always be borne out empirically), and the successful course is one in which "something happens" to the students. As with all other interpersonal activities, however, success is affected largely by the resistance exercised or experienced by the participants.

In most college courses, the resistance is minimal. Students are there to learn; they are often paying hard-earned money for the privilege, and they want something (if only the credential) from the experience. They are likely to be willing to give up ignorance or long-held views for the sake of attaining knowledge or a degree. But the teacher of ethics, and particularly the teacher of religious ethics, is confronted with a host of additional sources of resistance. What these are, and how to begin to counter them, are the main subjects of this paper.

The Secular Context

I am going to speak here only of essentially "secular" universities in the United States in the 1980's. What are the major sources of resistance to the teaching of religious ethics in such settings? I would suggest four closely related sources:

First, one feature of secular culture is its preference for pragmatic considerations. The removal of religious institutions and beliefs as the major determinants or definers of conduct often leaves a vacuum, which is generally filled by a rather unexamined commitment to "what works." The resulting instrumental orientation of many contemporary students makes the teaching of religion in general, and of religious ethics in particular, a somewhat idiosyncratic (and perhaps even suspect) task. It is not so much that such subjects are bad or dangerous, as that they are seen as useless and irrelevant.

We should not make too much of this problem, of course. Many students do not fit into this description, and many others are "ready" to be convinced that the pursuit of knowledge, values, or commitments are valuable for their own sakes. Yet, the contemporary teacher must recognize that many, if not most, undergraduate students will approach her/his course with an attitude of skepticism.

Second, and perhaps even more disturbingly, many students do not approach the study of religion as a neutral subject. A course in religion is different from a course in mathematics or biology, or even from one in psychology or political science. Many students have had extra-curricular experiences with religion, and come to a college course with a host of presuppositions and attitudes about the subject. In a society which prides itself on the pluralism of religious traditions, and in institutions which pride themselves on maintaining a stance of "objectivity" toward the truth-claims of these traditions, the teacher confronts students who are primed to resist both the religious attitudes of their peers and the entire "academic" approach of their professor. Little wonder that so many students feel betrayed by a course which "doesn't feel like my Sunday School class."

Third, the study of ethics in a pluralistic society confronts an ill-defined relativism built into the very fabric of the culture. Americans pride themselves on their "tolerance," a value which is then equated with an inability to distinguish between good and bad, right and wrong, or even better and worse. Pluralism need not lead to relativism, but it is not easy to convince students of this point.[1] As a result, the attempt to convince students that they even *have* ethical beliefs or theories may be resisted more strongly than any effort to impose a particular value stance upon them.

Fourth, and at a somewhat broader cultural level, the American social context makes it more difficult to think of ethics and religion as mutually reinforcing, or even as connected at all. Many Americans are brought up to distinguish sharply between religious and moral commitments, a distinction which would be meaningless in most other cultures. This is a particular problem for young students who may be questioning the nature of their religious identity, and who may need to assure others (and themselves) that they are still "good" persons even if they turn against their religious commitments. The very existence of a course in "religious ethics," therefore, may be experienced as a challenge to their new-found respect for the possibility of an atheistic morality.

These factors must be taken into account by anyone contemplating teaching religious ethics in secular modern settings. One must be endlessly sensitive to the threats posed by such courses, as well as to the opportunities they provide to challenge students to grow, to change, and to reflect.

These problems are intensified when we attempt to teach about non-Christian religious traditions. The teacher who wishes to teach about Jewish ethics, or even to incorporate Jewish ethics into a broader course, must deal with some additional problems: (1) Students often bring specific stereotypes with them about Judaism, stereotypes which must be confronted and discussed in class.[2] (2) Judaism must be approached historically in order to understand its ethics, and this is difficult in a culture which is proud of its uniqueness and in which the study of history is often ignored. (3) Judaism resists the search for easy answers; indeed, the entire process of Jewish interpretation seems posited on the view that, if there is even one "correct" answer, we are unlikely ever to be able to find it. For students who are uncomfortable enough with the ambiguity of their developing beliefs, this openness is particularly frustrating. (4) In important respects, students raised in a broadly Christian culture will tend to understand Judaism in more familiar Christian terms, a fact which poses enormous barriers to taking the Jewish tradition on its own terms.

This last point raises a more troubling issue. It could be argued that the entire concept of "Jewish ethics" is itself a creation of Christian theology. Whether the normative teachings of Judaism can be separated from other fundamental aspects of the tradition is open to doubt. One could make similar claims about Christian ethics, in the sense that the ultimate justification and grounding of ethical judgment usually entails a theological claim. But there are important differences between the ways the two traditions approach authority, the relationship between Scriptural writings and ethical reflection, and the attempt to be a "good" religious person. The teacher must continually wonder whether the very categories adopted in the classroom may not themselves be determined by one of the religious traditions under consideration, perhaps to the detriment of the other.

We have identified a number of resistance-creating factors, and have indicated how the teacher of Jewish ethics may face even more significant problems. How, then, are we to proceed? What methodological suggestions derive from the awareness of these problems? What pitfalls — what opportunities — await the person foolhardy enough to venture into this field?

Let me make several suggestions, drawn from my own limited experience. I must preface the following comments with the obvious caveat that teaching styles differ, and what works for one person may not work for another. Our abilities, our interests, and our fears as teachers are as divergent as our personal religious beliefs. A teacher deeply committed to a religious tradition may have to work harder to be objective in the classroom; at the same time, other teachers with the same religious commitments may be so eager to avoid indoctrination that they are willing to share less of their own beliefs. My comments, therefore, as all such suggestions from teaching professionals, should be understood in terms of my own efforts to discover a style of teaching which allows me to provide students with the opportunity to reflect upon significant religious and ethical issues.

Pedagogy and Relativism

Let us begin by considering how to confront the relativism issue in classes of religious ethics. Perhaps the most important methodological issue here revolves around the teacher's ability to communicate to students two apparently contradictory facts: (a) the students are allowed, expected, and encouraged to disagree — on questions of value and opinion — with the teacher and with one another; and (b) the teacher may believe that some of those values and opinions are better than others, or even (horror of horrors) that some of them are simply wrong. A teacher who communicates only (a) risks reinforcing the pervasive relativism, while the teacher who communicates only (b) skirts with indoctrination or narrow-mindedness.

How can both messages be held together? Several methods seem helpful in this regard. First, the teacher must be willing to share her/his own position on sensitive religious and ethical issues. This is a highly controversial point, of course; numerous colleagues (excellent teachers all) have disagreed sharply with this view, believing instead that students could only be led astray by the teacher's inevitable authority. Although I recognize the dangers, the alternative costs are far worse. Students must learn that a person can have strong views, be willing to express them, and still be able to tolerate disagreement and listen to opposing views. The act of teaching is inevitably a modelling of attitude and action; if we want our students to learn to think for themselves, we must communicate to them that we are willing to do so as well.

In my own teaching, I have adopted different strategies to deal with this problem. I do not reveal to students my own religious beliefs or identity, unless they ask. On occasion, however, I will share with them answers to religious problems which have helped (or hindered) me in my own religious searching. For example, I always raise the theodicy problem in my courses, because this problem is so central to ethical understandings of human nature and freedom. Many students have never confronted this problem before, or at least never *felt* it as a challenge to their faith; the teacher should indicate to the students some potential escape routes from the apparently inevitable loss of traditional faith which seems to follow from the problem. What better way to indicate that some of these escape routes can in fact work, than by indicating points in one's own life where they may have mattered?

Similarly, the complexity and ambiguity of searching for an answer to ethical problems such as abortion or euthanasia can lead to a despairing "what's-the-use?" syndrome. After forcing students to see the other side, and to confront the weaknesses — logical, emotional, and pragmatic — of their own views, I invariably share with them my own highly tentative "solution" to the problem. In doing so, the students can recognize that someone can see various sides, be drawn to conflicting arguments, and still stand somewhere.

Of course, this strategy "works" only if carried out in a highly sensitive and cautious manner. I am not sure I always succeed; some students seem overwhelmed by my position, and assume that they must adopt it (in spite of continual warnings on my part that they should not draw that conclusion), while others resent even this amount of personal opinion coming from their instructor. I am willing to risk these failures, because I am even more worried about the students who leave an ethics class with the conviction that "anything goes."

Another way to confront the relativism problem is to convince students that they are not in fact relativists themselves. This is usually an easy task, with well-chosen examples. Few students will say that there is nothing wrong with a teacher assigning grades on the basis of physical attractiveness, for example; even the potential beneficiaries of such a policy are likely to see something unjust or inappropriate about such a policy. By choosing such examples, and asking repeatedly whether they really believe there is nothing right or wrong about such actions, the teacher can break through the most naive versions of relativism fairly quickly. (Of course, in doing so, we may leave the student even more confused, unless we can quickly present some alternative ways to assess the correctness of a policy.)

There will always be a few students who will hold out for the relativist answer, and there is no easy solution here. One method which has worked on occassion is to isolate those students, and ask them to defend their position to the rest of the class. One of two results usually occurs: either they present a cogent rational defense of relativism, which the other students quickly recognize as a non-relativist position based on certain absolute claims about truth, human nature, or reality; or they refuse to give any reasons, often leaving the other students highly frustrated and allowing the teacher to discuss the role of "giving reasons" in ethics. In neither case, however, would I try to make light of the relativist position, or to prevent students from voicing it continually during the course.

The teacher confronts a different problem, of course, with the student who is thoroughly convinced of the rightness of a particular religious tradition, or of a particular ethical policy. In such cases, I have found that the "devil's advocate" strategy is seldom an effective one, simply because it is so easy to see through. I have preferred to adopt two approaches in such cases. First, I will allow the other students to raise objections from their own traditions, beliefs, or ethical commitments; the teacher can be a more effective facilitator of such discussions, and help point out the conceptual weaknesses of the position, by urging the students to battle it out. Second, and with great trepidation, I will "take on" such a student in class, questioning assumptions, uncovering inconsistencies or historical mistakes, or presenting equally plausible interpretations. Such students are seldom "convinced" by such challenges, but they often do return later to continue the discussion, and the other students in the class often benefit from such dialogues. (Once again, of course, such moments must be carefully chosen, and handled with as much sensitivity as can be mustered.)

I have discussed the relativism problem at some length because I perceive it as a common and difficult issue in contemporary education. I am not arguing that a relativist position cannot be defended, or that such arguments should be read out of the classroom. But I am suggesting that teachers of religion and ethics must self-consciously develop ways to deal with the more naive forms of relativism they are likely to encounter from undergraduate students, and to clarify in their own minds whether, or how, such arguments are inadequate.

The Case for Cases

A second methodological problem concerns the way in which ethical decision-making is to be addressed in the classroom. Should we present the great ethical theories, examine their religious (and non-religious) foundations, and assess them logically? Should we present the historical positions of the major religious traditions on various ethical issues, and seek to ask how these are to be understood and applied today? Should we look at specific cases of ethical decision-making, and struggle to decide what we, as actors, would or should do in such situations?

We should do all of these things, and any ethics course which omitted one of these tasks would be remiss. But where should the teacher begin? How do we introduce these problems to our students? In spite of some obvious problems with a case-method approach, I have continued to find that specific examples provide the best way to engage the students in such issues. I tend to choose readings which use specific cases; I build case discussions into my lectures and in-class sessions; and I expect students to grapple with specific issues in their writing assignments.

Several cautionary notes concerning the use of case materials are in order, however. First, the cases should be selected not only to reveal the ethical complexity of the problem, but also to make the student feel that such problems must be faced in human life. For this reason, I tend to stay away from using overly dramatic scenarios at the beginning of each unit. When discussing world hunger, I will begin with some fairly common dilemmas of sharing possessions, and move gradually to the broader issues of a rich nation sharing its food resources with a starving country. Similarly, ethical dilemmas of conflicting loyalties are best introduced by asking students to choose between returning a book to a friend and studying for an examination, rather than by asking immediately about civil disobedience in a national context.

Second, case studies can obscure as much as they reveal, unless the teacher carefully sorts out the most relevant aspects of the case. Cases should be introduced with sufficient detail to enable the student to be put imaginatively into the shoes of the actor, but not so detailed as to allow the student to escape from the ethical dilemma. We need to know whether the woman in an abortion example is married or unmarried, young or old, rich or poor; we probably do not need to know at the outset (and are perhaps better off not knowing) if she is a Protestant or a Catholic. We want to avoid the student responding simply by saying: "If I were in her position, as a Catholic, I would probably oppose abortion."

In short, cases are indispensable tools, but they must be selected carefully. The instructor must consider the nature of the case, the implications the students may draw from it, and precisely which ethical dilemmas it is expected to reveal. In addition, the teacher should be careful not to leave the impression that the examination of ethical issues is purely a matter of "hard cases"; the role of theory, of historical study, and of analytical discussion should be emphasized as well.

Another important tool is the religious tradition's own ethical self-examination. There is a temptation to focus on the sorts of "secular" issues or cases which fill our modern newspapers, and which are likely to be most on the students' minds. But a course in religious ethics should raise ethical problems which confront religious communities, and should use the collected arguments of these traditions to reveal such problems. For example, Jewish writers have struggled with "in-group/out-group" issues; are my obligations to my neighbor any different if he/she is not Jewish? Such dilemmas, and the debates about them in Jewish literature, can help students both understand the complexity of ethical questions of "special relations," and appreciate the distinctive ethical issues which may confront particular religious communities.

In this connection, it is very useful to read apparently conflicting accounts from the traditional sources. Students assume that religious traditions are monolithic, and nothing undermines this assumption as effectively as reading three or four interpretations of the same biblical passage, or a running argument concerning a point of Jewish law. Such tactics also can create the opportunity to delve behind specific cases or passages, to ask about underlying ethical themes or values. Students should be pushed — in class discussions, in papers, and on examinations — to look behind the answers to a case, and try to discover the foundation upon which the writers are attempting to stand.

Strategies for Reflecting

It might be helpful, at this point in the paper, to turn to some more specific suggestions of teaching methodology. One's selection of specific methods should depend upon which approaches will best lead the student to reflect upon the important ethical issues of the course. I will look briefly at four questions: How should the instructor select reading materials? How should historical materials be presented? What written assignments are most useful? What other teaching strategies might be important in the religious ethics course?

Reading Assignments

The selection of reading material is one of the most difficult problems for any instructor, and this is particularly true in the area of religious ethics. Textbooks are notoriously superficial, primary sources are difficult, and most secondary treatments are either boring or too difficult for undergraduate classes. I have tended to use a combination of sources, usually including a "Reader" of important primary source materials, some biblical selections, and other types of writings.

Among the most successful reading assignments I have used are works of literature. I regularly assign at least one novel in every course, and often use an additional collection of short stories. These work well: the students enjoy them, they can generate exciting and productive discussion, and they provide the basis for more interesting examination or essay questions. Several criteria for the choice of such literary works suggest themselves: the situation should present some sort of clear ethical issue(s), the characters should be diverse and identifiable, the book (or article) should be short enough to be read within a week or two, and the instructor should enjoy the material. (This last criterion mitigates against using the same book every time.) If these criteria are met, such materials can provide enormously important insights into ethical issues.

Thinking Historically

Most of the introductory books written about major religious traditions take a historical approach. While this is important, there are other strategies for getting students to think historically. I routinely deliver two lectures on each religious tradition, while the students are reading more thematic selections from the sources. I expect them to be able to identify themes with the historical development of the religious ethic; it is crucial, for example, to communicate the connection between the value of freedom and the Exodus, or between the role of fidelity in marriage and the Covenant Event in the Jewish self-understanding of history.

There is an interesting methodological problem here, of course: Should the "history" be presented to students as if it "really happened," or as the religion's claim about its history? The choice is a significant one, and must be handled carefully to avoid either reductionism or naivete. My strategy is usually to begin by indicating that the early "history" is not history as the students may study it in other college courses, and that we often have no extra-biblical evidence for the events we are recounting. At the same time, I impress upon them that we are attempting to understand the way Jews (or Christians) have traditionally understood their own history, and the effect of this self-understanding upon their ethical standards and actions. In this way, we can proceed to take seriously the tradition's historical roots, without assuming that the specific historical claims are either true or false.

There are some specific problematic areas here. Some students may insist that the biblical account of creation is "true," or that Jesus "really did rise" from the grave. Such problems can be handled differently according to the class context, but I believe that the teacher has a responsibility to present the more "secular" or scientific understanding as the one which is adopted *for the purposes of the course*. This last phrase is all-important; students should feel that they may believe whatever they wish about Jesus' resurrection, or about Moses receiving the Law at Sinai, but that the course will deal with such "events" primarily as claims that religious communities have made. A teacher who has developed adequate rapport with the students, and who is able to distinguish between "what I believe" and "what this course is about," should be able to avoid the obvious pitfalls of these discussions.

The other comment I would make about the methodology of teaching history is that it is easy to make it boring. Students often resent a historical approach, and a course on ethics should use history only insofar as one cannot appreciate ethical reflection without it. It is usually a mistake to begin a course with historical material, or to spend too much concentrated time on it in any one unit of a class. But historical perspectives are essential, and the teacher should struggle to find ways to introduce them throughout the course.[3]

Writing and Reflecting

All courses are expected to help students learn how to think, but this criterion is perhaps even more critical in the field of religious ethics. We are usually less concerned about giving out information, or about memorization, than we are about teaching a sensitivity to issues, an ability to think clearly, and a willingness to examine one's own assumptions. There is no substitute for written essays as a teaching tool for attaining these goals.

In-class essays, essay examinations, and essay assignments are all important tools here. The instructor must indicate at the outset, however, precisely what the criteria of assessment will be. Students will tend to simply repeat lecture notes or reading materials, and few of them have much experience with careful argumentation or exposition. The teacher should indicate what a good essay looks like, and that clarity and conceptualization are more important than "getting the right answer." It is often useful to share the best (and not-so best) essays in class early in the semester, to provide a point of comparison. In addition, personal appointments with students are often very important for identifying the weaknesses in such essays.[4]

Essay examinations should be as creative as possible. It makes little sense to ask memorization questions; instead, I always present the students with a case or problem of some sort, ask them to apply the ideas of several figures we have studied, and then to analyze and assess the various arguments and draw their own conclusions. This is the opportunity to communicate to one's students that the study of ethics is a challenging and open-ended task, and that their "success" will be judged in terms of broader criteria than they may be used to in their other college courses. They will resist the openness at first; I always have at least one or two students demanding to know "what I have to do to receive an 'A'" and being disappointed by the answer. But it is imperative that the study of religion and ethics not be turned purely into a matter of memorizing what various writers have said.

Other Strategies

There are other strategies for a course in religious ethics. Small group discussions are often extremely useful, although they must be structured very carefully. Organized debates in class can reveal interesting issues, although I personally am somewhat uncomfortable simply "assigning" students to defend specific ethical positions. Guest speakers are particularly useful in such courses; I regularly bring a draft resister (or at least a member of a religious peace group of some sort) into class during the discussion of pacifism and religious disobedience to authority, and the discussion clearly troubles the students more than if I were to present the pacifist position to them.

Another method I have used is to develop brief surveys of student opinion on the ethical issues we are addressing. The survey can be administered in class very quickly; I routinely ask about fifteen or twenty questions, five dealing purely with descriptive background information (gender, religious affiliation or preference, etc.) and others (using a five-point agreement scale) dealing with the ethical issues under consideration for that part of the course. Tabulation is quite simple, and the "data" can then be used to begin a discussion of both what the students think and why they think it. It is particularly useful to reveal to the students that, in most cases, they are not alone in their views.

Perhaps the overall methodological considerations here would hold true for most humanities courses. Using a variety of teaching styles, presenting material systematically in a way that engages the students gradually, forcing them to think about the fundamental issues of the class, and being willing to enter into the fray on occasion oneself — such recommendations are standard fare for the college teacher. I would suggest that such criteria are particularly important in teaching a subject which is at once so commonly misunderstood and so deeply felt (or rejected) by many college students.

---

[1]See the interesting discussion in Bernard Rosen and Authur L. Caplan, *Ethics in the Undergraduate Curriculum* (The Hastings Center, 1980), especially pp. 45-46.

[2]I have occasionally asked students to list their stereotypes of different religious groups. As the blackboard is invariably completely filled with the traditional views of Jews, Catholics, and other groups, it is clear that such underlying perspectives die a very slow death.

[3]One useful approach is to view the biblical evidence as stories that communities tell about themselves; in this way, students are free to believe or disbelieve the historical nature of the claims. I usually present much of this material in the tone of a "bedtime story," exaggerating the characterizations and tying the narrative together. Although some students resent this as "making light" of their sacred text, others report that the material has "come alive" for them for the first time. Once again, sensitivity is important here in determining how far the instructor can go.

[4]I provide a lengthy assignment sheet for take-home essays. Students may write three or four short essays in a semester course on different topics; when the

assignment is very structured and explicit, they tend to feel much less anxiety, and the resulting papers are of much better quality.

As a side note, I might add that, as a teacher, I must continually remind myself how terrifying the prospect of writing an essay is for many of my students.

Part Three

TEACHING JUDAISM TO NON-JEWS: CLASS STUDIES

Chapter Nine

Teaching the Intertestamental Period to Christian Students

Ellis Rivkin

I.

The Hebrew Union College-Jewish Institution of Religion is a seminary for the training and ordaining of rabbis for the Reform Movement. As such, it has from the days of Kaufman Kohler been noted for its advocacy of the historical-critical method and for its espousal of a form of Judaism which welcomes the findings of modern science as a mode of divine revelation and the scientific method as the most reliable instrument for the discovery of truth and for the building of knowledge. By according to the individual and his or her conscience the highest of values, many spokesmen for Reform Judaism have been willing to reach out to Christianity as a daughter religion, take a new and more sympathetic view of the historical Jesus as a Jewish teacher, and encourage fruitful dialogue between Christians and Jews.

With distinguishing features such as these, it was not surprising that Dr. Julian Morgenstern should have given his blessings to the establishment of a graduate school on the Cincinnati campus which would be open to qualified students irrespective of their religious affiliation. This he could do because the disciplines cultivated at Hebrew Union College were regarded as scientific disciplines taught by professors who took great pride in their commitment to the search for truth and knowledge for their own sake — a search uninhibited by any pre-committment to traditional notions of revealed truth. And since for those professors *torah-li-shemah* (i.e., study for its own sake in the sense of truth and knowledge) was their highest religious commitment, there was no question that they could teach, not only Semitic languages, but Bible and Rabbinics as well, with scientific objectivity and trans-denominational dispassion.

Dr. Glueck's confidence that the faculty of a rabbinic seminary could teach its disciplines to all-comers was confirmed in the years that followed by the steady stream of Christian students who took advantage of the opportunity of studying at the Hebrew Union College at the feet of highly competent Jewish scholars who could be counted upon to teach Semitic languages, Bible, Mishnah, Talmud and even, with Dr. Samuel Sandmel, the New Testament no differently than these disciplines would be taught at Harvard, Yale, or Johns

Hopkins. So successful indeed has the Hebrew Union College been in attracting non-Jewish graduate students that they have always outnumbered the Jewish graduate students. It is thus fair to say that a rabbinical seminary has given birth to a sound and healthy graduate school made up for the most part of students who are non-Jewish.

Of these non-Jewish graduate students, a large majority are not only Christians who have been ordained and hold BD degrees, but are also affiliated with conservative denominations. As such, they regard both the Old and New Testaments as, minimally, bearing true witness to the divine word, and maximally, as being, literally, the divine word. For such students the claims of the historical critical method have to be continuously adjudicated in the light of their faith commitment. Also, as believing Christians, they have to determine where Jews and Judaism fit within the divine plan. Bound as they are in some way to the authority of Scripture as determined by their faith commitment, they understandably are wary lest they be subverted by the authority of critical scholarship.

What, then, draws conservative Christian students to the Hebrew Union College whose graduate school faculty is, with perhaps one or two exceptions, one and the same as the rabbinical school faculty? Some are drawn because the College offers a very strong program in Ancient Near Eastern languages deemed by them to be necessary for a fuller understanding of the biblical text, as well as courses in Bible which focus primarily on the text and its meaning. Some also are drawn by the rich offerings of the school in the fields of rabbinics — tannaitic, talmudic and midrashic literature, Dead Sea Scrolls, and the apocryphal and pseudepigraphic literature which Christian scholars deem to be essential for understanding the Jewish backgrounds of Christianity and for the light that they shed on the meaning of New Testament texts. Others are drawn to the offerings in Hellenistic Jewish literature and in the history of the intertestamental period.

But whatever the reasons, there appear to be two overriding considerations: (1) The Hebrew Union College Graduate School is one of the few graduate schools which, because it is built on the rabbinical school and because its graduate faculty and its seminary faculty are one and the same, offers Christian students a graduate complex which is admirably designed for their needs: Semitic languages, Bible, intertestamental literature, rabbinics and history. (2) The Hebrew Union College Graduate School has earned for itself the reputation of being a school whose faculty regard themselves as scholars who pursue their disciplines in a thoroughly scientific manner, free of any doctrinal pre-committment or bias. What these Jewish scholars bring to their disciplines through their Jewishness is a deeper knowledge and understanding of the meaning of biblical and rabbinic texts which comes from having been exposed to these texts from within Judaism, yet filtered through minds committed to the spirit of free critical inquiry. A Christian student, no matter how conservative, thus has ample reassurance that he will get from the College that which he seeks:

mastery and proficiency in the handling of texts and context in a supportive intellectual and spiritual climate free of indoctrination or anti-Christian bias.

How, then, can these goals be achieved in view of the fact that the biblical, intertestamental, and New Testament texts are taught by professors who adhere to historical-critical principles, principles which carry with them implications that may very well collide with principles dictated by one's faith commitment? For strictly text courses in Bible, where language may be the crucial focus, such a collision may indeed be avoided. As for courses in Bible where higher criticism comes to the fore, avoidance may be an option, or a choice of this rather than that biblical book may confront the student with fewer critical issues. But when it comes to history, it would seem that collision is inevitable. Having had to face this problem for more than thirty-five years, I should like to share with others an approach that has proved to be fruitful in the teaching of Christian students — and the teaching of Jewish students as well.

II.

I offer a graduate elective course entitled "Reconstructing the History of the Intertestamental Period," which is divided into four segments spanning four semesters over a two-year period. Each segment is open to students irrespective of whether they opt for the other segments as well. The first segment deals with the finalization of the Pentateuch, the dissolution of prophecy, and the establishment of the Aaronide system as the normative form of Judaism. The second segment deals with the rise of the Pharisees and the collapse of Aaronide hegemony. The third segment deals with the apocryphal and pseudepigraphical literature, while the fourth segment deals with Hellenistic literature and Christian origins.

The basic philosophy which energizes these courses may be best summed up by paraphrasing the Karaite Anan ben David's exhortation: Search out the sources for yourself and do not rely on scholarly authority, not even that of the professor himself. Students therefore are not allowed to read secondary literature until the sources have not only been read by the students, but have been thoroughly discussed in class. Only when the students have gained full control of the sources, do they turn to the secondary literature and write a critical analysis of important scholarly contributions.

At the outset the students are asked to read the sources as though they had just been discovered, as though there was as yet no secondary literature, and as though the only tools at their disposal were those which they themselves shaped and fashioned to solve the problems which the sources raise. To do this, the sources are read in class, and the class as a whole determines what mental steps seem to be dictated by the sources themselves. Only when there is unanimity that the sources do indeed require us to take the next step, is that step taken. When such agreement is not forthcoming, note is taken of this fact and this item is set aside as a problem for which, at the moment, critical minds seem to be unable to find a solution.

Casting aside secondary literature temporarily, and exclusively concentrating on the sources themselves has a salutary effect. It puts them on the same plane as the professor and seasoned scholars, and by doing so energizes them to use their critical faculties without their being paralyzed by feelings of inferiority, and of ignorance. Instead, the students feel that they are engaged as is their professor and other scholars in the search for knowledge and truth — a search which may, but need not be, successful, as the history of scholarship makes only too abundantly clear. For conservative Christian students, this approach is reassuring because only the sources are studied and analyzed; no scholarly presuppositions are imposed; no thought step not dictated by the source itself is taken; and students' voices do not go unheard, irrespective of their belief systems, during the process of jointly adjudicating what the texts do or what the texts do not mandate for them.

Fortunately, a focus on the sources without prior recourse to the secondary literature is well within the parameters of possibility. and this for two reasons: First, the total corpus of extant sources for the biblical and intertestamental period is so small that each and every student can read through all the sources that are pertinent for each segment of the course. Second, the sources by their very nature preclude any definitive resolution to the problems they raise. The Pentateuch, for example, does not tell us explicitly that it is a composite work; that this layer was early and that layer late; that the layers were joined together by this individual or that, this group or that, this class or that. The history of Pentateuchal scholarship itself seems to mandate that the Pentateuch and its problems be reviewed afresh by temporarily imagining that secondary literature did not exist. For Pentateuchal criticism has not displayed itself as successive building blocks to knowledge and understanding to which the next generation of scholars will add blocks of its own. Rather does Pentateuchal scholarship show itself to have been a series of scholarly forays which have as yet failed to achieve their strategic objectives. Indeed, the only secure beachhead which has been fully secured is that which holds that the Pentateuch is a composite work.

The fact, then, that the corpus of sources is manageable, and the fact that even the most brilliant scholars over more than two centuries of critical scholarship have been defeated by these sources give the students the courage, on the one hand, to try again, and gives them at the same time the consolation that when they fail, they will find themselves in the goodly company of the Kuenens, the Grafs, the Wellhausens, the Albrights, the Noths, and the Kaufmans. Students will realize that the search for knowledge and truth is a risky undertaking, an undertaking where success is measured far more by the quality of the critical effort than by one's success in coming up with a definitive solution. The history of the scientific enterprise makes it only too clear that though there can be no finding without questing, questing in itself offers no sure road to finding. Yet it is a road that no truth-seeker can avoid taking.

III.

How, then, do I try to achieve my objectives over a four-semester period? Let me start with the first segment of the course, a segment which seeks to establish the structure of Judaism which emerged with the promulgation of the finalized Pentateuch and to set this structure off sharply from the structures of Judaism which both preceded the promulgation of the Pentateuch and which followed.

To accomplish this task, it is esential to determine what this structure was, drawing on some source which comes from a time when there can be no question that the Pentateuch had indeed been finalized and promulgated, and a source which is self-validating as to its right to bear witness. Such a source is to be found in the Wisdom of Ben Sira. Although scholars may argue as to when Ben Sira originally wrote his book, there can be no argument that it was written *after* the Samaritan schism (c. 350 B.C.E.), a schism in which both sides simply took for granted that the Pentateuch was God's immutable revelation.

As for self-validation, the author of Ecclesiasticus is not only a Scribe dedicated to the pursuit of Wisdom, but a devoted student of the Pentateuch (cf. Sirach 39:1-11, 44 ff) and a participant observer of his society who draws vignettes of the peasant, the artisan, the Scribe, and the High Priest of his day. With such, Ben Sira can serve as the jumping-off point for reconstructing the Judaism to which the Pentateuch had given birth.

It should be noted that Ben Sira's self-validation is the first exposure of the students to a methodology that focuses exclusively on the sources themselves. Ben Sira is not validated as a source on the say-so of scholars, nor on my say-so as teacher, but by Ben Sira himself. The students read Ben Sira and discover for themselves that the Pentateuch is the book of God's revelation to Moses and that the incumbent High Priest Simon, whether Simon I or Simon II, is exercising prerogatives set down in the Pentateuch. This discovery requires no previous knowledge on the part of the students, no exposure to secondary literature, no dependence on the teacher's expertise. All they need to know is the text of Ben Sira, the text of the Pentateuch, and Josephus' account of the Samaritan schism in *Antiquities*.

Exposed to these texts, students agree that Ben Sira must have written his book *after* the finalization and promulgation of the Pentateuch; that he venerated the Pentateuch as the word of God and meditated on it day and night; and that he stands in awe of Simon, the High Priest of his day as God's anointed and of the sacrificial cult as the divinely ordained mode of worship. They also see for themselves that Ben Sira makes no mention of living prophets, multiple shrines, or synagogues, though he does make mention of Scribes who pursue Wisdom, whose source, like the Law of Moses, derives from God Himself.

Building on this mutually agreed-upon knowledge, the next step is to ask the question as to how Ben Sira read the Pentateuch. Did he read the Pentateuch as though it were the undifferentiated word of God, or did he read it selectively? Did he read it literally, or did he bring to his reading concepts and notions which he superimposed on the text in such a way as to radically modify or distort the simple meaning of the text?

To answer these questions, we turn to the text itself. The students find for themselves a clear, unambiguous answer in Chapters 44-49 where Ben Sira sings the praises of the great spiritual leaders of biblical days. There are, to be sure, Adam, Seth, Noah, Abraham, Isaac, Jacob, Moses and Aaron, and all the others; but though they receive their due, the due they receive is by no means equal. Thus, understandably, Moses is singled out for his having been chosen by God to give the people God's revelation. But what is striking is that Moses pales before Aaron. Moses, for Ben Sira, may have given God's revelation, but that revelation was Aaron!

The centrality of Aaron is made clear not only by the twenty-one verses Ben Sira lavishes on Aaron as against the skimpy few, five in all, that he gives to Moses, but by the glorious portrait that he paints of him and by the authority over God's revelation that God had bestowed upon him and his descendents for all time. Of all the episodes of God's wonder working in the wilderness, the only one which Ben Sira recalls is the revolt of Korah and his campaign against Aaron's priestly monopoly, a revolt which God punished so severely.

Since, then, the primacy of Aaron and of his priestly descendants is there to be seen, spelled out clearly and unambiguously, the students have little choice but to acquiesce to the fact that the system of Judaism that Ben Sira took for granted as the system which God had mandated for His people was a system which had at its center the sacrificial cult and had at its head Aaron and Aaron's sons. And that this system was not simply an ideal hope, but in actual operation, is confirmed when we read Chapter 50, a chapter in which Ben Sira gives us a glittering description of the High Priest of his day, Simon I or Simon II, carrying out his priestly duties and performing his role of grand expiator by entering the Holy of Holies as prescribed in Numbers.

It thus becomes obvious that even though Ben Sira had the completed Pentateuch before him, and though he clearly affirms that it was God's revelation given through Moses, he focuses exclusively on the cultus and the Aaronide priesthood. Ben Sira does not focus on Deuteronomy, where the entire tribe of Levites are given altar rights, and where Moses, in his deathbed blessing, assigns to Levi authority over the revelation; nor does he focus on those texts in Exodus and Numbers which allow multiple altars and provide for no priestly class whatever. Rather does Ben Sira focus exclusively on the Aaronide system.

Since this is literally so, the next logical step is to enter the Pentateuch with Ben Sira as our guide and select all those passages which clearly identify themselves with the Aaronide system. In the course of doing so, the students can see for themselves that Ben Sira was accurately reflecting the focus of the Pentateuch itself, since far more verses are devoted to Aaron and the Tabernacle in Exodus through Numbers than to the non-cultic, non-priestly materials in these books or to the Levitical priests in Deuteronomy, and since far more space is given to God's anger at Korah and his fellow Levites' rebellion against Aaron than to His anger at Aaron for building the golden calf. Note also should be taken of the fact that non-Aaronide Levites were barred from priestly functions on pain of death and their fire pans of rebellion were to be hammered onto the altar as a warning as to the dire fate that awaited anyone who dared challenge the Aaronide monopoly over the altar.

Once again the minds of the students have been confronted exclusively with the sources. As such, their minds can no more legitimately challenge the fact that Ben Sira focuses on the Aaronide segments of the Pentateuch, that the Pentateuch itself from Exodus through Deuteronomy has thousands of more verses devoted to Aaron and his sons and the cultus than to any other leadership group, and that God's anger with Korah and his fellow rebels was greater than it was for the building of the Golden Calf, than a mind can challenge legitimately a geometric proposition and its logical consequences. Yet this acquiescence is an acquiescence that comes from the sources themselves, unmediated by the secondary literature and unmediated by the Professor, whose primary function has been the exposure of the students to Ben Sira and to the Pentateuch.

The next mental step is to read through Exodus-Deuteronomy to determine whether the Pentateuch provides for any system of authority other than Aaronidism. Here again it is the sources, not the secondary literature, that clearly reveals that in Exodus and Numbers there is an authority system that invests power in a prophet — Moses — a power symbolized by the simple tent of revelation (Exodus 33:7-11) which has no cultic function whatever — but invests no power in priest or king. One finds Joshua, and not Aaron, as Moses' understudy. Multiple altars are not only allowed, but encouraged. Yet Ben Sira chose to ignore this system of authority and opt exclusively for the Aaronide.

So, too, when the students turn to Deuteronomy they see without benefit of secondary literature that the Aaronide system is nowhere referred to; that the entire tribe of Levi are blessed with altar rights and not just Aaron and his sons; that the revolt of Korah and God's subordination of the Levites to the Aaronides is nowhere to be found; and that kingship, nowhere to be found outside Deuteronomy, is given Yahwistic legitimacy. It is thus evident that Ben Sira gave no more preference to the authority system recorded in Deuteronomy than he had given preference to the prophetic system of authority recorded in Exodus and Numbers.

The upshot of focusing exclusively on the sources turns out to be that the unmediated texts reveal three systems of authority — prophetic, prophetic-levitical-monarchical, and Aaronide — only one of which, the Aaronide, is regarded by Ben Sira as normative, and operational in his day, even though all three systems are recorded in the Pentateuch as equally revealed by God to Moses.

The sources thus seem to leave us no choice but to conclude that in the time of Ben Sira the system of Judaism which flourished was exclusively the Aaronide system.

We must then ask: How far back does this system as normative and operative go? To answer that question we turn from Ben Sira to the third division of the Canon, the Hagiographa, and look first at Chronicles, Ezra and Nehemiah since they were written after the Restoration. In these books, we find that the Aaronide system is normative throughout. According to the Chronicle's reconstruction, the sons of Aaron enjoyed a monopoly of altar rights from the very moment that the cultus was established in Jerusalem, and according to Ezra and Nehemiah (e.g., Neh 10:38, 12:47), the Aaronide system was normative in the post-exilic period as well.

At this point, the students are asked to compare the reconstruction of the period of the monarchy in the books of Kings. Again, neither secondary literature nor the authority of the teacher is needed to convince the student that whereas the Aaronides are everywhere to be found in Chronicles, they are nowhere to be found in Kings. Not even Zadok, the first High Priest, is linked to Aaron. Indeed, Zadok sports no genealogy at all.

This absence of Aaronides from the book of Kings thus raises questions as to what priestly system did function during the monarchical period — a question that is addressed not by some magisterial decree, but by a look at other biblical sources, namely the prophetic books, beginning with the post-exilic prophets. Here the students can see for themselves that though Levites as priests are mentioned in Malachi, Zechariah, and Ezekiel, the Aaronides are nowhere mentioned in these books. Indeed, Ezekiel, who strips the Levites of their priestly rights, assigns these rights to the sons of Zadok not on the ground that they are the sons of Aaron who had been given exclusive rights to the priesthood when he had crushed the rebellion of Korah in the wilderness, but on the ground that the sons of Zadok were the only levitical priests who had kept their charge and had not profaned God's holy sanctuary.

And when the students go back further to Jeremiah, Isaiah, Micah, Hosea, and Amos, they discover that Aaronides are nowhere mentioned, and that Aaron is only mentioned once (Micah 6:4), but only alongside Moses and Miriam in the wilderness, and not as a priest at all.

Moving back from Ben Sira and Chronicles-Ezra, in which sources the Aaronide system is normative, the students discover that the Aaronides disappear with Malachi as though the Aaronide layer of the Pentateuch did not exist. Instead of the Aaronides, students find the Levites serving as priests as mandated by the book of Deuteronomy. It is as though these prophets were fully aware of Deuteronomy, but not aware of the Aaronide texts that loom so large in the finalized Pentateuch.

And when the student pushes back to even earlier sources, he/she discovers that no prophet before the time of Josiah makes any reference to Levites. Indeed, the cultic system that they castigate is one where multiple altars are the rule and where priests are neither Levites nor Aaronides, but just priests — exactly as one would have anticipated from the texts in Exodus that allow for multiple altars, but do not provide for a priesthood.

Confronted with this fall-away of the Levites, the students are then asked to take a close look at the account of Josiah's reformation as is given in II Kings. Here they see for themselves that the discovery of the book, its authentication, its promulgation, and the tearing-down of the high places involve the collaboration of a High Priest, a prophet and a king, two of whom, the priest and the king, are legitimatized as exercising authority alongside the prophet by divine command or sanction as revealed through Moses in the wilderness and recorded by him in the book of Deuteronomy, but are not recorded in the prophetic level of the Pentateuch, a level which bestows upon Moses exclusive power and authority and which mandates neither priesthood nor King.

Having made this journey of discovery, the students are then confronted with the delicate question as to how they are to account, not for the secondary literature, but the sources. These sources reveal that although the Aaronide system flourished in the time of Ben Sira, and that it was the normative system for the authors of Chronicles and Ezra-Nehemiah, there is not a single prophet who ever makes mention of Aaronides, nor are there any references to Aaronides in the books of Kings.

The students have also noted that though prophets refer to Levites from the time of Josiah, no prophet refers to Levites before Josiah. These pre-Josianic prophets are only aware of high places and their priests. For them, sacrifices had seemingly not been demanded by God in the wilderness and therefore had no covenantal status.

The students also have seen for themselves that there are three mutually exclusive authority systems in the Pentateuch — the prophetic, the prophetic-levitical-monarchical, and the Aaronide. At no time have they been coerced by scholarly authority. Secondary literature has been excluded from the discussions. The professor has at no time pressed his own interpretation on the students. His only function has been to see to it that the sources are read — and read in full - and discussed in class. Indeed, his only determinative role has been the decision that the first source to be read be Ben Sira. But even this decision was acted on only after the class had engaged in a free and open discussion and had agreed that the rationale was one to which they could give their assent.

Once the sources have been read and discussed by the students, they are ready to tackle the secondary literature with the assurance that they know from first-hand reading what the sources say. They are urged to weigh and measure every scholarly opinion in the light of the sources and render a critical judgment accordingly. They are also encouraged to come up with alternative solutions to the problems raised in class and in the secondary literature.

IV.

This method of focusing exclusively on the sources is one that *ab initio* is deeply appreciated by all students irrespective of their denominational commitment. It is especially appreciated by conservative Christians, since throughout the course, the texts are treated with respect, and allowed to present themselves without scholarly intervention. The problems which arise are problems that arise from the texts themselves, and the solutions are left open so that the students can deal with them with their faith and through their faith. Though in the course of discussion possible solutions may be suggested, they are never imposed.

This method which has been spelled out with respect to how the sources lead us to conclude that the system of Judaism which flourished after the finalization of the Pentateuch was the Aaronide system, is the same method that is used in the three subsequent segments of the course. To deal with the problem of the Pharisees, we begin exclusively with the sources that are self-legitimizing because they specifically refer to the Pharisees and Sadducees: Josephus, the New Testament, and the Tannaitic literature, and we allow the sources to lead us to the next logical steps that have to be taken. Similarly, the apocryphal and pseudepigraphic literature is read without scholarly intermediation or intrusion. The same holds true for the Hellenistic literature, the Letter of Aristeas, III and IV Maccabees, the Wisdom of Solomon and Philo.

With every source emerging out of intertestamental Judaism absorbed, with every form and mode of Judaism elicited from these sources clearly in mind, and with every literary form and mode familiarized, the students are then ready to bring all their source knowledge to bear when they begin their study of the Gospels, Acts, and Epistles of Paul and the other books of the New Testament with the professor's admonition: "Search out the sources, and rely not on my opinion."

Chapter Ten

Theological Education and Christian-Jewish Relations

Eugene J. Fisher

Introduction

Since the publication of my book on *Seminary Education and Christian-Jewish Relations*,[1] interseminary programs have been put on across the country devoted to the issue of integrating better understandings of Christian-Jewish relations in theological curricula. These have taken place in such diverse areas as Dallas, Boston, Chicago, Los Angeles, and Washington, D.C.[2] A distinctive feature of all of these colloquia is their ecumenical as well as interreligious structure. In several cases, students and faculty of various Christian denominational institutions have been brought together for the first time to work together on a theological and methodological challenge that confronts all Christian denominations equally.

At one time it may have been popular to view the rise of the concepts of civic tolerance and religious pluralism as solely and directly the result of the Protestant Reformation or, alternatively, of the "secular" Enlightenment. Such a simple view of Western history, recent work has shown,[3] is no longer acceptable. Anti-semitism, the teaching of contempt against Jews and Judaism, can be found in the works of the Reformers and Enlightenment philosophers no less than in their medieval scholastic forebearers.[4] Shared theological anti-Judaism, then, remains a sort of inverted symbol of the unity of Christians. The first great schism experienced by the Church came with its split from the Jewish people. Understanding that split, and the tragic implications of the violent rhetoric with which the early generations of Christians interpreted the meaning of the Church's break with Jews and Judaism, therefore, is of central, not peripheral, importance to the Church's self-understanding today. Ecumenism and Christian-Jewish dialogue are two sides of a single coin.[5]

The thesis raised by this paper is that the question of the relationship of the Church to the Jewish people is integral to every area of the core theological curriculum, from sacred scripture and liturgy to systematics and Church history. The reason for this can be found in the fact that the Church in the first instance (i.e., from New Testament times) defined its identity against its understanding of the identity of the Jewish people as "people of God" (covenant/election).

Though the question of reformulating the relationship challenges Christian theology "at the very level of the Church's own identity," to cite the words of Pope John Paul II, it has seldom surfaced, except in a negative way, in Christian theological curricula. The methodological implication of this view, if correct, is not merely that courses in rabbinics need to be added to the traditional Christian theological curriculum.[6] This is a necessary step, since so much of what we say about Christianity depends on what we say about Judaism. So our traditional ignorance of rabbinic Judaism is an increasing problem methodologically. Beyond such additions to the curriculum, however, the argument is made that each course as currently taught must face a series of challenges raised from within by the contemporary reassessment of the relationship between the Church and the Jewish people, both "people of God."

Such a reassessment of the basic grounding of Christian theological enterprise in the light of its Jewish origins and present dialogue with Jews and Judaism, it is maintained, is a necessary ingredient of the theological renewal called for "in our age."[7] It would seem appropriate, then, to indicate at least some of the challenges raised in the various core areas of the theological curriculum.[8]

1. Sacred Scripture

The immediate and most central question facing biblical theology (and with it systematic theology, of course) is the relationship between the Scriptures. The classic Christian position, heavily influenced by Marcionism, is embedded in the very terminology used to name the two major collections of the Christian canon: "Old Testament" and "New Testament." This terminology in itself implied a theology of discontinuity between the Scriptures, and leans heavily toward a theory of supercessionism (Christianity has superceded Judaism in God's favor and plan for sacred history) if not necessarily abrogationism (God has cancelled the "old" covenant with the Jews in favor of a "new" one in Christ Jesus). The distinction between the two is that in the supercessionist theory one can, albeit only with difficulty, preserve the testimony of such texts as Romans 9-11 by arguing that God's covenant with the Jews has not been abrogated or cancelled, but merely subsumed into that of the Church as the new people of God. The abrogationist model, however, is compatible only with the ancient Christian "teaching of contempt"[9] that viewed the Jews as "accursed" by God and relegated them to the scrapheap of sacred history. Such a view, of course, implicitly eviscerates the Christian claim to covenant at the same time as it denies that of Judaism. For if God could abrogate His/Her covenant with the Jewish people for their sin (in "rejecting" Jesus), the continued sinfulness of Christians equally questions any Christian claim to covenant.

To reject flatly the Hebrew Scriptures or God's covenant with the Jewish people, therefore, is to destroy the essence of Christianity, which is one good reason why the early Church rejected Marcion when he took the abrogationist model to its logical conclusion. Marcionism, however, proved not so easy to defeat. Supercessionism, while more subtle, maintains a great deal of its dynamic. Thus modern scholars can speak of Second Temple Judaism as "late Judaism," implying that Judaism "died" for all practical purposes with the coming of Christ and the destruction of the Temple in 70 C.E.

The tendency to dichotomize the relationship between the Scriptures remains a strong one: "old" vs. "new," "law" vs. "grace," "love" vs. "mercy," etc. Many New Testament scholars, such as Rudolf Bultmann,[10] can speak of the Hebrew Scriptures as a mere "propadeutic" to the New Testament, as if they have no intrinsic value as God's Word save as a background paper or proof text for the New Testament.[11] Others can maintain, seemingly with a straight face, that any sayings of Jesus which are congruous with those of contemporary Judaism or rabbinic dicta are, *by that very fact*, eliminated from consideration as authentic *logia* of Jesus. Though he cautions against taking the principle too far, Reginald Fuller, for example, can affirm this strange-sounding *a priori* as a "valuable" criterion:

> We can eliminate any material [in the Gospels] which can be paralleled in contemporary Judaism, for here too the presumption is that the sayings in question have, historically speaking, been erroneously attributed to Jesus. This material would include sayings which are paralleled in Jewish apocalyptic and in Rabbinic tradition.[12]

Christian New Testament scholarship has the tendency as often as not to place both biblical and rabbinic Judaism in the procrustean bed of its own internal, Christian dichotomies, as E. P. Sanders has shown so effectively in his analysis of Christian use of rabbinic sources.[13] One example here will stand for many more.[14] It is common, Sanders points out, for Christian scholars to juxtapose divine mercy and justice, using the contrast to "prove" that rabbinic Judaism subordinated the former to a legalistic view of the latter. But the actual rabbinic pairings, as Sanders notes, are between God's "quality of punishing" *(middat pur'anut)* or "quality of justice" *(middat ha-din)* and God's "quality of rewarding" *(middat tobah)*, or "quality of mercy" *(middat rahamin)*, with the latter greater than the former.[15] Sanders summarizes, counter the notion of rabbinism as a system of "works of righteousness" so often imposed on it by Christians:

> The statements of reward and punishment [in Rabbinic] literature do not indicate how one earns salvation. Their opposite would not be that God is merciful and saves, but that there is no correspondence between God's rewards and man's behavior: that God is arbitrary ... Mercy and justice are not truly in conflict, nor is strict reward and punishment for deeds an alternative soteriology to election and atonement.[16]

In a remarkable essay in the Stimulus volume, *Biblical Studies*,[17] Joseph Blenkinsopp points out the critical difficulties experienced by Christian scholars seeking to develop an adequate "Theology of the Old Testament." His conclusion is that the endeavor as a whole has reached a point of crisis: "If the general impression given in this essay is overwhelmingly negative, and if we have said little positively about the relation between Old and New Testament, we can only plead that we are as yet nowhere close to knowing how to write an Old Testament theology.[18] Again, underlying theological *a prioris* and an essentially apologetical stance *vis à vis* the Hebrew Scriptures surfaces as the *bete noir* of Christian efforts.

Blenkinsopp discerns a depressingly deep strain of anti-Judaism even in the best of Christian experts on Jewish biblical writings, such as Julius Wellhausen, (whose meaningful effort framed much of the methodology for succeeding generations of scholars), Gustav Friedrich Oehler, Wilhelm Vatke, Hermann Schultz, Walter Eichrodt and Gerhard von Rad. The methodological manifestations of this are several, but curiously unified in rhetoric. Wellhausen, for example, writes of Second Temple Judaism (which he identifies with "Early Catholicism," thus writing off Roman Catholic tradition at the same time) in the following way:

> The Creator of heaven and earth becomes the manager of a petty scheme of salvation ... The law thrusts itself in everywhere, it commands and blocks up access to heaven; it regulates and sets limits to the understanding of the divine working on earth. As far as I can see, it takes the soul out of religion and spoils morality.[19]

Schultz, who can speak blithely of "the petty Pharisaic view of life," sees in the Second Temple period the victory of "unhealthy" over the "healthy" elements of religion, by which he means of externalism and legalism over the "inward religious assurance which is the gift of prophecy."[20] Schultz is even capable of inventing a socio-psychological analysis: "the consciousness of inward emptiness, and the feeling that the Spirit of Jehovah had departed, kept on increasing."[21] The writers of this period, Blenkinsopp notes, tended to structure their approach to Jewish history "on the procrustean bed of Hegelian dialectics,"[22] following the philosophical fashion of the times, Social Darwinism.

A generation later, and following a philosophical trend less Hegelian but no less strictly formed by *Heilsgeschichte*, Walter Eichrodt can state of Second Temple Judaism (of which early Christianity was a part):

> Thus at the very heart of the desire for salvation we find once again that inner disintegration of the structure of the Jewish faith.[23]

Psychology still seemingly in vogue, Eichrodt speaks of "the inner schizophrenia of Jewish piety" which was overcome in Jesus.[24]

The enterprise of Old Testament theology, as Blenkinsopp has shown, has proven incapable of overcoming its own sense of the discontinuity between the Scriptures save through "a typological linking of Old and New Testament and a virtual bracketing of post-biblical Judaism" as well as of the wisdom writings which form the bulk of the third part of the canon.[25] Theories which cannot encompass large sections of the biblical canon and which are forced to rely on a reed as thin as typology to achieve any sense at all of the continuity between the Scriptures are, from a Christian point of view, very seriously flawed. In learning how to write biblical theology, Blenkinsopp concludes:

> It seems that first we must take Tanakh seriously on its own terms which ... involves coming to terms with the Second Temple period inclusive of early Christianity ... It involves further, as a necessary consequence, coming to terms historically and theologically with Judaism which, far from declining or disappearing at the time of early Christianity, only reached its most characteristic expressions several centuries later.[26]

One could add, as another way of saying the same thing, that the problem of discontinuity is heightened by the tendency to define the biblical-theological endeavor solely in Christological terms. Christian scholars often look, whether in biblical or rabbinic Judaism, only for parallels to the New Testament, allowing the categories of Christian theology to determine what they find and thus missing or even distorting central elements of sources which they are attempting to understand. Such a reductionist approach to the sources impoverishes Christian thought even today, and has led to some odd pairings in the standard lectionary.[27] Samuel Sandmel once lamented the tendency of the Christian scholar "to create his own categories and to superimpose these on Judaism or else make Judaism fit into them."[28]

2. Systematic Theology

The attempt to form an adequate biblical theology is intimately linked with the conceptual attempt to formulate a way of articulating in positive terms the relationship between the Church and the Jewish people as people of God. Pope John Paul II succinctly frames the issue in a 1980 address:

> The first dimension of this dialogue, that is the meeting between the people of God of the old covenant *never retracted by God* (Rom 11:29), on the one hand, and the people of the new covenant, on the other, is at the same time a dialogue within our own Church, so to speak, a dialogue between the first and the second part of its Bible.[29]

This statement effectively challenges both the abrogationist and the supercessionist approaches to the relationship that have dominated so much of Christian thought historically. The abrogationist approach, on the basis of Romans 9-11, is clearly rejected as inadequate: the Jews are in a covenant "never retracted by God." The latter theory, which might be interpreted broadly to avow some sort of notion that the Jewish covenant has been "subsumed" into the Christian covenant, is challenged by the introduction of the notion of dialogue at this level. Jews, the Pope states, clearly exist as a people, whole and integral unto themselves. This very real, historical people, in continuity with their biblical forbears, just as clearly exists in covenant-relationship with God.

Since being "people of God," with a divine mission in and for the world, is likewise the essence of the Church's own claims concerning itself, the Church must listen with care to the Jewish witness to the world in order to develop an adequate ecclesiology for itself. Rabbinic Judaism, which developed alongside early Christianity and reacted in its own unique fashion to many of the same events and pressures (i.e., the destruction of the Temple, the need to respond to Hellenistic philosophy and culture without accepting its pagan elements, the crisis of faith and reason, etc.), clearly has much more to say to us spiritually than simply becoming a backdrop for better understanding the New Testament. Israel's struggle with the One God has direct, not indirect or ancillary relevance to the Christian struggle to remain faithful to the God of Israel.

In its divergencies as well as in its parallel solutions to common dilemmas the spiritual riches of the Tannaim and the Amoraim, the medieval Jewish philosophers and the Hasidic masters witness directly, on the level of faith to faith, to Christian thought today. As the Vatican's 1974 Guidelines for Catholic-Jewish relations pregnantly suggest, "the problem of Jewish-Christian relations concerns the Church as such, since it is when 'pondering her own mystery' that she encounters the mystery of Israel."[30]

Not only the mystery of the Church (ecclesiology), but the mystery of Christ itself is centrally affected by the reformation of attitudes toward Jews and Judaism currently under way. A full appreciation of the Incarnation, for example, requires coming to grips with the fully Jewish particularity of Jesus' humanity rather than glossing it over as we have tended to do in the past.

Along with Christology, traditional eschatology will need to accommodate on a more radical level the "not yet" aspect of the New Testament kerygma. It is this aspect that Christians have most been tempted to ignore in their proclamations of the gospel to the world, sliding, at times, to the point of identifying the Church and the Kingdom.[31] The Jewish "no" to Christian claims about Jesus must be seen as a continuingly valid (and necessary) witness to us to avoid the dangers of triumphalism. Theologian David Tracy articulates succinctly both challenge and hope for future theological research:

> For myself, the suspicion which the Holocaust discloses for traditional Christological language is this: does the fundamental Christian belief in the ministry, death and resurrection of Jesus Christ demand a Christology that either states or implies that Judaism has been displaced by Christianity? ... For Christians to retrieve the reality of the not yet as a historical reality is to recall that the concept Messiah cannot (by being spiritualized) be divorced from the reality of Messianic times ... However influential in later Christian history, theologically pure fulfillment models and a-historical Messiah models are not the only New Testament models that can be employed ... The always/already/not yet structure of belief pervading Israel's covenant with God and Israel's expectation of Messianic times remains the fundamental always/already/not yet structure of Christian belief as well.[32]

The challenge, as this passage illustrates, extends into all areas of Christian doctrine. The promise/fulfillment model, so popular as a frame for interpreting the fundamental thrust of the Bible, needs to be re-cast more accurately along the lines of a "promise/confirmation" assertion, as Paul van Buren has suggested. Christians, no less than Jews, await the fullfillment of the Messianic times. And Jews, no less than Christians, are filled with the spirit of God's grace in and through Israel's covenant with the One God. To dialogue with Jews is not, then, to encounter a people who can be adequately counted among the "un-evangelized" or the "pre-evangelized." The Jews *are* God's people, and as such are *already* "with the Father" even as they (no less than we) await the End Time in divinely-inspired hope and expectation.

Missiology, then, needs to take seriously the implications of the renewal of covenant theology in our time. As Daniel Harrington has shown, the key phrase of the risen Lord's commission to the disciples in Matthew 28:16-20, *Matheleusate panta ta ethne* (Mt. 28:19) may perhaps most accurately translate as "make disciples of all the gentiles (*goyim*)."[33]

A number of recent works by Protestant and Catholic scholars have begun the task of systematically reformulating Christian teaching. These should be required reading in all theological schools, since they are among the truly pioneering efforts of our times. A handy overview of the field can be found in John Pawlikowski's *What Are They Saying About Christian-Jewish Relations* (New York: Paulist Press, 1980).

Solid contributions to this growing field of renewed Christian thought have recently been made by the following. These do not necessarily resolve all the myriad questions that will emerge as the effort progresses. But, together, they establish a new *status questions* for contemporary Christian theological efforts. Clemens Thomas' *A Christian Theology of Judaism* (New York, Paulist Press, Stimulus Books, 1980) assesses biblical and doctrinal theology to the present, noting where further work is necessary. John Pawlikowski in *Christ in the Light of the Christian-Jewish Dialogue* (Paulist Press, Stimulus Books, 1982) develops a solid Christological model which avoids the pitfalls of past triumphalist excesses while maintaining (and, in a number of ways enriching) traditional creedal claims. Joseph E. Monti's *Who Do You Say That I Am?* (Paulist, 1984) seeks to develop a "non-negating" Christology based on a dialogic model of theological methodology.

Finally, Paul M. Van Buren's *A Christian Theology of the People Israel* (New York: Seabury) undertakes the ambitious task of rethinking all the basic categories of classic theology: creation; covenant; religious anthropology; evil and hope; election; the people of Israel; Land and Torah; Jesus and Torah; and Jesus and Israel. In the process he carefully reconsiders the implications of the writings of St. Paul, which remain crucial to the discussion.

3. Liturgy

Retrieval of the Jewishness of Jesus and the covenantal validity of Judaism has enabled scholars today to see more clearly the roots of Christian liturgy in Jewish practice and the living spiritual bonds that link the Church to the Jewish people. Jesus, again, was a Jew who prayed as a Jew, and who taught his disciples to pray as Jews. Each of the elements of the Our Father *('Avinu)* finds close parallels in biblical and especially rabbinic literature.[34]

The Christian order of the Eucharist takes its form by combining elements of the traditional synagogue service (readings from Scripture, Psalms and homilies on the text) with elements from the Passover meal (bread and wine, berakoth, hallel, etc.).[35] Likewise, it is not difficult to discern the Jewish origins of much of the Christian liturgical cycle.[36]

But it is not simply a matter of historical understanding to study the interdependence of the parallel developments of Jewish and Christian liturgies over the centuries. It is equally a matter of surfacing immense spiritual riches within the present age that is the potential of a dialogical approach to the seminary curriculum. Some of this potential is illustrated in the essays included in the volume, *Spirituality and Prayer: Jewish and Christian Understandings*, edited by Leon Klenicki and Gabe Huck (Paulist Press, Stimulus books, 1983).

4. Church History

Several very important new works have come out since the publication of my *Seminary Education* text which have greatly expanded our knowledge of the history of Christian-Jewish relations, which is to say our knowledge of the history of the Church. John Gager's *The Origins of Anti-Semitism: Attitudes Toward Judaism in Pagan and Christian Antiquity* (Oxford University Press, 1983), for example, reveals the surprisingly positive attitudes of many pagans toward Judaism and their attraction to it. This corrects the notion that Gentile Christians simply brought anti-Judaism from the pagan world into the Church when they entered. One must, then, look to specifically theological Christian motivations to understand fully the phenomenon of Christian anti-Jewishness.

Gager's concluding portion on St. Paul (pp. 174-264) is extremely helpful in understanding the precise character of the Apostle to the Gentiles' "argument" with Jews and Judaism. No New Testament course can any longer afford to ignore these new insights, and those of other scholars such as Stendahl,[37] Sloyan,[38] Sanders,[39] Koenig,[40] Gaston,[41] and Davies.[42] It may not be too great an exaggeration to state that the present re-evaluation of a key theme of the Pauline corpus may be viewed in the years to come as the most significant in Christian history since Martin Luther.

Robert L. Wilken's *John Chrysostum and the Jews: Rhetoric and Reality in the Late 4th Century* (University of California Press, 1983) sets Chrysostum's justly infamous anti-Judaic polemics into the context of the inflated rhetorical style of the time. Once again, as with Gager, we see the attractiveness of Judaism and not only for pagans but for Christians as well. Chrysostum's invectives may well have been aimed not primarily at the Jews as such but at the members of his own Christian community attracted to the synagogue.

Jeremy Cohen's *The Friars and the Jews: The Evolution of Medieval Anti-Judaism* (Cornell University Press, 1983) likewise clarifies our historical understanding, pointing out the radical shift that took place in the Christian ideological stance toward rabbinic Judaism from the relative tolerance that characterized the Augustinian and classical papal legislation on the Jews to a form of intolerance which justified in theological terms the efforts made from the 13th to the 16th centuries to "cleanse" Europe of its Jewish population. This shift in attitudes, Cohen argues, was coincident with, but by no means coincidental to the rise of the mendicant orders.

Heiko Oberman's *The Roots of Anti-Semitism in the Age of Renaissance and Reformation* (Philadelphia: Fortress, 1984) picks up almost exactly where Cohen's study leaves off in the 16th century. He shows convincingly the continuity between the negative attitudes of the later medieval period sketched by Cohen and the equally negative polemics (and actions) of the great Reformers and humanists of the age. The Reformation challenged many aspects of its medieval heritage, but not its virulent anti-Judaism. It was only in a later period, when Christians too began to see themselves in exile, Oberman concludes, that they were able to see in Israel's exile any other than "the marks of a God-sent punishment"[43] and were therefore able to glimpse the notion that a state of diaspora did not necessarily mean the ending of God's covenant with the Jewish people — or with themselves as Church.

Finally, Alice and Roy Eckardt in *Long Night's Journey into Day: Life and Faith after the Holocaust* (Detroit: Wayne State University Press, 1982) grapple with the implications of Nazi genocide for contemporary Christian theology.

Conclusions

It is hoped that the above survey, by no means complete (even on those four issues it does pick up), will serve to whet the appetites of faculty and students for the tasks ahead — and the spirited riches to be gained through them. Again, the point has not been simply to suggest the addition of another elective or hiring a Jewish faculty member, though such advances are by no means eschewed. Rather, it is up to teachers and students alike to seize the opportunities offered in every course in the core curriculum and ponder together what that course would be like if it truly sought to take seriously God's covenant with the Jewish people, and Christian treatment of God's people up to the present age.

---

[1]Eugene J. Fisher, *Seminary Education and Christian-Jewish Relations* (Washington, D.C.: National Catholic Education Association, 1983).

[2]With the exception of the Boston efforts, sponsored by the Boston Theological Institute (and spearheaded by Krister Stendahl of Harvard Divinity School and Daniel Harrington, S.J., of Weston School of Theology), these programs have been co-sponsored by the theological schools involved and the American Jewish Committee (AJC). Reports on the AJC co-sponsored workshops can be found in the 1983-84 issues of AJC's Interreligious Affairs Department *Newsletter*. Reports on the progress of the B.T.I. efforts can be found in the "Ecumenical Events" section of the *Journal of Ecumenical Studies* (Vol. 20, no. 3, Spring, 1983), pp. 358-360.

[3]E.g., Heiko A. Oberman, *The Roots of Anti-Semitism in the Age of Renaissance and Reformation*, transl. by James I. Porter (Philadelphia: Fortress Press, 1984), and Arthur A. Hertzberg, *The French Enlightenment and the Jews: The Origins of Modern Anti-Semitism* (N.Y.: Schocken, 1970).

[4]Cf. Jeremy Cohen, *The Friars and the Jews* (Cornell University Press, 1983).

[5]Eugene J. Fisher, "Jewish Christian Relations and the Quest for Christian Unity," *Journal of Ecumenical Studies* (Vol. 20:2, 1983), pp. 235-244.

[6]Jacob Petuchowski eloquently argues the case for inclusion of rabbinics in Christian theological curricula in "Judaism in Christian Theological Education," *Harvard Divinity Bulletin* (April-May, 1984), pp. 10-12.

[7]Reference to *Nostra Aetate*, no. 4, the Second Vatican Council's Declaration of the Jews which, in 1985, celebrated its 20th Anniversity.

[8]These are developed more fully, and with bibliographic reference, in my book, *Seminary Education*, cited in note 1, above. This paper will update rather than repeat that bibliography. The curriculum model I have followed is that typical of Roman Catholic seminaries. Some adjustments may have to be made to the particular academic divisions pursued in Protestant and Orthodox theological seminaries.

[9]For a definition of this term, cf. Jules Isaac, *Jesus and Israel* (N.Y.: Holt, Rinehart, Winston, 1971).

[10]For a spirited discussion of Bultmann's theory on the relationship between the Scriptures, see the essays in B. W. Anderson, ed., *The Old Testament and Christian Faith* (London: SCM Press, 1963).

[11]E.g., W. Vischer's essay, "Everywhere the Scripture is About Christ Alone," in *ibid.*, pp. 90-101.

[12]Reginald H. Fuller, *The New Testament in Current Study* (N.Y.: Charles Scribner's Sons, 1962), p. 33.

[13]E. P. Sanders, *Paul and Palestinian Judaism* (Fortress, 1977).

[14]Other examples are given in Eugene Fisher, "From Polemic to Objectivity? A Short History of the Use and Abuse of Hebrew Sources by Recent Christian New Testament Scholarship," *Hebrew Studies* journal (Vol. 20-21, 1980), pp. 199-208.

[15]Sanders, *Paul and Palestinian Judaism*, p. 123.

[16]Sanders, *Paul and Palestinian Judaism*, p. 182. Sanders' treatment of Pauline theology, included in the last section of the cited volume, is expanded and, to my mind, helpfully clarified in his more recent *Paul, the Law, and the Jewish People* (Fortress, 1983).

[17]L. Boadt, H. Croner, L. Klenicki, ed's., *Biblical Studies: Meeting Ground of Jews and Christians* (N.Y.: Paulist Press, Stimulus Books, 1980).

[18]Joseph Blenkinsopp, "Tanakh and New Testament: A Christian Perspective," *ibid.*, p. 113.

[19]Julius Wellhausen, *Prologomena to the History of Ancient Israel* (1878, Engl. transl. by Robertson Smith, New York: Meridian Books, 1957), p. 509.

[20]Hermann Schultz, *Old Testament Theology* (1869, 1896; Engl. transl. of the fourth German edition, Edinburgh: T. & T. Clark, 1892), Vol. 1, pp. 321-331.

[21]*Ibid.*, pp. 1, 406.

[22]Blenkinsopp, "Tanakh and New Testament," *cit.*, p. 103.

[23]Walter Eichrodt, *Theology of the Old Testament*, transl. by J. A. Baker in two volumes (Philadelphia: Westminster, I 1961, II 1967) pp. 11, 464.

[24]*Ibid.*, II, 315.

[25]Blenkinsopp, "Tanak and New Testament," cit., p. 113, refers to Gerhard von Rad's *Old Testament Theology* (New York: Harper and Row, 1962), G. Ernest Wright, *God Who Acts* (London: SCM Press, 1952) and R. E. Clements, *Old Testament Theology: A Fresh Approach* (London: Marshall, Morgan & Scoft, 1978). Von Rad, he notes, simply ignores the Second Temple period, while Wright and Clements omit entirely treatment of the Wisdom writings

[26]Blenkinsopp, "Tanakh and New Testament," *cit.*, p. 113.

[27]Cf. E. Fisher, "Continuity and Discontinuity in the Scriptural Readings," *Liturgy* (May 1978), pp. 30-37. This reductionist approach to Hebrew sources is particularly striking in H. Strack and P. Billerbeck, *Kommentar zum Neuen Testament and Talmud and Midrash* (Munich: 6 Vol's., 1922-61).

[28]Samuel Sandmel, *Two Living Traditions* (Detroit: Wayne State University Press, 1972), p. 230. For an overview of other relevant questions and opportunities facing biblical students as a result of the Jewish-Christian dialogue, see Eugene Fisher, "The Impact of Christian-Jewish Dialogue on Biblical Studies" in Richard Rousseau, S.J., *Christianity and Judaism: The Deepening Dialogue* (Ridge Row Press, 1983), pp. 117-138.

[29]John Paul II, "Dialogue: The Road to Understanding," *Origins* (12/4/80). The talk was originally given to representatives of the Jewish community in Mainz, West Germany on November 17, 1980. Italics added.

[30]Vatican Commission for Religious Relations with the Jews, "Guidelines and Suggestions for Implementing the Conciliar Declaration, *Nostra Aetate* (no. 4)," Rome, December 1, 1974.

[31]New Testament scholar Daniel Harrington works through these and related points in illuminating fashion in his two recent works, *Light of all Nations: Essays on the Church in New Testament Research* (Wilmington, Delaware: Michael Glazier, Inc., 1982) and *God's People in Christ: New Testament Perspectives on the Church and Judaism* (Fortress, 1980).

[32]David Tracy, "Religious Values After the Holocaust," in Abraham J. Peck, ed., *Jews and Christians After the Holocaust* (Philadelphia: Fortress Press, 1982).

[33]Daniel Harrington, "Make Disciples of All the Gentiles," in *Light of All Nations*, p. 111. On the missiological issues in general, see Martin A. Cohen and Helga Croner, editors, *Christian Mission — Jewish Mission* (New York: Paulist Press, Stimulus Books, 1982).

[34]Cf. M. Brocke and J. Petuchowski, *The Lord's Prayer and Jewish Liturgy* (New York: Seabury, 1978) and A. Finkel and L. Frizzell, *Standing Before God: Studies in Prayer in Scriptures and Tradition* (New York: KTAV, 1981.

[35]Sofia Cavalleti, "Christian Liturgy: Its Roots in Judaism," *SIDIC* (Rome: Vol. 6:1, 1973), pp. 10-28; Asher Finkel, "The Passover Story and the Last Supper," in M. Zeig and M. Siegel, eds., *Root and Branch* (New York: Roth Publ., 1973, pp. 19-46; and Anthony Saldarini. *Jesus and Passover* (New York: Paulist Press, 1984).

[36]L. Bouyer, "Jewish and Christian Liturgies," in L. Sheppard, ed., *True Worship* (Baltimore: Helicon Press, 1963), pp. 29-44; W. O. Oesterley, *The Jewish Background of the Christian Liturgy* (Oxford: Clarendon Press, 1925); and Eric Werner, *The Sacred Bridge: Liturgical Parallels in the Synagogue and the Early Church* (New York: Schocken, 1970). The second volume of Werner's classic study is due for publication at the time of this writing.

[37]Krister Stendahl, *Paul Among the Jews and Gentiles* (Fortress, 1976).

[38]Gerard Sloyan, *Is Christ the End of the Law?* (Westminster, 1978).

[39]E. P. Sanders, *Paul, the Law and the Jewish People* (Fortress, 1983).

[40]John Koenig, *Jews and Christians in Dialogue: New Testament Foundations* (Westminster, 1976).

[41]Lloyd Gaston, "Paul and the Torah," in Alan T. Davies, *Anti-Semitism and the Foundations of Christianity* Paulist Press, 1979). Cf. also Harrington and others mentioned above.

[42]W. D. Davies, *Paul and Rabbinic Judaism* (N.Y.: Harper & Row, 1984).

[43]Heiko A. Oberman, *The Roots of Anti-Semitism* (Fortress, 1984), p. 141.

Chapter Eleven

Team-Taught, In-Class Dialogue: A Limited But Promising Method For Teaching Judaism

James F. Moore

There are many ways of teaching theology and, in particular, Jewish thought. None, however, is more productive and satisfying than a team-taught setting in which a Jewish scholar and a Christian scholar construct a course designed to maximize classroom dialogue. Though such a setting is an optimum arrangement for teaching Judaism at an undergraduate level, so many factors work to make such a consistent course offering difficult that an in-class team-taught dialogue is rare, at least at undergraduate institutions. Dialogue classes would be even rarer on the campus of a private, Christian denominational university since not only are the normal logistic, curricular, and financial problems evident in such a program but the typical commitments to safeguard traditional ways of teaching theology are generally heightened.

Because of the obvious roadblocks usually facing the development of a program of in-class Jewish-Christian dialogue, we consider ourselves fortunate to continue into this academic year just such a program at Valparaiso University. Though much formal planning and consistent urging is necessary to create any university curricular offering, the pattern of in-class, team-taught dialogue (now in its sixth year) is as much due to happy coincidence and general good fortune as genuine foresight. Given that fact, this pattern of teaching is offered as an exciting model for teaching Judaism though I fully understand that recreating such a model elsewhere depends upon the coincidence of similar circumstances.

The initial part of our good fortune is the easy proximity of a synagogue (one of the Reform Jewish tradition). That, in itself, may be comparable to many other locales; however, three additional factors serve to make this proximity work to our advantage. First, the Rabbi at the synagogue has been trained in a program that already prepared him in the study of Christianity and in contemporary Jewish-Christian dialogue. One of his teachers, Rabbi Samuel Sandmel, had been a forerunner of what has blossomed into a full-fledged program of study at the Hebrew Union College. Second, the congregation together with the Jewish Chautauqua Society has been willing to do what is necessary to release the Rabbi for the time necessary to take on a part-time teaching load. Third, the curricular structure at Valparaiso is flexible enough to guarantee the space, the faculty and the students for team-taught courses in our department.

We are also fortunate that we have had students whose interest and initiative has led us toward an expanded offering in studies in Judaism. Though our students may be no different than other undergraduates, the initiative taken by a few has consistently reinforced for the administration and our department the need for courses in Judaism, especially the team-taught courses of in-class dialogue. The active role of our students has undoubtedly made the program more feasible for our administration, flexible to a point, but nevertheless consistently conscious of financial and scheduling pressures.

A Model for Dialogue

Even with the good fortune of coincidence, a clear model for such classes must be developed in order to take full advantage of a potential for dialogue. Indeed, the model I present is both a pattern growing out of classes and a formal structure by which we can judge the effectiveness of such offerings. A pattern of teaching has clearly developed in a hit and miss fashion from the actual experience of teaching (more on those specific experiences later). This means that the pattern I propose is both a product of experience and a process in need of refinement with each new class experience. Yet we need some pattern for us to assess adequately the success of dialogue classes.

The model for teaching is a broad model for dialogue that may be a useful way of conceiving all theological work. This model has four basic points that are separate yet integrated, important on their own but also part of a leveled, developing process of inter-religious communication. Those points are:

1. Openness to listen to another view
2. Openness to accept truth in another view
3. Openness to learn about one's own tradition
4. Openness to risk change

In fact, the last of these points may well be a presupposition for all dialogue preceding the other three basic points. The experience of the class setting, however, tends to show that students, and, even, professors are unaware of the risks involved prior to becoming engaged in dialogue. The risks may range from a jumbling of views, to doubt about any truth, to challenges and judgment of peers. For the undergraduate student, all of these risks as well as others are real and can be devastating; nevertheless a student may tend to enter a dialogue class with a certain amount of naive confidence, a confidence that change can be warded off if necessary, that the student can remain aloof.

There are some university settings in which the instructors may also wish to give the appearance of remaining aloof. Attempts to conduct class in a sterile, analytical fashion, however that may satisfy certain images of religious studies on the undergraduate level, is ultimately dangerously naive in the context of a dialogue class. Perhaps the instructors can maintain such an objective relationship to their subject matter, but they must realize that many students cannot. In addition, the dynamic created between instructors in a team-taught situation intensifies the apparent threat to the personal religious faith of the students.

The belief that even the instructors can remain fully objective in the context of an in-class, team-taught dialogue on Judaism and Christianity may also be a myth. Either the instructors will force objectivity robbing the class setting of the dynamic of true dialogue (and thereby the risks that accompany dialogue) or the instructors will remain unaware of their own personal prejudice, how that view affects the communication of the material and the course of the dialogue, and how instructors' views affect the attitudes of students toward the material and toward the dialogue. There is a thin line between forcefully expressing the views of a tradition and actually seeking (at the very least) the intellectual conversion of one's dialogue partner.

Nevertheless, the main intent of a dialogue may be simply the passing on of information (point one of the dialogue aspects given above). The instructors may aim to do what they can to remove barriers to understanding so that students can actually listen to another view. Among Christian students at Valparaiso, views of Jews and Judaism are formed by Christian teaching and Christian teachers with varying degrees of sensitivity to Judaism. Our students are undoubtedly representative of Christian students elsewhere. Thus, a seemingly simple matter such as the use of "scripture" not only produces surprises for our students as they are confronted by the views of a Rabbi but also makes obvious the stereotypical Christian interpretations of specific scriptural texts that make a genuine understanding of Jewish views on the same text most difficult. For example, how is it that Christians read Genesis 3? Our Christian students will learn and be surprised that many Jews (if not most) do not read Genesis 3 as a fall of humanity. Unless treated with sensitivity to these matters, and even if treated with sensitivity, discussion on a single chapter such as this reveals the spontaneous dynamic that occurs in a dialogue setting and, of course, the potential confusion and struggle among students who are trying to grasp a new, even foreign, viewpoint.

Of course, for the student to meet the confusion of the moment, the student must be capable of reflective thinking. The student must be able to step away from his/her own view in order not only to hear someone else speaking but also to recognize how that different view challenges or supports one's own view. For this reason, our dialogue classes have usually been limited to upper-division students (juniors and seniors). In addition, classes have usually been limited in size to allow for the necessary time for in-class discussion and reflection.

Usually if the student can move to the point of reflection, he/she has already become open to possible truth in another viewpoint -- truth that is not solely based on perceived agreement with one's own view. Such a step is difficult since most students (especially if they are not theology or religious studies majors) lack the capability of making sound judgments on truth claims. Rather, most students experience moments of brief insight, have a sense of accommodation for views similar to or not in contradiction to their own, and operate on opinion or some limited level of awareness of acts (i.e., attitudes toward ancient Judaism based solely on the Christian Gospels). Thus, the team-taught dialogue class can be an especially sensitive tool which could help students make clear distinctions, recognize differences that actually exist, and challenge oversimplifications with both real data and the personal contact with a representative from another religious tradition.

Assignments can be used to enhance this type of student development. Our classes have utilized short reflective essays to zero-in on typical trouble areas enabling students to see more clearly where stereotypes are mistaken and more sensitivity and awareness can lead to a better judgment. We could hardly expect students to completely resolve truth claims; however, instructors can by their own modeling lead students toward a greater openness and, thereby a fairer judgment of the facts.

Of course, the whole matter of dealing with truth claims may only be a by-product of a dialogue course. Perhaps the most satisfying aspect of the team-taught dialogue courses has been observing students relearning their own tradition simply by being exposed to alternative points of view. This relearning process is bound to be an integral part of Jewish-Christian dialogue since beginning students will inevitably discover that Judaism clearly presented gives insight into much of early Christianity. Of course, the role that instructors play in this process of relearning is significant since the in-class dialogue can model for students the kind of openness to another that is required in dialogue or for the student to be opened up to genuinely new insight about his/her own tradition. Though our experience is limited in this regard, Jewish students may discover some things about their own tradition by simply being opened up to the fact that early Christianity was in fact an outgrowth of the Judaism of that time.

Despite the satisfying experience just described, we also know from our classes that students experience frustration and, even, anger during a transition from a more exclusivist view toward a more inclusive view. In addition, dialogue produces many gray areas in which the distinctions between views and, thus, truth claims is difficult to determine. For most undergraduate students the likely response is a relapse into a hardline, exclusivist position (a more comfortable position to inhabit). Although the upheaval may be a long time coming, every class we have taught has experienced a mid-stream, watershed discussion experience in which students express their frustrations and then experience the possibilities of the kind of open discussion and thinking that the instructors have set as a primary objective. While the initial frustration may be directed at instructors (students hope that the instructors will "settle" things), the movement toward new openness depends upon the instructors' willingness to model the struggle that must take place in dialogue (e.g., if the dialogue presumes that a perspective of covenant as perceived from each tradition may also each be legitimate, then the struggle becomes how can different views of the same truth claim be legitimated and made understandable).

The pattern of the development of feelings has been consistent for us. What usually transpires through the latter half of a course is a new form of discussion raised to the level of dialogue simply because the frustrations of the students have been met in the open and new possibilities for open dialogue have been discovered by the students, themselves. Because of this new-found solid ground, we have found in most cases that our students are made more firm in their own tradition while at the same time more open to the views of others. In order to assure that development toward more open dialogue, instructors will have to build into the course schedule that possibility for open expression of frustrations. Of course each instructor will be faced with a decision on course objectives. We would suggest by our experience that the objectives include this effort to enable students to broaden their understanding of their own tradition (a very personalized objective, to be sure) and to appreciate more fully another tradition, even struggling with the possible truth in that view (for most of our students this means a Christian gaining more appreciation and sensitivity toward Judaism but in another setting the situation could be reversed as has been shown in the programs at Hebrew Union College mentioned above).

Dialogue on Suffering: A Case Example

Though the above outline is a bit sketchy, the four points of openness do offer a means for judging the relative success of a dialogue course. Objectives may, perhaps even should, be constructed to account for the development of openness in students on the four different levels. However, in the context of a particular course offering, other objectives often take precedence. There may be material objectives, the desire to cover a certain amount of information or span a breadth of viewpoints. In the case of the program at Valparaiso, recognition of the importance of devising objectives aimed at the growth in the student's openness has come with experience over time.

One of the most recent courses offered in the team-taught Jewish-Christian dialogue format took a shape that may be the most promising approach we have yet tried. The course (again, with a limited, general enrollment) focussed on a single theme of particular interest to students and for dialogue -- the theme of suffering and evil. Since this course is the one most familiar to me (because of my direct involvement) and offers exciting avenues for future classes, I offer this course as a case-example for our discussion.

Constructing a course on a theme such as suffering may seem fairly simple at first. The issue of suffering and evil has been subject to treatment by both Jews and Christians of every persuasion throughout the nearly three thousand years of written tradition. However, three major factors made the formation of the course outline more difficult than, at first, seemed. First, though much has been written on the subject, very little has been written with the relationship between Judaism and Christianity in mind. Any reading (except for a few) would have to be supplemented with attention to the differences that a setting of dialogue makes. Second, though the history has been long, clearly approaches to questions surrounding the theme of suffering and evil would differ depending upon whether the commentator is Jewish or Christian. Most specifically, Christians have often used the broader resources of Western philosophy to fashion a dogmatic, theological approach to issues. While Jews have also used philosophical resources (e.g., Philo, Maimonides, and Buber), Jews rarely see their task as dogmatic theological. Instead, Jews are inclined to respond with a philosophy of life and action, often rooted in the Rabbinic tradition. Comparing materials from different traditions requires the time-consuming task of developing some kind of basic, comparative vocabulary. Third, the event of the Holocaust is so recent that almost every approach to the subject of suffering and evil must be seen as outdated given the impact of the Holocaust, for both Jews and Christians, on precisely the subject of suffering and evil.

Of course, these three problems can easily be opportunities for creative work. Both students and instructors can observe with every class the new ground being broken -- the active, creative work of theology and theologians. Though the result of the class may not be, of itself, earth-shaking, the impact on the interest level of the students is immediately evident -- students feel like they are in on something *new*. In addition, the newness (in these various ways) of the focus for discussion allows for creative flexibility in class discussion. With the awareness that the class is doing a "new thing," all participating can treat the class as an experiment with greater freedom for suggested interpretations, possible problematics, and potential solutions; a flexibility that might be impossible if the literature were more extensive.

Naturally the choice of reading already limited by the structure of the class period and the length of the semester also must be scrutinized by the criteria of dialogue, of different approaches and of the critical theme of the Holocaust. We found early that some of our choices for reading were appropriate and others were not. Few could be given a completely satisfactory mark. This means that class discussions could not merely presume the reading material but must also provide critical guidance for students as they read. For example, the recently reprinted edition of Arthur McGill's *Suffering* (Westminster Press) while perhaps appropriate in some instances proved wholly unsuitable for a dialogue setting. McGill's casual, even naive, certainly uncritical use of language and Biblical texts makes his book an affront to Jews and an embarrassment to Christians who aim at dialogue. Such matters could hardly be left to the students' discretion since the use of language (often missed by students in its subtlety) is at the very heart of concern for dialogue. Other materials such as Dorothy Soelle's

Suffering and Harold Kushner's *When Bad Things Happen to Good People* are fair resources for discussion but still exhibit severe limitations for the furtherance of either dialogue or theological thinking.

Thus, an initial decision made for this course was to design the course precisely with the purpose of constructing a theology in dialogue. Though traditional texts were used (including biblical texts), we intentionally worked a "theological" interpretation of the texts based not on historical tools but on theological criteria. On my insistence, we left large blocks of class time for this ongoing constructive task that aimed at two major goals: (1) developing a sound theological response to suffering and evil given the resources of both Jewish and Christian tradition as well as meeting the critical criteria of the Holocaust, and (2) building a setting for dialogue in which potential new areas of investigation could be uncovered. The last four weeks of the course were specifically set aside for a presentation of a finished theological position (from each instructor), insofar as a finished position could be developed given the work of the semester.

Needless to say, the initial weeks of the semester were needed to introduce students to the language of the traditions (especially to Judaism although that could be reversed if the student situation were reversed) and to the style of approach demanded by the type of class being developed. The early time was spent formulating definitions, fielding questions, responding to puzzled frustrations by students, and setting the tempo of the course. Anyone who attempts a dialogue course such as this would find this time most valuable and necessary eliminating the waste of time later in the course. Still, the agenda and material of the course was academically challenging, personally stimulating (even threatening to some) and theologically productive (each student was given ample opportunity to develop the necessary tools to form a personal theological response to the myriad of questions that the material of the course raised.) The work of the course was rigorous, demanding more of students than they had encountered in nearly every other course at the university, including honors courses. Students can and will be interested in dialogue to the point of extending themselves beyond what they normally do, which is one of the most appealing features of this style of teaching.

The most threatening challenge for the student may have been whether they would be willing to set aside the necessary time and energy to do the work for this single course in theology. The results, however, were astounding. Obviously, some students handled the load better than others.

A third of the class struggled and some of those did not do well in terms of grade (though some growth was obvious even in these students). Most of the students did remarkably well precisely because they did decide to throw themselves into the matters of the course with an energy that perhaps surprised them. Student evaluations at course-end were nearly unanimous, this course was the most stimulating and personally interesting course of their college careers. Despite background, students gave what the course demanded. No doubt, the combination of instructors representing the two positions and traditions in dialogue contributed that important factor that generated this interest and productivity. I suspect that few courses, outside of those offered by professors of extraordinary charismatic appeal, could stimulate a similar level of interest no matter what the institutional setting might be.

Naturally, such an interest level bodes well not only for classes in dialogue but for an entire Jewish studies program. Since undergraduates choose courses not only to fit schedules but also because of reputation, the success of dialogue classes continues to stimulate extraordinary interest in other Jewish studies classes. In addition, student papers and evaluations show nearly unanimous success in instilling a more sympathetic view toward Judaism among our predominantly Christian students. Some sample comments are: "Helped me to understand the Jewish beliefs," "the ability to question our faith while examining the Jewish faith was a tremendous strength," "I find myself more sensitive to Jewish views," "broke through walls that separate Jews and Christians," "dialogue is such a great atmosphere for learning," "the strength lay in the dynamic of dialogue." Each of these comments comes from a different student and, though from the same class, is quite typical of comments from students in the other five classes we have offered here at Valparaiso.

Stimulating Faculty Interaction

The unique character of our whole program in theology and religious studies certainly affects both the chance of success, among students, of the dialogue class setting and the nature of the success. Our courses are often a part of a general education curriculum and objectives are basically aimed at the lay reader in theology. That our requirements guarantee a certain pool of students makes selectivity in determining enrollment more likely. That our school is a private, denominational institution makes certain objectives more acceptable (perhaps) and certainly guarantees a mix of students fairly committed religously with personal goals and beliefs at stake when studying any area of theology (that is especially the case in Jewish-Christian dialogue classes).

Even given these factors, though, the form of team-taught dialogue classes gives potential for success because (especially with limited enrollment) the student is engaged in a course with faculty interaction (as one student remarked in evaluations, "This was my first college class" meaning that the class moved students beyond the ordinary, the usual student-professor relationship). Many students may find that such a course is their only opportunity to observe faculty interacting with one another. Of course, it is possible to naively romanticize such an atmosphere, but I suggest three concrete factors that make such interaction especially useful for the teaching of Judaism.

First, the interaction between faculty members makes each faculty member more immediately accountable for their arguments. For a subject matter that has historically been colored by a full range of prejudices and stereotypes even for the most sensitive academic, the setting of dialogue becomes an invaluable check upon areas of misunderstanding, loose thinking and unclear conclusions. Fortunately, for student and faculty alike, this immediate accountability stimulates on-the-spot creativity that may seem, at first, overly spontaneous but over the course of a semester creates a valuable mood of genuineness of trust (both for students and faculty).

Second, the interaction in dialogue exposes more readily the active work of the theologian. What may be left implicit otherwise in the way a thinker develops a theological view usually becomes more explicit in the process of review and critique regularly present in a team-taught dialogue setting. For the faculty involved, the setting of dialogue allows an academic a rare opportunity for self-criticism not only materially but methodologically. For example, assumptions about how Christians form their views and treat scripture may differ radically from the actual work of a dialogue partner. Such assumptions cannot be held long in the process of dialogue. For the student of Judaism (especially Christian students), this on-the-spot self-critique of approach becomes a critical learning experience. Students see firsthand how the way theology is done can affect the conclusions offered. For Jewish-Christian dialogue such self-analysis is a basic since conflicts in view may be as much rooted in method as in content.

Third, the process of interaction involves both students and faculty in a growth process. Perhaps the student will encounter the rare experience of witnessing professors involved in a process of learning as well as teaching. Indeed, all teaching may ideally aim at student-professor interaction in which the professor as well as the student learns; however, the setting of team-taught in-class dialogue is more likely to assure that ideal. Such a setting of professors learning and being encouraged to creative, spontaneous interaction is valuable for the teaching of Judaism on the undergraduate level (especially in the context of Jewish-Christian dialogue) since students can be, in the process, led from set views toward a willingness to be open; from organized, rigid perspectives toward a growing, adapting process.

This last factor of discussion seems especially appropriate for a Jewish-Christian dialogue that takes seriously the challenges of the Holocaust. Few scholars are ready to settle for accepted understandings of either Christian or Jewish tradition given the critical questions arising from the Holocaust. In order to bring students to see the perplexities of the post-Holocaust religious world, those students must first be opened up from standard, limited, rigid ways of thinking even about their own faith. Students are well served if they can recognize the necessity for re-evaluation of the tradition and can be led toward creative reassessment of the relation between Jews and Christians. The pattern that the style of team-taught, in-class dialogue offers of necessary self-criticism and openness pushes students toward that point of critical re-evaluation better than any other approach to religious students that we have found. The results of the written work from students indicates to us that the spontaneous, process nature of dialogue, while frustrating on the one hand, produces startling results in growth of understanding and personal flexibility, on the other.

The Inherent Dangers

Naturally, there are dangers, unique problems associated with a dialogue setting. The dialogue may provide a setting that is too open-ended making the learning of information more difficult. The balance between informing students and engaging them in discussion is a delicate one, especially in a general education setting. Such a balance is always a problem for teaching undergraduates but may be especially problematic for the teaching of Judaism among Christians. Our experience has been good, thus far, but we remain fully aware of this danger. The reverse would surely be the case for a Jewish student being introduced to the Christian tradition. Thus, one of the severe limitations of the dialogue model is that it demands students who can cope with openness of dialogue and still independently learn data that can keep them abreast of the information critical for advancing the dialogue. Students who are not good independent learners may find this style too much to handle.

There is also the special danger associated with dialogue between two scholars. Conclusions reached may be representative of only a certain small circle of Christians or Jews. Given the spontaneity of dialogue, students may forget to realize and analyze the great plurality of views in both the Christian and Jewish traditions and, above all, those views that might differ considerably from the views of either dialogue partner. The impression of a too easy unanimity of views is a particularly difficult problem requiring constant monitoring by the professors involved since in some cases such unanimity will not reflect the actual relationship between Christians and Jews outside of the academic sphere. Perhaps a careful selection of readings can help to give a more balanced perspective on the plurality of Jewish and Christian views.

Another problem may be the possibility that the personalities of the participating professors can dominate the class setting. True of any course, the affect of personality may be especially evident in dialogue. The unequal balancing of personalities or the obvious clash of personalities may deprive the students of an objective judgment about either tradition and/ or the developing relationship between the two traditions. Great care must be exercised in order to guard against the temptation to make the interaction rather than the subject matter the main concern of the class. While spontaneous interaction can be a great benefit to students showing the potential of dialogue, interaction can also detract from the importance of reflection on the issues at hand. This is a problem that cannot be totally avoided but could become a severe limitation unless the instructors are consistently concerned to raise up the issues of dialogue rather than to put forth themselves. Our experience has been quite positive in this regard mainly because we have taken great care in the choice of participating professors.

Worth the Work

Despite the dangers, as listed above, and others that may be evident from descriptions elsewhere in this essay, the team-taught in-class dialogue may be the most ideal way to teach Judaism on the undergraduate level (especially in a private, Christian university). Given attention to clear objectives, student-centered sensitivity, spontaneous interaction between professors, awareness of the structure of dialogue, and careful balance between providing information and processing ideas in dialogue, the potential for team-taught classes seems unlimited. Especially for the teaching of Judaism, the team-taught situation seems most adaptable and most challenging for the student and offers a unique opportunity for stimulation of creative, accountable thought on the part of participating faculty. There are some situations in which the team-taught in-class dialogue may not yet be appropriate or even the most beneficial way for teaching Judaism (thus, we would call this a limited proposal) but for the setting where the majority of students are Christians and, perhaps, in some limited occasions for classes where the majority of students are Jewish, the team-taught, in-class dialogue is a most promising model, indeed.

Part Four

INNOVATION

Chapter Twelve

Not By Words Alone

Jo Milgrom

A determined process of individuation characterizes Genesis 1. The verb "to distinguish" appears repeatedly in Days 1, 2 and 4, as does the phrase "of its own kind," like a refrain in Days 3, 5 and 6. Everything is individuated in chapter 1 except the human being, whose sexual distinction is completed in chapter 2. Mircea Eliade comments on this ordering:

> ... out of the chaos of undifferenti matter God brings order by distinguishing and separating the elements: light and dark; sea, land and sky; solid, liquid and gaseous; animal from plant; then in all their details each form of life in its own kind; and man and woman. Only when everything is distinct and separated from everything else can a new order be established; the opposites can come together in a new relationship; man with woman; human with animal and plant. It is as if spirit and soil had to be separated from one another in order after their 'divorce' to become 'married' again. A law of creation seems to appear: the substances must be sorted out, separated and opposed in order to connect again in a new way; as with the individual human being, the differentiation of sex becomes more and more precise before the opposite poles can unite for a new generation.[1]

This humanistic principle extracted from a linguistic and stylistic examination of the biblical text is one of several to be highlighted in this essay to demonstrate how modern sciences related to biblical study can be focused so as to educate the spirit as well as the intellect of the learner. The reader is invited to participate in a creative process in which the learner leaves the text, experiences some aspect of its essence personally, and returns to the text with a new and deeper knowledge.

Thus, for example, the student who created light from darkness by tearing and pasting black and white construction paper discovered Eliade's insights on a more profound level than had the lesson ended with textual analysis alone:

> My immediate impression was that of the paper folded back on itself, closely adhered with no space between it. The relationality of light and dark — the inseparability of the concepts. Then the two sheets are wrenched apart, seen as distinct in a false way. If I come to know the

> terms that way, I must backtrack to the relationality. It has struck me again and again in life how much of my first encounter defines what something 'is.' To know something is to first separate it off and then the relationality must be perceived. The separateness, the naming can only be a tool for discerning connections.

Another principle derived from the first days of Creation is that of the honored element of chance in creativity. The great "unlimiteds" are named and thereby limited. Thus Time (light and dark) becomes Day and Night, and Space (the deep, water, chaos) becomes Land, Seas and Sky. Why then does each day end with the refrain, "and it was morning and it was evening"? Why not, "and it was day and it was night"? The creator/author saw their inseparability. Where day meets night, the threshold of transition chanced to come into being: evening and morning, more palpable than the illusory horizon that joins the sky to the earth. This is beautifully illustrated in the tear art of student RG whose darkness ripped away to reveal light, inadvertently casts the shadow of transition [fig. 1].

Thus one creative process in my class is an impromptu art activity in which graduate theological students and faculty, untrained in art, explicate a biblical passage by manipulating colored construction paper. The exercise demonstrates the way in which spontaneous artistic creativity can release a level of personal insight which in turn evokes deeper meaning from the text. Thus defined, visual art is simply part of the midrashic method whose persuasive function was eloquently defined by Judah Goldin:

> ... text and personal experience are not two autonomous domains. On the contrary, they are reciprocally enlightening. Even as the immediate event helps make the age-old sacred text intelligible, so in turn the text reveals the fundamental significance of the recent event or experience.[2]

The Method: Synectic Metaphor

At the appropriate time, after some textual study, I distribute construction paper, inviting the students to select three or four colors, and instructing them to tear and paste forms according to the requirements of the specific text (see below). Tearing is the mode, without scissors or knife, since tearing without tools is the least intimidating art exercise. Clearly the forms are coarse, and chance plays its inevitable role. In this kind of exercise I emphasize that there is no correct or incorrect way and that aesthetics is not a goal since we are all untrained in art. My purpose is to show that the soul brings forth images which the rational mind may at first consider worthless, but which once evoked have the power to become personal symbols which can mediate the paradoxes of our lives. However, in order to produce these forms, we must act like children; we must unpretentiously peer over the rim of our past with the arts as our guide, in order to rediscover the shared universal images.

I was inviting my students to play, which in the creative process means allowing one's self to float, to consider associations apparently irrelevant to the problem at hand, to daydream to no immediate benefit. This "play" is part of the science of synectics (creative metaphor) whose pioneering uses in science and technology have been advanced by William J.J. Gordon who writes that in synectic theory, play with apparent irrelevancies is used extensively to generate energy for problem solving and to evoke new viewpoints with respect to problems. Play generates energy because it is a pleasure in itself, an intrinsic end. Gordon also claims that while the kinship of art and play has been overemphasized, the kinship between play and all forms of creative adult behavior has been overlooked.[3]

The students shortly reassemble, lay their art out on the floor, prepared to talk, to listen, to interact and finally to write. Their creative work is thus processed on three levels. At each point something reveals itself: first, in the act itself, then in the verbal reflections, and finally in the making of a written record. For many students, text and personal experience achieve a new synthesis. In some cases motifs appear which enable me to lead organically from the art work to subsequent levels of textual and artistic exploration. It is these latter that confirm the hypothesis that the individual creative experience is a legacy of the collective unconscious and a reflex of the divine creative process. Some of the responses are profoundly personal, even therapeutic. If nothing else were to come of it, the sheer disarming effect, the creation of an almost intimacy, the opening up of other ways of seeing, is worth the break with formal structured procedures.

The Lesson: "God Saw That It Was Good"; "And It Was So"

For this lessen I chose to focus on the cunning repetition/ omission of two recurring phrases: "God saw that it was good," and "And it was so." Could the periodic presence or absence of those phrases tell us in greater depth what they meant? Here too the textual study would culminate in an art activity, a "self-portrait" of the student reflected in "good" and "so."

The first step was the search within each day's creation for "And God saw that it was good," with the following results:

Day 1: the light of Day 1 was "tov" (good); *Day 2*, no "tov"; *Day 3*: "tov" appears twice; *Days 4 and 5* "tov" appears once; *Day 6*: "tov" appears twice, but not in regard to humanity. The second appearance is "tov m'od," very good, in v. 31, referring to the total creation.

The second step was to examine the absence of "tov" on Day 2 to see if that shed any light on the absence of "tov" in the creation of humanity on Day 6. A naming process comes into being with creation: It is possible to "see" light once it is set against darkness, so both, having been distinguished from each other, can be named respectively, day and night.

Now on Day 2, God, in the manner of a metal worker, makes a firmament (*RAQIA*, hammered metal), which is like a lid on a pot. It is the lid on the earth which separates the upper waters from the lower waters. The image is the biblical portrayal of the three tiered universe.[4] Firmament and upper waters are now distinguishable, so the firmament is named, and sky comes into being. But the waters are not named on Day 2 because they are not yet distinct down below. They still cover everything.

Day 3 opens with the gathering together of the waters under sky enabling the dry land to appear. At last the waters and the dry land have been separated out from each other. Once distinguished as separate entities, they can be named: oceans and land "And God saw that it was good." The "aha" experience comes when the class realizes that the waters could not be named on Day 2 because they were not finished. Aha, so "tov" means finished, does it. And by association to Day 6, the incompleteness of the human being is immediately perceived.

But we are not through. There is the matter of "And it was so." We learn that "so" comes from the Hebrew root *KOON*, meaning to be fixed, to have a fixed place and function, and we follow the same sleuthing procedure through Genesis 1. Our findings are equally intriguing. The light of Day 1 is not "chen," nor the fish/fowl nor the human being.[5] The light of Day 1 stands in a class by itself. Its place and role are part of the mystery of God's immanence. In the instances of fish/ fowl and the human being, we understood that unfixedness means freedom, and the class was invited again to scour the text for the compensation provided against the security of fixedness. "And God blessed them," vv. 22 and 28. The pattern emerging from this analysis of Genesis 1 thus projects a world in which it is better for one species to be free, incomplete and therefore blessed, than for everything to be absolutely certain, unmysterious and predictable.

The time had come now for the class to leave the written word and to image once again through paper play. The instructions were to show yourself through freely torn and pasted forms, as being free (unfixed), incomplete, but blessed.

Student 1 (CF) chose a background of red for what she identified variously as her awareness, knowing, hope and experience [fig. 2]. She wrote as follows:

> I started with my incompleteness — it was shaped as a pit whose bottom was ragged, mysterious and extended beyond the edges of my awareness. Overlayed on my incompleteness was blessing — shaped like a green, lifegiving, growing tree, its roots extended even further beyond my knowing than my incompleteness — and grew up beyond my hopes extending beyond the edge of my experience. Supported by the tree of blessing, a small three dimensional winged 'freedom' poised partly within my range of experience, partly extending beyond what I have known.

CF's self-portrait is a tree. The three required elements, incompleteness, freedom and blessing overlap and are therefore part of the tree. Incompleteness is part of the root system. In the text we say it exactly that way — that the 'absence' of "tov" is 'ever-present', fundamental to the structure of Genesis 1. The blessing of unfathomable proportion exceeds her consciousness. Yet it allows the incompleteness its space. Though she describes the latter as a rough pit, it is also a well that nourishes the root system, which in turn is balanced (upper left) by the three dimensional, butterfly shaped fruit of the blessing tree, her transformative freedom.

A note rather than a footnote is in order here about the tree as self image. The image of the Cosmic Tree belongs to a coherent body of myths, rites, images and symbols which comprise what the historian of religion, Mircea Eliade, calls 'symbolism of the Center'. It is an image which structures experience of the physical world and the world of the imagination and the spirit. Like the Tree, imagination connects heaven and earth; it is rooted below and it unites the luminous world of consciousness to the dark underworld of the unconscious. Like the Tree, the individual draws nourishment from the 'heavenly' immaterial world of the intellect and the 'earthly' material world of the senses. Like the Tree, the individual experiences periodic autumn, and again regeneration and fruitfulness. Thus the Tree is an archetypical 'axis mundi', (an axis of the world linking heaven and earth) and like the Tree, the centered individual needs to see him/herself as a discrete vertical link between heaven and earth.

In sum, the arborescent motif is one of the primary visual images used as early as the fourth millennium BCE, reflecting the human need to grasp the essential reality of the world.[6]

Because the arborescent motif is part of the shared treasury of human images, it is fitting for the reader to place the work of CF into the iconographic context which the doer herself achieved intuitively, by reading *The Tree of Life* (note 6). However, I will add to that treasury here with an analogous modern work unknown to the student, done some 25 years earlier by a gifted young artist whose eight original wood cuts, *The Psalm Book of Charles Knowles*, done as a senior project at the Putney School in Vermont, can be seen at both the Museum of Modern Art in New York and at the Israel Museum in Jerusalem[7] and fig. 3.

As a visual response to Psalm 1, the text of which he printed on a hand press and placed on the page facing the woodcut, Charles Knowles did a self-portrait of the artist as a tree. He saw himself as the "happy/fortunate man" of Psalm 1:

> like a tree planted by the rivers of water
> that brings forth his fruit in his season
> His leaf shall not wither
> Whatever he does will succeed.

His self/tree is sturdy, deep rooted and abundantly fruitful in his season, wholly successful. But there is a strange scattering of stuff to the left of the tree and close to its roots. Contrasting with the fortunate/happy man are the "ungodly who are like the chaff which the wind drives away." The chaff is the "ungodly" part of Charles Knowles, the chaotic, disorderly, even demonic, the incomplete part of the person, close to the roots, the hidden part of us, the mysterious shadow source that nourishes the creative freedom/fruit.

Where the modern psychologically aware individual sees the human self in arborescent forms, the ancients saw the original, divine Self providing human nourishment. The first of two Egyptian illustrations from the 2nd millennium BCE shows the breast of the goddess held in her hand, as it emerges from the tree to suckle the young king; the second shows the figure of the goddess herself as the trunk of the tree of divine blessing presenting oval cakes and bread to the man and woman[8] [figs. 4 and 5].

As the tree is a primary symbol in the human imagination, so the seed and the spiral/serpent, evident in the work of Student 2 (LB) who writes:

> Surrounding, enfolding and grounding me is God's blessing; it gives me life; it holds me up and envelopes me because it is God's love. That's what the blue circle is. Attached to the blessing, springing forth from it is my freedom spiraling up. It doesn't just shoot up straight, but spirals up enfolding in its own right other people, touching them and all of life at many points. The spiral goes up but sometimes folds in on itself making me confined and two dimensional. I have the freedom to confine myself. In the center the seed, the egg. It is potential, not complete. It is also secure in the blessing and touched by the freedom. There is freedom and choice in my incompleteness. I can choose which way to go ...

The spiral emerging from the egg has at least two powerful meanings. First, it recalls the serpent of the Garden in Genesis, and throughout the Ancient Near East, associated with feminine regenerative power; and because the feminine means ultimately association with the earth, the ambivalent and ambiguous serpent represents both life and death, the marriage of opposites, and their synthesis into a higher form.

Second, the spiral points to the labyrinth representing the long and difficult initiatory journey of the hero, and all the demons, battles and fears to be conquered en route to the sacred center and one's final reward, another motif that has traveled through time from hoary beginnings to the present.[9]

Student 3 (GN) is an older, mature and beautiful woman, a gifted photographer of modest achievement. She expressed her incompleteness in an irregular, roundish green form representing her scattered efforts in "umpteen different directions," describing the form of

> green for growth, but not necessarily upward like a tree — moss, fungus creep along the ground — a base, with edges torn into rays, irregular and going into all kinds of directions, thick and thin, and splintered and bent but all ending, sometimes cut straight where the paper's edge is — as if cut off by time, in nothing.
>
> And then there is the white form: a spiral, an irregular path in the form of a helix, arising from the torn and splintered green base, woven unevenly as if the path were again submerged (lost in the morass of my disorganized aimless activity) but then emerging again, winding its way upward, folded into rough steps, uneven and rocky, but upward still, sometimes smoothly, briefly, and then an abyss, but reaching up in the end.
>
> First the white helix ended in an oval knob. But then from this shape a hand arose, primitive and knobby (arthritic?), but still a handstretching upward — trying to reach — what? Some sort of resolution, knowledge, wisdom, heaven? Or with bent fingers reaching down trying to create; a hand trying to bless the mess which I have created? Or maybe forgiving too.

GN is not a theology student. She participates in adult education in the Jewish community. But the text of Genesis 1 was the same. The identity of her work with the preceding examples and with those from ancient art and mythology only reinforces the power and presence of the common treasury of images, the blundering journey which is both ascent and abyss, the hand that started out as an egg, that must create to live [fig. 8].

Forgiveness was part of the closure of the activity. I related the reading of Genesis 1 to Rosh Hashanah, which marks the creation of the world, and which therefore incorporates *t'shuvah* (repentance) into creation. A better translation is "turning" or "changing." In experiencing the freshness of primordial beginnings, everything can return to its original perfection. It is as though chronological time is suspended and through transcendent liturgical time one can wipe the slate clean and start anew. It was thus possible for the students to view the incompleteness in their forms as an opportunity for *t'shuvah.*

I was not surprised to see both Christian and Jewish students in both religious and secular contexts drawing on the same universal imagery, without sectarian differentiation. And I expected and received from some of the seminary students' transference from Genesis 1 to Christian symbolism.

A final example, Student 4 (EH), writes:

> The first piece I tore seemed to take on a life of its own ... the form that emerged was a pink flash of lightening. At first I attempted to place it in the background traditionally (sic) as coming diagonally from the sky down to me. But it would not fit that way. Instead it needed to go up from the lower left hand corner toward the right top corner — Then I had to remove the backing paper and let the lightening go off into space —

> my sense of freedom, creativity, is never quite complete — and yet at times it flashes strongly up and out.
>
> The blessing started with the color blue which has always had significance in my life, and as I tore it became an empty tomb with a spiraling 'stone' — always coming into place, yet always being removed. Later I had to tear out the background center of the tomb to make it both 'completely' empty and completely filled. My life has been such a series of experiences of moving into darkness/death/tomb and yet such a series of resurrection/renewal/new birth/light/. The blessing is that no matter how deep the darkness/death/burial comes now, I have experienced so much of resurrection I know it will always come again.

Student EH understands the caveat, the powerful thrust of creativity which is electricity to be harnessed, which doesn't always know its own structure and goal (flying off the edge of the paper), the arbitrary "curse of the blessing." But that erratic force is balanced by the rhythmic filling and emptying of the tomb, expressed by the ebb and flow, the serpentine movement of the spiral. As we have seen, the serpent is an image of periodic renewal particularly associated with the feminine. In this instance, EH uses her large faith to harness the rhythms so the filling can surpass the emptying, and can keep a watchful eye on the incomplete freedom flashing up on the left.

These several self images were evoked spontaneously in a single class meeting of 90 minutes duration without prior preparation on the part of the students. My expressed purpose was to show imaginative ways of eliciting creative metaphors from a biblical passage; but something more inevitably happens during the process. With all the levity (nervous and relaxed) that breaks out when (graduate theological) students are forced to abandon a cognitive mode of learning in order to tear construction paper to make a visual midrash, pre-verbal revelation takes place which then begins to surface through dialogue, achieving even greater clarity in the later writing. Powerful metaphors embedded in the biblical text resonate with human nature and experience. The archetypal images cited here have turned up before in my classes, and as I have indicated, have happened a great deal more in human history, in the search for symbols. Genesis 1 is just the beginning.

Edward Edinger nourishes this discussion with his applied definition of symbol, basically meaning that which has been thrown together, from the Greek, sym = together and bolon = that which has been thrown. The symbol in Greek antiquity was a coin which, to conclude a transaction, would be broken, buyer and seller each retaining their half. The halves, when brought together, gave proof of the transaction. The symbol, he concludes, "was originally a tally referring to the missing piece of an object which when restored to, or thrown together with, its partner recreated the original whole object ... The symbol thus leads us to the missing part of the whole person. It relates us to our original totality, it heals our split, our alienation from life .... it relates us to the suprapersonal forces which are the source of our being and our meaning. This is the reason for honoring subjectivity and cultivating the symbolic life."[10]

Creation = Revelation

Eventually I knew I was headed toward a connection between Genesis 1 and Exodus 19-34, *Mattan Torah,* revelation in the giving of the Torah. The first step would be the realization in more than a cognitive way, that the light of Day 1 (different from the solar lights of Day 4) was the revealed presence of God. (The word "divine" comes from a Sanskrit, "div," meaning light.) This time the exercise would be to create light out of darkness. The materials would be only black and white construction paper. What would be the procedure? It was the first class meeting and the people did not know one another.

Someone who enjoys reading aloud volunteered to read Genesis 1 slowly and dramatically. She was to pause after each day's creation to allow the class to visualize and personalize the increment of that day's creation. For example, to recall not just abstract sky, but a certain sky of a certain moment in your life; not just bird, but your experience of a particular bird — the tail of a peacock in the San Diego Zoo suddenly came to mind — or the embryo of a dead bird, random death on the sidewalk. It is the particularization that restores awe to what we mistakenly see as ordinary.

When the six days had been completed, we began a subtraction process in order to arrive at the conceptually impossible-nothing of Day 1. First we visualized our lives without anything man-made. Although the manufactured world is not part of the primeval week, this is an essential, enormous and shocking imaginative leap since civilization initially does mean artifacts. It helps to start thinking of ourselves without the house and car. Bit by bit we are denuded of the telephone, the sofa bed, University Avenue, Safeway, Tahoe and Jerusalem, till we are naked in the wilds. Only then can we start to subtract all other people, then our pets, sunlight, etc., personalizing as we did when we added it all up till we are left utterly alone in the world with the eight nouns of the first two verses of Genesis: water, darkness, deep, formlessness, the spirit/wind of God, sky and earth. Only then does God say, "Let there be light."

Each participant then receives a selection of quotations on light from the *Zohar* and *The Book of Human Destiny* (see Appendix.) for private meditation, and sheets of black and white construction paper from which s/he is to create light by tearing and pasting forms.

The student (NR) produced a black horn spewing white steamers of light/sound. She wrote:

first last
speak listen
front back
light dark
form empty
good bad

create kill
white black
hungry full
slow fast

stop
start
stop
start.

Stark contrasts of color, form, and movement allowed her to express revealed Light as the consciousness of all the ultimate dualities of life and death, which is the central preoccupation of religion everywhere. Human thinking requires binary opposites, what something is, and is not. But religion seeks to deny the link between the dual pair, life and death. It does this by creating a mystical 'other' perfect world where the dead are perpetually alive. Ironically because this other world is perfect, God comes to be associated there, not here. Thus, the eternal quest of humanity, to bridge the gap between man and God.[11]

Thus the Zoharic statement that the Divine Light of Day 1 is called *Ohr Ganuz,* hidden light. The presence of evil in the world causes its concealment. But it is kept in reserve for the righteous in the world to come. The rich dualities illustrated by the tear art and poem of student NR accessed these concepts to the class in a memorable way because they came about organically from within the class, rather than in the traditional format of frontal lecture.

The student (SW) tore a small triangular shaft of light whose tiny sharp point (she exploited the finished edges of the paper) emanated from the corner of the black page. She wrote:

> Wherever God is is Center — Darkness and light, dynamic, impacting on each other — The moment of creation of light — dramatic, perhaps as a beam piercing the darkness — or subtle like the infinitely quiet approach of dawn — so that blackness fades or yields to the radiance which comes from the God-Center.
>
> p.s. The available medium offers a real challenge to create the dynamic in-motion condition of the exercise.

Thus Light is God's presence, God's space. SW has found a way to distinguish between ordinary space and sacred space, and a way to connect with sacred space. Her shaft of light operates as an axis mundi, as we saw earlier, the like function of the tree. Eliade reminds us of this principle, that all space is not homogeneous, and that the religious person strives to transcend secular space because h/she cannot live without the divine connection. The question, how did our ancestors bridge the gap gets the same answer that we need to hear: You metaphorically reach up and poke a hole in space, and plug in. "On the most archaic level of culture transcendence is expressed by various images of an opening. Communication with the gods happens via an opening." (Eliade, 26) That is why comparative religion has a variety of terms for that tiny opening and the growth of the connection: "Hidden Seed," "Divine Egg," "Root of Roots" (Cook, 9).[12]

Thus Creation is Revelation, and the Divine Light of Genesis 1 is the same Light that beamed from Moses' face (Exodus 34), so frightening his congregation he had to mask himself when he addressed them; the same beams of light became his enigmatic horned attribute made famous by Michelangelo but seen regularly from the eleventh century on.

Enter Moses At Sinai

In an important little paperback called *On the Kabbalah and its Symbolism,* Gershom Scholem focuses on the revelation at Sinai as an issue of the relationship between authority and mysticism. The authority aspect is clear. Israel receives a sharply defined set of doctrines, a calling to the human community, whose direct meaning negates any mystic formula subject to infinite interpretation. The mystic aspect arises when we ask what was divine about that revelation. When Israel received the Ten Commandments, what actually did they hear? Some traditions say they heard it all; others, that they heard only the first two and were so terrorized by the Divine presence that they implored Moses to mediate the remaining eight.[13]

Rabbi Mendel Torum of Rymanov (d. 1814) had a different approach. For him it was both an acoustic and a linguistic problem. What could God sound like? His solution was that Israel heard only the *aleph* of the first word, *anokhi,* "I." Readers of Hebrew understand the enigma of that answer since the *aleph* is a silent letter. Scholem explains that the *aleph* may be said to denote the source of all articulate sound, the potential sound of a divine larynx, as it were, about to speak. In this way, Rabbi Mendel transformed the revelation at Sinai into a mystical revelation "pregnant with infinite meaning but without specific meaning." It remained for Moses to translate the non-verbal into the human linear language of the receivable Torah.

Outside circles of traditional Jewish learning, yet strangely akin to Jewish mysticism, welcome support comes from psychologist, Dr. Gerald Epstein, encouraging a view of Divine revelation not as *verbal* (linear, sequential, rational, intellectual, logical), but as *imaginal* (experiential, acausal, non-rational, intuitive and associative). In his book, *Waking Dream Therapy,* Epstein synthesizes traditional psychotherapeutic methods with the insights of Eastern psychology:[14]

> It is well known that many religious and spiritual experiences which convey knowledge to the individual such as Moses at Mt. Sinai are not describable in words and frequently are attainable only when the content of linear thought is slowed, stopped, emptied ... It is only when such non-linear thinking is embraced that a holistic (incorporating the concept holy, healthy) experience can happen. It is here then that a possibility of healing asserts itself through an experience which abrogates the activity of linear thought. (p. 51)

Psychology is no stranger to visual imagery. Both Jung and Freud evoked active imagination and visual scenes from their patients. However, Epstein's method is particularly welcome because he counsels that restoration of health is a process that includes the holy, a concept that has generally been ignored by most Western therapies.

"If therapy tries to invalidate man's relationship to God, it does so at the expense of dissipating our fundamental wholeness. If this is the case, then the whole picture of a man's potentials cannot be addressed." As Epstein restores the healing perspectives of religion within psychology, my approach affirms the neglected functions of psychology in the study of religious texts and experience.

Imaging: Meeting Up With God

Preparation for the black/white construction paper activity included the above discussion on the non-verbal aspects of revelation, and also a brief reading of Exodus 19 in which I emphasized the word *va-yeherad,* to convey the emotional readiness for the divine encounter. Both the mountain and the people shook, trembled, feared. The instructions this time were to tear and paste forms which conveyed the encounter of the human and the divine. A paradigm for this encounter also included midrashim on the radiance of Moses.

The desired effect of this paper-tearing exercise is to lift the participant from the enclosure of historical sequence — to free the imaginal life from the familiar over-rationalized word view of a problem. The resulting images concretize one's emotions opening the individual to the intelligence of the heart. Imaginal seeing is a vision that allows one to get outside of one's personal self and to see one's self from a non-habitual vantage point. What is thus seen brings with it the power to alter one's habitual relations. (Epstein, 18)

Two of the participants were in striking contrast with one another. The first merely tore the shape of a crown. Her simple and direct comment was that the exalted experience had left her feeling every inch royalty. The second student, JH, used the white paper as the background for the Divine, and placed himself in a corner, a tiny frightened owlish face around pinpoint pupils wreathed in black hair and beard. He said that confronting the Divine reduced him to a nothing. Both had achieved a personal analogy in a blurt of association, integrated, compressed and poles apart. Remarkably, the specific yet universal responses of the two, in their polarity, explicitly echo the psalmist. Grandeur and self-effacement meet under the sky in Psalm 8:

> When I consider your heavens, the work of your fingers
> the moon and stars which you have ordained
> what is man that you are mindful of him
> the son of man that you pay attention to him
> Yet You have made him little less than divine
> and crowned him with majesty and splendor.

The particular yet universal responses of these two persons enabled us to view Psalm 8 in a midrashic relationship to both Genesis 1 and Exodus 19. Psalm 8 is the affective, emotional response of awe and appreciation to the cognitive, discursive accounts of creation and revelation. Thus three diverse biblical passages are brought into a direct relationship to each other by creative analogy, and a personal connection with a sacred text is bonded in which cognitive and experiential modes successfully complement one another.[15]

Student 3 (VS) produced two tearings, a 'before' and an 'after' [fig. 7]. She wrote with great excitement about the feeling of coming face to face with the Divine, of the intimacy within her in the attempt to make contact with a real feeling lying dormant yet yearning to be brought to light.

Concerning the 'before' tearing she wrote:

> I thought of God as an encompassing radiance — the whole sheet of white paper, and then added the black square of mankind's ignorance and separation from the Divine, due to his lack of insight and understanding. Within the darkness I placed the white square of man.

Concerning the 'after':

> Moving to Moses' confrontation I felt that his direct contact with God left his usual 'self' shattered as physically represented by the trembling of the earth. Within him then appeared God through the revelation on Mt. Sinai, as the Divine is in all of us. Through the shattering of his earthly self appears the divine, as described by the light shining from him. The experience was very strong and moving.

Between the pride of Student 1 and the humility of Student 2 is the introspective sensitivity of Student 3. Only with the "shattering" of the ego can the inner square of humanity be illumined by the Other light. The liturgy of the High Holy Days refers to Psalm 34:19 expressing the same sentiment, "the Eternal is near the broken-hearted," the wrench that makes it possible for one to experience *t'shuvah,* a turning around, a reversal of orientation, healing in the vocabulary of Epstein. When the imagination confronts vital human issues "the exalted state ... adheres to the standards of holiness," says Rabbi Abraham Isaac Kook, leading modern mystic cited by Epstein (p. 163).

In this final example, Student 4 (JB) is responding specifically to midrashim on the verse, Ex. 34:29, "And Moses did not know that the skin of his face beamed." Using black as background he placed upon it a large eye and eyebrow. Within the eye, functioning as its pupil was a human figure from which emanated four rays. In answer to my question, how did the art connect you to the text, and how did it expand your self-perception, he wrote the following:

> I am Moses. I am glorified and made radiant to the extent that I enter up into presence of God. I am God. I am source of light and channel of the radiant presence of the divine to people broken and hiding in the shadows.

Following this poem, his second statement was an analysis of the process:

> My mind moved from *'ohr* = skin to a resonance with *ohr* = light (homonyms in Hebrew), to a further connection with *ayin* = source, eye. In putting together the picture of the eye I was struck by a hesitation to make the figure in the eye Moses or God. I became comfortable with the ambiguity of the God-man tension in experience: that glorification is to be found only in this tension.

By means of symbolic synectic analogy accomplished through black and white paper-play, JB confronted the paradox of God's being both our center and our circumference simultaneously (I am Moses, I am God). The greater the consciousness of that interplay, the firmer the reality of that inner-outer dual presence. The four rays and eye are also identified as a mandala quaternity image which conveys a sense of stability and rest, a glimpse of static eternity (Edinger, 182). Thus the man-God tension expressed verbally by JB achieves visual equilibrium even before he articulates it, "I became comfortable with the ambiguity of the God-man tension in experience: that glorification is to be found only in this tension" [fig. 8].

I strive to validate the student's artistic expression with parallels drawn from recognized artistic and literary sources which express similar concerns even though there may be great disparity in talent, training and artistic experience. Thus, for example, in this instance I was able to bring a work by surrealist artist Salvador Dali in which Michelangelo's radiant (horned) Moses is placed within the eye of God. I do not believe the student had any knowledge of Dali's work [fig. 9].

The art activity has a remarkably freeing effect. Intimidation in the face of an ancient and enigmatic literature is dissolved as the biblical text is seen as a vehicle of human emotive expression unlimited by chronology and accessible to all. And an openness to visual art flowers out of the unexpected revelation of one's own begotten forms, both representational and abstract, a boon for modern art which so often meets with alienation from the uninitiated.

At the point in the curriculum when the more traditional disciplines are engaged, they too are to be seen as only a partial view of the biblical perspective one acquires on the nature of learning and the learner. The Kabbalists who flourished in 16th century Safed worked out the last word on the rabbinic principle of the infinite meaning of Torah: The 600,000 Israelites who left Egypt received the Torah at Sinai and sparks of those souls are present in every succeeding generation in Israel. Consequently there are 600,000 aspects and meanings of Torah, each enclosing the root of one of those primordial souls. "In the Messianic age every Israelite will read the Torah in accordance with the meaning peculiar to his/her root. Thus also is the Torah understood in Paradise." (Scholem, op. cit., 65) So the Rabbis and the mystics, both creatively orthodox, view as an ideal not only the infinite faces/facets of the Torah, but the infinitely individual needs of the learner as well.

---

[1]"The Myth of Alchemy," *Parabola* III, 3, p. 28.

[2]From the Introduction to *The Last Trial,* by S. Spiegel (New York: Schocken, 1967).

[3]*Synectics, the Development of Creative Capacity* (New York: Harper and Row, 1961). The word synectics comes from the Greek meaning a kind of metaphor, a joining together of different, apparently irrelevant elements. It is a theory for the conscious use of the pre-conscious psychological mechanisms present in human creativity. My adaptation of the synectic principle seeks to define complex biblical concepts by means of familiar forms achieved through pre-verbal free association: the raw material of creative midrash, a dramatically new expansion of hermeneutic method. Thus the difficult becomes familiar, and the familiar, surprising and unique. For further application of synectics in Jewish education see "Synectics: An Approach to Teaching Midrash" by Rabbi Alvan Kaunfer, *The Melton Research Center Newsletter,* Fall, 1980 (now called *The Melton Journal),* where I first learned of this science, and my earlier article on synectic midrash, "Hand-Made Midrash," *The Melton Journal* 17, winter 1984.

[4]"Cosmogony," T. Gaster, *Interpreter's Dictionary of the Bible* (Nashville: Abingdon, 1962), for a clear illustration of the three tiered universe after the imagination of the ancients.

[5]*The Lion and the Ass,* R. Sacks, unpublished manuscript. I am in debt to Prof. Sacks for his many insights into the creation narratives.

[6]*The Tree of Life,* R. Cook (London: Thames and Hudson, 1974), p. 8ff. The thirty page essay and many pictures epitomize the comprehensive nature of the symbol, dealing with Tree as Center, as core image of Imagination, of Fertility, of Ascent, of Sacrifice, of Knowledge, of History, of Inner Necessity.

[7]*The Psalm Book of Charles Knowles,* by Charles Knowles, facsimile edition (New York: Viking Press and Pinnacle Press, 1959).

[8]*The Symbolism of the Biblical World,* O. Keel (New York: Seabury Press, 1978), figs. 253, 254.

[9]The reenactment and therapeutic application of the spiritual journey via the labyrinth is excellent reading in *Rosegarden and Labyrinth A Study in Art Education,* by Seonid M. Robertson (Dallas: Spring Publications, 1982); among others, a Renaissance drawing of the labyrinth in the legend of Theseus and the Minotaur in Cook, op. cit., pp. 62-3.

The ancient motif of serpent and egg can be seen in Phanes' birth from the world egg (ca. 117-138) celebrating the birth of the year-god Aion, on January 6, a date later assigned to the Epiphany and (originally) the Nativity of Christ and to his Baptism as well, *The Mythic Image,* by Joseph Campbell (Princeton: Bollingen, 1975), p. 34, fig. 6 and *Jewish Symbols of the Greco-Roman Period,* E. R. Good enough (Princeton: Bollingen, 1958), vol. 8, fig. 159.

[10]*Ego and Archetype,* E. Edinger (Baltimore: Penguin, 1973), p. 130.

[11]*Genesis as Myth,* E. Leach (London: Jonathan Cape, 1969), pp. 7-10.

[12]*The Sacred and the Profane,* M. Eliade (New York: Harvest HBJ, 1959) Chapter 2, "Time and Myths."

[13]*On the Kabbalah and its Symbolism,* G. Scholem (New York: Schocken, 1969), pp. 29ff.

[14]*Waking Dream Therapy,* G. Epstein (New York: Human Sciences Press, 1981).

[15]For a comprehensive and unsurpassed collection of the traditional midrashic sources in English, see *Legends of the Jews,* L. Ginsberg, (Philadelphia: JPS, 1909); also *Encyclopedia of Biblical Interpretation,* M.M. Kasher (New York: American Biblical Encyclopedia Society, 1953).

APPENDIX

Reflections on Light

The Book of Human Destiny by Solomon Goldman (Philadelphia; JPS, 1949) (selections are cited below as in above volume)

Sight is an absolutely spiritual phenomenon: accurately and only to be so defined; and the "Let there be Light," is as much when you understand it, the ordering of intelligence as the ordering of vision.

Ruskin, *The Eagle's Nest*

The history of Genesis or the old mythology repeats itself in the experience of every child. He too is a demon or god thrown into a particular chaos, where he strives to lead things from disorder into order.

Emerson, *Nature, Addresses and Lectures: The Method of Nature*

Can the man say, *Fiat Lux,* Let there be Light, and out of chaos make a world? Precisely as there is light in himself, will he accomplish this.

Carlyle, *Heroes and Hero Worship,* III

Say not, let there be light, but darkness visible.

William Hazlitt, *On Reading New Books*

Then I saw
How order might — if chaos wishes — become:
and saw the darkness crush upon itself
contracting powerfully; then it was as if
it killed itself, slowly: and with much pain.

Conrad Aiken, *The Room*

The splendid discontent of God with Chaos, made the world; and from the discontent of man the world's best progress springs.

Ella Wheeler Wilcox, *Discontent*

Form
Let chaos storm!
Let cloud shapes swarm!
I wait for form.

Robert Frost, *Ten Mills: Pertinax*

Selections from *Zohar, The Book of Enlightenment* translated and edited by Daniel Matt (New York: Paulist Press, 1983) and from other midrashic sources.

It is written, "God said, 'Let there be light,' and there was light." Rabbi Yosi said, "That light was hidden away, and it is reserved for the righteous in the world-to-come, as they (the Rabbis of the Talmud) have explained, based on the verse, 'Light is sown for the righteous' (Psalms 97:11). Indeed, for the righteous. That light never shone except for the First Day; afterwards, it was hidden away and shone no more."

Rabbi Yehudah said, "If it were completely hidden away, the world would not exist for even a moment. Rather, it was hidden away and sown like a seed, which then gives birth and produces seeds and fruits. Thus the world is maintained. Every single day a ray of that light shines into the world and keeps everything alive, for with that ray the Holy One, may He be blessed, feeds the world.

"And in every place where Torah is studied at night, one thread-thin ray comes out from that hidden light and flows down to those studying ...

"Since the First Day the light has never been fully revealed, but it does indeed function in the world. Every day it renews the Act of Creation."

(Zohar II 148b-149a)

I have been taught by my teacher that Adam somehow resembled that first light which was hidden away. Afterwards, a thread-thin ray appeared to give "breath (or "soul," Hebrew: neshamah) to the people on earth and life to those who walk thereon: (Isaiah 42:5).

Understand this, for the secret is essentially one.

I cannot expand this, for thus have I been commanded.

(Shimon Lavi, Ketem Paz ("Finest Gold," Commentary to the Zohar written ca. 1570), Djerba, Tunisia, 1940, p. 121b)

For with the appearance of the light, the universe expanded;
With the concealment of the light, all individually
existing things came into being . . .
This is the mystery of the Act of Creation.
One who is able to understand will understand.

(Shimon Lavi, Ketem Paz 124c)

The light which God created during the Six Days of Creation — with that light Adam could see from one end of the world to the other. However, God hid that light away from the righteous to enjoy in the life-to-come.

Where did He hide it? In the Torah. Therefore, when I open the Zohar I see the entire world. (Israel ben Eliezer, the Baal Shem Tov)

FIGURE 1

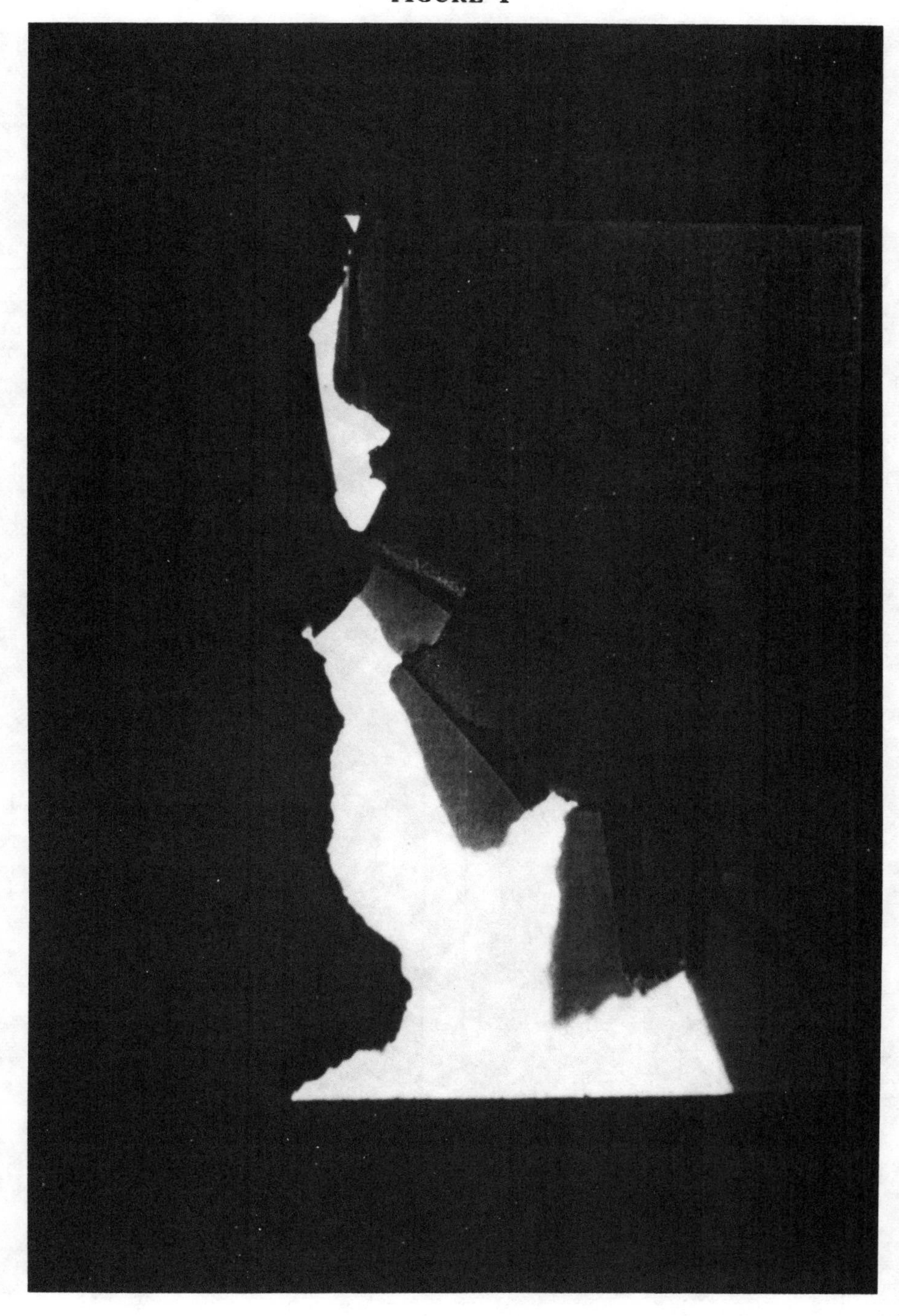

FIGURE 2

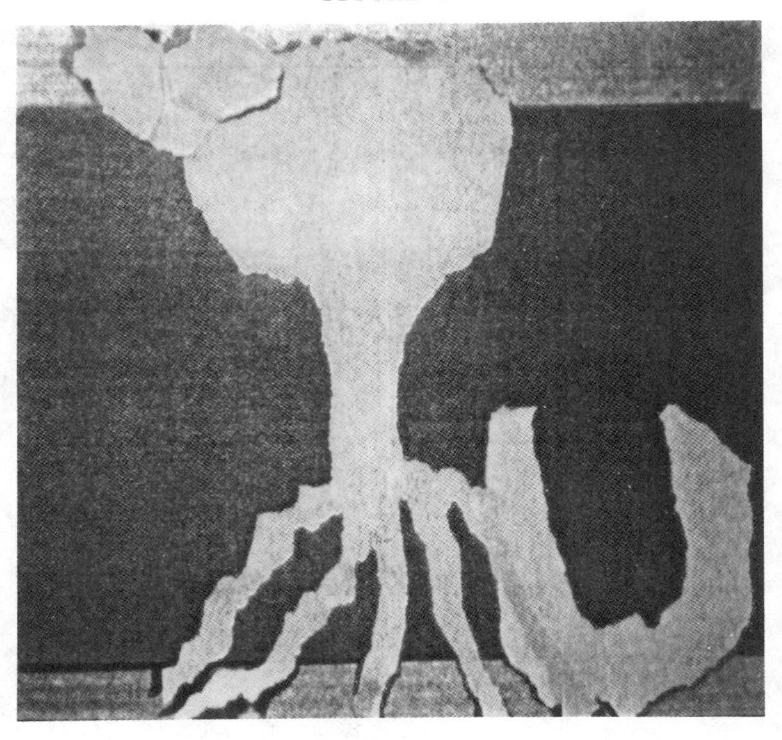

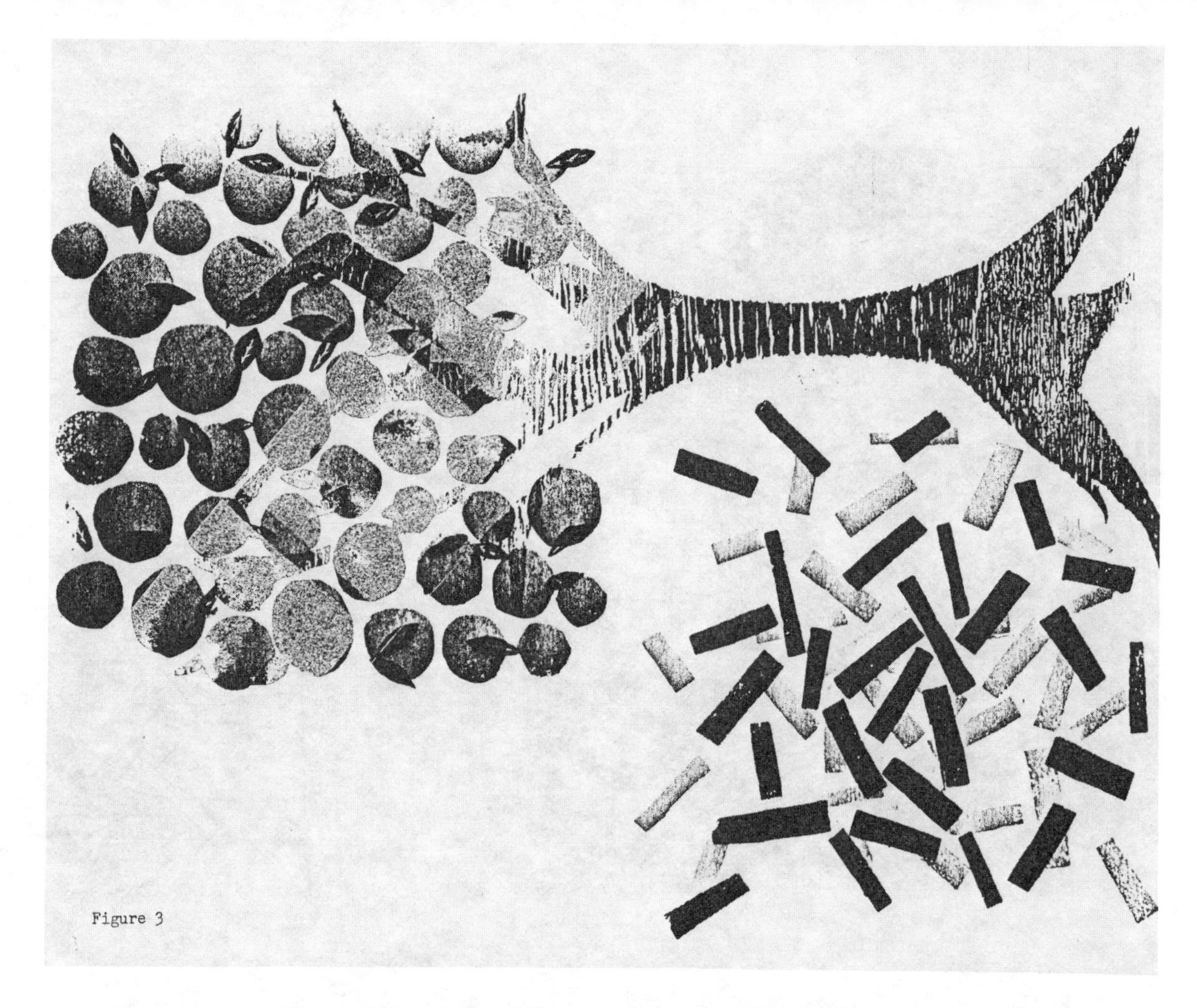

Figure 3

Figure 4

Figure 5

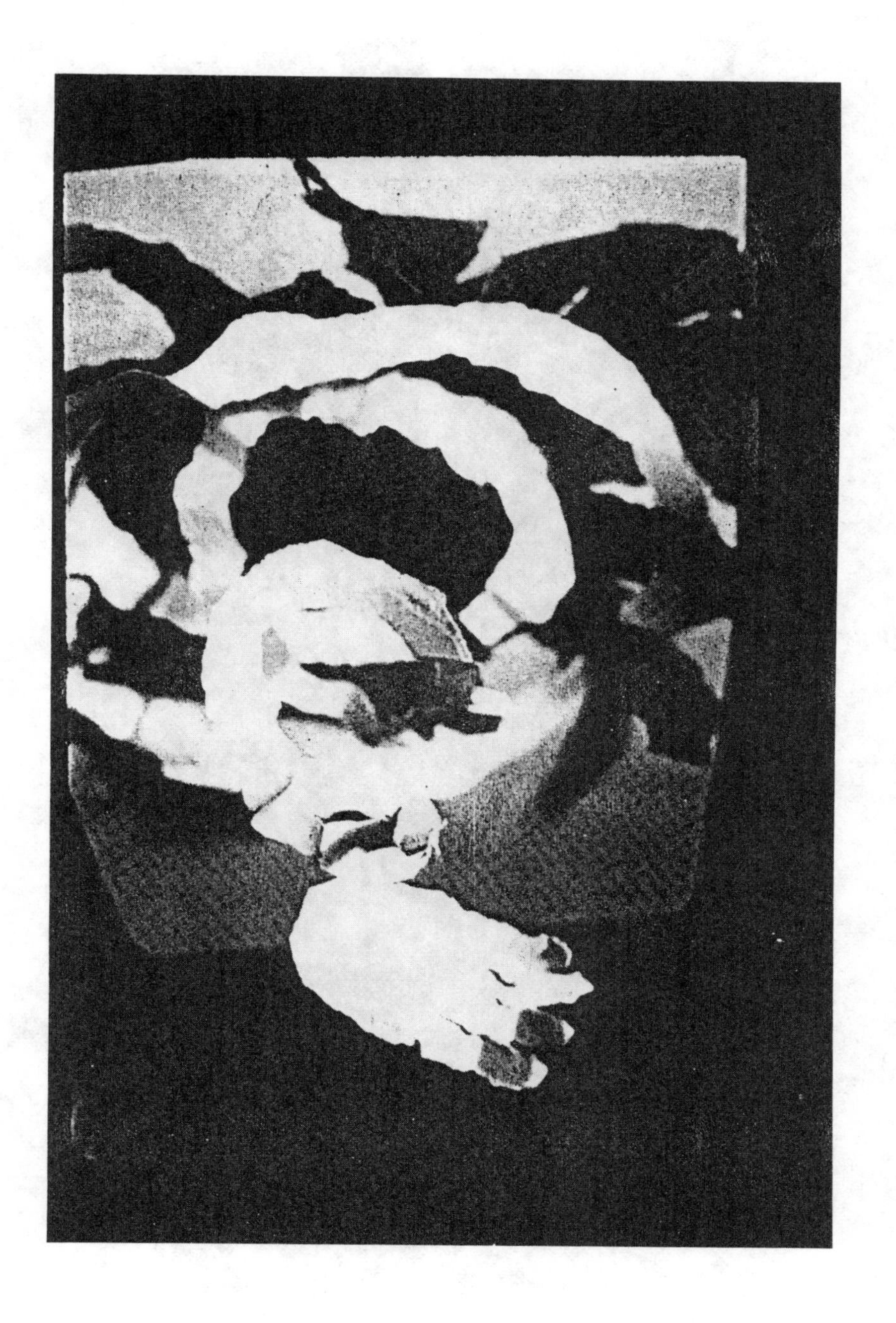

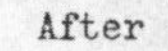

Figure 7 Before After

Figure 8

FIGURE 9

Chapter Thirteen

Wrestling With Torah, God and Self

Arthur Waskow

One of the most ancient and most characteristic forms of Jewish thought is *midrash:* the profoundly playful discovery of meaning between the lines of a tale or a text. This paper is concerned with teaching various kinds of students how to make midrash of their own — thus teaching them both a fuller understanding of the place of this approach in the history of Jewish thought, and a deeper understanding of their own world, of themselves, and of their relationship to Jewish culture.

Why Teach How To Make Midrash?

In the Biblical era of Jewish thought and history, passages of what to a modern, critical eye look like midrashim on previous texts were interwoven with those texts so as to appear within and as part of broader texts — all of which became canonized as Revelation. In the Rabbinic era, the midrashic process was understood as the discovery — "uncovering" — of previously hidden aspects of God's Revelation at Mount Sinai. Thus the midrashic wrestle within and with Torah was truly a wrestle with God — the very process that in the Biblical tale transformed Jacob into Israel, and thus the people Israel into "Godwrestlers." The midrashic process became a way for Jews to encounter and enrich such issues as, "How did the world come to be?" "What is the place of human beings in the world?" "How ought the rich and the poor, parents and children, people of different cultures, women and men, to understand and relate to each other?"

In the modern era, many Jews have not viewed Torah as the Revelation of Divine truth and have therefore not seen the midrashic process as a guide to thought or action. The "scientific" paradigm — including the "scientific" politics of Machiavelli, Mill, and Marx and the "scientific" psychologies of Freud, Pavlov, and Piaget — has turned many away from wrestling with a text, to analyzing data — as a path to profound truth.

If this "scientific" worldview were a sufficient guide to how to seek truth, it would be unlikely that we would want to teach how to make midrash. It would be more likely that instead we would encourage students to read and understand and place in historical perspective the recorded midrash of the Biblical and Rabbinic eras. Imaginably, we might ask students to make some midrash of their own so as to understand more fully how the ancients did it — but learning how to make midrash would not be the main goal.

But we are no longer unambiguously convinced by, living within, the paradigm of "science." In recent years there have grown both practical and philosophic doubts about the efficacy of the scientific method as the sole path to truth. Some philosophers have suggested that "science" is itself a "text," with all the problems of truthfulness that arise in any text. And at the same time, literary philosophers have begun to recreate a sense that truths about the world and about the self can emerge from a reader's engagement with a literary text. In a new sense, therefore, it begins to seem possible for the midrashic process to put the midrash-maker in touch with God — if by "God" is meant in part, the root of reality, the ground of truth, the mystery beneath and within mastery.

So — out of these and other currents of what may begin to be understood as a post-modern era — there has emerged new interest in the midrashic process: not only in analyzing its place in history, but in taking part in the process, in the present and future.

This beginning of a shift in approach from the modern, scientific worldview to a post-modern one offers an opportunity in the study of Judaism: an opportunity not only to learn *about* a characteristically Jewish path of thought, but to join in it and enrich it. The midrashic process is a particularly apt one to renew in this way, for within itself is the assumption of open-endedness, unveiling, enrichment. To "return" to this ancient process does not require returning to an ancient mind-set, for midrash is intrinsically the discovering of what was previously covered — hidden from sight. Whether the newly discovered meaning is in some sense "really" new — or was always there — it is certainly newly understood. So this process (perhaps unlike some other elements of Biblical and Rabbinic life-paths) can be rejoined by renewing, reinventing Judaism — instead of by restoring Judaism as it was before the modern era.

The midrashic process of "wrestling" with the text can change both the text and the reader. For even the most ancient and well-known of texts can take on new meaning when looked at under new light, and even the most modern and enlightened reader can change her or his behavior and worldview through opening up to texts that have been "reread" in many different times and cultures.

Teaching how to make midrash is therefore both cognitive and affective, both historical and value-generating, both "teaching that" and "teaching to." The fact that students learn to create and self-critically examine their own values is one of the most valuable aspects of teaching how to make midrash — but it also raises a problem. In most situations, teachers will find that in order to teach others how, they will themselves become models of midrash-makers. The process is so value-laden and value-generating that teachers should take special self-critical care that in the process of *imparting* their own values they do not *impose* them upon students. This can best be achieved by explicitly informing students that the teacher's midrash is only one among many possibilities — not *the* correct midrash — and that students' midrashim — even contradictory ones — may bear within them the sparks of truth.

Indeed, the most authentic truths about one's self may be expressed by the bent of one's midrash — so the process may be an important index to what perceptions human beings in general or a particular human culture as a whole share, and what perceptions are individual.

The reasons for teaching students how to make midrash can therefore be summarized as follows:

1. Exploring a form of truth-seeking through relationship with a text that might complement or absorb the scientific method and make possible a post-modern world that serves human needs more fully than science and modernity have done.

2. Reconnecting some of the severed strands of Jewish culture, thus revitalizing that culture as the bearer of Jewish peoplehood and renewing the ability of Jewish people to live under new conditions without abandoning its past.

3. Opening up to individual students and groups of students a way of exploring, debating, and sharing their own values and perceptions of the world — and revising these not only in the light of each other's responses but also of the responses of many generations of Jewish thinkers.

4. Through empathetic involvement, coming to understand more deeply the history of Biblical and Rabbinic uses of midrash.

How Is Midrash-Making Taught?

The basic approach to teaching how to make midrash is very simple: a group of students read together a passage of Torah, and respond to it. ("Torah" should be broadly understood: the "Torah" may be a passage from the Bible, the Talmud, the Zohar, a Chassidic tale or sermon, or a modern Jewish philosopher like Buber or Heschel.) The three main tasks of the teacher are selecting the Torah passage; encouraging and shaping the responses; and sharing similar or quite different midrashim on the same story, classical midrashim from Jewish tradition.

Drushodrama

One powerful technique for evoking responses and new approaches is to take a reasonably dramatic tale of Torah, to read the story together up to some climactic moment, and then to stop — and ask the group to choose roles in the story and to *act out* what happens next.

For example: the story of the Binding of Isaac (Genesis 22). Read until God has completed the command to Abraham, or until Abraham sacrifices the ram: Then stop. Ask for volunteers to act out Abraham, Isaac, the ram, the wood, the donkey, the boys down the mountain, Sarah, God. Give the volunteers a limited amount of time to share a sense of what they want to do; then press them to begin. (They will often be mildly embarrassed and reluctant.) More interesting midrash usually emerges from the flow of action than from the talk of "getting ready." As an example of what can happen: a 10-year-old boy, playing Isaac on his way down the mountain after the Binding, begins to stumble. "Wait! says the teacher; "What are you doing?" "Mmmm ... " says the boy. "I'm ... broken." "Of course!" say the others. "Just because Abraham didn't kill him doesn't mean that everything's OK." And then the teacher weaves this response together with the classsical rabbinic midrash that the aged Isaac of the Jacob-Esau story had been blinded not by old age buy by the flash of the knife above him at the Binding.[1]

For another example: choose the story of Jacob's intended marriage to Rachel, when Leah is substituted. Read till the verse that says "Look! In the morning, it was Leah!" Ask people to play Jacob, Laban, Leah, Rachel, God.[2]

This last example suggests an important element to take into account when planning drushodrama and other forms of making midrash: That one of the most intense buried energies within the Jewish people is that of women seeking to link their own spiritual experience to that of Jewish women in the past, by uncovering the hidden experience of the women of the Bible and of Rabbinic history. Focusing on stories of such women as Sarah, Rebekah, Rachel, Leah, Dina, Shifra, Miriam opens up new areas for midrash that have been little explored by the male-dominated tradition. Indeed, one experience with drushodrama paints the moral. [3]

The passage addressed was Genesis 34, on the rape of Dina. After the group read the story together, the teachers (a man and a woman) asked for an open discussion. Slowly there emerged a sense that the most puzzling aspect of the story was the silence of Dina. So the teachers asked whether someone would come forward to be the voice of Dina. A man volunteered, but the teachers asked him to wait until at least two women had spoken for Dina. A silence gathered in the room, and finally one woman took a deep breath, rose, shut her eyes, and said:

"Raped.

"I have been raped three times in this story.

"Once. I was raped by Sh'chem.

"Twice. I was raped when my brothers ignored me, refused to ask me what I wanted — and murdered all the men of Sh'chem.

"Three times. *The Torah itself is raping me.*

"Still raping me. Because it does not speak my voice."

And she sat down, in tears. The room was deathly silent. After several minutes the teachers asked whether any other women wanted to speak in Dina's voice. Again there was silence. Finally one of the teachers asked, "Do I take it that all of the women here think that Dina's voice has already spoken — that there are no other words they want Dina to say?" The women nodded.

Afterward, the woman who spoke for Dina said that she lost all consciousness of being "herself" and really did "become" Dina.

It is this process of "becoming" a character in the story that most powerfully breaks through both personal embarrassment and the cultural distance from Biblical life. The "becoming" seems to be accomplished more easily by drushodrama than by more verbal midrash-making because the physical and the emotional as well as the intellectual aspects of the "reader" are engaged.

In another version of this approach (which might be called "drushodancing" or "drushodreaming") the teacher, a professional dancer and choreographer,[4] had the group read together the Biblical portion *Korah* concerning the rebellion of Korah and others against Moses and the affirmation of Aaron's priesthood through the blossoming of an almond branch.

After the reading, the teacher moved the group outdoors onto a small open field, led some simple movement exercises, and then asked everyone in the group to "become" some character from the Korah portion (human, animate, or inanimate — the almond branch, Moses, the mouth of the earth that swallowed Korah, etc.).

Each person was to find a comfortable place in the field and begin through any combination of mime, gesture, dance, chant, and words to express the character s/he had chosen, intermittently chanting the character's name: "Korah! Korah!" "Almond branch! Almond branch!" and so on. Whenever the actor had "had enough" of one character, s/he was to move to a different place and become a different character. Actors could, if they chose, interconnect with each other — "Korah" with "the mouth of the earth," for example — but were not required to do so.

Then the enactment of the portion began, and went on for about 30 minutes. Since there was no time sequence, but all and any part of the portion was enacted in any order or simultaneously according to the individual desires of the actors, the reenactment was more like a collective dream than a drama. After about 30 minutes, the teacher ended the reenactment and led a discussion of what had just happened. Not only did individuals report an extraordinary sense of more deeply understanding various aspects of the portion, but the group as a whole noticed and reported a sense that out of the seeming disorder of the reenactment emerged a different order — one governed not by the chronology of the portion but by a reordered "psychological chronology." For example, the group found itself moving together, late in the reenactment, to become a forest of blossoming almond branches — an effort, the individuals reported, to affirm life and fruitfulness after a searing set of encounters with frustration, pain, and death.

In this enactment, as well as in a number of others, actors who chose to become "God" reported afterward that their previous semi-stated theological assumptions were shaken by the experience. God often came to seem almost powerless, unable to reshape and channel the intense interactions of other participants — sometimes reduced only to the role of comforter, as in rubbing the shoulders of a Leah deeply pained by Jacob's rejection and Laban's manipulation. "The pain of God" was often reported — arising from God's witnessing of His/Her creatures' own creation of injustice, hunger, etc., and God's inability to change the situation — even by direct intervention and exhortation.

Verbal Midrash

Forms of midrash-making that are more purely verbal can also be taught in much the same way. Most of these forms are somewhat closer to the classical rabbinic forms of midrash. Indeed, a group of students can be taught to wrestle with the classic four "levels" of understanding Torah that were summarized in PaRDeS: P'shat, the apparent surface meaning; Remez, allegory; D'rusha, reading between the lines; Sod, the mystical meaning:

For *P'shat,* students can be asked to read a passage and after locating it in its historical context, suggest how they would apply this understanding in contemporary society. For example, together read the Jubilee passage in Leviticus 25 about periodic redistribution of land, annulment of debt, and rest for the land. Discuss how this worked, or failed to work, and how Jeremiah, Isaiah, Hillel, and others responded to it. Then ask the question: How would you imagine using these ideas today? What is the relationship of these approaches to technological and economic development? capitalism? socialism? communitarianism? to modern patterns of work and leisure?[5]

Similarly, ask students to take a single sentence or paragraph about God, the world, the meaning of creation, etc. — from a rabbi, a kabbalist, a Chassidic rebbe, a modern Jewish philosopher. Then ask them to write a similar sentence of the same pattern, expressing *their own worldview* while coming as close as in good conscience they can to the formulation they have just read. This exercise will teach them to understand both their own selves and the model passage more deeply.[6]

For *Remez,* (allegory), the *locus classicus* is the rabbinic reading of the Song of Songs as a poem of the love between God and Israel. But the technique can be applied in many places. For instance: ask students to examine the "descent" into and the "ascent" from Egypt/Mitzrayim/the Tight Spot as a descent into and ascent from spiritual narrowness in a single individual. How do these spiritual changes happen? Does the exodus from Egypt draw on the archetype of conception and birth — new life from a tumultuous passage through a narrow space?

For *D'rusha,* reading between the lines, there are several techniques — some old and some rather new.

The group can read a passage together and focus on the key-words that are repeated and emphasized as keys to interpreting the text.[7] Usually this approach requires using Hebrew text alongside an English translation, since most translations ignore the punning repetition of Hebrew roots in different forms, and instead use the most appropriate English word for that form. Thus rarely do translations of the Isaac story translate the various forms of the root Tz-Ch-K, "laugh," in such a way as to make clear that it is used over and over in different ways: *Yitzchak,* Isaac, "Laughing Boy"; *mitzacheyk,* mock by imitating laughter; and in various places, to laugh joyfully, laugh bitterly, etc. Asking students to look for these keywords and interpret the passage from their usage is one way to teach midrashic process.

Another is to examine a story for a spiral or cyclical pattern like a palindrome ("Madam, I'm Adam" — reading the same, backward and forward), and then to interpret the story by seeing what its center and its end/beginning are.

Still another, perhaps the most frequent approach of classical rabbinic midrash, is to ask students to tell — instead of acting out — what "happened" between two verses, or even two words, of a text. What happened *between* the moment when Moses lifted his rod at the edge of the Red Sea, and the moment when God said "Tell my people to move forward."

Another approach is to ask students to look at passages that seem to be related only by proximity — not by meaning — and work on what meaningful relationship they might in fact have. For example, various passages of the initial part of the Talmud — *Berakoth* — are about night, dreams, sleep, death. The transitions seem at first to be free associational or even accidental, one comment by a rabbi followed disjointedly by another, from the same rabbi. But on reflection, are these passages joined by a sense of relationship between sleep and death? And — taking into account the larger pattern of emotional response to the sometime fluidity, sometime obsessiveness of the Talmud text, is the text itself dreamlike? Does the Talmud begin with a section on night, sleep, dreams, and death because (in contrast with the Bible) it is the Torah of night and dreaminess?

Another method of verbal midrash-making is to read together a passage of Torah and then to go around the room, asking each student simply to share aloud one *question* that occurs to them out of or about the text. Such questions may be ethical, historical, literary, esthetic, psychological, philosophical. "Answers" — responses to one's own or others' questions — are to be avoided, at least until all students have had their chance to a question. In some situations, indeed, simply sharing the questions may be a more powerful way of learning how to make midrash than hearing specific "answers."

It should be explicitly stated in advance that any who are unwilling to pose a question may pass their turn, and then reclaim the right when everyone else is finished. It rarely helps the midrash-making process to force midrash out of a student. The few with inhibitions will learn more from listening than from being forced.

Finally, *Sod* (mystical) readings of the Torah are built on the sense that all of Torah is itself a Unity, the Name of God, the Architect's blueprint for Creation — perhaps, in modern terms, the DNA-code of the Universe. Having said this, how can students wrestle with a particular text of Torah?

The classically kabbalistic way to do this was to see the text as talking not only about the histories of human beings, but more importantly (in a kind of code) about the "evolution" (so to speak) of God. The dialectical relationships and recombinations among the *S'phirot,* the internal aspects or emanations of God, could be discerned encoded within the stories of life-struggles of the Biblical heroes and peoples. Through this reading, any particular passage could be seen as a discussion of the inner life of God.

For students to enter this form of midrash-making, they would need first to learn the classical symbolic identifications of particular S'phirot with particular Biblical figures (the S'phirah of *hesed,* loving kindness, with Abraham, for example) as well as the identification of particular S'phirot with particular colors, virtues, vices, etc. They might also become sufficiently intimately acquainted with the Biblical texts to see particular Biblical women as additional symbolic representations of the S'phirot, alongside the traditional men. Then the students, looking at the interplay of both the new and traditional S'phirah-symbols, might be able to enrich their (and our) understanding of the interplay of Divine energies and aspects.

Secondly, a quite new way of developing the *Sod* aspect of midrash — a way that is influenced by modern psychological consciousness — is to understand the readers' own emotional responses to the texts they are reading as a reflection of the inner meaning of the texts themselves. Thus the Architect's blueprint of the Creation becomes actualized, embodied, in the Creatures' responses to the blueprint — Torah.

How could this self-reflective form of midrash-making work?

One of the most powerful texts to approach in this way is the *Sotah* chapter (Numbers 5) on how to respond to the jealousy of a husband who without evidence accuses his wife of adultery. Many groups will explode — some readers out of a scornful sense that the passage is sexist, superstitious, magical, irrational, and others from a sense that the text is holy, truthful at some deeper level, not to be ignored or scorned. Let the explosion gather force. Then ask the students to reexamine these explosive reactions *in the light of the text.* Were they becoming "part of the story" — quarreling, like the Sotah and her spouse, over jealousies and angers that no evidence could resolve? Is the next passage —

on Nazirite status — or the next — on the identical gifts of the twelve tribal leaders to the Mishkan — so written as to soothe the turmoil? What is the relationship between message and medium in Torah? Can Torah "reach out" to create the effects in its readers that it wishes, or is Torah itself "recreated" by its readers' responses?

This approach to midrash-making bears some analogies to a classical kabbalistic understanding of the relations between human action and Torah. Primordially, said some Kabbalists, the Torah was encoded in a steady stream of letters (perhaps even arranged in an order different from the Torah that we know). This primordial Torah underwent a reshaping when Adam and Eve ate from the Tree of Knowing Good and Evil. Not only did the Torah itself then begin to describe that very choice in the Garden, but only then does it come to describe all the mitzvot that human beings must obey in order to walk a holy path in the world outside Eden. If the Torah can be conceived as shifting its form and word in response to the choices and action of human beings, then the meaning of Torah can be understood to grow in part from the responses of human beings to its texts.

Finally, this very strand of *kabbalah* which sees the primordial Torah as transformed by Eve's and Adam's choice in the Garden also expects the transformation of our present Torah, when the days of Mashiach arrive. Then the "white fire" of the spaces on the parchment that surround and pierce the "black fire" of the letters will take its rightful place as Torah, not just blankness. This notion of a newly understood Messianic Torah opens up the possibility of asking students to imagine how the Torah of the Messianic Age will read. What hints in the present "black fire" point to the future reshaping of the "white fire"? And if human action transformed the Torah once, could *action* along the lines of these imaginings transform the Torah again?

Obviously, such speculations bear the risk of dissolving altogether the meaning of Torah and of wrestling with it — just as such speculations by kabbalists of the past bore such risks, and sometimes even actualized them. Yet under the transformed conditions of modern and post-modern Judaism, such imaginings and speculations may help us leap across the precipice of death on which we find ourselves.

The Meaning of Midrash

There is indeed a story in the Torah which points in a richly fruitful way toward the importance of making midrash in a moment of world upheaval, in a moment on the precipice.

At the beginning of the story of the Flood, God "saw that every urge of the thoughts of the (human) heart was only evil — everyday." (Genesis 6:5) So God decided to blot out the human race and all life on earth. Then comes the cataclysm of the Flood, the salvation of the human race and every other species on Noah's Ark, and God looks again and says (Genesis 8:21), "Since the urge of the human heart is evil from youth upward, I will never again smite all life as I have done."

What has happened? God has become a midrash-maker. There has been a great upheaval. What to do with the Torah that has come before the upheaval? Shall it be ignored as irrelevant? Shall it be upheld as absolute? God does neither. God quotes from the Torah as it has been before the Flood — and gives its meaning a new twist. Before the Flood, God sees that the human heart has an urge toward evil. After the Flood, God sees again that the human heart has an urge toward evil, and quotes the earlier verse of Torah to affirm the truth — but then transforms its meaning. Before, this was a reason to blot out all life; after, a reason not to.

This is what midrash does: it neither ignores the earlier Teaching nor stays imprisoned by it. It learns from the wisdom that comes from before the upheaval — and learns to go beyond that wisdom.

And midrash-making is what the human race needs today. We have come partly through a great upheaval — the modern age, when our world was flooded with new knowledge and new powers that threaten still to drown us and destroy all life in a Flood or Fire.

What shall we do? Reject and ignore all the Teachings that came before the upheaval of modernity? Or restore our life-paths as they were before that flood?

Neither. We need to learn from and transform those Teachings, to do midrash on them. That is why the process of teaching how to make new midrash on the ancient teachings is now one of the crucial acts of intellectual empowerment required in our time.

The learning itself, of course, comes as a midrash on the ancient story of the Flood.

---

[1]The class was led by Arthur Waskow in the Fabrangen Cheder in Washington, D.C., in 1975.

[2]See Ruth Sohn, "Searching in the Text," *Menorah,* January-February 1983, pp. 5 ff. for a description of several teachings through "drushodrama," at the National Havurah Summer Institute in 1982, including a session on the Leah-Rachel story.

[3]Phyllis Berman and Arthur Waskow at the National Havurah Summer Institute at New Paltz, NY, 1984.

[4]Liz Lerman, artistic director of the Dance Exchange in Washington, D.C. led this teaching in the spring of 1982.

[5]See Arthur Waskow, *Godwrestling* (Schocken, 1978), pp. 110-127.

[6]This technique was used by Arthur Green in a class on the development of Chassidic thought at the Reconstructionist Rabbinical College in 1983.

[7]Everett Fox, *In the Beginning* (Schocken, 1983), explains how Martin Buber and Franz Rosenzweig developed this approach.

Chapter Fourteen

Reflections On A New Integrated and Interdisciplinary Approach to Undergraduate Studies: Jewish and Western Civilizations[1]

Steven Lowenstein, Joel E. Rembaum and David Stern

A two-year Core Curriculum in Jewish and Western Civilizations is the basis for lower division study in Lee College, the undergraduate program at the University of Judaism. Like its more famous counterparts in general education at other American universities — Columbia, The University of Chicago, and St. Johns — this interdisciplinary Core Curriculum aims to educate its students in the intellectual traditions of our culture through the intensive study of the great classical texts in the humanities and the social sciences. It emphasizes the acquisition of basic skills: the critical reading of primary sources and written and oral expression.

Recent years have seen a revival of interest in general education, partly in response to the increasing professionalization of American higher education. With the growth of Jewish Studies in the past decades, there have also appeared courses and curricula that present the history of the Jewish people and of Judaism from different perspectives. The Lee Core program is the first curriculum to combine the study of Western civilization with the study of Jewish history and culture and to apply to both elements the methods and aims of general education. The program was conceived out of a commitment to general education and with the belief that Jewish history cannot be understood outside the context of world history. It thereby aims to educate students in the essential pluralism of Western intellectual and cultural traditions. In pursuing the comparative study of Jewish and Western civilizations, the Lee program tries to show how these two cultures developed, at once influencing each other — with the influences going both ways — and differing. Beyond the question of influence, though, the program's study of Western and Jewish civilizations in unison allows it to avoid the provincialism that so often attends the usual survey courses in Western Civilization: the lazy assumption that all civilization is Western; that the cultural values and intellectual axioms of the Western tradition are the right, if not the only, ones; and that, indeed, in the study of human culture there exists a single line of truth.

This is where the interdisciplinary side of the Lee Core program proves so crucial, for aside from studying the same problem from different cultural perspectives, it also tries to look at each civilization from the changing viewpoint of different intellectual disciplines — to see how, for instance, a historian might view an age and its dilemmas in contrast to a poet or a religious thinker, and then to show how these disciplines themselves developed in response to varying historical and intellectual circumstances.

Thus, three principles comprise the basic framework of the Lee College Core Curriculum: first, a commitment to general education, its methods and goals; second, applying those methods to the study of Jewish and Western civilization together; third, teaching through an interdisciplinary approach to the study of both civilizations and their institutions that introduces the student to intellectual and cultural pluralism.

This paper will analyze the structure of the Lee Core Curriculum and its rationale. It will also examine how various components of the Core have been taught and the degree to which the program's goals and expectations were met and how effectively its underlying principles were realized.

Structure

The Lee College Core Curriculum is a four-semester sequence designed primarily for freshmen and sophomores. For its students, the Core is the center of their studies (though they usually take two or three other courses). In terms of class hours alone the course is very intensive: four meetings a week, each meeting an hour and a half — or six clock-hours of seminar-style class a week. Preparation is equally rigorous: the average reading assignment per class is between fifty and one hundred pages, and, in addition to mid-term and final examinations, short papers are assigned every two to three weeks. During the first year a course in English composition is tied to the Core so that the papers written on the topics studied in the Core are then used as the subject-material for composition exercises. Finally, the course is team-taught, with one instructor having major responsibility for each semester and a second instructor assisting and attending the class approximately half the time. In addition, outside lecturers — from the University and elsewhere — are brought in to teach special topics.

The Core course is not merely the student's main introduction to Jewish and Western cultures in various ages; it also serves as the foundation of the student's entire undergraduate program. Its purpose is two-fold: (1) to introduce the student to a body of knowledge; and (2) to help him or her hone their thinking processes. In creating the curriculum, the faculty tried to strike a balance between the need to transmit information and to teach method. Because of this need for balance, they did not wish simply to present the material to the student through a pre-digested survey (which, despite its limitations, might have been the best way to get the material across), but instead, chose to base the course almost exclusively on primary sources. This choice was necessary in order to accomplish the goal of imparting skills in reading texts, analyzing and evaluating arguments, and placing them in their proper contexts. However, since the texts have to be studied in considerable depth, it was required to limit the number and size of the texts to be covered. This, of necessity, renders the task of "coverage" more difficult. The program has to limit its coverage by selecting relatively short periods and a few disciplines to cover and by choosing only a few texts within each discipline. Often the process of reduction was more difficult to undertake than the initial selection and assembling of significant texts.

As its title suggests, the aim of the two-year sequence is to study the two civilizations that are its subjects. The program, however, is not a history-course (though its over-all perspective is historical), nor is it a survey. It does not attempt to cover *all* of Western and Jewish civilizations and their histories. Rather, each of the four semesters focuses upon a specific historical period of fairly restricted scope — usually a century or two — and within that period, it concentrates on a selected number of topics viewed from different disciplinary perspectives. The periods and the topics studied in each have been chosen for their representative value and intellectual significance. Thus, the first semester treats Late Antiquity, roughly from 50 BCE to 250 CE; the second, the High Middle Ages, the 12th and 13th centuries; the third, the early Modern Period from 1720 to 1780; the fourth, the Modern Period from 1870 to 1920.

The relationship between the historical organization of the program and the methods of the other disciplines is a complex one. Since history can include virtually any subject matter, there is a temptation (especially for those of the faculty trained as historians) to view the entire program as a history course and to see each thinker, for example, or text in terms of its reflection of its period. Yet the course's purposes go beyond this, since the goal of the Core Curriculum is to give the student an idea of how specific disciplines work. Thus, within each teaching team there may be historians, but there also may be philosophers who are interested in the ideational content of a text or experts in literature who closely examine the form and literary content of the text. The students, it is hoped, benefit from being presented with such different approaches and learn that the same texts can be used in a variety of ways.

Because disciplines such as political thought, philosophy, literature and art are presented within a chronological framework, the Core program is a compromise between history and the other disciplines. The Core courses, by concentrating on four specific periods, provide a historical focus while, at the same time, rejecting the usual historical concentration of the flow of events between epochs in favor of a concentration on specific ages which are widely separated. Students are given an understanding of the historical process in an unusual way. Through an intimate knowledge of the "spirit" of four ages, they get an idea of the profound differences between the periods. The transitions between the periods may be brief and sketchy, but it is assumed that students can easily fill in the historical lacunae. It is far more challenging to comprehend the "spirit of the age."

To some extent there has been a tempering of the purist tendency merely to present texts and expect the students to decipher them and thus learn the art of reading and analyzing without the crutch of prior guidance in "the right meaning." Students, before reading, need to know some of the cultural background of a text, its use of vocabulary and, perhaps, some specifics about the author and his or her intentions. Otherwise a student, especially a beginner, can simply find the text undecipherable or totally misread it. Thus, the second year students, reading Montesquieu's *Persian Letters* without being told that the "Persian Authors" were merely literary devices for the purposes of Montesquieu's criticism of European culture, did not know how the excerpts they read fit into a study of Enlightenment views of religious tolerance. Similarly, it was necessary to provide at least some summary transition between the periods so that the student could come to the new period with some idea of the issues to be confronted. In dealing with the Enlightenment, for instance, the students "coming from the Middle Ages" required considerable background information on the Protestant Reformation, the Scientific Revolution, religious wars and the rise of absolutism. With all due emphasis on the unbiased reading of texts, the need for proper preparation before reading readily became evident. Instead of merely giving snapshots of four distinct eras, the faculty chose to "run a movie" which is stopped at crucial points for closer study. The somewhat static picture of each age is thus still incorporated into a dynamic (and thus very historical) framework of introductions to each semester.

Example I: Jewish and Western Civilizations 101 – Late Antiquity

The first semester's Core, focusing on Late Antiquity, was designed as the beginning of the course for two reasons: first, it is in this period that Judaism — as we know it and as it continued to develop in the subsequent centuries — first emerges in a recognizable shape; second, because it is also during this period that the Jews first intensively confront Western — that is, Greco-Roman — civilization in ways that are historically significant for both cultures.

The course is divided into four sub-units. The first of these is a kind of "mini-introduction" to the period and its historical background. This introduction begins in the first class with pre-history and, in the succeeding ten classes, it traces the histories of Israel, Greece, and Rome up to the beginning of the Common Era. Following this broad historical survey an overview of Late Antiquity, its major historical developments and institutions, is attempted. This overview has a certain sociological bent to it. There are, for example, sessions dealing with the Rabbinic sage and the Greco-Roman philosopher as two ideal social types of the period; another class treats gentile views of Jews in the Greco-Roman world and Jewish views of gentiles; a third session deals with the spectrum of types of Judaism in Palestine and in the Diaspora in Late Antiquity.

The purpose of this unit is strictly introductory. Its aim is not mastery of the vast amount of historical material covered in it; rather, it is designed to provide the student with the historical background and resources he or she will need in order to situate the texts read later in the semester in relation to the historical and cultural events surrounding them. Unlike the readings in the other units, those in the introduction are for the most part from secondary sources; in the first semester, Robert Seltzer's *Jewish People, Jewish Thought* and M. Chambers *et al.*, *The Western Experience* are the texts.[2]

Following the mini-introduction come the three units that are the actual core of the program and its comparative, interdisciplinary study of Jewish and Western civilizations in Late Antiquity.[3] The discussion that follows details the structure and analyzes the logic of two units in the semester of Late Antiquity and highlights the strengths of the comparative approach and the kinds of problems it raises. It has been noted that the units are organized according to disciplines. The disciplines commonly used to organize our universe of knowledge, and which are used in the Lee Core Curriculum to organize its educational universe, are those which traditionally distinguished between the different branches of knowledge *as the Western tradition has defined them.* These disciplines, however, are not Jewish ones.

The first unit of the Late Antiquity Core course focuses on the Western discipline of Historiography. This is hardly the same as the Jewish discipline with which it is linked, *'aggada.* Part of the problem here is generic. We know what the various genres of Western literature are — what distinguishes a historiographical text from a literary or philosophical one. Even if the actual dividing line is sometimes fuzzy, we have enough of a sense of what a historiographical text is to say what it is and what it is not. More importantly, historians pursue their task and write history with a sense, a consciousness, of their discipline and its requirements. Yet there is no discipline comparable to historiography in Rabbinic Judaism; there is no justification to claim that a Rabbi, in speaking about the past, believed himself to be speaking about it in the way a historian like Tacitus would have. In fact, there is much to prove the contrary. Of course, Rabbinic literature has its own disciplines, its native genres; if we can recognize the difference between *midrash* and *mishnah*, so did the Rabbis. But what does Jerusalem here have to do with Rome, or *'aggada* with historiography? If there does not even appear to be a Rabbinic historiography, how then compare Western and Jewish historiography?

In the posing of this question, Josephus intentionally has been overlooked. He is, of course, a Jew in Late Antiquity with a Western historiographical consciousness. Josephus is read in the unit under the section sub-titled Secular Historiography (in contrast to Sacred Historiography). But among the Jews of his time he is the exception to the rule. There was, in fact, no solution to the methodological and procedural problem outlined above except to acknowledge it and then to bracket the entire notion of historiography as a discipline within the larger question: How is the past treated in Late Antiquity and what significance is attached to it? The present division of the unit into two sections, secular and sacred historiography, effectively posites the existence of different ways of treating the past in Late Antiquity. This allows for the demonstration that Western historiography is only a single way of treating the past, while the various approaches grouped in the rubric of sacred historiography — apocalyptic and Christian, as well as Rabbinic — are others, equality valid yet different. Ultimately, then, this unit is about the problem of understanding the past in Late Antiquity rather than historiography. It is meta-disciplinary.

In addition, comparative study takes place within the sub-sections. The secular historiography section is subdivided into two topics: the history of the emperorship and the Jewish War. The unit was structured this way to reach certain objectives. Particularly for freshmen and sophomores, there is little purpose in studying historiography without history. Yet the fact is that the ancient historians we read are also our primary sources for the history of Late Antiquity, and the task of defining their historiographical approaches is not simply a speculative question; it is also the first thing modern-day historians must do if they wish to use these texts as sources for a history of Late Antiquity. To get this point across to the student seemed necessary, and there was no better way of doing it than by comparing different writers on the same topic — Tacitus and Suetonius on Tiberius, Josephus and the Rabbis on the Destruction. As they learn about the historian, the students also learn the history. In this case, it is even possible to bridge the divide between the secular and the sacred.

The structure of this unit can be said to be one of the real strengths of the first semester core. In contrasting these different ways of looking at the past, in showing how a discipline may be a cultural construct, in discussing the purposes for which the past is remembered and how these can differ between cultures, an entire agenda of questions is opened that continues to occupy us for the remainder of the semester.

The unit on Law and Religion poses a slightly different problem — the definition of *halakha* as law. This is not so much a disciplinary question as it is one of understanding the subject itself. In its original form, the unit on Law (not Law and Religion) consisted in its entirety of eight classes of comparative study of Roman and Jewish law around a series of legal topics: jurisprudence, family law, torts, and property. The readings were all from primary sources, either *Mishna* or the Roman legal codes of Ulpian and Gaius, while the unit's goal was first to teach the student to treat a legal problem as a lawyer would, and then to compare the different approaches that Jewish and Roman law take in dealing with a legal question. These classes were taught by a member of the University of Judaism faculty who is both a Talmudist and a lawyer, and the unit was quite successful in reaching its educational goals.

At the conclusion of the semester, however, the question was raised whether in comparing Jewish to Roman law we had adequately defined *halakha*. The legal topics we treated, for example, were the topics that naturally allowed for comparison. But what about all the other areas of *halakha* — the laws of purity, ritual ceremony, holidays, and so on — which are equally intrinsic to Jewish law but have no counterpart in a Roman legal system? In comparing Jewish and Roman law, our study had often dwelt upon the difference between a right-oriented legal system and a duty-oriented one. Yet even this comparison did not really touch upon the most salient feature of *halakha*: that it is a religious, not just a legal, system.

Asking this question, however, opened up an entirely new avenue of approach to the question of law in religion. The attitude of *halakha* towards law is not the only religious perspective on law in Late Antiquity. As an alternative to the Rabbinic view, the Pauline critique of *halakha* immediately came to mind; it also happened to be a topic central to the development of the early Church, yet another phenomenon of Late Antiquity. Realizing the importance of addressing the early Christian attitude toward law, the unit was redesigned.

As it now stands, the unit on Law and Religion is a kind of three-pronged exercise in comparison. Following an introductory session on law and morality, four sessions are devoted to a comparison of Jewish and Roman law on the topics of jurisprudence and judicial structure, and family law. These comparative sessions are then followed by a class devoted specifically to the question of the extra-legal, religious significance of *halakha*. With other texts, chapter 8 of *Berakot*, which deals with both blessings and questions of purity, is read and the meaning of the halakhic concern with purity is discussed. This class also serves as a bridge to the final sessions which treat the Pauline critique of *halakha*. The Gospel of Matthew, first read in the historiography unit, is reexamined to compare Jesus' attitude towards *halakha* with Paul's, and the difference between them is discussed in the context of the theological and historical development of the Early Church. Finally, the unit concludes with an attempt to provide a response to the Pauline critique from the Rabbinic side — that is to say, a defense of *halakha* (though not an apology for it). The pluralism implied in the Pauline attitude toward *halakha* is also contrasted with the opposition to law that Paul's position was interpreted as having in the later Church.

The history of this unit on law is similar to that of the unit on historiography. What began as a comparison between two systems became a somewhat farther-reaching study — via comparison — of the idea of law itself, its definition in different systems, its function, and its efficacy. The unit as it now stands is, admittedly, not what it was. Its educational goals have changed. There is, for example, less emphasis upon mastering the "lawyerly mind." On the other hand, the present unit can be said to be truer to its material and offers a more comprehensive view of *halakha* in addition to providing an original perspective from which to consider the Pauline critique. *Halakha* is no longer viewed in splendid, or not so splendid, isolation but against the backdrop of Roman law. The conventional and tired critique of *halakha* as legalistic, as obsessed with the letter of the law rather than its spirit, takes on a rather different meaning when it is set against the legalism of Roman jurisprudence. Upon completing the unit, the student is better prepared to deal with the variety of functions law may serve, and with the special status it came to have in the development of Rabbinic Judaism and Christianity amid their dispute over the value of *halakha*.

Example II: Jewish Western Civilizations 103-104 – The Modern Period

Besides having to select a significant sample of texts from the myriad of possibilities and to balance a historical approach with an inter-disciplinary one, the Lee Core program has had to integrate Jewish and Western cultures. The relationship between these two cultures has varied widely, yet never so greatly as during the two periods discussed in our second year, 1720-1780 and 1870-1920. It was, therefore, necessary to vary the degree and type of integration between Jewish and non-Jewish material in the curriculum. On the one hand, an effort was made to give adequate treatment to both cultures in each period; on the other, it would sometimes distort the nature of the period to give equal treatment to both. Making Western civilization revolve around the Jews would falsify the nature of the interrelationship between the two cultures. Nevertheless, disciplines and texts were selected so that balanced emphasis reasonably could be made. On occasion that meant creating units with little or no Jewish content and, on other occasions, the choosing of issues especially relevant to Jews.

The positions of Jews in the two periods dealt with in the second year were very different. In the mid-eighteenth century the gap between Jews and the vanguard of European society (especially in intellectual life) was especially great. In a way, the third semester provides a necessary corrective to the overall impression given in the other semesters of integration between Jews and non-Jews. The student is made aware of the gap between the mental worlds of 18th century Jews and Enlightenment thinkers and the fact that there were issues in the general world for which there were no obvious Jewish parallels.

It is sometimes difficult to be fair to both cultures. On the one hand to concentrate on the *maskil* Mendelssohn as the Jewish counterpart of Kant, Hume, Rousseau, and Voltaire would distort the picture of 18th century Jewish thought regarding which Mendelssohn was quite atypical. However, to confront profound Enlightenment philosophy and theories of toleration with Jewish folk religion and absence of toleration would unfairly depict a contrast between forward looking Western Europe and backward Jews. A variety of steps was taken to solve this dilemma. The disciplinary section on intellectual thought (epistemology and proto-anthropology) did not include a Jewish element, since no Jewish text dealt with issues similar to those of Kant, Hume, Vico, and

Voltaire. The comparability came in other places. First, the autobiographies of Benjamin Franklin and Gluckel of Hameln introduced students to two very different mentalities with intriguing points of comparison (business life, moral theories, role of family). In addition, a study of religious movements showed both the Enlightened and the un-Enlightened side of European thought. The tales of the Hasidim and theories of man of Luzzatto could much more legitimately be treated in a unit with Jonathan Edwards' fire and brimstone sermons, Cotton Mather's view of witchcraft, or Blake's romanticism than together with a study of philosophy. By not comparing Jewish religious culture with high intellectual thought but rather with works on a somewhat more popular level, a legitimate comparative evaluation could be made.

In the political sphere, too, there was little point in forcing a Jewish element into a discussion of basic social contract ideas. It was, however, legitimate to discuss Jewish institutions in the context of the survival of the estate system in the 18th century rather than look for some obscure Jewish political theory. In the treatment of politics, emphasis was placed on an issue which could be justified as intrinsically important to the Enlightenment and especially relevant to the Jews — toleration. Perhaps the faculty's special interests influenced the choice of this subject and its being structured in a way emphasizing the Jewish example, but the subject itself did not have to be artificially foisted on the Enlightenment. The study begins with various Enlightenment theories on toleration (Lessing's tale of the three rings, Voltaire's intolerant tolerance, Montesquieu's relativism) which are then compared with actual practice both in the treatment of Jews and of Christian minority religions. This teaches important lessons about the gap between theory and practice, the role of social conditions in the toleration issue, and the different types of intolerance (French Protestants recognized as Frenchmen but denied the right to worship; Jews permitted to worship but restricted as a foreign social group). It also gives students a more realistic basis for comparing Jewish and non-Jewish views. When dealing with Jewish views of tolerance no attempt is made to whitewash the Jewish attitudes. Though the class reads a large part of Mendelssohn's *Jerusalem*, which is clearly in the Enlightenment tradition, the assignments also include Mendelssohn's correspondence with Jacob Emden on *hasidei umot ha'olam* which shows that traditional rabbis did not even understand Mendelssohn's categories in discussing toleration.

Whereas in the third semester the gap between Jews and non-Jews is so great that the Jewish material receives less than parity and the faculty had to look carefully to find fields in which Jewish texts legitimately could be integrated, the fourth term presents a totally different problem. Especially in Western Europe, Jews were so deeply integrated into the intellectual life of the West that it was often difficult even to decide if something was a phenomenon of Jewish or general history. On the one hand, the Jewish issue (in anti-Semitism and Nietzsche) loomed large even in non-Jewish society; on the other, the Jews as a group were becoming harder and harder to recognize. The course deals both with overtly Jewish phenomena like Zionism, the Bund, stories by Peretz, and the philosophy of Hermann Cohen as well as ambiguous cases like Kafka and Freud. In general such "borderline" cases are considered as part of Western history.

The difficulty in determining whether a specific phenomenon should be defined as an aspect of Jewish culture or of general Western culture itself has emerged as a significant issue. Thus, for the first time in the four semesters of the Lee Core Curriculum the students can address the question: What difference did people's being Jewish make with regard to their functioning as members of Western society? Having asked the question students and faculty alike soon realized that on occasion it can not be answered. After an analysis of various texts under the rubrics of political ideology and cultural ideology and after a unit on the transition from representational to modern art (in which little overtly Jewish material is presented), two sessions are devoted to the issue of "The Non-Jewish Jew." Deutscher's famous easy by that name is read. This matter, so crucial to the whole enterprise of the fourth semester, does not fit into the Core's disciplinary framework but does shed light on much that was covered before.

In contrast to the eighteenth century, a period of comparative stability in which it is relatively easy to grasp the general outlines of the dominant Enlightenment philosophy, the period from 1870 to 1920 was a period of rapid change, much of it in direct reaction to the liberal ideology which dominated the mid-nineteenth century. Though the reaction against liberalism provides a convenient focus for much of the semester, it produces a technical problem. Without a good exposure to the literary sources of liberalism it is sometimes difficult to see all the issues raised by its critics on the right and left. In addition, the socialist ideologies of the period, for all their importance, are still divergences of opinion from the theories of Marx which were promulgated, in the main, before 1870. It therefore becomes necessary to provide a great deal of background on Marx and the liberals, which, if included in the course would greatly reduce the amount of time for the materials concerning our own period. As a temporary solution, an elective course is given simultaneously with the third semester's Core which covers the basic liberal and Marxian economic texts, enabling students to tackle the late nineteenth century material with the proper background. It remains to be seen if this solution will be permanently satisfying.

By their very nature, text-oriented courses tend to stress the thinking and action of elite groups, who alone created articulate texts. This is to some extent unavoidable, though recent trends towards social history "from below" have caused many historians to take an interest in non-elites. The core courses, both in the social unit of the medieval term and, to a lesser extent, in the religious section of the eighteenth century semester, try to deal with groups somewhat different from those in the forefront of intellectual life. Although a planned unit on popular culture in the third semester core proved to be unworkable, the inclusion of works like the Hasidic tales and Gluckel's memoirs do bring the students into contact with thought that could hardly be called elite intellectual. Still, in future revisions the possibility of offering somewhat less of an elite orientation in at least some of our units will be reconsidered.

Program Evaluation

Is the Lee Core Curriculum a successful program? This is a question difficult to answer simply. The program is, after all, still in the experimental stages. As yet Lee College has not attracted a sufficiently large number of students of the proper caliber to test the curriculum under more ideal conditions. As a course in general education — in acquiring skills in reading primary sources and in writing about them — it has succeeded inasmuch as the students certainly have improved. Whether or not this improvement meets the faculty's highest expectations is a matter that will have to wait until more students complete the Core Program and continue in upper division courses. As a course on the culture of a given age, each core segment is successful in establishing certain broad lines and facts about the period.

A number of pedagogical issues are raised by a course as rigorous and challenging as this one, especially since it is directed toward college freshmen and sophomores. Even in the second year, the students are often overwhelmed by the quantity and difficulty of the material, although the quantity is less in the third and fourth semesters than in the first two. Certain texts, Kant's epistemology, for example, still intimidate the students. Shorter or simpler alternative readings have been explored. To give a mere outline of Kant's philosophy of the mind through lectures would defeat the purpose of the curriculum. Assigning fewer pages but analyzing them in greater depth may be a solution. Despite six clock hours of class time a week the term still passes at breakneck speed. Students frequently get to read the text only once and often too rapidly. The faculty steadily has been moving toward reducing the quantity of reading and increasing the amount actually gone over in class. The tension between coverage and teaching techniques of textual analysis is ever present. Teachers constantly are faced with the dilemma of deciding how long to allow the students to struggle with a difficult concept before they step in to explain it. Sometimes it requires considerable self-discipline on the teacher's part not to step in too soon in the interest of covering the material. Perhaps the six hours of classroom work should be increased to eight so that the texts can be covered at a somewhat less breathless pace.

Although students sometimes feel that they have not acquired the total mastery of the material presented or that they do not remember it in sufficient detail, this may be less of a problem than it appears to be. One of the purposes of the Lee Core curricular exercise, besides the development of techniques or the acquisition of data, is to stimulate the student's own personal and philosophical growth through exposure to new ideas. It has always been the stated or unstated goal of general education to affect the values of the students. Especially in the early part of their college career, intellectually aware students should be starting to form their own philosophies of life. It is our hope that they will incorporate the insights of the texts they have studied into their worldviews. Even when students only partially have worked out all the implications of a text or have forgotten some of the details, study has been worthwhile. A text studied at the age of 19 can, if the student has been stimulated, be better understood years later when the student has acquired more life experience. The Lee Core Curriculum is intended to help stimulate and begin this process of value formulation and introspection. The end of its two years should mark the beginning and not the end of the students' thinking about the issues raised.

The model we have presented has two aspects — its specific content and its general philosophy. The idea of comparative study, exposure to original sources and various disciplines, and the choice of limited time periods has wide applicability and is subject to various means of realization. Since the Core Curriculum as presently formulated it is still somewhat experimental, revisions will be made on an ongoing basis. Alternate models incorporating the same basic philosophy are certainly possible. Once could alternate the periods covered and the disciplines presented. For instance, the third and fourth semesters could have alternative forms covering the Renaissance-Reformation period and the period between the French Revolution and 1848.

Lee College students sometimes have floundered in a sea of texts and sometimes have been discouraged, but they frequently exhibit enthusiasm, and debate in class is often lively. Most of the students seem to enjoy the course; a few have found the program positively exhilarating. The faculty certainly has enjoyed teaching it. Occasionally students will tell their instructors how they used the work of a thinker discussed in class in an argument on some contemporary issue. If students can still engage in this type of discussion in our overly professionalized, career oriented university world, we surely have accomplished something.

---

[1]This essay is based on papers by Steven Lowenstein ("Modern Age") and David Stern ("Late Antiquity") delivered at the 14th annual conference of the Association for Jewish Studies, Boston, Massachusetts, December 19-21, 1982. They have been revised by Joel E. Rembaum.

[2]In the other semesters, the introductory section serves the same purpose, in addition to bridging the gap between the period studied in the preceding semester and the one about to be studied. In the second semester, for example, the period between the third and twelfth centuries is surveyed.

[3]The disciplinary units vary from historical period to period, both to expose the student to as many disciplines and approaches as possible and to cater to the strengths of the period. After all, it is impossible to study the Middle Ages without looking at Religious Art. How else can one possibly understand the medieval Church? The need to do this, however, created a problem of balance on the Jewish side. Sometimes a comparative approach cannot be a balanced one.

There are, however, certain lines of continuity: Late Antiquity and the Medieval Period both contain units on Literature, and in the course of the year the students will be exposed to several literary traditions of heroism. They also will read the three great epics in these periods that are modelled upon each other — the *Odyssey*, the *Aeneid*, and *Dante's Inferno* — and thus will be directly exposed to the meaning of literary tradition.

Glossary of Terms

aharonim: "later authorities"; term used to describe rabbinic literature and authorities from mid-15th century to the present day.

'aggada: telling, narrative discourse; sections of the Talmud and Midrash devoted to ethical and moral teaching, legends, folklore, etc., as opposed to legal discussions *(halakha).*

amora (pl. *amoraim*): speaker; later scholar of the Talmud whose discussion(s) is found in the *Gemara.*

'Avot: "Fathers" (also known as *Pirkei 'Abot:* "Chapters of the Fathers," commonly referred to as "Ethics, Sayings of the Fathers"); tractate in the fourth Order of the Mishna (*Nezikim,* "Damages") containing maxims of tannaitic masters to demonstrate the continuity and weight of tradition (= pharasaic Oral Torah). The five chapters of Perek plus a sixth one (*Kinyan ha-Torah,* "Acquisition of the Torah") are traditionally read in and of themselves on Sabbath afternoons between Passover and Pentecost.

'Avot de Rabbi Nathan: best known classical commentary on *'Avot,* containing 40 chapters and composed during the amoraic period.

Bar Mitzvah: son of a commandment; ceremony at which thirteen-year-old boy is called up in the synagogue to read a portion of the Torah and prophetic reading to mark his entrance into religious maturity and responsibility; an adult male Jew who is obligated to fulfill the religious dictates of Judaism.

d'rash: seeking; homiletic approach in reading Scriptures with the intent of squeezing the inner essence from a text by means of very close critical analysis. The *d'rash* (*d'rusha*) is more eisegesis than exegesis and is the main vehicle by which the classical sages developed the *Haggada* and *Halakha.*

gaon (pl. *geonim*): eminence, excellency; title used for the heads of the leading Babylonian academies of Sura and Pumbedita between the 6th (end of talmudic period) and 13th centuries (beginning of the rishonic period) and stands for *resh yeshivat geon Yaakov* ("head of the academy which is the pride of Jacob"). The descriptive quality of *gaon* today is an outstanding talmudic scholar or genius.

Gemara: completion; mainly a scholarly discussion on the contents of the *Mishna* but also includes topics of history, legend, myth, ethics, nature, and science. The Gemara supplement to the Mishna was developed in two centers, Palestine and Babylonia, from ca. 200 to 500 c.e. *Mishna* and *Gemara* together form the Talmud.

Ein Sof: limitless, infinite; kabbalistic phrase to describe the essence of God as known only to God (= transcendental God.)

hesed: lovingkindness, mercy; the fourth S'phirah in the kabbalistic S'phirot, identified with the divine name El; some additional associations: Abraham, Water, South, Right Arm.

halakha: way or path from *halak,* to go; legal discussions and pronouncements.

Hallel: praise; hymns of praise consisting of Psalms 113-118 and recited on certain festive days of the year. During the last six days of the eight-day Passover holiday (and on Rosh Hodesh, a minor festival at the start of a Jewish month), the first eleven verses of Psalms 115 and 116 are omitted (="half-Hallel").

hasidei umot ha'olam: "pious of the nations of the world"; righteous Gentiles have a share in the world to come (cf. *Sanhedrin* 13:2). Today the term is frequently used to describe non-Jews who risked their property and lives to secure safety for Jews under Nazi tyranny.

Haskalah: enlightenment; 18th-century movement that began in central Europe which (a) encouraged Jews steeped in Orthodoxy to broaden their knowledge of the world through secular studies and (b) appealed to Jewish masses to become active participants in European enlightenment and emancipation.

hiddush (pl. *hiddushim*): originality, new insight.

Kabbalah: tradition; the whole of Jewish tradition as found in the Talmud and Midrash; later usage, the esoteric and mystical teachings within Judaism.

Ketuvim: Writings; third division of the Hebrew Bible commonly known as Hagiographa (Daniel, Job, Psalms, etc.).

lishmah: for its own sake; *torah-lishmah:* study for its own sake in the sense of truth and knowledge.

maskil: enlightened one; advocate of Haskalah (Enlightment).

Mahzor: cycle; the festival prayer book for major holidays, including Rosh Hashanah and Yom Kippur.

middat ha-din: the quality of justice; in Jewish ethics justice and mercy are seen as the pillars supporting human society, and the former is the requisite for a world at peace; in Jewish theology *middat ha-din* is aligned with *Elohim* (God) and teaches His divine justice and authority.

middat ha-rahamin: the quality of mercy; usually applies to the ineffable name YHWH and stresses God's revelation to mankind and acts of lovingkindness and mercy.

middat pur'anut: the quality of punishing; usually applies to God's attribute of justice.

middat tobah: the quality of rewarding; usually applies to God's attribute of mercy.

Midrash: biblical inquiry; an attempt to explain the biblical text in as many ways as seemed possible to the inquiring mind of the Jewish sage. Thus *Midrash* has a variety of interpretations and includes exegesis of Scriptures, sermons, and nonlegal discussions. The genius of *Midrash* lies in its *Haggada* (nonlegal ethical and hermeneutical pronouncements) peppered with philosophical wisdom and a vast amount of folk tradition), though parts of Midrash are legal in nature and very close to *Halakha* (legal; Jewish law). *Midrash* may also characterize collections of accepted rabbinical pronouncements intimately related to Scriptures, from the dawn of the common era to the 10th or 11th centuries. Some of the more significant compilations are: *Midrash Rabbah* on the entire Pentateuch and the five *Meggilot* (biblical books read on certain festive occasions), *Mechilta* on Exodus, *Sifra* on Leviticus, *Sifre* on Numbers, *Mechilta* on Deuteronomy, *Pesikta* on the festivals and special days, and *Tanhuma* on the entire Pentateuch. In present usage, Midrash may also describe a process in which a contemporary relates directly to the Bible and offers existentially observations justaposed to the text which may or may not be consistent with the accepted classical Jewish interpretations as found in the Midrash, Talmud or Codes.

Mishna: repetition; authoritative collection of Jewish law, tradition and teaching which was originally handed down in a repetitive oral form but was later compiled into a written collection in ca. 200 c.e. by Judah the Prince. The Six Orders of the *Mishna* deal with agricultural laws of the Land of Israel, Sabbath and festival rulings, laws of family, marriage and divorce, civil and criminal law, laws pertaining to Temple and cultic sacrifices, and legal decisions dealing with personal cleanness and religious purity.

mitzvah (pl. *mitzvot*): commandment, good deed; usually, any proper human activity which represents an obligation to and fulfillment of the teachings of the Written and Oral Torah.

Ohr Ganuz: hidden, treasured light; zoharic reference to celestial light ("Let there be light") of day one of creation.

PaRDeS: garden, paradise; mnemonic device explaining four types of Bible exegesis: *p'shat, remez, d'rash, sod;* generally, esoteric teachings and speculations.

p'shat: literal meaning of a biblical text with special emphasis on its historical, literary, and linguistic context.

Pharisee(s): separatist; major Jewish party in ancient Judaism, characterised by strict observance of categories of purity and advocacy of God's revelation at Sinai to include Written and Oral Torah, the latter against their rivals, the Sadducees. Their beliefs include immortality of the soul and resurrection of the dead, free will, and divine providence in nature and history. Their successful legislation of Torah and Prophets in and out of synagogues became the norm for later rabbinic Judaism. Unjustly maligned in the New Testament and in the writings of the Church Fathers, the Pharisees have been misunderstood and damned by centuries of Christian laiety and scholars. This image has only recently been corrected.

remez: hint; scriptural exegesis bordering on the allegorical and philosophical.

rishonim: "first authorities"; term used to designate early authorities in relation to a specific scholar and time in regard to halakhic understanding of Torah;

now used to describe rabbinic literature and authorities between 13th (end of geonic period) and mid-15th centuries (start of the acharonic period).

Rosh Hashanah: "head of the year"; Jewish New Year, observed by most Jews as a two-day holiday which falls out at the beginning of the Hebrew month Tishrei (September), and ushers in Ten Days of Penitance (Tishrei 10 = Yom Kippur).

Sadducees: major Jewish party in ancient Judaism supported primarily by aristocratic and priestly social classes. The Sadducees rejected much of the methods and ideals of the pharasaic Oral Torah, and insisted on the authority of the Written Torah alone as interpreted within priestly circles. Their influence was exclusively connected with the Temple cult, which suffered irreversible harm when the Second Temple was destroyed by the Romans in 70 c.e.

sod: secret; in esoteric teachings, the inner essence and mystical meaning of a biblical text.

Siddur: order; Jewish prayer book for weekly and Sabbath prayers.

S'phira (pl. *S'phirot*): number, emanation; term used in Kabbalah for the ten emanations through which the *Ein Sof* manifests itself. Concept implies Neoplatonic and Gnostic influences.

Talmud: Mishna and *Gemara* together form the Talmud. The rabbinic academies in Palestine and Babylonia produced two kinds of Talmud, *Yerushalmi* (Talmud of the Land of Israel) and *Bavli* (Babylonian Talmud). Since its completion in ca. 500 c.e., the *Bavli* has emerged as the more authoritative and the one universally studied in Jewish academies, schools, and seminaries. The primary source for Jewish law and lore in the past 1500 years, the Talmud is second to the Bible in authority.

TaNaK: Jewish acronym for Hebrew Bible; each letter stands for one division of the Bible, viz., *T* for *Torah* (Pentateuch), *N* for *Nevi'im* (Prophets), *K* for *Ketuvim* (Hagiographa).

tanna (pl. *tannaim);* teach by repetition; early scholar of the Talmud whose comments are found in the *Mishna.*

Tanhuma (*-Yellamdenu)*: name given to various sermon-type midrashim preached in the ancient synagogue prior to the Torah reading; *Tanhuma*= Rabbi Tanhuma bar Abba (5th-century Palestinian *amora)* and *Yellamdenu* (*Rabbenu)*= "may our masters teach us." Features of *Tanhuma:* halakhic question, several proems, exposition of the first verses of the Sabbath Torah reading (following the Triennal Cycle), eschatological conclusion.

Torah: in a restrictive sense, the Pentateuch; in a broader sense, the whole Hebrew Scriptures; in common usage, the pharisaic notion of total revelation, the written Scriptures and related authoritative rabbinical commentary (= Oral Torah, i.e., Talmud, etc.).

Tosefta: addition; a collection of tannaitic supplements which parallel the Six Orders of the Mishna.

t'shuva: repentance; denotes the inner change of heart and the outward change of direction conditioned by one's freedom of will to turn from evil and return to God and the proper path of *Torah* (Written and Oral).

Yad (*ha-Hazakah*)*:* "strong hand"; name for the authoritative work on Jewish law by Maimonides (1135/8-1240) and contains 14 (*yad* =14) parts; the classic is commonly known as *Mishneh Torah.*

Yalkut Shimoni: the best known and most comprehensive midrashic anthology of the Bible, following the order of scriptural verses, attributed to a 13th-century "Rabbenu Simeon chief of the preachers of Frankfort." The *Yalkut,* which gained universal recognition by the 15th century, contains thousands of 'aggadic and halakhic statements on most chapters and verses of the Bible.

yeser ha-ra: the evil urge or inclination; in rabbinic psychology, it implies weakness of the flesh.

yeser ha-tov: the good urge or inclination; the disciplined character of a righteous, virtuous individual conditioned by the precepts of Torah.

Yom Kippur: Day of Atonement; solemn fast day of repentance which falls out on Tishrei 10 (September).

zaddik: righteous one; in Hassidic circles, synonymous with the *Rebbe,* the leader of a Hassidic court.

zedakah: acts of righteousness; generally used for charity and philanthropy but applies to any proper social action.

Zohar: brightness (cf. Daniel 12:3); major work of the Kabbalah traditionally attributed to the second century *tanna,* R. Simeon ben Yohai, but mainly composed and edited by the 13th-century Spanish kabbalist, Moses de Leon; written in Aramaic, the work is primarily a mystical commentary on the Pentateuch and portions of the Hagiographa.

Index

Source Index